PAIN SO DEEP BUT FAITH STILL STRONG!

SHANNON HAMMONDS

inspired by the Holy Spirit

NEWMAN SPRINGS PUBLISHING
320 Broad Street
Red Bank, NJ 07701

First originally published by Newman Springs Publishing 2024

ISBN 978-1-68498-169-4 (Paperback)
ISBN 978-1-68498-170-0 (Digital)

Printed in the United States of America

To the Most High, to my parents, Willie and Edith Hammonds,
both of my sons, Timark and Shaquille Hammonds,
who always believed in me when I
sometimes didn't believe in myself
To my grandchildren, Dajohn, Nevaeh, and
Brooklyn, who are the joy of my life.
Thank you, Jesus!

If Only You Knew

If only you knew what I've been through,
the hurt and pain I cannot explain,
the things that I've seen,
and the places I've been even within!

If only you knew it's nothing for me
to give you my last
when you sometimes just give me your a———.

If only you knew what God has brought me
through and the blessings He's given to me
after all of my pain and miseries!

If only you knew how much love I have for you and
the hatred you have for me,
but that's okay, you see.
This is the way God created me to be—
to love even my enemies!

If only you knew how much praying I do,
not only for me but always for *you*!

If only you knew!
If only you knew!
If only you knew!

Me!

The year was February 13, 1971, the day that I was born into this world. It may have been one of the coldest months of the year but one of the *best* months for any Black man or woman to be born in. The month of February is best known for our Black History Month, a month celebrated for our Black African Heritage history and a month celebrated for love! I was born the day before Valentine's to the proud parents of Willie and Edith Hammonds, and this was supposed to be one of the happiest days of my parents' lives—well, at least for my dad anyway! As the years went by, I always felt as though I was what they called in most families the black sheep and was proven to be right by my mother at the age of thirteen when my mother and I engaged into a heated argument. I remember my mother telling me these words as though it was yesterday: "That's why I never wanted you anyway!"

I said, "Well, why you had me?"

She said, "Because I got scared and jumped off the abortion table and ran out of the room!"

My mother told me something that would stick with me for the rest of my life. Words of pain that ripped through my chest and sent chills all over my body. Words that could have destroyed a person's life forever, but not this person. It made me stronger, and it made me the person I am today. But there was a reason my mother said the things that she said and felt the way that she felt. I would learn it all, only to realize that I wasn't a *mistake*, but a child sent from God! After going through what I've gone through and seeing what I've seen, I now realize that God had his hands on me the whole entire time!

After giving birth to a beautiful baby girl, my parents named me Shannon Rena Hammonds. I was told by my mother after bringing me home from the hospital that she handed me over to my dad, who was taking a nap on the sofa from a hard day's work. My dad has an auto body shop and has been working on cars before I was born.

"Here, take her since you wanted her so bad!" my mom said to my dad.

He woke up, took me in his arms, laid me on his chest, and we both fell back to sleep. Most of the time, my daddy's chest was where I slept, and that's why I became daddy's little girl!

I was a daddy's girl, the baby of three, well, of four, because our daddy had another daughter who was older than all of us from another woman. I followed my daddy with every step he made and cried hysterically if he would go anywhere without me.

"What y'all doing to my baby that she crying like this when I leave?" my daddy would say.

"Well, take her with you when you leave if you think somebody is doing something to her," my mom would say.

As long as I've lived, my dad has never beaten me. The reason is because my mom told us that one day my dad was getting ready to spank my sister who was around four years old at the time, and she decided to run from our dad. As he was chasing her, she fell down a flight of steps, and our dad thought that he had killed her. The fall caused her to have a cut above her eye, which she still has to this day. Our dad was so disturbed after that, he decided to let our mother handle all the spankings—more like beatings, which she did like a pro.

My dad is a country man who was born and raised in Allendale, South Carolina, to the proud parents of James (Monkey) and Nancy Hammonds. My dad's parents taught their four children that in order to love someone else, you must first love yourself. And if you're not going to share and give to *all*, then don't give to any. My grandparents may not have had much to give, but they made sure that we had what we needed.

Allendale, South Carolina, is my dad's home, a place where we visited often. I still remember my granddad (Monkey) who was slim, tall, and very handsome. The reason they nicknamed him Monkey was because of his big ears, which my brother inherited as well. My granddad worked at the Coca-Cola plant for many years and was well-known and liked by just about everyone in that town. My grandmother (Nancy) stayed at home taking care of the children, the cooking, cleaning, and helping out around the farm. Back in those days, that's what most women's job consisted of.

We visited our grandparents often, and I was one of my grand-mother's favorite. I remember my grandmother telling me, "Baby, you know you and me are just alike. They call us both ugly in the family."

I guess my grandma knew that I was always getting picked on, and I knew she told me that just to make me feel better. My grand-mama loved me so much. I remember how she used to always make her famous delicious homemade six-to-eight thin-layered jelly and chocolate cake that was out of this world, and she always made sure she made an extra cake just for me, which made all the other grand-kids mad. Now I was never big on cakes, but candy was a different story, and I have yet to meet anyone who could top my grandma's cakes. I used to laugh when the other kids ask Grandma, "Grandma, how come Shannon get a cake all by herself?"

"Because I said she can get one, that's why!" And that was the end of that conversation, and because they used to pick on me, I didn't share my cake with any of them, which made them even madder!

Since our granddad worked at the Coca-Cola plant, he kept the cooler in the shed stocked with sodas. Granddaddy would tell all the grandkids about seven of us to go into the back of the barn in the shed and get ourselves a soda, which, you know, we all grabbed more than one! Alone with our sodas, Grandaddy gave us Krispy Kreme donuts that were kept in the refrigerator, but after warming them up in the oven, you would have thought that we had just brought them straight from the store. So all night long, we would sneak in and out of the shed for sodas while eating hot donuts straight out of the oven while watching scary movies until we all feel asleep. That was the good ole days!

I remember having to wake up very early in the morning to draw water from the well to bathe in before eating breakfast. That was something country folks didn't play. Lying around all morning, I wish you would, you're getting a stick upside your head! Grandma also sent us out to the chicken coop to get some eggs so she could cook for breakfast, and she would always say, "Don't y'all go out there messing with my chickens!" Grandma loved those chickens.

"Grandma, the chickens always messing with us!"

"No, they ain't," she would say. "Now y'all gone on out there and do what I say!"

We would be scared going into that chicken coop because those chickens and hens always tried to attack us once we got inside, so the seven of us would draw straws, and whichever two had the shortest straw would be the ones going in to get the eggs while the rest of the gang all laughed. We would run into the coop so fast trying to get as many eggs without dropping them and trying to get out as quick as possible without getting attacked by the chickens. It was fun but scary at the same time.

We didn't have hot running water, so Grandma had to get the water from the well and heat it up on top of the stove to pour into a tin washbasin so we could all wash up. Grandma would line us all up, seemed like from youngest to oldest, and she would wash our face, neck, ears, hands, and arms one by one in the same water. This particular weekend, my uncle, my mom's baby brother who was raised with us like a brother, had decided to come down with us to visit my grandparents. On this particular morning, like all other mornings, my grandma sent two of us out to go and pump the water from the well so she could heat it up on the stove to wash us up for breakfast, and my uncle was the last one and the oldest to get washed up. It was so funny, I'll never forget it. I remember it like yesterday.

My uncle told my grandmama, "I'm not washing up in that same dirty water that everybody else done washed up in!"

My grandma told him, "If my grandkids are good enough to wash up in it, so are you, and if you're not, then don't come back to my house!"

My uncle told my grandma while rolling his eyes and head, "Don't worry, I won't." And he didn't!

Back in those days, butchering hogs every year was like a ritual, and I loved going to the country to be a part of the festivities. On this particular weekend, it was just my dad and I who drove down to Allendale to help with butchering the hogs. Didn't I tell you I'm a daddy's girl, and a country girl at that! The grandchildren's job was always cutting up the hog's skin to make pork cracklings. I remember my auntie, my dad's only sister, gave me something in my hand and told me to throw it in the fire, and that's just what I did, threw it in the fire. My aunt screamed at the top of her lungs, you would have thought I threw a child in the fire, "I told you to throw the meat in the pot, not in the fire! You don't listen!"

I'm a child, and I only did what she told me to do. It was only just one tiny piece of meat! That day, I realized that Black country folks didn't play when it came to their food. After getting home and telling my mom what had happened, which I should have kept my mouth closed, I think that was my last time going down there to help butcher hogs, you know how those mammas can be when it comes to the in-laws. Please don't give them a reason. "That's what you get. You should have stayed your a——— at home!"

She never stopped me from going down to my grandparents' house to visit, no, never that, because when it comes to family, blood is always thicker than mud! In my book!

My parents have been married for over fifty years and counting, even after all the cheating, lies, and infidelities, on my dad's end, of course. My mom said that even though she and my dad don't get along, they may as well stay together because neither one of them has anywhere else to go. She said when she met our dad in Allendale, he was a very hardworking, faithful, loving, and respectful country man until he moved to the city, got with his cousin, and got introduced to the city life. Now he's trying to be, as she said, "a city slicker." My mother's family is also from Allendale, and that's how both she and my dad met while visiting her mother's family.

My mother, along with her five brothers and three sisters, was born and raised in Columbia, South Carolina, to the proud parents of Frank and Earlene (Mama) Geiger. I never got a chance to meet my granddad because he died before I was born. I saw a picture of him when he was younger. He was very handsome, and the lead singer in his band. My granddad was a light-skinned, slim man with curly hair, and his features put you in the mind of Mista's dad in *The Color Purple*. Yes, the one who told Mista when they were eating at the dinner table, "Mary, what, Mary Agnes, Mrs. Mary, who gives a damn. Boy, you gonna sit there and let this lil nappy-head gal cuss you out like that. You sitting at the head of your own dinner table, and you acting like a waiter!" Yes, that was one of my favorite scenes.

My grandmama, Mama is what we all called her always, told me to *pray!* Mama may not be here with us today, but she always told me to go with my first mind because that was Jesus talking to you. Mama was my best friend, and I could talk to her about anything. She was there to listen as well as give me her advice on many things, especially when it came to my mother and me. The relationship and bond that I had with my grandmother was so close that I didn't look at her as my grandmother but as a mother, the kind of mother that I was looking for in my own mother at the time. Our mother was the Terminator in the house, and she didn't play. I remember getting backhanded in my face with blood coming from my mouth because I left a little bit of Kool-Aid in the jug in the refrigerator. I told my mom that the reason I left some Kool-Aid in the jug was because I didn't want to drink all of it. I wanted to save some for someone else, but she didn't believe me. She said I only did it because I didn't want to wash the jug, which wasn't true at all since I was the one mainly washing the dishes anyway.

Our dad was the chastiser with that mean and stern look on his face like James Evans on *Good Times*, the kind of look that said, "If you move while I'm talking to ya, I'll kill ya!"

I mean, he will have us, my brother and I, especially me standing there listening to him lecture us for hours and you better not slouch or doze off because if you did, that was another hour or two of him talking! My mother was so stern when it came to me that if I didn't look just like her, I would have thought that I was adopted. Mama also knew that my mother was hard on me, definitely harder on me than she was with my brother or sister, and that's why I felt as though I was the black sheep!

One day, while I was visiting Mama, she told me, "You know I asked your mama why she was so hard on you?"

"What did she say, Mama?"

"She said that she was hard on you because she wanted to make you strong for the outside world."

I told Mama, "My mama is gonna make me so strong that one day I'ma whoop that behind."

Mama looked at me with a strange look, and I looked back at Mama, and we both laughed! My dad was who they said that I get my comedian side from. That maybe somewhat true, but I think I may also get some of my comedy from Mama. Mama was never trying to be funny. She was just funny, and you couldn't help but laugh at her. One thing you better not do is piss Mama off because she'll never let you forget it. I think that's where I also get my stubbornness from. It could be three months later, and you and Mama could just be sitting around having a good ole time, and out of nowhere, Mama would bring up that same subject that you or someone else has pissed her off about three months ago.

"You know, I just didn't like what you said or what you did!"

"Mama, that was three months ago!"

"I don't care. I still don't like it!"

Mama was a diabetic who had to get her right leg amputated, then her left toe, then half of her left foot. Every time I visited Mama, I made sure that I rubbed her legs to keep her blood circulating.

"Thank you, baby. That feels so good. I still have ghost pain here in my right leg. I call it ghost pain because sometimes it still feels like that leg is still there."

I remember Mama saying that she wished she had her legs, so she could go to church, but instead, Mama stayed home in her wheelchair looking out of her window while listening to the pastor preach on TV or listening to gospel songs on her radio.

Mama was a strong believer in Jesus, and I remember her being so excited about my aunt, my mom's baby sister, whom Mama was living with at the time. I remember Mama telling me, "You know,

7

your aunt got church on her mind." Mama said that since they moved, they were closer to the church, which was right across the street from their house, and that my aunt told Mama that she was going to start going to church!

I told Mama, "Now, Mama, how come Auntie got church on her mind now because y'all only moved one block over, and if she didn't have church on her mind then to go, then she ain't got church on her mind to go now!"

"Yes, she do now!" Mama told me. I was wrong. My aunt went one time, bless her heart.

I hate that Mama is gone and no longer with us, but I love that she's not in any more pain nor do she have to try to hide her pain pills that she said my uncle and auntie used to steal from her for their addiction. I remember one day, while over at Mama's house fixing her hair, something I did on a regular basis because I'm also a cosmetologist, my uncle came over to see how Mama was doing. Well, while Mama and I were in the kitchen getting ready to wash her hair, she asked me in a low voice, "Shannon, where Charles at?"

I said, "In the room, watching TV."

"Charles, come here, Charles. Help Shannon stand me up here to this sink so she can wash my hair." So my Uncle Charles came in to help me stand Mama up to the sink, and as I started washing Mama's hair, she said, "Oh, thank you, Charles. I don't know what I would have done if you wasn't here!"

My Uncle Charles looked over at me and said, "The same thang you been doing when I wasn't here!"

I could have fell out. I laughed so hard to myself, looked over at my uncle, and cracked a smile and kept washing Mama's hair.

I didn't know Mama was trying to keep my uncle out of her room and away from her pills that were in her nightstand, but he had already beaten her back in the room. I rolled Mama back in her room, and my uncle was sitting on her bed, close by her nightstand as if he was watching TV. We were behind him, and Mama started pulling on my pants leg. She was trying to tell me something in a low voice, but I couldn't hear her, so I bent down so she could tell me in my ear, "Go over there and get my pills."

I said, "Ma'am." Even though I heard Mama, I didn't wanna walk over there to get Mama's pills out of her draw and my uncle getting mad at me, so I pretended that I didn't hear her, and I said again, "Ma'am." Mama got so mad at me and said, "Go and get my pills, stupid!" and started wheeling herself over in her wheel chair to get her pills. In a softspoken voice, she said, "Excuse me, Charles. I need to get over here and get my pills. Oh, my legs hurting so bad, I need my pills for my pain."

I said to myself, "Mama, ain't crazy. She knew my uncle was stealing her pills, but it's sad that she has to hide or explain why she needs her medicine."

There was another funny time when I went over to Mama's house just to check on her, and she and I were in her room talking, and my aunt went to the mailbox to get the mail. She walked back to her room to watch TV. After looking at the mail, she hollered, "Mama, the pastor done stopped by the house and thought you wasn't home and left your money in the mailbox in an envelope. I didn't hear nobody knocking on the door?"

Once a month, Mama Pastor would stop by the house to check on Mama and see how she was doing since she wasn't able to attend church and leave her a couple of dollars. I don't think there was no more than maybe twenty-five dollars. My aunt couldn't wait to open up the envelope, thinking it was some money.

"No, Mama, it ain't no money. It's a paper about your tithes that you paid into the church and what you can file on your taxes."

Mama said, "Well, you know I ain't filing no taxes, but what it say?"

"It say…um…that, you…um…" My aunt was trying to read the letter while trying to watch TV both at the same time, but she was more into the television than trying to read the letter for Mama, and Mama couldn't understand what she was saying, so Mama asked her again, "What does it say?"

"Um… It's talking about…um…just the…um…"

"Shannon, go and get that letter. Carolyn don't know how to read!"

I went and got the letter and started reading it to Mama. The letter said that Mama only paid $250 in church tithes and that she could file that on her taxes. Boy, Mama was hotter than a firecracker!

"Carolyn, I know dog gone well I put more than two hundred and fifty dollars in them people's church! Now you must have been spending my money because I give you fifty dollars each month to take down to that church, and the only time I was unable to give you money is when I was in the hospital for those two months!"

My aunt claimed she took the money to the church each and every time Mama gave her the money. "No, you didn't. You spent my money, and those people gonna put me out the church!"

I told Mama, "Them people ain't gonna put you out no church because you didn't pay your tithes!"

"Yes, they will now. Don't tell me those people will put you out of the church if you didn't pay your tithes. Don't tell me 'cause they will!"

I said, "Mama, if those people put you out the church, then those people are not Christian folks!"

"Yes, they will now!"

My aunt said, "Well, Mama, you have a hundred dollars in the bank, do you want me to take some of that money down to the church?"

"I got a hundred dollars in the bank?"

"Yeah, you want me to take that down to the church?"

Mama said, "Hell no, don't take those people none of my damn money!"

I coulda fell out! I laughed so hard to myself, and I said to myself, "After all that fussing about her money and the people putting her out the church because she didn't pay her tithes." After that, Mama ain't had nothing else to say about no kind of money. I see Mama wasn't crazy about giving those people at the church her money, plus she knew my aunt was stealing her money and her pain pills! Sad!

Mama had many grandchildren and great-grandchildren before she left us, but only the two of us really took the time out to spend with Mama, and you know I was one of the two. I would always visit or call Mama if not every day every other day, and if Mama didn't hear from me in about two days, she would get worried and reach out to me. I loved sitting around Mama, just the two of us talking, and we always had a good time. I enjoyed sitting around my elders talking and listening to their stories. I guess that's why I was told that I had the knowledge, wisdom, and conversation of a very mature young lady for my age. I learned through the years while sitting around Mama and my elders that you not only hear a lot, but you learn a lot of valuable information that will take you a long way through life trials and tribulations!

Now pictures are images that speak a thousand words, and looking back over our pictures, you would have known that my family didn't have much but each other and our dog. I remember only going to the movies with my family once, and that was to see *Grease*. I loved that movie. When my parents brought the record of the soundtrack, I played that record every day and would act out each scene to the song. "I got chills, they're multiplyin', and I'm losin' control, 'cause the power you're supplyin', it's electrifyin', electrifyin', electrifyin'... You're the one that I want!" Don't you get me started with my *Grease* because I would put it down!

Looking back at our family pictures, I realized that it's clear to see that we were definitely living a lifestyle of the show *Good Times*! I saw a picture of me when I was around two years old. My hair was nappy and short! My uncle, my mom's baby brother, used to call me TWA (teeny-weeny afro). He would joke about me, saying, "That lil monkey of a child hair so short, you can't even roll it with rice!" The reason my hair was so short was because when I was two years old, my mama put a hair relaxer in my hair, not a relaxer "just for kids" but a "just for grown people" relaxer because my hair was so nappy for a little girl, and that took all my little bit of hair out! Well, don't blame me because my hair was so nappy...I got it from my mama! So my nickname from my family was TWA (teeny-weeny afro), but my nickname for myself was Ugly Duckling, because that's how I felt about myself. When people would ask what happened to my hair, my uncle, my mom's baby brother, would tell everyone that I stuck my head out of the car window and the wind just blew all my hair off my head!

So now after taking my little bit of hair out with a relaxer, my mother decided to start straightening my hair with a hot comb when I was four. She was burning up my scalp with all that hair grease on my head, and you couldn't jump or say nothing about being burned because you would get pop with the back of the comb on the back of your head, arms, or legs. "Sit still. Ain't nothing burning you. It's just the grease!" Yeah, cooking my head like an egg! I didn't have much hair up there, and you trying to catch what little I did have with this hot comb basically straightening my scalp because there wasn't much up there since you took it out with the hair relaxer! Then after she was finished, I used to hate when she would put a stocking cap on my head to keep my hair together for school the next day, and it wasn't like a new stocking cap. It wasn't even a stocking cap. It was a pair of her old pantyhose, one that she had been wearing to work every day and didn't have any use for them anymore. And so she would cut the legs off, tie each leg hole in a knot, and make it out of a stocking cap, putting the butt part on my head that smelled like butt! Now I could see if she washed the stockings first before she put it on my head, but women weren't washing their stockings. They would just wear them until they couldn't wear them anymore. Some would wear them until they got holes in them. I don't know how many times my mama wore those stockings, but it had to be a lot because all I smelled was ass. You should have seen my face looking like someone farted right in my face, and I was only four, so I had better not open my mouth to say nothing!

My family and I moved around many places. My sister and brother weren't like me. They were quiet and stayed in the house. Not me, I'm a people person. I got out to explore life and to have fun because just sitting in the house was just too boring. My mother wasn't a people person. She was mean. She was so mean that when people would see me, they would ask me if my mom was still mean. She was so mean that she even had a problem of me speaking to other people. It never fell anywhere we went if someone spoke to me and I spoke back, she would say, "You just know every damn body!" It wouldn't matter where we were or who spoke to me, she would always say, "You just know every damn body!" This went on for a long time until I just got tired, and one day, when someone spoke to me and she said, "You just know every damn body!" I said, "Well, I can't help if people speak to me. Maybe if you and my daddy didn't get us put out everywhere we went, then I wouldn't know every damn body!"

It came out before I knew it! My mama gave me that look like, "Heifer, I'll kill ya!"

The first place I remember us living in were Latimer Manor apartments as a little girl around the age of two. This was the place where my dad chased my sister to spank her, and she fell down the flight of stairs. I only remember two things when we lived there.

One was helping my sister fight this boy who was picking on her, which my sister didn't need any help. I think the boy liked her, but I didn't know it then. All I remember was grabbing hold of his leg, and I tried to bite a plug out of it! After that, we all became friends, and years later, I saw that same lil boy who's a grown man now. He said that he still had that bitemark on his leg when I bit him and showed it to me to prove it. I got a little scared. I thought maybe he wanted some retaliation, but we just laughed about it. He asked me how my sister was doing. I'm sure everyone's family is the same where you have siblings fighting each other, but we ain't gonna let nobody else put their hands on them. It will be like what Della Reese said in *Harlem Nights*: "Let's get it on sucka!"

What I also remember about living there was when Mama's apartment caught on fire! At the time, my auntie was babysitting me, my sister, and brother while our mother and Mama went to the garage sales. I remember my aunt telling us to come outside because there was a building on fire. The fire was about four or five apartments down but in the same building. While we were standing outside, watching the fire, this lady had to jump out of her top window. The fire kept burning one apartment after another until it started burning Mama's apartment. The next thing I knew, my auntie screamed, "My money!" and told us to stay back. But when she tried to run back into the apartment, the firemen stopped her. When Mama and our mother came back home, Mama was hysterical but more about her money that she had auntie put up for her, which they found still stuffed under the mattress.

Years later, my auntie told me that she had hoped that she wasn't the one who started the fire where one person died because of it. She said that she had just brought her a leather jacket that she said she was looking fly in, and she wanted to go out to show off her jacket. She said that she had friends who lived a couple of apartments down, and she went there to see if they wanted to hang out. She even told them that she would pay for them to get into the club, but they didn't want to go. They wanted to stay home to get high from smoking weed and get drunk from drinking alcohol. My auntie said that she was disappointed but stayed there with them and got high. She said that she remembered, while smoking the weed, the seeds were popping everywhere, and she didn't know if maybe they popped on the carpet or between the sofa while slowly burning, causing the fire to start or if it was because of someone else who was there that may have started it after she left. The fire originally started in that apartment. She also admitted that she wasn't running back into the apartment to get Mama money but her leather jacket. She said after thinking about her jacket, she forgot all about Mama's money.

The next place I remember us moving to was a house on Monstella Street, which was just right around the corner from Latimer Manor. My uncle Greg was living with us at the time, and because we were all so close in age, people really thought he was our brother! It was funny back then when people would ask if he was our brother, and we would tell them, "No, he's our uncle!"

"Uncle?" People would look at us like we were crazy! Yes, my uncle was only a couple of years older than my sister. My uncle was also the snitch and the breakfast cooker, and boy did my uncle know how to cook some pancakes. We loved his pancakes so much, my brother and I wish that we could have that rather than when our Mama would leave our sister in charge of the cooking the dinner if she was coming home late.

Our sister was another Thelma on *Good Times*. When our mom came home, she asked, "How was the food?"

I would say, "Wasn't nothing good but the Kool-Aid, and that wasn't sweet enough because the fried chicken still had blood on the inside!"

My uncle was the snitch and the tape recorder, and he would record my brother and me fighting, but my sister did come to my rescue and tore my brother behind up over me! But as soon as our mom walked through the door, the first thing my uncle would do was say, "Here you go, E!" That was our mother's name. We called her E short for Edith. It was just the way we all grew up. Just about all of my mom's brother's and sister's children all called their parents by their name, and we all called our grandmama Mama! Our mama couldn't get in the door good enough. Here comes our uncle. "E, I got something I need for you to hear!"

My uncle had recorded us fighting each other in the house, and boy did we get our behinds tore up! We used to get mad at our uncle, but what could we do. He was our uncle, and he didn't record us all the time, only when the fighting got pretty rough with his dirty and sneaky self!

When I was five, my mother was taking us to school. Don't you remember fussing with your brothers or sisters about who was getting in the front seat or who was sitting by the window. I was and still am the kind of person who always spoke their mind regardless of who you were. My dad knew this and would tell you, "One thing about Shannon, she doesn't bite her tongue for no one, not even her mama or me, so I know she's not going to bite it for you." But to my mother, she considered it disrespectful, but I wasn't trying to be disrespectful. I was just trying to have a voice and get my point across! I know parents might say a child doesn't have a voice or a point to get across, but sometimes as parents, we should give our children a chance to speak in order to know what's on their mind, instead of wondering what's on their mind. Give them a chance to explain themselves. I know it may be hard, but it will be worth it at the end!

My brother and I were arguing about who was sitting next to the door, and I won, of course, and wasn't aware that my door was not all the way closed. So on our way to school, my mother made this quick right turn. My door flew open, and I flew out of the car, rolled across the street, and balled myself up in my fake squirrel fur, I mean, my fur coat, into this ten-foot ditch! I heard my mama, brother, and sister screaming. They stopped the car, and everybody jumped out and ran to see if I was okay. I jumped up with mud all on my clothes, face, and my fur coat. I was okay. I was just crying and upset that I couldn't find my money that was in my hand! Child, I had about fifteen cents that I was crying about. God is good because it could have been another car coming in the opposite direction and ran me over! Thank God! Yes, I am a blessed child!

While living there, I became best friends to my first white girl-friend Vicky! Vicky and her brother used to live with their grand-mother, and boy was Vicky's grandmother big as a house, and their house was nasty! It was nasty because they loved cats. They had so many cats that all you saw and smelled was cat poop and cigarette smoke all over the house. I couldn't stand it, and I couldn't stay in there long either! I also had a little crush on Vicky's brother. He was about four years older, but he was cute, dusty, and dirty. To be honest, really the both of them were dusty and dirty. Poor lil thangs. But they were cool and my only friends.

I remember Vicky's brother and I were sitting in my dad's Road Runner. I always admire that car. My dad was in the army, and after getting out (going AWOL, but you didn't hear that from me), my dad opened up his own auto body shop, which he still has to this day. And yes, my dad is very good at what he does, and I bring him plenty of business, but my mom tells me all the time, "I don't know why you keep telling people your daddy fix cars! You know he slow, and if something happened to their cars, they're going to blame you. That's why I don't recommend no one to go to his shop, so you need to stop it!"

I'm a daddy's girl, and I still tell people till this day about my daddy if they need their car fixed! I do remember years later while driving my car, I had my best friend Tonya and her daughter's father both riding in the backseat. I was so mad about my brakes on my car that I just hollered out, "I'm tired of having problems with these brakes. every time I take them to him, it's not long that I need some more brake pads. Now the next time I take my car to him and he don't fix them right, I'm taking his ass to court, and I'm not playing!"

Tonya said, "Well, who you had fixing your car?"

I shouted, "My daddy!"

Tonya and Tony fell out laughing! I wasn't joking. I was dead serious!

I ended up losing my friendship with Vicky because my dad busted her brother and me in his Road Runner kissing, which was my very first kiss. My dad ran him home, and I was not allowed to go back down to Vicky's house again. I don't think that Vicky was able to come back to my house either, so my next best friend was Alfreda from next door. Alfreda also was living with her grandmother, and you know with a name Alfreda, you knew she was Black. I kinda felt sorry for Alfreda because her grandmother was very strict, it made me appreciate my mean mama! Alfreda and I stayed best friends for a long time until we moved away, but while we were there, I remember my dad every Easter buying us these colorful chicks. They were so beautiful—blue, green, pink, purple, red, and yellow.

My dad was a good dad, a hard worker who provided for his family, and he made sure he gave us what we wanted as well as needed. I remember him bringing home some fireworks for us to shoot, well, not for me because I was too young at the time, and he told me that he didn't want me shooting any of them. On this particular day, our mom dropped both my sister and brother off at the Laundromat just around the corner from the house. While my mom was in the other room, getting more dirty clothes to take the Laundromat, I decided that, since my brother or sister wasn't home, I would go and sneak into their room and get me some of their fireworks. The pants that I had on didn't have any pockets. I took as much as I could carry in my hands, and what I couldn't carry in my hands, I put some in my mouth.

So I sneaked to the kitchen while my mother was still in the back room, and the way our kitchen was made was the stove was close by the door, next to the storage room, which lead to the backside of the house. Because I didn't have a lighter to light my firecrackers, I turned on the stove and opened the door, so when I light the firecracker, I could just throw it out of the side door. I was so excited, my hands were sweating. I couldn't wait to light my very first firecracker. I put the firecracker stem in the fire on the stove, and I saw it sparkle, so I hurried up and threw it out the side door! *Pow!* I was ecstatic. I turned my head around to see if my mom was coming. She wasn't, so I started giggling and decided to light another one. I was scared but brave at the same time. I threw it out of the side door. *Pow!* And I turned around to see if my mom was coming. What I need you guys to understand is that I was still standing in front of the stove. The fire was very close to my face, and I had the fire turned up high. So when I turned around to see if my mom was coming with the firecrackers still in my mouth, one caught on fire. The next thing I knew—*pow!*—right in my mouth! Oh, you should have heard me. I started screaming at the top of my lungs, and my mama came running around the corner flapping her arms like a chicken with the head cut off screaming.

"Oh my baby teeth, my baby teeth!"

It wasn't my teeth. It was just the paper and smoke from the firecracker flying everywhere!

After she realized it wasn't my teeth, she gave me some ice in a rag and told me, "Now go and sit your a—— down somewhere!"

It didn't matter what happened to me. The *only* thang I got was some ice in a rag and was told to go and sit my a—— down somewhere! But the most hurtful thing in the whole situation was when my mom and I went to go and pick up my sister and brother from the Laundromat. I was sitting in the backseat with the rag over my mouth, and my sister and brother asked my mom what was wrong with me, and my mom said, "Well, show them your mouth."

When I took the rag from my mouth, my lips looked like two butts together I thought they were going to feel sorry for me, but they all just laughed, I mean, even my mama, like it was the funniest thang they had ever seen! But that's okay because after my dad heard about what happened to me, my sister and brother couldn't have any more fireworks for a long time. Now who got the last laugh!

Living on Monstella Street is when I remember meeting my oldest half sister for the very first time. I didn't consider her our half sister. She was our sister and she fitted right in with us as if she grew up with us the whole entire time. To be honest, my oldest sister from my dad and my sister from my mom both looked more like sisters than we did!

When I was five, Mama was living on Read Street, and if you're from our town, then you know back in those days, Read Street was one of the toughest streets to be on, unless you lived on that street, then other people would watch out for you. My mom took me and my brother who's two years older than me to visit Mama. My brother decided that he and I would walk to the store down the street. As we were passing by this church called Daddy Grey about a half block from Mama's house, we saw some people in the back of the church waiting in line to get into this pool. My brother and I both looked at each other and said, "I want to get in the pool." So when we walked to the back to get in line, we saw three men standing in the pool helping people one by one into the pool.

My brother went before me. When it came around to me, the first man said something to me while putting his hand on the top of my head, and the next thing I knew, he was pulling me down underwater. I was wondering what was taking him so long to bring me up out of the water. Then the next thing I knew, the second man was taking me through his legs, and now I was starting to panic. I felt like they were trying to kill me, so I did what any little girl would have done. I started biting my way up out of there! The man started jumping and yelling, "She's biting me! She's biting me!" They hurried up and snatched me up out of that water.

My brother and I went back home to Mama's house, soaking wet from head to toe. As soon as we walked in the house, Mama and our mama said, "What happened to y'all? Where y'all been at to be wet like that?"

"We went to the church down the street and saw these people getting in the pool in the back of the church, and we wanted to get in the pool."

My mama said, "Get in the pool? Y'all ain't did nothing but get baptized!"

My mama and Mama laughed so hard like that was funniest thing they have ever heard. I didn't think it was funny because I really felt those men in the pool was trying to kill me. You ain't gotta keep somebody that long in the water to baptize them! This was my first time getting baptized, and do you know after I got baptized, the devil started bothering me!

It is said that the devil doesn't want the unsaved he wants the saved. He wants those who God has chosen to serve in his army, the ones God chosen to use for his service in building up his kingdom to help those who were lost, blind, deaf, and confused and the devil hates it! He'll do anything to get that person off the path God has for them, and I do mean anything!

I remember a couple of months after my brother and I got baptized in the pool at the back of the church. I was talking on the phone to who I thought was my cousin! Believe it or not, I know people have heard of the sayings that if you hear your name being called, don't answer because it might just be the devil. I do believe when people are trying to get close to God, the devil comes in disguises being busy in doing everything he possibly can to discourage that person from getting closer to God. But little does he know when he has scared you so much, all you wanna do is run to God!

I remember receiving a phone call as though it was yesterday. I was about five or six years old, and I was at home when the telephone rang. My cousin Linda was telling me that Mama told her to call me to tell me to come over because she was baking some cookies. I promise you, I heard Mama in the background as clear as day!

"Yes, Shannon, I'm baking some cookies. Tell your mama to bring you over and get you some."

At that moment, I yelled out to my mother who was in the other room. "E! Mama want me to come over and get some cookies!"

My mother walked in the room "What?"

"Linda is on the phone. She said Mama said to bring me over there because she baked some cookies."

My mother looked at me for a moment and then said, "Okay."

Once we got to Mama's house, my cousin Linda was there, and I said, "Mama, where the cookies you told me to come and get?"

Mama looked at me like I was crazy. "What cookies?"

"Linda called me, and I heard you in the background telling her to tell me to come over and get some cookies?"

Mama said, "I didn't bake no cookies."

And my cousin Linda said, "And I sure didn't call you!"

Mama said, "Nobody called you, that phone call came from the devil himself!"

After Mama told me this, I felt as if I was going to faint. Chills went all through my body to hear that I actually spoke to the devil! That's how the devil works? As soon as I got baptized, the devil was knocking at my door because he wants the saved. He wants the ones Jesus is calling. That's why you have to stay prayed up at *all times* because the Word is Jesus's armor of protection!

I was a tomboy growing up, and when we would go over to Mama's house, I would run outside on the back porch just to swing on her clothesline pole. On this day, we went over to Mama's house, and I went straight outside on the back porch to swing on her clothes line pole. When I jumped to grab the pole, my hands slipped, and I fell backward, hitting my head on the edge of the cement step! I jumped up, screaming for my life at the top of my lungs. I grabbed the back of my head and ran into the house. When I took my hand off the back of my head, it was full of blood, and I went to show my mother. She looked at me, turned around, went into the kitchen, got a rag, put some ice in it, gave it to me, and told me, "Now go and sit your a—— down somewhere!"

I looked at my mama wide-eyed as if "You not going to take me to the hospital?" Now I know I needed about six or seven stitches maybe more than that! But all I got was some ice in a rag. Now where was the love in that? I guess in the rag. That knot is still in the back of my head to this day! I want to say either my mama didn't have the money or Medicaid to take me to the hospital because I just don't want to believe that she just didn't care enough about me to take me to the hospital because she just didn't *feel like* going! Black people, yes, I'm talking about us! I've heard people telling their children, "Now you hurt yourself if you wanna because I *ain't going to no hospital!*" Come to think of it, that's exactly what it was. She didn't *feel like going to no hospital!* That's a shame!

Saxon Homes was the projects where we grew up, and every project had their sets. Whichever projects you grew up in, then that's where you were considered family, and we didn't mingle too much in other projects because we knew that we may had to fight someone who lived there who we didn't like. Growing up in my days was fun and exciting. People didn't fight with guns or knives, and if you did, then you were considered a coward! We may have fought like cats and dogs, but we were able to walk away to see another day, another day to come back and redeem ourselves just in case we lost that fight, and normally the person you fought, you both became the best of friends.

Drew Park was our hangout spot. It was a park with a recreational center and a big swimming pool out back! Drew Park was where I first joined the Girl Scouts! The one thing I always wanted to be was a Girl Scout, and they organized one over at the park. One day, we had a Girl Scout's meeting, and the meeting was held inside the center at the park. After the meeting was over, our leader decided that we could have a little fun, so she decided to turn on some music to have a *Soul Train* dance line. Dancing was one of the things that I loved and was very good at it if I may say so myself. Anytime I heard music, I would start dancing to the beat. It didn't matter where I was at. It could be in the grocery store. That was my cue to get down, and each time I would get down, my mom would tell me to "sit your a—— down somewhere before I tear it up!"

I would stop, but it wouldn't take me long before I was back to getting down, and I mean real good too! So when my mom came over to the center to check on me, it just so happened that she walked right in when it was my turn to go down the *Soul Train* line. She saw me getting down. She snatched me so fast up out of the line, and out the center we went. It was embarrassing, her pulling me by my arm across the street.

"I'll be damned if I spend any more of my money on you just to show your a—— dancing instead of you doing what you are supposed to do." She didn't even give me a chance to explain. I don't believe I was in Girl Scouts but a week or two!

Drew Park was where I learned how to play dominos, best known as bones! If you knew how to play bones these days and time, people would look at you as if you were one of the coolest persons in the room! I mean it's really nothing to playing dominos but counting! If you knew how to match up the end of a domino to match another end of a domino, that was already played on the board to total up an *even* number. Then you get the points. It's that simple, and I still have the hardest time trying to teach someone the game! I'll just tell them, "Well, maybe this isn't for you. Just try tic-tac-toe or something. You might like it."

Drew Park was a place where all the kids hung out every day, and everybody played with everyone without having any problems except this one day I'll never forget. I was over at the center just like on any other day, and it was this guy who came into the center. He was drunk, and one of the staff who worked there asked this guy to leave, but he wouldn't. The staff asked him again, but still the guy wouldn't leave. The drunk guy started getting loud with the staff. Then he started messing with some of us kids in the center for no reason, so the next thing I knew, the staff walked off. When he came back, he came back with one of those hard drinking glass Coca-Cola bottles in his hand, and he took that bottle swung it backward. He smashed the bottle so hard in the drunk man's face, I never saw anything like that ever in my life. It was like I was watching wrestling on TV. Blood was just pouring down his face like a river with glass sticking out of his face! I said that I knew the staff was trying to protect us kids, but at the same time, for him to have done something like that, he had to have had an anger problem!

Carver Elementary School was the school we all attended, my sister, brother, and cousins. We all gave the school the same address, which was my Auntie Betty's address. Our family wanted all of us to attend the same school, not because it was a good school, only because they said they wanted all of us to stick together. Just in case someone tried to bother one of us, we were all together to help one another. It was the school that I remember having my first crush on my PE teacher. He was one of the reasons I liked going to school. Now ain't that something! Carver Elementary was the first school I remember that sent home permission slips from the principal to the parents in requesting permission to paddle their children if they were sent to the office. Well, you know I got rid of my slip real fast, but it didn't matter because everybody else went home with theirs. I personally think the school should have kept the paddle concept in the schools because it only took me once to go to the office to feel the burn, and you better not flinch or that was an extra lick added on to the ones you were already getting! That butt-whooping was a blessing for me because "If Only You Knew."

During this time, in my classroom on certain days, two students were allowed to take a pet home for about two or three days at a time, so it was my turn to take home a pet, and I decided to take home Henry, our gerbil. Henry was cute and soft, and I was playing with Henry in the kitchen throwing him up in the air and catching him when he came down. While I were throwing Henry up in the air, I was wondering to myself, "What would happen to Henry if I decided to just not catch him? Will he land on his feet?"

So I decided not to catch Henry, and Henry did not land on his feet. Henry went splat on the floor! Henry was all over the place, and his blood was so stank. The smell was horrible, nothing like anything I've ever smelled before. I ruined it for everyone in the class. No one was allowed to take another pet home again. So you know I was hated by all the kids in the classroom. Everyone called me Henry the Gerbil Killa!

One day, I was the last one to have come out of the little girl's restroom. I remember our janitor being this big, tall, ugly, drippety-drip Jheri curl man who walked in the little's girl's room right after I came out and stopped me. He stated that I didn't flush the toilet after I used it. Hell, there was about seven bathroom stalls in the girls' restroom. How would he know which one I used. So because of one toilet not being flushed, the janitor made me clean up the entire girl's restroom toilets and all! If I only knew, we could have sued! Sued them for having me clean up those nasty toilets!

But you talk about somebody *hot*, my daddy! Remember I'm a daddy's girl, and when my daddy came up to the school, both my daddy and the janitor was toe to toe and nose to nose in the principal's office having it out until the principal was about to call the police. My dad told the principal, "Well, call the police because what the hell he doing going behind my child coming out of the bathroom and sitting in there with her while she cleaning it up!"

I had confidence in my daddy because I knew my daddy was a tough man who put you in the mind of James Evens on *Good Times*, especially when he gets mad. But I was afraid for my daddy at the same time because this janitor was big, tall, and *ugly* with his scary curl looking like a lion, tiger, and bear. Oh my! At the end, the principal apologized to my dad and me, and do you know I still see that janitor with the same Jheri curl to this day! He's a baseball referee. I should have knocked him upside the head with one of those balls that came over the fence, but I remember I'm a child of God now. So please be patient with me 'cause GOD is not through with me yet!

Carver Elementary also was the school where I had to learn how to fight. I was getting tired of the kids always picking at my navel. When I was born, my mother told me that I was born with a hernia in my navel. My navel was so huge to where you could see it through my shirt, and if my shirt came up, then the kids would always say, "Oh, Shannon, you have a wee-wee." I told my mom how the kids would always pick on me about my navel looking like a penis. My mom told me, "The next time a child pick on you about your navel looking like a wee-wee, you shake it at them like a wee-wee." Well, I did, and this little boy tore my little butt up, so my mom started tapping Kennedy half dollar coins on my navel every day to help my navel go down, but that didn't work because as soon as I got to the candy store by the school, I would pull up my shirt and rip the money right off my navel to buy some candy. Every day, I came home without the coin on my navel. My mom tore my butt up, but I didn't care because candy was my weakness! I loved candy like crazy. I loved it so much I remember stealing a classmate's bag of candy out of her book bag. She knew I stole her candy, but I didn't confess to it, and I felt really bad because she was my only friend in the class. I knew I was wrong, but that didn't stop me from keeping the bag of candy! I can't say I don't know why I stole her bag of candy because I do. I love candy, and I can't say I know where I picked that bad habit up from. Maybe it was in my blood because stealing sure ran on my mom side of the family.

I remember as a little girl around three or four, I know my mom would probably say she doesn't remember this or she didn't do this, but I remember it like it was yesterday. You know kids remember *everything*! I remember my mom taking me to the store to buy me this bathing suit, but she didn't buy it. She stuffed it under my dress that I had on and told me, "Don't you say nothing."

And I didn't until now! But I can't put my stealing on my mom or anyone else as long as I knew right from wrong, and we parents tend to do that to our children. "I don't know where they got that bad habit from?" Well, maybe they got it from you, from seeing you or maybe you used to steal. It's in your blood and now theirs! "I got it from my mama!" Just like fighting, my dad told me that I was like my mom. When she was growing up, she was a little feisty something, and she didn't back down from anyone!

On this particular day, I remember coming home from school, and I remember this little girl wanting to fight me. Why, I don't remember. Probably me running off with my mouth as always. Well, anyway, I told myself that I was not going to let anyone else beat me up again, so I picked up some dirt and kept it in my hand. As soon as this girl approached me, I threw the dirt in her face, and she blocked the dirt from going in her eyes! At that moment, I said to myself, "Uh-oh, my plan didn't work. Here comes another a——— whooping!"

When I got home, my mom asked me what had happened to me, and when I told her, she walked me back around the corner and told me if I didn't fight this little girl back, she was going to whoop my a———! So I did what any child would do. I fought for my life, and after that, this little girl and I became the best of friends! That's why I love what Tupac the rapper said in one of his rap songs, and I find it to be true growing up: "Your best friends become your enemies and your enemies your best friend." Once we became friends, then her friends became my friends, and we all became the best of friends.

I remember one day, my girlfriends and I were all walking home from school taking the same routine that we normally take every day. On this particular corner, there's a barbershop, and this barbershop had one apartment next to it. For the longest time, we never knew who stayed in that apartment nor did we care. Until one day, we all came around the corner walking home from school. We saw a black man, butt naked, heavy Vaseline greased down from head to toe, standing in his doorway playing with himself! We all screamed and ran across to the other side of the street! Coming home from school the next day, we saw the same naked man greased from head to toe playing with himself in his doorway. Again we all ran to the other side of the street. So the next day, I told my girlfriends that I was tired of looking at that nasty, disgusting pervert who waited until we got out of school to be in his doorway waiting for us to walk by. I told my girlfriends that I wanted them to walk by like we normally do but on the other side of the street, of course, because once he saw us, we knew that he was coming out. I had a big surprise waiting for him. So sure enough, like clockwork, my girlfriends all walked by while I stayed behind, and he came out like he normally did, looking all greasy and nasty. While his attention was on my girlfriends, I came from around his door, got right in front of him, and rocked his butt up with a bunch of rocks. You should have seen how he fell down on the ground, kicking and screaming like a girl while I was tearing his butt up with those rocks. Then the police pulled up, jacked his butt up, and took him off to jail, just like he was, butt-naked! My girlfriends and I laughed for days!

After that, I was considered as one of the toughest girls in the neighborhood. I thought I was so tough that I started picking on this guy we all called in the neighborhood Johnny the Water Maker, and if you lived in Saxon Homes, then you would remember who Johnny the Water Maker was. I don't know why they called him Johnny the Water Maker. The only thing I could think of was just that his pants was always high water, and he had a switch in his walk, a girly switch, and a switched when he talked (crazy and slow), and he didn't bother anybody that I knew of. But one day, I decided to bother him. That man chased my little bad behind all the way home screaming and yelling, "Mama!" You would have thought I was a track star and him too because he was right on my heels. I just knew he had me. I think that day was the fastest I ever ran in my life. He didn't catch me, and I learned my lesson that day. I never messed with Johnny the Water Maker ever again!

I was never a bully, but after my mom threatened to whoop my behind after the last incident, I told myself I wouldn't back down from anyone else again. I remember this cross-eyed, half-blind little boy who wore these thick bottle eye glasses. He started messing with me. For what reason, I don't remember. I just remember him following me and taunting me at the same time all the way home, and as soon as I got close to my auntie's house in Saxon Homes, I got big and bold because I knew I was home. Before he could say another word, I turned around and clocked that boy so hard upside his head that I knocked his glasses off his face. Then I realized that he couldn't see without them because he was down on the ground, trying to feel for his glasses, so I took my foot and stomped on them to pieces. I'll show him messing with me!

The next thing you know, the little boy's mother came back with him to talk to my mom about me stepping on her son's glasses, and she needed to pay for them. I thought for sure I was going to get in trouble about his glasses, but my mom told his mother that she wasn't paying for nothing, and her son didn't have any business bothering her child and that I should have whooped his a—— and if she didn't get out of her face that she was going to whoop her a——! Like I said, I got it from my mama!

At the age of seven, one weekend, we were spending the night over to my Auntie Betty's house in Saxon Homes, something my sister, brother, and I did on a regular. Our parents would drop us off because they worked on the weekend, and they needed our auntie to watch us. My auntie's house was the babysitting house for all of us cousins as well. The babysitting house, card playing house, drinking house, party house, just the all-around fun house for us! I remember having my one and only birthday party at my auntie's house. On this particular weekend, it was on a Sunday, and there were at least five other people in the house at the time—my auntie, my two cousins, my sister, brother, and me. The spirit of the Lord woke me up from out of my sleep from everybody else and said, "Get up. Put on your clothes and go down to the church!" Now no one in my family that I knew of at the time were churchgoing folks, never went to church, never took us to church, and never talked about church, so out of all of my family members, what made God decide to choose me to wake me up to be the one to go to church? I guess I would soon find out. I knew it had to be God at the time because we've never went to church, so how would I know what the church looked like?

I got up, got dressed, and walked by myself about two blocks around the corner from the house to the community church. The Lord got me up early enough to make it to Sunday school, something I've never done before. He took me straight to where they were having Sunday school service in the basement of the church. I walked straight down to the basement with other people as if I had been attending that church all along. After Sunday school was over, I walked back upstairs into the church sanctuary to stay for their regular Sunday services, and I had one of the most wonderful times of my life! When I started walking back home, I saw people running around like ants. My family saw me and said, "Where have you been? Everybody have been looking for you!"

I said in my baby voice, "I went to church."

"Church!"

As I look back on that day, I now know that God had his hands on me. He had a plan for my life, and he was preparing me for my future!

My first day in church, I was hooked, and from then on, the Lord was waking me up every Sunday so I could attend Sunday school and Sunday services, and I always went by myself! I remember Mama saying, "Ain't that something that child wake up every Sunday like that just to go to church." I remember my mother saying, "Oh, the only reason that child going to church is to eat up those people's snacks down there!"

I said to myself, "Well, maybe I did like eating their snacks, but I still raised my hand to read the Bible." What my mother and family didn't know was that I was really listening and enjoying everything that was being taught to me in Sunday school, and I proved it to her one day when I was misbehaving. Right when my mama swung the belt to beat me, I started singing this church song: "Please be patient with me. God is not through with me yet." When Mama heard me singing, she told my mama, "Don't you beat her. Leave her alone

29

and let her sing the song." I sang that song like my life depended on it because it did, and Mama rocked and sang alone right with me. When God gets through with me, I shall come forth as pure gold.

I knew from then on that if I did something wrong, all I had to do was sing my way out of it. I wasn't a child who was extremely bad. I was just the kind of child that always spoke up or defended myself, but if you let my mother tell it, I was someone who was back talking and being disrespectful toward her. On this particular day, I'll never forget it, I got in trouble again, and right before my mother was getting ready to beat me, I started singing my song "Please be patient with me. God is not through with me yet." My mama looked at me and said in a stern voice, "If you sing that song one more time, I'll kill ya!" When I saw the look my mother had in her eyes when she said this, I said to myself, "Oh, she ain't playing!" So I didn't sing that song again until I got grown!

You know I believe that I was born an actress because I could remember any time when my mother was getting ready to beat me, I told myself, "Okay, get ready" because right when she swung that first lick with the belt, I would always, I mean always, fall to the floor kicking and screaming. You would have thought that my mama was killing me, but that didn't stop her from tearing my behind up! So one day, my mom was getting ready to beat me with a belt, and as soon as she lifted the belt up to hit me and was about to bring it down, I was already on the floor kicking and screaming like someone was killing me! The belt never touched me, and when I finally opened my eyes, my mother was looking at me like, "What the hell, so you been faking all this time!"

I said to myself, "Oh, Lord, I done fell too quick, she done bust me!" I guess she had to laugh to herself because she told me to get up off the floor before she killed me!

When I was a young girl, my Auntie Zena, my dad's only sister, used to call me Free Love, and I asked her once I got older, "Why do you call me Free Love?"

She said, "Because it didn't matter who you met or what you had in your hand. You would always ask someone, even a stranger, you want this or that you would give them your last!" Wow, wasn't that something. That's why I thank God for giving me the heart to show love and to give love!

I don't remember a whole lot about myself when I was attending Carver Elementary School. I do remember my parents allowing me to go on my first and only field trip to Charleston, South Carolina. I remember her packing a small portion of food with me to eat on the trip. It had to be a very small portion, or I was just greedy because when we made it to Charleston, I had finish eating just about all my food. I remember sitting around hungry, looking at all the other kids enjoying their food their parents packed for them which seemed as though their parents packed their foods for days, and do you know those selfish kids didn't offer me any of their food. I guess they said I shouldn't have eaten all my food coming down the road!

I remember being in love with Smokey Robinson. Where girls my age was like, "Who? What? You're in love with who?" Now I know that man was just too old for me, but I didn't care. And when I found out that Smoky Robinson had the same horoscope as mine, Aquarius, I just knew it was meant to be! I remember having a school performance at school, and there was this all-female dance group of some of the cool girls from Saxon Homes practicing for the performance. I found out that they were going to perform in their Nickle-bottom pants, now called capris, and they were going to sing the song "Square Biz" by Teena Marey. I begged and begged my parents to let me practice and perform with the group because I too wanted a pair of capris. My mom told me no all the way up until the last two or three days before the show. I did get to perform in the show, but I was so embarrassed because I couldn't remember the steps or the words to the song. The only thing good that came out of it all was me having a pair of the Nickle-bottom pants!

I'll never forget my fifth-grade teacher that I felt at that time loved me more than my own mother! She was and will be the only teacher I ever loved like a mother. I wish there were more teachers like her in this world today who really truly made a difference in a child's life! A teacher who not *only* loved to teach but one who loved the children she taught! She gave you a listening ear, good advice, and a big hug at the end.

Another teacher I remembered was my math teacher who just knew she were the finest thang walking the face of this earth with all that black lipstick on her lips, which she didn't need because her lips were big enough! Now she did have a very nice thick Coca-Cola bottle shape on her. I remember her acting like she was so professional as a teacher and her thinking that she was just the s——, I remember someone farted in the classroom, and she went off! "Somebody done passed gas with you stank a——. Didn't your mamas teach you any manners! Nobody wants to smell your stank a——. I wish I knew who did it. I would teach you some manners with your nasty self!"

It was so funny, I said to myself, "Now how did she just go from Mrs. Professional Teacher of the Year to Mrs. Ghetto Fabulous!"

There was another recreational center that we all used to play at right next to our elementary school. I believed that I was just around nine or ten years old at the time. On this particular day, we were all just running around, playing in the center as usual with my sister, brother, cousins, friends, and my sister's so-called boyfriend. The game room that we were all playing in had a piano in it, and my sister's boyfriend and I were playing together, chasing each other around the room, and then around the piano, from one end of the piano to the other. I was standing in front of the piano to see which way that he was going to come, not knowing that the piano had a broken leg. He was standing on the end of the piano, peeping at me. The weight of his body pushed the piano over, which fell down on top of me, and this was an old heavy-duty back in the day, school piano, the one that your chorus teacher played on.

The piano was so heavy that it took four men and my sister just to lift it up just a little bit while someone pulled me from under it. I was screaming at the top of my lungs because the piano keys that stick out from the piano landed on my knees! The man who pulled me from under the piano picked me up and handed me to my uncle.

Back in those days, my family used to call me Mickey. "Give it to Mickey. She'll eat it. Mickey eats *everything*. She likes it. She likes it."

So when the man gave me to my uncle, I was still screaming, and I guess my uncle wanted to shut me up because he handed me his icy lick-up, and I used to love some icy lick-ups. We all did. I remember we used to go to the candy house about two to three times a day just to buy some lick-ups. All they were, were just different-flavored and different-colored Kool-Aid, frozen in a small Styrofoam cup that were only 10 cents. Something our mama could have made, but black people were serious about their Kool-Aid. They were not going to waste their Kool-Aid talking about putting it in the freezer for us just to suck the juice off the ice. No, they told us, "You're not wasting my Kool-Aid putting it in no freezer so drank it like you been doing!" Because as soon as we sucked the entire flavor out of the ice, we would throw the ice at people or their cars and run! Yeah, we were bad kids!

As soon as my uncle gave me his lick-up, I stopped crying and started sucking on that lick-up like that was going to be my last lick-up in the world! I remember my mom taking me to the hospital and me not being able to walk after the doctor claimed that there was nothing wrong with me. They didn't even give me crutches to walk on. The doctor told my mother that nothing was broken on me, but I still couldn't walk and still couldn't figure out why the doctor said that there wasn't anything wrong with me.

I couldn't walk, so I crawled around the house like a snake while some of my mom's family members laughed at me. They laughed and pointed at me saying, "Look at that lil black monkey crawling around on the floor!"

Yeah, everybody thought it was funny, even my mom. Everyone except my brother! My brother got tired of everyone picking and laughing at me so he went outside and found me the right stick. This stick was the perfect stick, the right height, the right size, and the right design. This stick had the shape of the letter *V* at the top, and I now know that God placed that stick there just so my brother would find it for me. My brother took a cloth and wrapped it around the *V* part of the stick so I would be able to walk around comfortably without having to crawl around on the floor. That stick became my crutch. I'll never forget what my big brother did for me on that day, and after that, I loved my brother even harder because my right knee is still messed up to this day. Sometimes, my leg would collapse from under me, and I find myself trying to get up off the ground. It was embarrassing.

Another thing I liked about growing up in Saxon Homes was free lunch! Who remembers free lunch? Free lunch was something we definitely appreciated as a child growing up. I know I did. Free lunch was always given out on the weekend at the center in Saxon Homes, and my auntie made sure that we all got out in time enough to walk down to the center to get it! "Okay, y'all better get on outta here and go down there to get that free lunch 'cause I ain't cooking nothing so don't come looking in my face for nothing!" Free lunch was served early, and you had to get there early before all the lunch bags were gone because you better know it was a long line to get in when you got there, and some of us would get back in line hoping the people didn't remember that they had already given us a bag. We all would stand around opening up our bags just to see what we had like opening up a Cracker Jack box just to see what prize we got? Most of us liked the ham and cheese sandwiches or the grape juice, and if we had something in our bag we didn't like, we would try to find someone to trade with like we had a choice to be choosy!

Well, God allowed me to graduate from Carver Elementary, and now I must move on to middle school. Crayton Middle School, another school we all attended together. Only I had to be the *only* one to break the cycle when I got kicked out in the eighth grade. But before I tell you the entire reason, let me first ease you into it by giving you a little info on me growing up in my middle school years. I used to be a tomboy growing up, climbing trees, not carrying a purse and always fighting the boys. How I hated the boys because they used to try and feel my butt, and they weren't going to stop until they got a feel, and I wasn't going to stop until I got my man, I mean, little boy, and when I did, *pow wow* right in the *kisser*!

As a matter of fact, that's how I learned how to fight by fighting boys, especially my boy cousin on my daddy's side. Yeah, I definitely got tired of his bad behind beating me up every time he saw me for real! Each time we went down to the country in Allendale to my grandparents' house and he was there, he would always beat me up and always tell me, "I'ma keep beating you up until you stop crying and learn how to fight back." Until one day, I got tired, fought back, and had him running! I guess when you're scared, sometimes you don't have any other choice but to fight back!

While in the sixth grade, my cousin Beeve, who looked like a midget, was kinda slow, poor lil thang. I heard my auntie, the one who lived in Saxon Homes, used to drink a lot of liquor while she was pregnant with him. Well, Beeve and I both used to walk to the bus stop together and had started skipping school some days and staying at home. We would go off to school together and miss the bus intentionally, wait until everybody had left the house, and go back home to play who could make the hottest paper airplanes. Not just any kind of airplane, the glider airplane. I used to think my cousin was a little slow in the head, but if you think about it, I must have been slow too to play hooky from school just to stay at home to play paper airplanes all day.

I tried to use my cousin to go to the candy store for me, knowing we weren't supposed to be outside because we were playing hooky from school, but we didn't care because both of us were candy freaks. I gave Beeve a list of all the candy that I wanted him to bring me back while I sat at the house chilling watching cartoons! When Beeve got back from the candy store, there wasn't one thing in that bag I ask for!

I said, "Cuz, where's the candy I ask for?"

He said in his little slow (literally slow) mouse voice, "They didn't have it."

I said, "Okay, so where is my money?"

He said, "I spent it."

I said, "So where is the candy I asked for?"

He said, "They didn't have it."

I said again, "So where is my money since they didn't have the candy I wanted."

And he said again, "I spent it."

So I said, "Oh, I see. You spent my money on the candy that you wanted."

I realized my cousin Beeve wasn't slow after all, but I still tore his behind up and threw him in the closet underneath the stairs for spending up my money on the candy he wanted.

Anyone who has ever lived in Saxon Homes would tell you that under the stairs was a closet, a very dark and scary closet with no lights! I was so mad at my cousin. Even though he was about two years older but a lot shorter, I still tore his little behind up. Beeve was kicking and screaming trying to get out of that closet, but I was stronger. I had my back to the door so he wouldn't get out until we both fell asleep. When my aunt came home, I was watching TV, and she asked me, "Where is the Beeve?" That's the name she calls him, The Beeve. At that moment, I just remember I left the Beeve in the closet! Uh-oh! When I opened the door, the Beeve fell out the closet, balled up at the door, still asleep. At that moment, I knew it was time to make a run for it. My aunt looked at me and chased behind me with a knife talking about "I'll kill ya!"

I had to use someone else's phone to call my mom to come and pick me up, and when she did, boy oh boy did see come. She came to fight my aunt, her sister, for running me out of her house especially with a knife. They had a big argument because at that time, my aunt was a drunk, and she didn't care about cutting nobody, so she ran my mama out of the house with the same knife. Everyone was trying to hold my mama back, but she didn't want anyone to hold her. She said, "Don't hold me. She done pulled a knife on me and my child!" So when my mom got away and went back in the house, my aunt was passed out on the floor, drunk. I remember my mama leaning down telling her, "See, I could kill your a—— right now!"

I told myself, "Now I see where I get all this fighting in me from!" singing the song "I Got It from My Mama."

After that day, my cousin and I didn't cut school again, at least not from that school anyway! But being a candy junky caused me a lot, caused me to have to go to the dentist and get four teeth pulled at one time. You would have thought it would have stopped me from eating candy the way that I did, but it didn't. I was addicted, just like a crackhead addicted to crack! My auntie's house in Saxon Homes was where all the happenings were. I remember them having a card game playing for money, and my mom sent me upstairs to get her purse where she hid it, and it was a good thing she did because I caught the Beeve, who was a big rogue as Mama would say, about to go into my mom's purse.

"Why a rogue, Mama?"

"Because Mama said a rogue will steal any and everything that ain't nailed down!"

I grabbed my mom's purse and went to wailing on the Beeve. I ran downstairs to tell my mom what had happened, and Beeve ran downstairs to tell my auntie that I beat him up. Now my mom and auntie were about to fight again because my mom knew how much of a thief my cousin were, and she was glad I caught him going into her purse. But my auntie don't play with no one messing with the Beeve. "The Beeve don't have to steal a damn thang, and y'all can just get the hell out of my house!" My auntie was good for putting you out of her house, so we always were prepared for it!

I was over at my auntie's house watching TV, and my auntie was feeling good. Well, let the truth be told she was drunk, and she wanted me to put a relaxer in her hair. "Auntie, I don't think that you're able to get a relaxer in your hair today."

"Why not? I got some relaxer, and I need my hair done!"

What I really wanted to say was, "Auntie, you're too drunk to get a relaxer in your hair!"

When my auntie gets drunk, she won't sit still. She's all over the place, or she's passed out on the floor. "You just do what the hell I tell you and put my relaxer in my hair! Now how you like them apples!" That was one of my aunt's favorite lines, especially when she has told you off. "Now how you like them apples!" And when she was talking to me, she would say, "Now how you like them crabs!" because she knew that I love seafood and the blue crabs are my favorite.

I told my aunt to sit in a chair in her kitchen while I applied the relaxer. I worked it in, and right when it was time for me to rinse the relaxer out of her hair, she passed out at the kitchen table! I started panicking and saying to myself that if she didn't get this relaxer out of her hair, it's going to burn her scalp up! Poor lil thang don't know nothing because she's passed out! I kept screaming, "Betty, get up. I have to rinse this relaxer out of your hair. Get up!"

She was not bugging, and I was getting scared because it was over the time for me to rinse the relaxer out of her hair, and I was saying to myself, "I know that relaxer is tearing her scalp up by now!"

I decided to bear-hug her from behind and carry her to the sink, so now I'm behind her, trying to hold her up while trying to rinse the relaxer out of her hair, but her head wasn't in the sink. It was leaning on the side, resting on her arm. I'm trying to get her to get under the water faucet, and she's smearing the relaxer all over her face with her arm and all in her eyes. I'm like, "Oh lord, what in the world!" It took me some time to get that relaxer out of her hair, and that was the last time that I ever put a relaxer in her hair again. I'm surprised she didn't come out looking like Fire Marshall Bill on *In Living Color*.

I remember one of the funniest things that have ever happened to my auntie. She was so drunk one day talking about how no one loved her and everyone was full of s———. I watched her walk up the stairs and into the bathroom. She didn't close the door behind her. She was still talking to herself, so I decided to sneak upstairs behind her to see what she was doing. My aunt was standing in the mirror looking at herself, and then she started crying an ole ugly cry, and the next thing I knew, the mirror cracked in pieces! I've heard of a person being ugly and looking into the mirror until the mirror cracked, but I would have never believed it if I didn't see it with my own eyes! Now my auntie isn't an ugly woman, but when she gets drunk, that's just another whole look.

My family kept asking me what happened to the mirror, and I kept telling them, but they didn't believe me, but I knew the truth! My auntie is not an ugly woman. She was just like a lot of us who wasn't ugly until we got drunk. That *ugly drunk*, and please don't let us start crying. I can say now my auntie have been sober for over ten years. Thank you, God! But she's still cursing you out and putting you out! LOL.

My Uncle Greg, my mom's baby brother who was attending high school just a couple of streets over from my middle school, used to love to walk over to my school with a couple of his buddies just to check up on us, and it never seemed to fail that whenever one of the young boys from our school would see them, they would say something smart to them about them being too old to be at our school or something, and he would always tell them, "You just stay right there. I got somebody for you." So he would send someone to find me, and once I came to where he was, the first thing he would tell me was, "Lil niece, this little joker just got smart with me. Now I want you to slap the taste out of his mouth." And with no hesitation, I'll do it! Slap the taste out of one of my classmates' mouth! Then my uncle would get up in their face and tell them, "Now when I leave, if you put your hands on my niece, I'm coming back, and it's not going to be nice when I see ya!" This happened maybe about three or four times, and the boys never thought about hitting me back when they left! I never told my parents about what I did because for one, I was young and didn't know any better and scared about what they would have done if they would have found out.

I was thirteen years old when I first had *sex*! I remember going over to this boy's house who was around my age. He lived maybe a block away from my auntie's house in Saxon Homes. His mom was not home, and I remember going into his bedroom. We both started taking off our clothes, and I was nervous but curious. I remember him getting on top of me, and as soon as he started to penetrate into me, his mom came home. We jumped up. I grabbed my clothes and sneaked into the bathroom. His mom must have known something was wrong because she opened the door to the bathroom. But by then, I had already put my clothes back on. I was so embarrassed, and I didn't think about sex or a boy again until I called myself falling deep in love (puppy love) with my best friend's boyfriend. The same best friend in my early years who wanted to fight me and I tried throwing dirt in her eyes but missed, and she whooped my behind.

I felt bad that I liked him so much, knowing that he was my best friend's boyfriend, but I couldn't help it. He was just so...so fine, short but fine! He put you in the mind of a very, very short but fine Billy Dee Williams. I was so in love with him. I remember walking all the way to his house, which was about a twenty- to thirty-minute walk. I didn't care. I walked while listening to the Cindy Lauper song "Girls Just Wanna Have Fun" on my boom box. "Girls Just Wanna Have Fun" was the song that all the girls rocked to! Nothing ever happened between Keith and me, just conversation and laughs. I walked over there a couple more times, and he nor I never mentioned it to my girlfriend. It was just our little secret.

Years later, Keith got into some trouble and went to prison and because he was so fine but too little to defend himself. They turned lil Keith out and made him their woman! Poor lil Keith. I felt really sorry for him because when he got out years later, he had changed to wearing women's makeup, clothes, and high heels. I wouldn't have believed it if I didn't see it with my own eyes!

Drew Park started a swim team that a lot of my girlfriends from the neighborhood had already joined, so you know I had to join regardless if I were a good swimmer or not. My brother also joined the team because he wanted to compete against our cousin who had joined another swim team. We used to have fun at practice until one day, I almost drowned, and my mother had to come and curse the coach out to make him let me out of the pool! We were at swimming practice, and one of the games we played were shark. The way that you played shark was whoever was tagged shark had to swim underwater while holding their breath, and the only way you could come up for air was after you tagged a person who came up for air. But if that person went back down in the water before you tagged them, then you were not allowed to tagged that person!

It seemed as though everyone I swam to trying to tag them would go right back underwater, and I felt myself getting tired and weak every second, so I swam to the edge of the pool to get my breath and some energy. But each time I would swim to the edge of the pool, our coach would tell someone to push me back in. Don't let her get out. They was clawing my fingers off the edge of the pool and pushing me back in all the while I was trying to get my breath and keep myself up from drowning. All I could think of was that I was going to die, so I started screaming to some people who was standing on the outside of the gate watching us practice, "Somebody go and get my mama!"

And my mama came walking fast! "Why in the hell would you not let my child out of the pool. I want her out right now!" The coach asked my mom if she was just taking me out of the pool or off the swim team, and my mom told him that she was taking me off the swim team altogether. I was glad my mama came and saved me, but I was upset to be off of the swim team!

After that, I just decided to play tennis with one of my best friends just for fun. Tootsie and I were really good at playing tennis. We played all the time, and I really fell in love with it. I do believe that if my parents would have supported me in tennis even though I was just playing for fun, I too could have been another Venus or Serena!

I wasn't the kind of girl that liked putting on makeup until one day, while still in middle school, I walked into the girl's bathroom and started watching this lil white girl putting on makeup. You would have thought that she was a makeup artist. The way she was putting her makeup on was like nothing I've ever seen before.

She asked me, "Would you like for me to apply some makeup on you? I think you'll like it."

I said yes! Honey, that white girl transformed me into a black Olivia Newton-John on *Grease* that day! The next day, I applied my makeup on the exact same way and every day after that. Until many years later, it took a guy, a stranger, to tell me that I was beautiful without all that makeup on my face. Some people really don't need all that makeup on their faces looking like Ronald McDonald! My sisters, you're more beautiful without it! I never understood why some women would shave their eyebrows completely off just to draw them back on? Will that be you?

I'm an animal lover, and I love dogs. I remember one day walking around the corner to my uncle's house to play with my cousins, and I saw some baby puppies that was just born and left on the side of the road by their momma. Having the heart that I have, I just couldn't let those defenseless little puppies stay on the side of the road and get ran over. I found this card board box, and I scooped the baby puppies up and took them around to my uncle's house to show my cousins. As soon as my auntie opened the door, she said, "If you don't get those rats from around my house, child, I'll kill ya!"

I said, "Rats?"

"Yeah, rats. Don't you see how long their tails are?"

I dropped the box and started running. My auntie called me back, "No, you don't! You better get back here and get these damn rats out of my yard!"

I came back crying and scared. "Auntie, I don't wanna pick them rats up. I'm scared!"

"You picked them up and brought 'em round here. Now take 'em back from where you got 'em from!"

My cousins laughed at me so hard, I'll never forget it. You should have seen how fast I started running with the rats on the box. When I got back around the corner from where I found them, I threw the rats, the box, and kept on running! I was young. I didn't know any better.

By this time, we had moved about three to four times, and the neighborhood we had just moved in was pretty nice. This was my first time ever getting a bike and the last time. My parents brought us all bikes for Christmas so while I was enjoying riding my new bike for the first time up and down our street, there were some girls around my age sitting on their porch giggling, laughing, and pointing at me. I'm wondering what was so funny and why were they laughing and pointing at me. I didn't know them, and they didn't know me. Maybe they were jealous of my new bike. So I said to myself that since they were pointing and laughing at me, I would give them something to look at. I had decided to ride my bike past them without any hands, showing off. The next thing I knew, I crashed, me and my bike was on the ground twisted. I'm sure those girls were on the ground too laughing, but I didn't look. I couldn't hear, and I was in too much pain to even care. Plus I was scared and mad that I broke my first bike on the first day. My mom yelled at me and never asked if I was okay. She just told me that was the last time she wasted any money on another bike.

At this time, I didn't know that my parents were having marital problems until one day when I walked in on my mother in the kitchen cooking. She was mad, walking back and forth and telling my grandmamma (Mama) on the phone about how she didn't appreciate my dad doing what he did and that she was going to fix his a——! Now like I said, I just remember my mom cooking on the stove, but what she was boiling in the pot, I just didn't understand! She was boiling water. Then I saw where she put Clorox, lye, bleach, salt, and whatever else she thought was needed to go in it. I thought to myself, "What is she doing?"

So after the pot cooled off, my mama poured everything in a jar, closed it up, and placed it on top of the refrigerator. Later on that evening, when my dad came home, my sister, brother, and I were in the room, and we heard our dad and mom arguing. So my sister and I came out of the room to see what was going on, but my brother stayed because he felt like nothing serious was going on. It was just normal.

He just said, "Oh, they'll be all right." Maybe he knew something I didn't!

Our parents' argument turned into them fighting each other, and my sister and I were trying to break them up. My mama ran to get the jar off the top of the refrigerator that had the solution in it, and while she was trying to open it up, she and my dad were still fighting. She had the jar in one hand and hitting him with the other. While she was hitting him, she was trying to open up the jar at the same time, but she couldn't get it open. She put it on too tight or the solution in the jar had pressure on it where it was just too tight. Either way, she couldn't get the top off. I was in between the both of them trying to stop them from fighting! When my mom finally got the jar open, the solution went *everywhere*—some on my mom and me but mostly on my dad. They kept fighting until we all started feeling a little funny like something was on us like you had to stop and look up in the air like, "Why do I feel the way that I do, like my skin feels like it's burning. Something just ain't right!"

My mom looked at me. I looked at my mom, and we both ran out of the house screaming running to our white neighbor's house across the street. My mom and I went banging on her door screaming and yelling, "I'm on fire! I'm on fire! Somebody help us!"

She was so nice. She opened the door, grabbed us up, and threw us both in a tub of water. My mom and I looked like the mother and daughter on *Poltergeist*, all hugged up together when the mother went and got Caroline from the other side. And they both came back holding on to each other tight! That might have been the only time my mom and I hugged. That's a shame. We had to be on fire before we could get close like that! My mom and I stayed in that tub over an hour before we went back home to find my dad gone.

Hours later, my dad finally came back home. And when he walked through the front door, we knew that he had been at the hospital. I would not lie. My dad was bandaged up, wrapped up, and taped up from head to toe, looking like a real mummy. I turned and looked at my mom, and her eyes got big. My mom ran to her room, crying her eyes out, and I heard her saying out loud, "Oh my god, what have I done?"

I looked at my mom and rolled my eyes, saying to myself, "You know what you did. Got my daddy walking round here looking like a mummy!" Either she was hurt because she didn't know that she hurt my dad that bad or just scared thinking she was going to jail. Either way, I knew my mom learned a lesson that day—not to mix too many chemicals together the next time!

Even though we moved from place to place, most of our childhood time was spent at my auntie's house in Saxon Homes. There wasn't a day that didn't go by that all my girlfriends and I didn't hang out together. Either we were all at the park, at each other's houses, at the mall, at the movies, or hanging out at a basketball or football game. I remember some of us going to the New Edition concert that was downtown! "Cool it now… You got to cool it now… Oh, watch out… You're gonna lose control." New Edition was the new young group that all the young girls loved. Ronnie, Bobby, Ricky, and Mike. "If I like the girl, who cares who you like," and I was in love with Mike! We all picked our favorite singer, and if you thought about picking anybody's man, it might have been a fight! Like those guys really knew who we were, and we were really their girlfriends.

I remember us being right up front by the stage that you could almost touch their pants leg. I remember me throwing a flower, a teddy bear, or something on stage, and one of them in the group throw it off the stage into the crowd. I was so mad because all my girlfriends thought that it was funny, but my feelings were hurt because I thought I was doing something nice! I broke up with Mike that day and didn't want anything else to do with him until a week later. I was back in love, singing all their songs!

It didn't matter where we went or what we did. We all did it together, and everyone knew when you saw one you saw us all. There was about ten of us in the group, and we had decided to name ourselves the Fila Females because back in those days Filas was the thang. So we all decided to go to the mall to get our Fila tennis shoes and our Fila shirts! We were poor, so all I could afford was one pair of sneakers and one shirt while some of the other girls had different sneakers and shirts, but I learned later that they got their clothes and a lot of other things using their five-finger discount (stealing)!

Now, I'm not bragging, but I must say that all of us in the group were some attractive young ladies, and most of us had the most popular, coolest, and toughest boyfriends around the neighborhood, and they wasn't bad-looking. So because we came up with a name for ourselves, a lot of the other females in the neighborhood came up with names for themselves as well, like the Mackey Girls and the Gucci Girls, which all became our rivalry. We just laughed about them calling themselves Gucci when we knew and they knew that they wished they could afford Gucci. The Gucci Girls wasn't much to look at. Most of them were big, dusty, country, cornbread eating mashed potatoes with chicken on the side. But they wasn't someone who you thought that you could just run up on either. Those girls were from the streets and jail for shoplifting. Even though we all were from the hood, compared to them, we looked like 90210!

I'm not even going to talk about The Mackey Girls. Poor lil thangs is just what they were—*poo*. And they just wanted to fit in with a group of their own, but no one really paid them any attention but themselves. All eyes were on us the Fila Females and the Gucci Girls, and people all over heard about us that we didn't even know. We knew that they were all jealous of us because we were dating the popular guys! My parents didn't allow us to spend the night over to anyone's house unless it was family, so for my parents to allow me to spend the night with my girlfriend Tracey said a lot. I always spent the night over with Tracy and her sister Chrissie. Remember, Tracey was the one that I fought when we were younger, and I tried to throw dirt in her eyes, but she blocked it and wore my behind out. Yeah, that one. I wore that behind cutting, but then my mom made me go back because she knew Tracy tore my behind up, and like she said, "You better go back and beat her or I'ma beat you," and I fought for my life and won that fight, but afterward, Tracy and I became the very best of friends.

Sometimes we went over to Tracy's cousin Lisa's house and spent the night. The four of us were close like sisters. Their family loved me especially their Auntie Jackie who was also like an auntie to me. To me, Jackie was just one of the coolest aunties in the world, and when it came to the four of us, she didn't play with nobody bothering us! If Auntie Jackie saw us fighting some females in the neighborhood, she would yell out, "If y'all don't whoop their a——, I'ma whoop y'all a——, and I mean it!" So we had to fight as if our lives depended on it! Afterward, Auntie Jackie would take us over to her house, which was really nice and decked out, but all their places were nice and decked out. Tracy and their cousin Lisa. I guess just because they lived in the hood didn't mean that they had to look like the hood. We enjoyed chilling over at Jackie's house, mainly Chris and me staying up late at night drinking, getting high and listen to music until we passed out asleep.

When we created the Fila Females Gang, there was about fifteen of us just hanging out together having fun, and then we started bumping into the Gucci Girl Gang, which seemed like it was about thirty of them either at the mall or at a basketball or football game. And each time they would give us this look, we knew eventually one day we would have to fight! Our first fight with the Gucci Girls who were considered the toughest girls around because most of them were built like quarterbacks with shoulder pads looking like the Tasmanian devil, and they were not scared of us, our boyfriends, or anyone else, for that matter. The day came. I'll never forget. We were all at the mall, and it was time for the mall to close so we headed to the bus stop to catch the last bus going home, and who did we see coming to the bus stop to catch the bus as well—The Gucci Girls!

While we were all standing around waiting to get on the bus, I made sure that we all stayed together. Since the bus stop was full, I wanted to make sure we all had seats on the bus. When the bus pulled up, we were the first ones to start getting on the bus, when all of a sudden, someone behind Chris pulled her hair, and Chris screamed, "Ouch, someone is pulling my hair." Tracey, her sister, heard Chris scream. She turned around and saw one of the Gucci Girls pulling on her sister's hair, so Tracey took off one of her shoes and clocked the girl in the head. The female shook off the pain and started throwing blows, and the fight was on!

The bus driver started screaming and told us that we either were getting on or getting off. We all managed to get on the bus at the same time. There were pushing and junk talking to each other the whole ride about what we were going to do to each other, and as soon as we pulled the bell to get off at our stop, the bus driver passed it by. We all looked confused and wondered why he didn't stop at our drop-off. The bus driver took us further down the road and dropped us off on Read Street, and anybody who knows about Read Street knows that Read Street was one of the toughest streets in the neighborhood to walk on. I guess the bus driver said, "Since they want to act like hoodlums, they may as well get off on the hoodlum street and fight it out there."

We were only about ten minutes away from home, so when the bus stopped to let us off, I noticed that some of our girlfriends, the Fila Females, were scared to get off the bus. I didn't want the Gucci Girls to know that we were scared of them, so while still on the bus, I got up in the Gucci Girls' face standing in their way to block them so that I could let all my girlfriends off the bus first. When the Gucci Girls finally got off the bus, they started walking up on us talking crap, and I was the first one to punch one straight in her face, and the fight was on again! The bus driver looked at us, shook his head, and pulled off. We were scared because there was more of them. Then it was us, so we started fighting for our lives. We started getting the best of the Gucci Girls and chased them home through our neighborhood. Even though some of us may have gotten our behinds whooped that day, we all felt good that we fought together as a group.

After that fight, the girls all decided to make me our crew leader since they said that I was acting like the mother of the group, being protective over everyone and the one who stood up to the Gucci Girls. They wanted someone who wasn't afraid to fight. The news about us beating up the Gucci Girls spread all throughout our city, and people who didn't even know us would come up to us and say, "Y'all the Fila Females who beat up the Gucci Girls?" We would look at each other with pride and a smile on our faces and be like, "Yep!"

I was never a bully and don't believe in bullying anyone. I just made sure that no one bullied us, and I made sure that we didn't start fights, but we sure were going to finished them.

Our boyfriends were tough also, and I just didn't know how tough they were until one day, a couple of us decided to go to one of the biggest parties at this club house that was talked about all over town, and I wanted to make sure that I had on one of the hottest outfits there. One of my girlfriends told me that if I wanted a hot outfit to wear, just go to Rainbow City. I told her, "Rainbow City, that lil cheap clothing store. Everybody and their mama and grandmama along with me would be dressed a like girl, please!"

I decided to go to a store that sold a lot of military clothes, and I found a gray and black pants and jacket camouflage outfit with the matching hat and my black Timberland boots! I was the first one in my young days to wear an outfit like that. People at the party were checking me out I had "All Eyez on Me" like Tupac! There was this one guy who came up to me, looked me up from head to toe, smiled, and told me that he really liked my outfit and that I was the baddest thang rocking up in the house and that he was going to bite my style! I just smiled and thanked him like I was just the coolest thang around and told him that he could bite it like me wearing that outfit was nothing! Gurl, stop!

I don't know what made me decide on wearing a military outfit. I guess I just wanted to be different. That night, at the party, our boyfriends were all there as well wearing their long trench coats and looking like the black mafia gangsters as some would call them. I didn't know how much of a gangster or a fool I was that night until I reminded myself later on in life. That night, the police came into the party, and they started searching some of the guys, I guess, for drugs, guns, and whatever else. My boyfriend walked up to me, took off his long trench coat, and told me to put it on. The next thing I know he was giving me two sawed-off rifles and told me to put them up under my coat. I did what he said with no hesitation, grabbing both rifles putting them both under each arm.

I thought doing something like that made me cool and tough because we knew that the police officers weren't checking any of the women, just the men. Yeah, I was young and dumb, and I wonder how cool and tough I would have been if the police checked me that night. I would have gone to jail with someone else's gun! Stupid!

The police left without finding anything on anyone, and the party continued. After the party, our boyfriends went their way, and we went ours without a ride to get home. So we asked this guy who we didn't know to give us a ride home. There was about five or six of us and guess who got dropped off last? Me! Plus it was very cold that night, and he was telling me that he hoped where I lived didn't have a steep hill he had to drive up because it was cold. Betsy, his car, was acting up, and sometimes, Betsy would cut off when climbing the hill. I told the guy exactly where I lived, and all he had to do was just go straight, but instead he made a right turn into another neighborhood, which made me nervous, but I think he knew where he was going and what he was doing because on our way coming out of the neighborhood, there was this steep hill.

So now Betsy was stalling to climb this hill, and he started rubbing on the dashboard talking about, "Come on, Betsy baby. You can do it. Come on, girl!"

So Betsy cuts off in the middle of this dark road at about one in the morning! Now I'm really nervous and scared at the same time. Now we're just sitting there looking out of the window like two fools, and it was cold in the car. He said, "Betsy just needs to sit for a little while, and then she'll be okay. Since it's cold, I got a blanket in the trunk to keep us warm while we waiting for Betsy to rest." Then, he asked me to get in the backseat so we could lay down because it could be a minute before Betsy would crank back up. I looked at that fool, jumped out the car, and started walking home. About ten minutes later, guess who came pulling up behind me, blowing the horn talking about, "Get in. Betsy's good!"

I was still a fool because I got back into the car because it was cold and dark, but thank the Lord I made it home safely with the grace of God! *Thank you, Jesus*!

There was another crazy time when we the Fila Females all went to a home basketball game. After the game was over, our boyfriends decided to walk us home. There was about twelve females and four of our boyfriends walking home together. Out of nowhere, the Mackey Girls appeared.

The Dirty Girls is what we called them were on our tails with a little over twenty females and about five guys. They all just started talking big smack to us, and they followed us until we got to our neighborhood, and that's when just about all the Fila Females took off running and left about four of us to fight for ourselves along with our boyfriends. When the Mackey Girls and their boyfriends started walking closer toward us, my boyfriend pulled out a gun, handed it to me, and told me to shoot it in the air, but I didn't hear that part on the account of my attention on the crowd. All I heard him say was, "Shoot!"

I grabbed the gun, pointed it at the crowd, and shot two times. *Pow! Pow!* Everyone took off running! My boyfriend grabbed the gun and said, "I told you to shoot it in the air!"

I know God was with me that night because as many people that was in the crowd, and as close as I were standing when I shot the gun, I should have hit somebody, but I thank God I didn't! We all ran before the police came, but that was the very last time we had any problems with the Dirty Girls, I mean, the Mackey Girls! For the females that ran off and left us that night, we let them know that wasn't cool because it's supposed to be one for all and all for one, but we all still remained friends. But the females that stayed that night, we told them that we would have each other's back. We became even closer than ever.

By now, my family and I had moved again in another house for about the sixth time, what I could remember, to a neighborhood called Hollywood Hills. I didn't know during this time that my mother decided to leave our dad. She went on her own just to find a place for her and her children without my dad's knowledge. That's because he was staying out a lot and not coming home for days, so during his staying-out time is when my mother had decided to pack up all our things and moved us to Hollywood Hills. I'm a daddy's girl, so I asked my mom, "How will Bonnie know where we're moving too?"

She gave me that look and said, "Since you're so worried about your daddy so much, you can stay your a—— right here and wait on 'em!"

I just looked at my mom and shook my head like, "What is wrong with her?"

It wasn't long before my dad found out where we were staying. That's because he came to my school and picked me up. "Where y'all living at?"

"I don't know the name of the roads, but I can show you how to get there."

So I showed my daddy all the turns to make to get to our house, and when we got there, we both walked in the house, and all I remember him saying to my mama was, "Yeah, you thought you were slick and could leave without me finding out?"

My mama told him, "Go back to wherever the hell you came from?" My mama looked at me like, "So you brought him here. I'll kill ya!"

I looked back at her like, "You should have told me you didn't want him to know!"

All I know is he never left.

It was the month of May, the month we've all been waiting for. Our May Fest Festival, something our state have every year downtown at the Capital State House. Every year, it grows bigger and bigger. Everybody and their grandmama is going to be there, so you know the Fila Females had to make sure we all made our grand entry with some sharped outfits. We all went to the mall, and each one of us picked out a different pair of Jams shorts because that's what was rocking that year. Basically, some shorts that had a Hawaii style on them, and we each wore a plain-colored shirt that matched our shorts with the Fila Females embroidered on the back. We became very popular back in our day, so we had to represent, even still to this day, people still remember us as the Fila Females.

Our group was only organized because of our close friendship with each other, and because we all like Filas, so we had just decided to name ourself the Fila Females, and other females decided to copy after us but just with a different name. We were hated as much as liked because, like I said, everybody in our group were very pretty, popular, and we all dated the popular guys. So there were a lot of females that just didn't like us because of that reason. While we were walking around at the May Fest looking fly and enjoying the scenery, a group of females started walking toward us, and someone in our group started arguing with another female in the other group, and the fight was on!

It was a big fight. Every female was fighting another female. We won the fight not because I'm telling the story, but let the truth be told, we tore some butts up and high-tailed before the police came! I found out later that most of the girls we were fighting were from Hollywood Hills, the same neighborhood we had just moved to. I didn't care because even though we were living there, I didn't hang out there. My stomping grounds were Saxon Homes, and believe you me, if I had any trouble from the girls in the Hills, my girls from the Homes did not mind coming to give them a visit.

Yes, my girls had gotten tough, the same ones that used to run and leave us behind to fight by ourself. I had to toughen them up because since I was the leader of our crew, I told them either they were going to fight with us or get out the group because if they stayed and didn't fight, we were going to whoop their behinds. So they decided to stay. I believe some of them only stayed in the group for protection from other females because some of them were good at running off at their mouth with other females when they knew that they had backup, but like I told them, "If you kept your mouth closed, then we wouldn't have to worry about anyone bothering you!"

Like I said, we were not the ones who started the fight, but we sure finished them. I made sure of that! I told you I had to learn how to fight because my male cousin kept beating me up in the country until I learned how to fight back. In the seventh grade, there was this female bully named Alexandra who used to push us around, and I must say, we were scared of Alexandra because she looked rough and tough and all that stuff with her bad self. And she was known to beat up both guys and girls. I heard one day while in class that Alexandra wanted to fight me. My heart wanted to jump out of my shirt. I'm saying to myself, "For what? I've never done anything to her for her to want to fight me." We were in our last class of the day, so when the bell rang for us to go and get on the bus, everyone was standing around in a circle waiting for the fight to begin. I didn't want to fight Alexandra, but everyone else who was standing around was pushing us up to fight.

I was scared, and I didn't want her to know that I was scared, so I closed my eyes and starting swinging. (Why do some people fight with their eyes closed? I guess they don't want to see that a——— whooping coming.) I'm swinging, and when I opened up one eye, I was nowhere near Alexandra. I was swinging on one of my girlfriends who was trying to break up the fight. I knew my girlfriend wasn't going to fight me back, so I started swinging on my girlfriend, trying to show off because I'm hearing the crowd cheering me on. I knocked my girlfriend's glasses off, and poor lil thang wouldn't fight me back because she was too busy looking for her glasses. I just knew the fight was over, but when I opened my eyes, the bully Alexandra was still there waiting on me. Oh damn!

The next thing I knew, one of the guys who were standing around picked me up and threw me back into fight like he was throwing me back in the ring. I heard him say to me, "Get her, Tiger!" and the next thing I knew, I guess being scared must have given me the strength that I needed because I tore Alexandra's behind up! The same guy who threw me in the fight cheered me on, grabbed me by the arm, and picked me up like I was Rocky who just won a boxing match. All I know is that it felt good, and I didn't have any more problems out of Alexandra! The one thing that I kind of learned in that situation was that you can't always run away from everybody, and you can't fight everybody because fighting doesn't solve anything. But maybe it does sometimes when you have a bully who's always bothering you. Sometimes you may need to put that bully in their place to keep them off you and out of your face. It could also stop them from bothering others. But I wouldn't suggest you going up against a bully in these times and days because bullies are more afraid of the people that their bullying. Nor do the bullies fight fair anymore, fist to fist, the way that we used to fight back in the day. No, now bullies are fighting with knives and guns, and that's what we call a coward!

I remember these identical twin sisters from the same school. The way you could tell them apart was that one was bigger than the other. They were very pretty but loved talking smack to everybody, and I was always getting into a fight with them. I don't know why we didn't like each other. We just didn't. The only thing I could think of was that they had mouth on them, and I had a mouth on me. They didn't back down, and neither did I. They were tough because they didn't care nothing about those beatings I gave them. They just kept coming back for more, I guess, to redeem themselves. One day, while in school, they both started running up to me, and I started getting ready for another fight, but they started telling me that we were cousins! They said that they had gone down to the family reunion that our family had in Allendale, and they found out that they were my cousins on my dad's side of the family, and I was like, "What?" They said that they knew my dad and that my dad and their mother were first cousins. It's a small world. That's why my dad is always getting on us about going to our family reunion. He said that we could have passed someone on the streets not knowing they were our family. So after the twins and I found out that we were cousins, instead of us fighting each other, we ganged up together and started fighting other girls at school who didn't like us, and the three of us became tight as ever!

Fighting was not my hobby or sport; my hobby was reading, I love to read because reading took my mind to another place, and that place was whatever I was reading at the time. Even in class, I loved reading and always raised my hand whenever the teacher asked for a reader. And I was always disappointed whenever I didn't get called on. I was proud of having a library card, and my parents felt that I was old enough to catch the city bus downtown to the library where

I felt like a young adult finding books to take home to read and listening to the audio tapes while I read along in the book for about an hour or two while waiting to catch the next bus back home. Reading was and is exciting for me. I loved it. I love to see little boys and girls with reading books in their hands reading. It makes me smile and makes my heart happy.

Now in the eighth grade is where my body came into my maturity stage! This is when I started as most women or girls would say my "monthly." I don't know if you remember me telling you that my mother and I didn't have that mother and daughter relationship that most girls have with their mother, but it was something I desperately wanted to have with my mom but didn't. For what reason, I didn't know. All I knew was that I wasn't her favorite, and she let it to be known to me one day while over to Mama's house who now moved from Read Street to Fairfield Arms Apartments.

I don't remember why my mother was getting on me. I just remembered she and I had gotten into a heated argument, and her telling me, "That's why I never wanted you!"

And I said, "Well, why did you have me?"

"Because I got scared and jumped off the abortion table!"

All I could say to myself was, "Wow, what is that to tell your child?"

Was I that disrespectful that I deserve to be told that? I never really considered my mother as a mother to me, especially the way she treated me, and I used to tell myself all the time that if I didn't look so much like my mother, I would have thought that I was adopted! The first day I got my monthly, I didn't know what was happening to me because my mother never talked to me about that or what to do. I was just so embarrassed because I messed up my pants!

My eighth-grade teacher took me into the bathroom, so I could clean myself up. She told me to tie my jacket around my waist to hide the embarrassment of my pants, and she talked to me a little bit about why my body was going through changes. But I don't think she wanted to get too deep with the conversation because I guess she figured my mother would do that. As soon as I got to my auntie's house in Saxon Homes, where we all went after school, it was full of people, as usual, men and women family members and friends of the family. I remember walking up to my mother nervously while she was talking to my uncle, and I whispered in her ear about what had happened to me in school. You would have thought that she would have taken me somewhere private to talk to me, but instead, she told everyone in the room. "Shannon's period came on today." She sent me upstairs to the bathroom, and as I was walking up the steps, she threw me some pads and told me, "Now these are what you put on whenever your period comes on!"

I mean, really who does that? Embarrassing their child in front of all those people like that!

Maybe that's why I had so much anger inside me! Maybe that's why I was getting into so many fights! Now I didn't get to graduate from Crayton Middle school because my twin cousins and I got into a fight with some other girls in school, and we got sent to the principal's office. So while we were sitting in the principal's office, my twin cousins and me, the principal told us in a very mean and nasty tone, "I'm tired of y'all Gonzales Garden girls because my cousin was from Gonzales Garden's apartment, and y'all Saxon Homes girls always coming here fighting!" I didn't like what he was saying, like, "Y'all little project girls always getting on my nerves."

I was getting mad because he was trying to belittle us, so I told him real nasty like, "I ain't from no Saxon Homes. I'm from Hollywood Hills!"

He said, "Well, your a—— will be going to Alcorn!"

My mouth and heart dropped. I felt as if I was getting shipped overseas away from my family and friends. My twin cousins turned and looked at me with a smirk on their faces, and I wanted to hit them both in their faces. I bet I kept my mouth closed after that, but it was too late. He was transferring me to Alcorn Middle School, the school that I was to attend.

I went home, afraid of telling my mother that I had gotten kicked out of school because just about all of my family members went to the same elementary, middle, and high school, and I had to be the only one who broke the tradition! After everyone heard that I got kicked out of school, my uncle started teasing me about those same girls who we all fought at the May Fest Festival. Not only did they live in Hollywood Hills, but they all attended the same middle school that I was getting transferred to!

My uncle said, "Don't those girls you got into a fight with at the May Fest go to Alcorn Middle School?"

I said, "Yeah, and?"

Sounding all tough and bad, he said, "And you will be there by yourself…Ooh, those girls is gonna whoop your a———!"

I said, "Yeah, right. I'm not worried about that!"

But in reality, I was kind of nervous because it would be about ten girls to one!

My first day of school on my way walking to class, the first thing I see is two of the females whom we fought at the May Fest, and they stopped in their tracks. One female hit the other female on her arm to get her attention. When they stopped, they just stared down at me, and I stopped and stared back down at them. They went their way, and I went mine. A few more females were in a couple of my classes, but they didn't say anything. They just looked at me crazy. A couple of days later at school, I crossed paths with the same two females whom I saw on my first day of school. One of them looked at me and, with the motion of her head, said, "What's up." Not knowing what her "What's up" meant, I said, "What's up." Just in case there was some beef between us, I was letting them know "Yeah, I'm here, and I ain't scared!"

But her "What's up" was only her saying, "Hey, I'm Step."

And the other one's name was Tracey. The three of us got to talking about what happened at the May Fest. I found out later that they were just as scared of me as I were of them. I guess we all got some Rocky in us when we got our crew with us! I got to meet the rest of their female crew who I also became cool with, but I didn't tell my crew about me being friends with the females we fought at the May Fest. I was their leader, and I didn't want them to think that I turned against them for another crew—*never* because they were my sisters!

So now I had to finish up my eighth grade year at Alcorn, and every morning before going to school, my mother would drop me off at Mama's house who moved into these apartments not far from us or the school. As a matter of fact, the school was walking distance from Mama's house, and because my mother had to be at work before school started, she would just drop me off at Mama's house. And from there, I would walk to school with my cousin, who were living with Mama at the time. Every morning before we went to school, Mama would get up and fix us all some grits, eggs, bacon, jelly toast, and coffee! We would eat out breakfast, drink our coffee, and watch *The Price Is Right* with Mama before going to school. I started getting to the point that all I wanted to do was stay home with Mama and watch the soap operas!

Now going to school with my cousin every day was a job because she was like a chihuahua, the littlest thing in the bunch. She loved to bark, but as soon as you stomp your feet, they take off running! That was my cousin, always running off at her mouth with someone in school but ain't going to fight a tick! They said that's how my Auntie Tiny, her mama was, the first one to throw a lick and run! I remember my cousin and I walking home from school one day, and there was these two boys following us. But they were really following my cousin. For what reason I don't know, but as soon as we got close to home, one of the boys pushed my cousin, and she took off running, leaving me there to fight her battle. I wasn't just going to let this boy push my cousin, so he and I started fighting, and I ran to Mama's house, rushed inside the apartment, went to the kitchen, and grabbed a knife.

Everyone who was there wanted to know what was going on, but I didn't say anything. I just ran back outside and ran up to the boy so fast. He didn't know I had a knife in my hand because I had it hid behind my back, and before I knew it, I swung the knife faster than you could blink. He jumped back, and I was an inch away from cutting his nose off! My mom, auntie, and uncle were behind me telling me to give them the knife!

I'm sorry that happened because I don't bother anyone, and I could have really hurt that boy and been in jail, but I blinked out! I snapped especially when someone bothers me, and even though it was my cousin and not me, our family taught us that if anyone bothers us, fight them back! Our blood is thicker than mud so when you mess with one, you mess with us all!

I found out later that the other boy who was with the boy I got into the fight with, my cousin had a crush on him, and she hit 'em up side his head in school that day and ran! Love licks, that's all it was! His friend was fighting for his best friend about to get stabbed, and I was fighting for my cousin, about to go to jail, all over some love licks! We all became friends after that, and that same guy my cousin had the crush on turned out to be a very nice guy. He was friendly, sweet, and very handsome, and all the girls were crazy about him! That same young guy died at an early age around sixteen or seventeen when someone shot and killed him, and I think, over a girl! It was a very sad funeral because he was loved by many.

There was another time that my cousin got us in some mess while walking home from school. She was running off with her mouth again with some girls at school who stayed in the same neighborhood Mama stayed in. The girls were on our heels following us home, about five of them, and they and my cousin was exchanging words with each other until I got tired and mad from them following us so close. So I turned around and jumped in the argument and told them to get out of my cousin's face, and the next thing I knew, one of the girls threw the first blow, and it was on! I was fighting five girls all by myself while my cousin ran and left me behind. I thought that my cousin left me, but instead, she ran to our uncle's apartment who stayed in another apartment complex next to Mama's apartment. My uncle and cousin came running down the hill and broke the fight up! I'm not bragging, but they said that I handle myself with the five girls all by myself, and yes, we too later all became friends! One of the girls told me that they only wanted to be friends with me and not my cousin since I stood up to them. They didn't want to be friends with anyone who would leave them in a fight all by themselves.

I guess in those days, when someone saw that you would stand your ground and won't back down, they would rather be on your team or want you on theirs than to be against you! Like I said, my cousin was always the first one to run her mouth, the first one to start the fight, and the first one to run! There was another time my

59

cousin was running off at her mouth to what was supposed to be one of her girlfriends, and my auntie, her mom, heard her. My cousin was outside playing with this young girl until they both got into an argument, and my cousin ran into the house. Before closing the door, she hollered to the young girl, "Bump you, your mama, and your dog!"

Now my auntie heard what my cousin had said to the little girl, and my auntie knew that this little girl and her family were not well off when it came to money because of how they dressed daily and they smelled very poor—well, let's say poorer than us—but they were still nice people. My auntie thought that my cousin and this little girl were the best of friends, and for my cousin to mistreat this little girl like that, telling her that she never wanted to be her friend anyway and that her family were dirty and poor really pissed my auntie off. So my auntie started fussing at my cousin, "Yeah, I heard you tell that little girl 'bump you, your mama, and your dog' and how poor she was! You can't talk about nobody because you nasty leaving your nasty dirty underwear on the bathroom floor!"

I thought the whole thing was funny, so I did one of my uncle's numbers and started recording my auntie without her knowing it, cursing my cousin out, and then she got on the both of us like I did something to the little girl! My auntie was mad. "Now y'all ain't the prettiest kids in the world, and you don't look good, so why would y'all be out there treating that little girl like that with your ugly a——!"

I was laughing, and I couldn't wait until my mom came to pick me up, so I could play back the tape. When I did, my mom and Mama laughed so hard, but my auntie was still pissed off. She didn't appreciate me recording her like that like she was wanted by the FBI or something!

My cousin and I were very close even though she was all mouth and no action and always leaving me to fight her battles. We were still the best of friends. Since my cousin was staying with Mama for a little to attend school, I would sometimes spend the night on the weekends. Mama had a three-bedroom apartment where she had a room, and both of my uncles had their room. I'll never forget this weekend I stayed over to Mama's house and my cousin wasn't there.

I was in the room sleeping with Mama when I was awakened by someone touching me. It was my Uncle Curt, my mama's brother. His hands were inside my underwear, rubbing his hand up and down my butt, and I said, "What are you doing?"

My grandmother woke up and asked what was going on, and I told her what my uncle was doing, and all he said was, "Her panties were in her butt, and I was getting them out!" Mama believed him, and the only thing my mother said was that he didn't have any business in my underwear. I should have known something was wrong with my uncle because sometimes I would walk by his room and hear him having a conversation, I mean a serious conversation, and I would peep inside, but there was no one in the room but him!

Sometimes my uncle would just stare at me in a perverted way, moving his mouth as if he was talking to me without any sound coming out. The way he stared at me really freaked me out, and I was afraid and nervous to be around him. I never told my cousin what our uncle did to me. I just didn't really want to talk about it. My cousin and I were still very close, and she wanted me to stay over with her on some weekends, and I did but made sure that I stayed clear out of my uncle's way.

One weekend, while spending the night over at Mama's house, I woke up around two o'clock in the morning. I went downstairs to the kitchen to get me something to drink. I heard my cousin talking, and when I turned on the kitchen light, she was standing in the kitchen window talking to these two guys, so my little fast self got right into the window with her. I too started talking, well, flirting, with these two guys who neither one of us knew. We talked so long until our Uncle Greg busted us. Our uncle and the two guys got into a heated argument, and he ran them off, then got on the both of us and sent us back to bed. The next morning, he made sure that he told Mama, our mothers, and everybody else about what happened that night.

A couple of days later, our Uncle Greg decided to take our baby cousin to the park, which was only across the street from the apartments. It was on a Sunday, and every Sunday, Mama's house was packed because that's where all of the family meet up for Sunday dinner. My brother walked outside, and we all heard him yell,

"Somebody just jumped on Uncle Greg at the park!" Now I'ma tell you about our family! Our family is just like a lot of other families. You fight one, you got to fight them all! When people say our blood is thicker than water, well, water is not thick at all, so the relationship between you and your family may not be as close because our family is very close. Our blood is thicker than mud because that's how tight our family is on my mother's side!

When my brother yelled somebody was jumping on Uncle Greg, everyone ran out of the apartment like we were the Mafia because Uncle Greg was the baby boy of nine siblings, so believe you me, they weren't coming out to play no games! There was about ten of us that ran out to the park. My brother got to the park first, and the guy who caught my uncle off guard from behind had him pinned down on the ground. My brother ran and bulldozed the guy off our uncle. Now my brother was on top of that guy. Then another guy who was playing ball on the basketball court came and jumped on my brother. By then, another uncle of ours hit the guy that had jumped on my brother so hard in his face that all I saw was blood! Then the next thing I know, everybody on the basketball court jumped in the fight. There was about maybe fifteen of them to ten of us! Even our mom, my uncle's wife, and my two aunties were out there knocking heads.

After the fight was over, we all went back to Mama's house, but some people were missing! My auntie Tiny, uncle Charles, and his wife had followed some of the guys back to their apartment! These crazy fools done went up in the people apartment still fighting! Now I see where I get my craziness from, my mom's side of the family! After it was all over, we found out that the guy who jumped on my uncle's back was the same guy he ran off that night from talking to my cousin and me in the window, so you know we were in trouble!

Living in Hollywood Hills was okay. I was the new kid on the block, and it was a little different from our last neighborhood, which I liked better! This neighborhood seemed a little on the rough side. The one thing that I loved about the neighborhood was that around the corner from our house was a candy store, and you would think that I had a job with money I spent there. I was at the candy store every single day. I hate that I was addicted to candy like that, and it wasn't as if I didn't brush my teeth every day. It's just that I would go to bed at night eating candy and falling asleep with it in my mouth, not knowing the damage it would cause me later in life. I was young, and teeth at that time was not important, but I would learn as an adult that having teeth was very much important!

I became to be very good friends with the same girls we fought at the May Fest, but I became best friends with my neighbor next door. There were three sisters who lived next door to me, and their mom was one of the toughest moms I've ever meet. She didn't play, and she didn't allow them to play nowhere other than around the house!

My auntie still lived in Saxon Homes, and I still remained faithful to all my friends there, and they still didn't know that I was hanging with the same girls we fought at the May Fest. I didn't have a choice. I was the only one out of my group that lived there, and I didn't want to stay in the house when I was home! We all talked about that day at the May Fest and laughed about it. I'm glad they found humor in it because I sure didn't. I was still watching my back because I didn't know them like that to start trusting them. I ain't crazy. I might have been born at night, but I wasn't born last night!

As time went on, I became best friends with two of the girls I fought at the May Fest, Tonya who stayed a couple of houses down the street from me and Tree who stayed two streets over. I remember them asking me if I could go to the movies with them that day. I told them that if maybe they would ask my parents, they might let me go. I wish that I would have never told them to do that because that day, my parents were back at it! The fighting between my parents was still going on because it never stopped! I remember my two girlfriends walking up to the house to ask my parents if it was okay that I could to go to the movies with them in the middle of my parents fighting! While they went up to the house, I stayed at the edge of the driveway, afraid of what they might say. Sure enough, I heard my mom telling my girlfriends, "No, she can't go, and, Shannon, bring your a—— in this house!"

It's funny now when we joke about it, but it wasn't funny then. All I remember my girlfriends saying to me was "Bye, Shannon" with a smirk on their faces!

I looked back at them, rolled my eyes, and ran into the house, mad.

That wasn't the only embarrassing time that my parents got into a fight while we were there. My dad didn't come home for a couple of days, and when he did, my mom got so mad that she started throwing all his clothes outside on the porch. I didn't want the neighbors or any of my girlfriends walking by seeing my dad's clothes thrown out on the porch, so I went outside to bring his clothes back into the house. After the second or third time bringing his clothes back into the house, my mama started screaming at me, "If your a—— bring them clothes in here one more time, I'ma put your a—— out with him!"

After that, my dad got so angry that he went and got his gun, and my mom started screaming and running through the house as if he was about to shoot her. That's when I called my brother Skeet on the phone to tell him what was going on, and the only thang he said was, "Bonnie ain't gonna shoot nobody." Things calmed down that night, and so did my mom after she saw that gun. That was the last big fight that my parents ever had, but it didn't stop the arguments.

At the age of fourteen is when I met Jeff, my oldest son's dad. He lived on the street behind us, but he was always next door at my other neighbor's house where all the boys hanged out at! It was a couple of weeks before Christmas, and I told my dad that all I wanted for Christmas was a boom box."

All the cool kids had a boom box, especially after watching *Krush Groove*, break-dancin', and the Fat Boys at the movie theater. I was determined to get a boom box before all of my other girlfriends did, and my dad promised that he would get me one, so I knew that whatever my daddy said he was going to do, he was going to do it!

It was Christmas Eve, and I hadn't seen my dad all day. So I assumed that he was just working late and I'll just see him tomorrow, on Christmas Day, when I wake up with my boom box! So now it's Christmas day, and I'm sitting in the window waiting on my dad to come home, and I waited and waited and waited, and my dad never showed. I was so hurt and so disappointed. So the next morning after Christmas, I sat in the window still waiting for my dad to show up with my boom box, and my mother walked by my room door. She stopped and told me with a firm voice, "Now let me tell you one thang. I watched you sit in that window for two whole days waiting on your daddy. Now let me tell you something, as long as you live, don't you ever depend on no man, not even your daddy!"

A couple of hours later, my dad walked in the front door, and I ran out of my room with a big smile on my face to meet him, but he didn't have no presents—no boom box, no nothing. When he closed the door behind him, my mama was standing right in his face with her arms folded. The first thang my dad said was, "I was kidnapped!" My mama said, "Kidnapped? Who the hell wanted you and how did you get away?"

I said to myself, "Kidnapped. Oh hell, that must have been the only thang he could come up with. He musta thought of that lie when he hit the door!"

I was hurt and disappointed. I just went to my room. I don't know what other lie he told my mama, but whatever it was, she must have believed it because they still together like the couple on *In Living Color*: "We still together!"

After that, I became very headstrong and very independent. Fourteen was also the year that I heard a voice in my mind telling me to start writing my material down! I now know that it was the spirit of the Lord. I was outside in my front yard when a voice in my head told me to start writing down my material. I also remember that same day while watching television, there were something that caught my attention! I was sitting down watching TV, and a commercial came on about "giving back, helping others, give back to the community, and just give." Then a second commercial came on after that about the same thing, giving back, reaching back to help others. And then a third commercial came on after that about the same thing, to help those in need, and I took that as a sign from God that he was telling me that this gift that he has for me was not just for me. But he was giving me this gift to help others! God is not going to give you anything he doesn't feel that you are not going to bless others with because the *blessings* he has giving to you, he can surely take them away! I had to grow up quick! Someone once asked me how did God speak to me and how did I know that it was God. God made us in his own image, so God is in me, and we are one. So when I know that I'm trying to walk in the path of righteousness and since he is in me, he will speak to me spiritually within. John 10:14 (NLT) states, "I am the good shepherd; I know my own sheep and they know me." John 10:27 (NLT) says, "My sheep hear My voice, and I know them, and they follow Me."

I know by faith that God will lead me in the right path that I should go if I just continue to remain in Him.

I'm the baby of three, and I never had any birthday parties. Just that one in Saxon Homes at my auntie's house when I was younger. I never went to any of the school dances or played sports. I was just a tomboy. I remember my mom dressing me up in my sister's old prom dress. She made my face up and took pictures of me as if I was going to a prom. I didn't go anywhere. She told me to smile and took pictures of me standing in our front yard. I don't know if she wanted me to feel special, or she just wanted to get some more wear out of my sister's old prom dress since she brought it and couldn't take it back. Either way, I didn't go anywhere. I felt like an idiot and the black sheep.

My next-door neighbor Tammy's mom was so mean and strict and tore up Tammy's and her two sisters' behinds at a drop of a dime. Some of the things that they had gotten whoopings for was just unbelievable. She was definitely one lady I wouldn't want to mess with. Sometimes when I acted up at home, my mom would say, "I'ma send you next door, and let Tammy's mama deal with ya!"

I remember them having a plum tree in their backyard, and I asked their mom if I could pick a couple of their plums.

"*No!*" she said. The tree was full of plums leaning over the fence in our backyard, so late one night when I thought that everyone was asleep, I sneaked outside and stole a few plums off the tree. And their mom was so nasty that she must have counted the plums missing off the tree because the next thing I knew, she cut the whole tree down! Just nasty!

After about three months living in our new neighborhood, I was standing in my yard when Jeff hollered out to me asking me my name, and I told him, "Shannon."

He said, "Sade."

I said, "No, Shannon."

He said, "Sade."

So I said to myself, "Since he don't understand what I'm saying, let me break it down to him in a song." I started singing, "Let the music play. He won't get away, just keep it grooving, and he'll come back to you again, let it play."

He said, "Ooh, Shannon!"

"Yeah, Shannon."

Most times I had to sing that song to people who didn't pronounce my name correctly! I asked him his name, and he told me Jeff. He also asked me my age. I lied and told him that I was sixteen when I was only fourteen! I also asked him his age, and he told me that he was eighteen! I knew he was a little older than me, and that's why I lied, because I found him attractive, and I didn't want him rejecting me because of my age, and I was going to keep it as that!

I also found out that one of the girls we fought at the May Fest was his baby sister. As a matter of fact, she was the first one I met at the middle school, and she was the one who first said, "What's up" to me. I'm a people person, so anytime we moved into another neighborhood, I'm the one, out of my brother and sister, that gets out, explores, and makes friends, while my sister and brother just sits in the house. After meeting Jeff's baby sister again, she and I started hanging out, and we became the best of friends. And since he was her brother, I also looked at him as a brother because Step and our friendship were more important than me trying to hit on her brother.

Out of all the females I became friends with in the neighborhood, Step and I were the closest of them all. We just clicked like that. We became more like sisters, then friends. Once Tree and Tonya found out that Step and I became the best of friends, they warned me to be careful about getting involved with Step and her family. What they meant by it, I didn't know nor did I care. Step and I were inseparable. She was the baby sister I always wanted. I remember years ago asking my mom if she would have me a baby sister, and she told me, "Child, sit down somewhere. You almost didn't make it!"

By now, Mama had moved from out of Fairfield Arms Apartment into Ashley Apartments. I was good at styling hair because Step and I started styling each other's hair all the time and had gotten good at it. One day, my Auntie Carolyn, who's my favorite aunt and my mom's baby sister, came to pick me up so I could fix her hair. My Uncle Curt was there also. While my auntie was sitting in a chair facing the television, I was standing up behind her hot curling her hair. It was in the hot summer, and I had on a tank top shirt. While my arms were up, hot-curling my auntie's hair, the next thing I knew, my uncle walked up beside me, reached his hand in the side of my shirt, and touched my breast before I could say the word.

"What!" My auntie had jumped up like a wild cat with the house phone in her hand and knocked the daylights out of my uncle so hard upside his head. She said, "What the hell do you think you doing!"

I said to myself, "Now how did my auntie know what my uncle did to me. Her back was turned. She couldn't have seen what he did, and she didn't give me time to say anything before she went into action." Did something happen to her where my uncle tried to touch her, or she just knew that he was sick in the head! My mom never told my dad what my uncle did to me about putting his hands in my panties, but after this happened, she had no choice. My mom had to stop my dad for going over to find my uncle. My dad said, "He ain't got no business putting his hands down my child's shirt. You better get 'em before I kill 'em!"

I knew my dad meant just that! The one thing my mom always said about her three children to anyone was that we didn't steal, and we didn't lie. I remember one day my mom asking my dad did he take some of her money out of her purse because she was missing some, and he told her, "You better ask those kids in there."

"My kids don't steal. I can leave money on my dresser, and they wouldn't touch it. It's you I don't trust!"

We didn't steal because we knew that our mama didn't play. Plus we were taught that if we wanted something, all we had to do was ask.

I have become friends with most of the girls in the neighborhood that we fought at the May Fest, and all of them attended the same middle school. The school were having a dance performance, and each classroom could participate. Now that was right up my alley because I was a dancer and loved to dance. Remember I said I got my dance training from dancing every time I heard music. I didn't care if we were in the grocery store, I would dance my butt off. My mama had to always tell me, "If you don't sit your a—— down somewhere, I'ma tear your a—— up. You ain't outside, and you ain't in no dancing contest!"

In my classroom, I got together with three other girls, two of them were from the same neighborhood and one of them were in the fight at the May Fest. We decided to put together a dance routine and sing to the song by "New Edition (I'm Lost in Love)"! We were good! We tore that song up especially the lead singer Sam. People actually thought that she was lip-syncing, but she wasn't. Sam could really sing, and our routine was off the hook. We had a standing ovation!

The school performance went to our heads because after that, we officially had an all-female group, and because one of the females didn't live in our neighborhood, we just replaced her with the lead singer's younger sister, and Tree didn't have time to practice with us, so we just replaced her with Step, and it was on! We practiced our dance routine faithfully, and we heard about a talent show that they were having in Latimer Manor every weekend. This was the same neighborhood that I grew up in, so we decided to go one day to perform. We heard about this all-guy group who called themselves New Edition, and they were fine! There were five of them. They were all dressed really nice in their nice black slacks, white dress shirts, and tie, and we heard that they were unbeatable.

While we were in the bathroom practicing our routine, I was looking in the mirror at my Jheri curl, and it was looking kinda dry, and I didn't have any activator with me. So I decided to put a little water on it, but damn, I put too much water on my hair. My Jheri curl went from curly dry to a wet and limp scary curl! You should have seen me in that bathroom. My girlfriends would tell you the way I freaked out, you would have thought we were going on stage at the Grammy's!

"Oh hell, y'all look at my hair. I done messed my hair up. Now what am I gonna do?"

They all just looked at me like the show must go on because ain't nobody tell you to put all that water in your hair!

Well, the show did go on, and we went out there, and we sang the song by Klymaxx, "Meeting in the Ladies Room," "I'll be back real soon!" Our dance routine should have been in a video. It was very creative, and our lead singer blew them away! We won third place, and the New Edition guys won first place, but that was okay because there was about five to seven groups that performed that day! Our next show that we performed there, I made sure that I carried my activator this time because I was not about to have my Jheri curl dripping and slinging all over the dance floor. Plus I came up with the idea to add color to my hair by putting Kool-Aid in my hair! It didn't matter whatever Kool-Aid pack I stole out of my mama's cabinet, that was the color of my hair that day! On our next performance, we performed from the song "Bass Mechanic." We tore the house down! We practiced our routine faithfully every day. We all said that we were going back to take our first place from the New Edition boys whose parents must have had some money because here they were again, all dressed up in their nice suits, doing their New Edition routine, looking all fine and good, and we tore their behinds up and won first place!

Some younger kids won second place, and New Edition won third. You should have seen the looks on their faces. They did not like that nor us. This was their neighborhood, and they have been out here beating these other groups for the longest until we came from out of nowhere and blew them out of the park! At the end of the show, I really thought we were in a video when they had all of us to join hands and sing to the song "We Are the World." I felt so special, like we just won our first Grammy Award. They gave us a trophy with our name engraved on it. Lady Mechanics, that's what we called ourselves because we were bad, and I still have that trophy to this day!

The next thing you knew, other girls started hearing about us and wanted to always dance against us which were no competition! Our group became closer than ever! I'll never forget when my mom asked us, "Who drinking up my Kool-Aid!" And my brother Skeet said, "Shannon's using it to put color in her hair!"

I didn't know how my brother knew, but he knew. My mom said, "No wonder my Kool-Aid has been leaving quicker than I thought, but I tell you, let me see another color in your hair, and I'll kill ya!" That was my mom's favorite line to me: "I'll kill ya!"

I remember I had a real blinking problem. I was about ten years old. I mean, a real blinking problem for about a year. I would sometimes blink about ten quick blinks in a row before stopping. I remember my mom saying, "What is wrong with that child blinking like that. I'ma take her to the doctor to see what's going on!"

So when my mom took me to the doctor, I overheard the doctor telling my mom that the blinking problem was just a habit. That there was nothing wrong with me, and I was just doing it for attention! My mom said in a loud voice, "A habit!" When we left the doctor's office to get back in the car, both my mom and I got into the car at the same time, and we both turned around to grab our seat belts. When we turned around at the same time to put our seat belts in the holster, our eyes meet, and at that moment, I started blinking again furiously! My mama looked at me and said, "I just paid this man $50 dollars just so he can tell me that your blinking was a habit. If you blink one more time, I'll kill ya, and I mean it!" I didn't blink no more after that. I was even scared to blink our normal blink. I was looking like a wide-eyed crackhead!

The time had come for our graduation from Alcorn Middle School, and at the graduation ceremony, they were announcing and acknowledging some of the student's achievements and awards. To my surprise, my name was called to receive a third place award for best drawing! I drew a picture of my family tree with our names on the branches, and maybe because the tree really stood out with details of the branches, leaves, and roots, but I really didn't think anything of it when I was drawing it. It was a homework assignment, and I did what I had to do for my homework. I didn't really look at myself as being an artist. I just loved to draw!

Looking back over my life at the age of fourteen, I would ask myself, "Why did I keep having that same dream over and over every single night. It never failed!" I may sometimes have another different dream after this dream in the same night, but I was always having the same exact dream every night for a whole entire year! I would dream that I had two sons, and we were all sitting at the kitchen table. I was sitting in the middle, and my two sons were sitting on both ends, facing each other, and there were a silhouette of a man standing at the stove as though he was cooking, and we were waiting for him to serve us something to eat, and that would be the end of the dream! I had this same exact dream every night at the age of fourteen for an entire year, night after night, and after that, I never had the dream again!

I love my sister and her marriage. She and her husband have been married twenty-plus years, and the way that they met was through me! My sister's husband was a bag boy at a grocery store, and the one thing my sister didn't like was going to the grocery store with our mother. So one day, while going into the store, my sister's and the bag boy's eyes met, and after that, our mother didn't have to force her to go to the store anymore with us. Our mother told her, "Yeah, I see you don't mind going to the store now. There must be somebody in there you want to see?" And each time we went into the store, neither one of them said anything to each other. They just always smiled until one day, I told him, "You know my sister likes you?"

He said, "Oh yeah? Well, I like her too." And I told my sister what he said. The next time when my sister came in the store, he approached her, and their relationship began!

My sister was eighteen years old when I found out that she had eloped with the bag boy. One day, while in our room, I was listening to one of my sister's tapes that her boyfriend Carl had made for her and was sending them to her while he was on the ship, because now Carl had enlisted in the Navy and he was sending my sister tapes with different love songs as well as his voice talking, telling her how much he loves her and whatever else. Now my sister had gotten on me before about messing with her stuff, but she wasn't home at the time, and I wanted to listen to some music. So I put one of her tapes in, and at the end of the tape, Carl was telling my sister, "Now you know we've been married for four years, and nobody knows it yet."

I said, "What? Let me rewind that back."

"Now you know we've been married for four years, and nobody knows it yet."

I yelled, "E!" Don't forget *E* is short for Edith because we were all raised calling our parents by their name and our grandmama was Mama.

My mama came in the room, and I played the tape back. My mama looked at me like I was the one who just eloped. All she could say was, "Oh, ain't that something!" Now she was waiting for my daddy to get home! My parents couldn't wait until my sister came home, but she said the reason they had eloped was because she loved Carl, and she wanted to marry him, but she knew our dad was not having it! They fussed about it but later on ended up giving them a reception.

I have now graduated from middle school. High school, here I come! Eau Claire High School, one of the best schools that everybody wanted to attend. Shamrock, a four-leaf clover, was the school logo! I entered Eau Claire High School in the year of '86, which meant I had to leave two of our girlfriends who were in our dance group behind, Step and Van, Sam's little sister, because they were about two years younger than Sam and me, but we all still remained very close friends since we all still lived in the same neighborhood! The time I taught myself to drive was around fifteen years old. My dad owns an auto body shop that was his trade ever since he got out of the military and before I was born. He was always leaving spare keys around to the cars that he was fixing on, and one day, I decided to go hunting, trying every key until I find the right one!

I decided that I would take the car around the neighborhood to practice driving. I knew a little bit about driving because when we were younger, our dad would take us around in the neighborhood while sitting us on his lap and letting us steer the steering wheel while he was controlling the gas pedal until our legs were long enough to touch the gas pedal on our own. So I took the car for a little spin and made it back in one piece. It felt good, and I decided that I would take the car whenever I could to practice, and it started getting good. So good that I one day decided that I would pick up Sam and Van and let them ride with me. I decided to drive down the street that I lived on. I noticed that both of my parents' cars were both home, and I panicked and screamed and told Sam and Van, "Y'all gotta get out of the car right now. My parents are home."

And they were like, "What!"

I screamed again in a panic, "Y'all gotta get out of the car right now. My mama and daddy is home!"

I was doing about thirty miles per hour coming down a hill. I guess by now they were both just as scared as I was, and as I was getting closer by my house, I screamed again, "Y'all gotta get out right now!" but I was so scared that I wasn't thinking to stop the car and let them out. These two fools jumped out of the car while I was still driving. I guess they said, "Well, you said get out!" When I looked back, both doors were still open, the front and the back, and all I saw were these two fools rolling down the hill. It wasn't funny then because they both hurt themselves, not bad, just some scrapes and bruises, but it's still funny till this day every time I think about it!

Being a freshman in high school was exciting, different, and fun! I remember getting my class schedule, and one of my classes was in the basement! Everybody knew anyone going down to the basement were in a special or slow class, but my class was a workshop class. People didn't want to hear that if you were in the basement period, you can say what you wanted. You were in a slow class. And if anyone saw you going down to the basement, they all laughed at you, so you know I was always late going to that class. I waited until the bell rang, and everybody was in their classes before I turned the corner to go down to the basement! At high school, they not only had a cafeteria to eat in, they had a food stand out back that mostly the cool students who had money would eat at because in high school, only the nerds or the poor people ate free lunch in the cafeteria.

I remember one day, Tree and I decided to get something to eat at the food stand in back, and Tree had already gotten her food and was waiting on me to get mine. The next thing you know, something had dropped in her drink that splashed so hard, it made her drink splash in her face. We both were like, "What was that?" and when we looked up, a pigeon came by and s—— on her head. And anyone that knows that when a pigeon sh——, they sh—— a lot. Tree reached in her hair to feel all the pigeon's s—— in her head, and all she could say was, "What the hell! I don't believe this!" Everybody that was out there laughed so hard at her including me. Some friend, I was, but it was too funny, I couldn't help myself! We still talk about it till this day. Well, I still bring it up because it's still funny!

I met a lot of friends at school, and one of my good friends was a guy who years later had a sex change and became one of the most well-known sensational drag queen performers all over the US! He and his group are best known to performed in South Carolina at the Comedy House as the Cabarea, imitating and lip-syncing to Patti Labell, Tina Turner, Beyoncé, Diana Ross, and many, many more! In high school, he and I would sometimes hang out together, and I would sometimes go over to his house. One day, I was in his room sitting on his bed, and he just started crying. I really felt sad for him. He started telling me that he tried talking to his mother about the feelings that he was having about him liking other boys. He said that he knew that he was a boy, and he didn't know why he would have feelings for boys instead of girls. I asked him what did his mother say when he tried to talk to her. He said that she only told him to go and sit down somewhere because he didn't know what he was talking about and that she didn't want to hear it! I wasn't judging him. I only felt sorry that his mother didn't want to listen to anything he had to say.

So see, parents, this goes back to me telling you that it is very important to listen to our children. I saw a commercial on television many years later showing clips of the Cabarea performing at the Comedy House. I heard that his performance was amazing, and I really wanted to see him after all these years, so I made plans to attend. The performance was amazing, and it was a sold-out show. The money that the people in the audience were giving to each dancer, you would have thought that they you were at a strip club, so I told myself, "Stop being cheap and pull out some money!" People were throwing twenty-dollar bills at them as well as putting their money in the performer's outfits, and they each had someone out there picking the money up as fast as someone was throwing it down! I said to myself, "I know. That's right. Better get that money!"

I had a great time, and I was proud of him. I never said that I approved of him being a drag queen. I was just proud of his performance. When I went backstage to his dressing room to see him, he told security to let me in because I was his classmate and friend. We were the only ones in his dressing room. We were both so happy to see each other after so many years. We hugged, and he spoke about his mother who was there for the very first time to see him since he started performing. He also told me that his mother never approved of him having his sex change, but she's now proud of him becoming one of the most talented drag queens, and the look on his face, you could tell that he too was happy. But he also felt that maybe she was just there for the money! He gave me that look, rolled his head and eyes, and we both just started laughing.

I said to myself, "Well, you know if she's just here for the money if she asked for some?"

High school had a lot of cute guys, especially this one guy I had a secret crush on named Jason, but he was liked by all the girls, so I stayed my distance but kept an eye on him! I remember they had an announcement over the intercom speaker about having a celebrity lookalike contest, and I was definitely a Michael Jackson fan to my heart. Plus I had the Jheri curl to match! So I went home and told my mama that I wanted to be in the celebrity contest at school and that I wanted to dress up like Michael Jackson. So my mom took me to the store and brought me the Michael Jackson outfit. I had the red plastic jacket with all the zippers, the black plastic pants, the Michael Jackson glitter socks, the one glitter glove with matching glitter glove earrings, and the penny loafers to match, but again, let's not forget about the Jheri curl, the most important thing that set it all off!

I just knew that I was going to be the winner of that celebrity contest, and by the looks of it, I was the only one dressed up in a celebrity costume. I only saw about one or two other people dressed up. I said to myself, "This must have been a joke, and the joke was on us new freshmen!" No, the joke was on me because I was just about the only fool who dressed up, and I don't remember them having the contest or who won? I was still saying to myself that if they did have the contest, I would have won, but the only thing I won was the

Funniest because everybody was pointing and laughing at me. At the same time, I felt like the guy on the movie *I'm Gonna Git You Sucka* when the guy got out of jail years later wearing his same clothes he went to jail in back in the '60s, and when he got out, it was the '80s, and he was wearing his pimp clothes with a pimp hat and high heel shoes that had gold fishes in the bottom of them like a fish aquarium! Everybody started pointing at him and laughing at the same time, and he started running, breaking up his fish shoes, leaving his fish behind on the ground! It was hilarious, but it wasn't funny when they all laughed at me!

I went home crying to my mama about how the kids at school laughed at me, and I was so embarrassed that I didn't want the Jheri curl in my hair anymore. So my mama decided that she would take me to the hair salon to the same lady who was doing my Jheri curl. My mom told her that she wanted to revert my hair from the Jheri curl to a relaxer, and after I was finished, my mom told me to walk home to my Auntie Betty's house in Saxon Homes since it was around the corner. The hairstylist didn't explain to my mom before she left that in order for me to revert my hair from a Jheri curl to a relaxer, she would have had to cut my hair down from where the chemicals of the Jheri curl stopped. When she was finished with my hair, this lady done cut all of my hair off, styled it like an old lady, and sent me walking home. I was mad as hell, and so was my mama! My mama took me right back to the hair salon and told the lady, "What did you do to my child's hair? The reason I put the Jheri curl in her hair was so that it would grow, and here it is, you done cut all of my child's hair off her head. I ain't paying you for this, and you won't get your hands back in my child hair again!"

And we walked out!

I was mad that the lady cut most of my hair off because it had grown to my shoulders. Now it was barely by the tip of my ear, but I was happy that I didn't have to wear the Jheri curl anymore even though people were still wearing them, mostly older people. I was just happy I didn't! It wasn't a week after I got the Jheri curl out of my hair that this guy in my class set my hair on fire! It was a classmate of mine; we both were in the same reading class together, and we both always cut up in class together with the jokes and laughs. He was someone I liked coming to class with just to get a good laugh. Our English teacher was also funny, naturally funny, even though he was gay. He was a funny teacher who didn't play, especially you getting in his class late after the bell rang.

In high school, they give you two bells over the intercom. One to let you know that you have three minutes to get to class and the second bell is the tardy bell. And if you are tardy, then you were sent to the principal's office with no exceptions! On this particular day, the first bell had already rung, and it was getting close to the second tardy bell to ring, and we were all rushing in behind each other trying to get into the classroom. And the next thang I knew, my English teacher was beating me in the back of my head and talking at the same time saying, "Oh, Jesus child, Lord, have mercy. What the world is going on!"

I didn't know what was going on. All I knew was that he was beating me in the back of my head, and I was like, "What the hell is going on?" When I looked back, my buddy whom I joke with in class had his hands up to his mouth and moving out of the way fast with a lighter in his hand like "Oh s——!" We both went to the principal's office, and the principal asked him, "What the hell was wrong with you, boy? And what had happened that you set this child's hair on fire?"

I was just lucky because I said to myself, "Damn, I just got my Jheri curl out of my hair a week before this happened, I could have been another Michael Jackson for real up in flames!"

I had a relaxer, which is still a chemical in my hair, and that's why my hair went up in flames so quick. I'm glad that my English teacher thought quickly and started beating the crap out the back of my head. I'm so thankful for him because he saved my life!

The principal sent my buddy in the back room of his office. Before my dad got there, he said, "I'm a dad as well, and I know how I might react if someone had done this to my child. I'ma be ready to hurt somebody!" My dad wasn't too upset because I told him that it was an accident and that he didn't mean to set my hair on fire. It could have been worse than it was. I didn't have any first-, second-, or third-degree burns, only my hair which was enough for me. After that, I found myself with a new hairstyle with just the back cut down really low! Years later, I ran into that buddy of mine who set my hair on fire with his wife and son, and when he saw me, he told his wife, "Baby, this is my classmate who I was telling you about when I was in high school, and I set her hair on fire!"

His wife said, "If I was you, I would have kicked his a———!"

I said, "No, because it was an accident!"

He said, "No, I was trying to set your hair on fire!" with a smile on his face.

I said, "What!"

He said, "Yeah, well, not really when we were rushing in class, I was behind you trying to light my cigarette, and when my lighter didn't work, I was behind you flicking it saying, 'I should set her hair on fire,' and the next thang you know, my lighter lit!"

He, his wife, and his son all laughed, but I didn't see a thang funny! I felt like it had just happened, and I was ready to jump on all their a——— for laughing! I played it off with a smile, but I was mad, and a little hurt now finding out after all these years later that he really meant to set my hair on fire. I said to myself while looking at him, "Lord, please forgive me with his cripple a——— arm!"

Something had happened to one of his arms years later where he had been in a bad accident because it was black and looked like it had been crushed and deformed. I just know that it wasn't like that in school. Please forgive me, Lord. I'm just telling my story because I know two wrongs don't make a right!

Step and I became the best of friends. We were so close that people thought that we were sisters. We became inseparable! They started calling us Salt and Pepper after the female rappers. We later found out the only reason they were calling us Salt and Pepper was because of our skin complexion! Step is light-skinned, and I'm dark. We looked at each other as in disappointment because we wanted to be known more of the female rap group than just some salt and pepper people put on their food. It didn't matter. We still called ourselves Salt and Pepper because they were one of our favorite female groups of all times. We wore our hair like Salt and Pepper, long on one side and short on the other! We even started dressing like Salt and Pepper with the hip-hop look. We were both one of the best female dancers around because we were always at home practicing our routine dances and always somewhere at a club on the dance floor, dancing together, performing our routine and always got the mean stares and the rolling of the eyes by the females that were there. But the guys loved us and were just amazed to see two females who could dance their a——— off!

The guys would first start checking us out smiling and rocking to the beat, and the next thing you know, they were out there on the dance floor trying to keep up with us. It was fun. We had a ball. Step's house was like my second home. If I wasn't home at my house, then my mom and dad knew that I was over to Step's house, and it was just one street behind our house. The more that I started hanging around Step's house and seeing her brother bean, the more I began to have a crush on him, and he knew it! Jeff was the one that introduced us to alcohol. Milwaukee Best was the first beer Step and I started drinking! Then we were introduced to cigarettes. Newport is what we started smoking, but Jeff told us that if we were going to smoke cigarettes, then we would have to smoke something smoother, like Salem Regular because Newport was just too strong for a woman and were more for a man! I knew that Jeff liked me too, but he treated me more like his sister than anything, and that was cool too!

I became really good friends with my neighbors next door. The Boys is who I call them. There was about thirty of them that hung together but only two that stayed next door. They were always doing something, shooting ball, playing cards, having parties, cooking on the grill, playing music, drinking, smoking, talking crap to each other, and it would sometimes end two and three in the morning. I sometimes found myself sneaking and peeping out the window, laughing at some of the things they would say as well as watching Jeff to see what female face he would be in. They were all good friends of Jeff, and they took the likes of me because I'm a people person. They said that I wasn't stuck-up like my sister or brother who stayed in the house and acted as if they were too good to even speak when they spoke to them!

I said, "Well, that's my sister and brother, and they're not as friendly as I am, and that's why my mama always use tell me, 'You just know every damn body!'"

I started going over to the Boys' house to play cards (spades) because we all loved a good game of spades. Now the two guys who stayed next door stayed with their mother and auntie, and we always respected the both of them because they both were churchgoing women who loved us, and even though they both smoked cigarettes, they didn't mind us smoking cigarettes or drinking beer, but they definitely didn't play us cursing in front of them or smoking that wacky-wacky weed, so we had to sneak behind the house to do that! I remember one day while going to the bus stop still in the ninth grade to catch the bus, and the Boys, who were older than us and already graduated, were on the corner that morning smoking their wacky-wacky weed. I decided to get a hit of it before getting on the bus! The weed was so good. I was high, high, high, high, high. I started walking down the hill to the bus stop. Then the bus pulled up, and everyone had gotten on the bus, and the bus driver was nice enough to wait on me. I wanted to run to catch the bus, but I was too high, and I felt like if I would have tried running down the hill, I would have fallen, and I wasn't about to be laughed at on that day.

So I started walking a little faster toward the bus, but the more I was walking toward the bus, the farther the bus was getting. I mean, the closer I tried to get to the bus, the farther the bus was getting. I felt like I was in *The Twilight Zone*. I just couldn't get to the bus to save my life, and the next thang you know, the bus just pulled off, and everyone on the bus started laughing. I was so embarrassed. I was like, "What the hell just happened?"

I had to go back home and tell my dad that I missed the bus! Another day came where I just didn't want to go to school that day. It was a rainy day, and it was pouring down hard. I just felt like staying home, so I went to the bus stop as usual. I turned around thinking that everyone should have been gone from the house. They weren't. I found myself hiding in our backyard, posted up against the house, looking like a fool under my umbrella getting soaked and wet while waiting for everyone to leave. It seems as though they would never leave, and I was getting tired of standing in the rain! Everyone finally left. Once I got inside, I took off all my wet clothes and got comfortable on the sofa with a blanket, pillow, and turned the TV on. It was about thirty minutes later that I heard my dad pull up outside.

I jumped up, grabbed everything, cut the TV off, and was like, "Oh s———." Where was I going to hide that he wouldn't know that I was there. He came in the house so fast, all I could think of was hiding in the closest thing next to me, which was the closet in the hallway, where we kept our dirty clothes in, and it was big enough to hide in. I decided to bury myself under the dirty clothes until he left, but it seemed as though he didn't want to go anywhere. He too made himself comfortable on the sofa and turned on the television! So I waited and waited, and while I was waiting for my dad to leave, the clothes on top of me was getting stinkier and stinkier.

I was like, "What the hell is that smell? Somebody's dirty drawls?"

I started feeling as though I couldn't breathe, and the smell wasn't making it any better, and I just couldn't take it anymore! I busted out of the closet with our dirty clothes all over me and with my best act ever!

"I can't do it. It's stank in there."

I told my dad that the reason I stayed home was because I wasn't feeling good, and I know that if I would have told E, that she would have sent me to school anyways! Now you know I'm a daddy's girl, and you know he either believed me or just shook his head to the bull———!

There was a female whose name was Rachel whom I took a couple of my classes with, and she and I became very close friends. Rachel and I started going to church together, and she was the first person to have ever taken me to a holiest church. I've never seen anything like it in my life. People were screaming, hollering, running around the church, falling out, lying on the floor. I didn't know what was going on. I was just nervous and ready to go and told myself this was my last time going with Rachel to that church. I'll find my own. I found myself going to different churches by myself because my family still wasn't going. On my sixteenth birthday, Rachel asked me what was I going to do for my birthday, and I told her that I was going to skip school, walk home, and find somewhere to celebrate because I knew that my family wasn't having anything for me.

She asked me if she could go with me, and I told her that it was up to her. So she too cut school, and as soon as we got close to my neighborhood, she had the nerve to ask me if I was going to walk her back to school, so she could catch her bus back home. I looked at her and told her that she must be crazy to think that I was cutting school just to turn around and walk her back to school.

"Ain't nobody told you to cut school with me. That was your choice!"

So she turned around mad and walked back to school because she knew that her parents didn't play! As soon as I got back in my neighborhood, I saw Sam's brother, Aaron, whom I also had a lil crush on. He was about three or four years older than me, and he was very cute! He asked me what was I doing today, and I told him that I was celebrating my sixteenth birthday!

He was like "What, okay come on to the house!"

So we both walked back to his house, and he said that he would roll up a blunt for us to celebrate my birthday with. I must say I really had a good time that day. Not only did we get high. We had sex off a song that became one of my favorite songs. It was the first time I ever heard it. "Computer Love"! Everybody loves "Computer Love"! Let's sing it together! "Computer love, computer, computer love. Computer love. Nothing but computer, computer love. Hey! You know I've been searching for someone to share that special love with me, and her eyes have that glow. Could it be a fantasy or my computer screen!"

Don't get me started. That's my jam. I *love* that song, and every time I hear it, it takes me back to my sixteenth birthday getaway!

When I got back to school the next day, my girlfriend Rachel was so upset with me that she didn't even want to talk to me after that, but I had to explain to her it was my day, and she wanted to follow me knowing she had that strict mama and daddy! I remember some of our classmates were talking about Rachel in class about how bad her breath smelled, and yeah, she did have some bad breath. I just thought that maybe she had a gum disease or something! Rachel was a very short dark-skinned female with a very cute shape and hips that all females my age wanted, something I didn't have. Her looks wasn't all that, but she was okay. Plus she had a big gap in the front of her teeth, and she was always spiting on you when she talked because she ended her sentences with the "shh" sound like the sound of a snake!

Because she was my friend, I felt obligated to tell her that people were talking about her, and she and this guy had started dating, so I wanted her to know so she wouldn't be all up in his face with bad breath. I didn't have the nerve to tell her face-to-face because I didn't want to hurt her feelings, so I wrote her a note instead and gave it to her in class. The note read, "Rachel, you are my friend, and I feel as a friend that I needed to tell you this because I didn't want other people talking about you behind your back, so I feel that I needed to be the one to tell you that your breath is stank, and people are talking about you behind your back!" After she read the letter, she looked at me with an attitude and got loud in class. I guess she was offended because she said "Shannon!" in a loud voice.

I said, "Shannon, what, your breath is stank. Would you have wanted somebody else to have told you? I was trying to help you out!"

She rolled her eyes, and after class, she asked me why I didn't tell her about her breath? I told her, "Hell I thought you knew!"

She forgave me, and we remained friends!

I remember running into David, a guy I used to have the biggest crush on growing up in Saxon Homes. David was about two to three years older than I and had all the girls running behind him because he was one of cuties and finest guys that I've ever met other than Keith, the one I said reminded me of a short Billy Dee Williams. I went to school with David's baby brother, and after David and I kept running into each other, we started hanging out and talking to one another on the phone as much as possible. I remember him taking me to meet his grandmother, the woman he said that raised him! I felt special that he would take me to meet his grandmother. He told me the reason his mother didn't raise him, his sister, or brother was because she was on drugs! Now I know we didn't have much growing up, but looking at David and seeing where and how he was living, we were still better off than he was, and my heart went out for him! I tell you, it's a privilege to still have your mother and father in the same household. It's a privilege to have a parent, period, in the household especially one that loves you!

One day, David called me up and told me that he wanted to know where I stayed and if it was okay that he came over. Well, like I said, I'm a daddy's girl, and I don't know how my daddy would have felt about me having a boy to come over to our house, so I figured the only way I would know was for me to invite him over, and I really liked David. I was willing to take that chance! I didn't want to say anything to my mom or dad until David got there. So he called me back to ask me what kind of car was in the yard so he'll know when he got on my street, and I told him a Bonneville. I didn't know that my parents had plans to go somewhere, and I was going to be home alone, so I knew that there was no way possible for David to come over since no one were going to be there! Oh no, my parents weren't having that, and I wasn't getting in trouble talking about having a boy in the house when I never had a boy in the house before and especially while they weren't at home.

I kept trying to call David to tell him that he couldn't come over since my parents had just left, but he didn't answer. I tried two more times and still no answer, so now I'm nervous because I knew I can't have this boy coming over to my house, knowing my parents were gone. I got a knock on the door, and it was David! I opened the door and talked to David through the screen door, told him that my parents weren't home, and I couldn't let him come in. Because it was hot, David asked me if he could have a glass of water, and I gave it to him while he was standing on the porch. He then asked if he could use the bathroom before he left. I was hesitant and said to myself, "Oh, Lord, now I know I ain't supposed to let this boy in my house, but I guess I'll just let him use the bathroom real fast, then he can go." I let David in, and I was walking in front of him to show him where the bathroom was at. Then David wanted to know which room was my room. Right there, why? So instead of him going into the bathroom, he pushed me into my bedroom where my sister and I slept, pushed me on the bed, and I jumped up and asked him, "What are you doing?" But he didn't say anything. He just started trying to take off my pants, and I started fighting him off me and telling him to stop, but he didn't because he was stronger than me.

He started ripping off my shirt, and I was fighting him to get him off me with all of my might, but it wasn't good enough. He was stronger, so he got the best of me, and he took my pants off and pushed my legs open with his legs. I couldn't close my legs, and he raped me! I laid in my bed and cried, and when he was done, he put on his clothes and left! I couldn't believe what was happening. I couldn't believe that the guy I was so crazy about all these years just raped me! I was so wrong about David, and I was too scared to tell my parents, the fear of me getting in trouble for letting him in the house in the first place and the shirt that he tore off me was really my brother's shirt. My brother was a sharp dresser and always wore the sharpest clothes. He's our mother's pride and joy, so he had the best!

I took my brother's shirt and hid it deep down in the bottom of my drawer. I had to somehow get my brother's shirt repaired before he found out! A couple of weeks later, my mom found my brother's shirt in the bottom of my drawer, held it up, and saw how it was all ripped up. She said, "What in the hell happened to this shirt, and why do you have it all stuffed down in your drawer like that?" She said, "Skeet, isn't this your shirt that you were looking for because Shannon had it tucked down in the bottom of her drawer."

"Yeah, that's my shirt I was looking for!"

I had to come up with the best excuse. There was one that I knew that she would believe. "Yeah, I wore Skeet's shirt one day and got into a fight with this girl." And my mom was like, "Well, looking at this shirt, she must of have whooped your a——!"

I was happy that my brother wasn't mad about his shirt. My brother loved me and I loved him. The only thing he told me was to ask the next time! I was so relieved that it was over until one day, while sitting at the table eating dinner, I started vomiting back up my food, and my mom was like, "What's wrong with you?"

"Nothing. I just don't feel well." So she told me to go and lay down. The next morning while eating breakfast, I vomit my food up a second time, and my mama looked at me kinda funny, and the first thang came out of her mouth was, "You better not be pregnant!"

I told her, "No!" with a sure and positive look on my face. She said, "Okay, I'm taking your a—— to the doctor, and we are sure going to find out."

Well, sure enough, my mom took me to the doctor to have a pregnancy test! I was told to go into the bathroom to urinate in a cup and to bring it back up when I was done. I was sitting on the toilet, trying to urinate into this cup, but I couldn't. I guess I was too scared because I really didn't know if I was pregnant or not, and I was scared because my momma was right there in the bathroom with me standing over me mad as hell! I sat there for about two or three minutes, and I told my mama, "I can't pee." So she did something that I would find out later that was an old trick to make you pee! She turned on the faucet and let the water run real slow, and damn, here came the pee!

When the test results came back, it came back positive. I was pregnant! The female counselor talked to us about me either having the baby or me having an abortion! It was settled. My mom told her that I was getting an abortion and for her to make the appointment, and when we got in the car, my mom backhanded me so hard in my face that blood shot out of my mouth! I still didn't tell her what had happened. I just later went to have the abortion, which was painful and hurtful!

Even though I was young, I still thought about my child dying that way, and they even had the nerve to show you the bag with all the blood that carried your unborn child in! Maybe they did it for a reason—to give you something to think about! The counselor told my mother that after the procedure they always recommend for the patient to lay down for about forty-five minutes before going anywhere, but my mom sent the counselor to come and get me up anyway.

"Baby, your mom sent me to get you. She said that you couldn't lay down and for you to put on your clothes because she had to go!"

I was so out of it, I could barely stand up to put on my clothes or even walk to the car, and my mom was not about to help me. She just told me to hurry up so that we could go! After the bad experience with me getting raped and getting an abortion, I didn't talk about the situation to any of my friends I just kept that secret to myself, something I will never forget! After that, my mom made sure that she put me on birth control pills!

I remember while being in school, I wasn't too smart about not sitting on the toilet seats. One day, while at home, I felt something crawling on me. I mean, crawling in my pubic hair! I went into the bathroom to see what was going on, and I started scratching myself, and when I did, I felt something under my fingernail. I thought that I scratched my skin off, but there was a bug wiggling under my finger, and I was like, "What the hell is that?" I started getting nervous because I'm wondering why would a bug be in my pubic hair? I looked down at myself really good, and I scratched some more like crazy. Another one! I was so scared, I didn't know what to do because I didn't know how the bugs got there, and I was too scared to tell my mama. So I called my cousin LuLu who was more like an auntie to me, and she works at a pharmacy, so I know she'll know what to do.

I told her that I found some bugs in my pubic hair and that I was too scared to tell my mama. She came over when my mom wasn't home, and she had me to sit on some newspaper and shave off my pubic hair, and baby, the bugs where crawling everywhere. I was like, "How did all these bugs been on me like that, like leeches, and I didn't know it?"

She wrapped the newspaper up and set it on fire outside. She then gave me some salve and told me not to bath down there to let the salve kill off any eggs that the bugs might have left on me! I didn't think she was going to tell my mom, but she did, and my mom was so mad. She said that I should have come to her, but how could I? I was too scared to get my head knocked off or get my teeth knocked down my throat as she would always tell me. I was just scared because I didn't want her to think that I was having sex.

My mom told me that it was embarrassing to her that I had to call my cousin instead of me telling her about me having crabs!

I said, "Crabs!"

She said, "Yes, crabs!"

I didn't know anything about crabs, only the live blue crabs that I love to eat and that's it! My mom told me that you can get crabs by sitting on toilets or by having unprotected sex with someone who has them! I told her that I wasn't having sex, and it had to come from me sitting on the toilets at school!

One day, while hanging over to Step's house, her brother, Jeff, asked me to ride with him to the store. I said to myself, "This is the first because he never asked me to ride anywhere with him." I felt a little special! On our way coming back from the store to get a couple of beers, Jeff decided to pull off on this backroad, known as the cut. Now I'm really wondering what was going on. He said that he just wanted to smoke a joint with me before heading back to the house. So we sat there tripping and laughing while smoking on a joint and drinking a beer! He said he wanted to get in the backseat, and I didn't ask any question because I had a big crush on him! Seem in my past I had a lot of crushes on a lot of guys, but that's all. It was just crushes. I was young and naive! He started kissing me on my neck, and I didn't want him to stop because it felt good. And then he started kissing me on my lips, and that felt good too. So then he started taking off my shirt, and I had to tell him that I didn't think us taking it any further would be wise, and he asked me why. I told him that I just recently had the crabs, and he said, "So?" I was like "So..." Well then, he must have really liked me that he didn't care that I had crabs! I should have known then that he was nasty and just didn't give a damn about himself or me! While we were talking, I don't know what made me open up to him about David, but I did. I told him something that I didn't tell anyone else. Maybe because I didn't want to go through something of what David took me through, but after I told Bean, he was very upset. He wanted to know where David lived because he wanted to pay him a visit, but I told him that it wasn't worth him going to jail over. Bean had a mean temper on him, and there was no doubt in my mind that if he would have found David, he was going to hurt him.

When I wasn't hanging out with Step, I was hanging out with Monica who lived in another neighborhood not far from us, only about a ten-minute walk. Monica and I were in a class together at Eau Claire, and that's how she and I became friends. Monica was very pretty who looked like Pocahontas with long hair and a cute walk that had a switch in it while swinging one arm. People used to ask me if she really walked like that. I used to question it myself in the beginning, but after hanging out with her for so long, I realized that it was her signature walk. It was so cute that guys and girls would imitate her, and she had a laugh so funny she sounded like Betty Ruble on *The Flintstones*. Monica was the baby of three, and she was her daddy's princess. Monica didn't have many friends. As far as I knew, I was the only friend coming over to hang out with her, and she wasn't allowed to go anywhere unless it was with her family! Monica didn't have a boyfriend at the time because she said that her dad wouldn't allow her to have one, so she had to sneak during school so see this guy whom she met. She said that she really liked this guy, and she thought that she was falling in love with him. She knew that her dad wouldn't approve of him, so she only saw him and spoke to him when she could!

Some months went by and I still never met this secret lover of Monica. One day, while changing classes, we stopped each other in the hallway to talk for a minute when she was surprised by the guy that she was secretly dating. He didn't attend our school, so he decided to come up there to see her since they had to sneak around, hiding from her parents. When he tapped her on her shoulders, she turned around and almost screamed. She was so surprised to see him. They hugged, and then he said, "What's up, Shannon?"

It was David, the same guy who raped me about seven months ago. I wanted to spit in his face and ask him, "Why in the hell did you rape me?" and to let him know that he had impregnated me after he raped me and that I had an abortion, but instead, I just said, "Hey, what's up?"

Monica said, "Oh, y'all already know each other?"

I said, "Yeah, we grew up in Saxon Homes together."

She didn't say much about it. Just "Oh yeah!" They seemed happy together, and I just left it like that! David threw his arms around Monica, and they walked off together down the hall, smiling into each other's eyes while I was left there standing alone in a daze.

After that day, Monica and I weren't seeing much of each other because she and David had started seeing more of each other. Monica had started skipping classes and started telling her parents that she was over to my house when she was really hanging out with David. I could really tell that Monica was falling deeply in love with David, and I believe that he cared for her too so who was I to stop that. I really cared about Monica as a friend, and I didn't want to hurt her by telling her what David did to me, and besides, she had something I always wanted from a guy—real love. One day, Monica's dad came over to our house looking for her, and my mom and I told him that we didn't see Monica any that day. Her dad didn't tell us that Monica was missing from home for about two or three days. Later, Monica came over to my house, and while she and I was in my room, my mom was watching television, and the news came on with a picture of Monica. The news said that Monica had been missing for about a week and that her parents were upset and have been looking for her and if anyone had seen her or know of her whereabouts to call. My mom jumped on that phone so fast we didn't know anything until her dad came to the house to get her. After that, I didn't see Monica anymore. I was sure that her parents were just trying to get her back focused and on track.

After passing to the tenth grade, we had to rezone to another school. We were so mad because the kids that lived across the street from us, I mean, directly across the street in the same neighborhood, could stay at the same school, but we had to get rezoned to Keenan High School, a school that was our rivalry, so you know we didn't want or liked going there! Some of our girlfriends stayed at the old school like Monica, Sam, her sister Van, and Tracey while the rest of us got rezoned—Step, Tree, Tonya, Regina, and Tammy, my next-door neighbor. Even though I became close friends with Tonya and Tree, my auntie still lived in Saxon Homes, so I still visited there often, and the girlfriends that I grew up with was still my sisters no matter what. No other females would come before them because I grew up with those females all my life!

Tree stayed two streets over from us, but she was always on our street, mainly at Tonya's house. Tree and Tonya were the best of friends before we moved out there. I remember one day, Tree, Tonya, and I were on our street sitting with one of the Boys! Tree and Tonya mainly drink. They didn't smoke weed or cigarettes like I did, especially Tree. Tonya would have a puff every now and then, but not Tree, and when someone would try to give Tree something to smoke, she would take it, but I would always snatch it out of her hand and tell them that she didn't smoke. I felt like I had to protect her because it was bad enough that I did, and I would tell her that she didn't need to do it. That's how much love I had for her even though she would laugh about it and still take a puff and pass it. I think she only did it just to fit in!

Now the Boys, most of them were good-looking and all of them were older than us from four years older and up! I remember both Tonya and I had a big crush on one of the Boys named Dean! Boy was Dean sexy and cute, and the four of us was sitting outside on this little hill in between Tonya and my house talking. Tree and Tonya knew that I was trying to wear Tonya out, and Tonya was trying to wear me out because we were both trying to have that alone time with Dean. Tree went home first, and guess who was the last woman standing?

"Bye, Tonya!" was what I told her. Tonya looked at me and rolled her eyes, but I knew we would still be friends tomorrow. Dean and I laughed about it and stayed maybe another five or ten minutes before I too went home, knowing that it was time for me to go. I just wanted to beat her at her own game!

One thing we always loved to do was go to the football games, especially when they had two of the most popular schools playing against each other. One day, while at one of the games, I had decided to walk on the opposite side of the field where the other team fans were sitting. When I got close to the end of the bleachers, I noticed some guys were in the bleachers fighting. When I got a little closer to be noisy, I realized that it was my cousin Kevin fighting against three other guys. Now anybody that knows my cousin Kevin, they would tell you that we were very tight. Our family called us partners in crime, and the next thang you know, I was swinging blows with my cousin, and we were fighting them off us! I guess because of the big commotion, his brother and my brother both saw us fighting on the other side, and they came running over, and after they jumped in, the guys took off! Yes, I was a fighter in my days. I was a tomboy who wore nothing but jeans, tennis shoes, and hats and didn't play no games!

Whenever any of my male cousins would get mad at their girl-friends, they would tell them because they didn't want to put their hands on them, "I got somebody for you, my cousin Shannon," and they would call me up to jump on their girlfriends, which I never did. I just laughed because I knew that they would be back with them again! My cousin Kevin and I were always partners in crime. I remember we went to this club together in his mother's car, and when we left the club, Kevin gave me the keys and told me to drive. But I guess I was more intoxicated than he was because when I pulled off, I hit another car. After that, we both sober up quick and was glad that no one else was outside to witness it. My cousin took over the wheel. We left like a thief in the night. My cousin took the rap for me and told his mom that someone must have hit her car and left the scene.

I found out that my cousin Charlene had two sons from Feet, one of the Boys in the neighborhood, and Feet wanted to introduce me to one of his cousins. Feet had a lot of cousins like a tribe, a cou-ple of tribes. As a matter of fact, their family was huge. Ant was his name. He was my age, and boy was he cute! It was like we both fell for each other the first time we met. Let's just say it was puppy love! Ant and I started hanging out a lot. We had a good time together. Our friends started noticing that we really liked each other. We liked each other so much that we started having sex like rabbits! I even remember us sneaking in his room a couple of times while his parents were at home and getting us a little quicky! We were young and wild and couldn't get enough of each other! We started hanging out over to his female cousin's house who were cool. We would smoke weed, drink, and play cards. Seems as though that was the thing in my days—smoking weed, drinking beer, and playing cards!

Ant and I wasn't a serious couple. We just used to mess around, and then I knew things were getting serious between us when we started being a little jealous of each other. I remember us being at this club, and this little, skinny, tall-looking girl started looking at me all crazy, rolling her eyes with some of her girlfriends like she wanted to fight me, so I stepped to her and asked her, "Do you have a problem? Can I help you?"

She just laughed and walked off! Ant was telling me not to worry about her because she was nobody and that she was just friends of the family and she always liked him and never said anything or acted like this until this day. Ant and I started arguing all the time over nothing serious. I think it was just puppy love we had for each other, and he never put his hands on me. He always said that I just was crazy. I remember chasing him around this car for about ten minutes. I was so mad, I wanted to punch him in the face, but he wouldn't let me catch him for nothing. He just thought it was funny.

Not long after Ant and I stopped messing around, Bean and I started, and that relationship was crazy! Even though Bean and I were messing around, my friendship and loyalty with his sister Step was more important than Bean and our relationship because I felt that Step and I became the best of friends before Bean and I even thought about messing around! I heard that Step and her family were church kids that grew up in the church, but they weren't going when I met them. Jeffery was his name, but we called him Jeff for short, and his older sister called him Bean. Bean was a tall, light-skinned man who was kinda on the mean side and had a nasty temper when he was drinking. Jeff's twin sister, Jen, was very pretty, and she put you in the mind of Pep the rapper of Salt and Pepper and Whitney Houston all in one! They were both slim, tall, loved basketball, and was good at it! Their family took me in like one of their own, and I loved them like my own family! Their mother Tiny was so cool and a trip. I used to remember her always saying that, "Nobody better not bother my b——," and her b—— were her kids! She was one of those mothers that allowed her kids to drink and smoke cigarettes around her. She

94

said that she knew that they were going to do it anyway so they may as well do it with her at the house instead of out in the streets!

Their dad was retired from the army, and everyone used to say that he didn't fit into that family because he was quiet and didn't raise hell like the rest of the family, but I think if you pushed him hard enough, you better get gone! Step was the baby of six. She was only fourteen years old, and she was spoiled rotten and got whatever she wanted. My two girlfriends, Tree and Tonya, felt like I turned my back on them since I was spending all of my time with Step and her family, and they told me that I was going to soon find them out. I told them that they didn't know what they were talking about, but hey, who knows because they knew them longer than I did! Step's mom loved to go fishing on the weekends, and she was going by herself until she started making Step and I go with her. At first, we were mad that we had to get up early just to go fishing with her mama. We weren't fishing. We would just sit around, tripping, watching her mom fish while we sat around, drinking with our cooler full of beer. Until one day, we both decided that we would grab a fishing pole and give it a try, and I tell you, that first fish got us hooked! After that, Step and I couldn't wait to get up early on Saturday morning with her mom, and I mean, we went early, but it was okay because Step and I was always looking forward to going fishing while drinking our beer and sneaking in the woods to smoke our weed. Her mama knew what we were doing because she saw us coming out the woods laughing and tripping the whole entire day! I always had fun when Step and I were together. There was never a dull moment. We were two of a kind, and we loved each other like real sisters!

Step and I sometimes hung out with Sam and her baby sister Van around the corner, the other two girls who made up our dance group at the park when we won the trophy against the New Edition boys. Sam was the first female I ever met that started wearing weave in her hair. Now Sam wasn't a bad-looking female, but she had some bad eyes. Her eyes were so cross-eyed that if you looked at them too long, your eyes started crossing each other. Sam's hair was very short, and she loved wearing her long weave. I remember one day while talking to Sam that I noticed something in her hair. I kept looking while she was talking, and I realized it was a big a—— safety pin! Sam had two big a—— safety pins one on each side to hold up one piece of weave in her hair! I looked and burst out laughing. I was rolling on the ground. I was laughing so hard. I was crying and couldn't stand up! Then Step came walking from around the corner. I jumped up off the ground and ran to get her. I couldn't talk from still laughing. All I could do was pull her by her arm and said, "Please come see this s——. You won't believe it!" When Step got in front of Sam, I just pointed at the two big a—— safety pins in her hair, and we both fell out on the ground rolling on top of each other! Sam realized what we were laughing at, so she said, while looking at us with her cross eyes, "Child, I didn't have any more sowing thread to sow my weave in, and y'all know I gotta have my weave!" The reason, it was so funny. Just imagine someone whose hair was so short, like my uncle would say, "so short you couldn't roll it with rice," and it was badly damaged, and she had this one twelve-inch weave on the side of her head with two big a—— safety pins holding it up! Just one piece of weave on her entire head. It was hilarious. I'll never forget it! I'm laughing hard about it right now!

One day, while walking over to Sam's house, I was stopped by this guy who lived in the neighborhood. He was an older guy whom I didn't know. I just only saw him a couple of times driving by, and I guess this particular day, he just wanted to stop me just to flirt with me. But I wasn't paying him any attention. We spoke for a little bit while he was sitting in his car. He left, and I kept walking to Sam's house! The next day, Sam called me on the phone at home and told me that Gena saw me talking to her boyfriend the day before. I was like, "Who? That guy in the car who stopped me?"

Hell, he stopped me, and I wasn't paying him any attention. Sam told me, "Well, make sure you wear some sneakers tomorrow because Gena told me that she was going to whoop your a——!"

I said, "What, well, I will be waiting on her tomorrow!"

So I decided that I would be the one waiting on her to whoop her a——. She talking about she was going to whoop my a—— over her ugly a—— boyfriend who stopped me. Child, please! So the next day, I put on my sneakers, and I thought of a plan, a plan that

I would blind her and whooped that a—— so good that she would think twice about ever wanting to fight me again. I decided to put some salt in my pocket, and when she got in my face, I would throw the salt in her eyes, blinding her, and then I would have the upper hand to whoop her a——! So I walked around to Sam's house, and Sam and her sister Van were both there waiting on me. I was waiting on Gena. I was talking big s——, and when she walked in the yard, I came outside and told her that I heard that she wanted to fight me, and she said, "Yeah, I'm going to whoop your a—— because I didn't appreciate you talking to my man!"

"Honey, he stopped me!"

"So? I don't care I'm still going to whoop your a——!"

"Well, bring it on!"

I made sure that I already had the salt balled up in my hand to throw it in her face, and as soon as she got up on me, I threw the salt. But she must have known I had something in my hand because she was like *The Matrix*. She blocked the salt with her hand and whooped my a——!

Gena was a couple of years older than me, and I was giving her all that I had, but it wasn't enough. All I could say to myself while she had me on the ground was, "Why ain't nobody trying to help me!"

Some kind of friends I had! I guess they were saying, "Hell, it was one-on-one, and there wasn't no need for them to jump in!" I told myself that I would remember that the next time if they were ever getting their a—— beat! I stayed into something just like my mama always told me!

There was another female named Angie in the neighborhood whom I hung out with every now and then. Angie lived right across the street from Sam, and one day, Angie was over to Sam's house filling out an application for a job. Angie was kinda on the slow side. She could barely read, and she stuttered when she talks. On the application, it asked her about her transportation and instead of her writing the word *bus*, she wrote, *bsa*.

I asked Angie what was that word she just wrote, and she said bus. I told her that wasn't how you spell "bus," and she told me that it was the right way to spell "bus." And I laughed at her so hard that she got mad and started talking s——. She was talking s—— and leaving to go outside at the same time, so when she walked out, talking s——, I slammed the door behind her. The door was made out of wood with a glass window pane. When I slammed the door, I was still laughing at her, and she got so mad that she punched the window pane with her fist and broke the glass, and a sharp piece of the glass landed straight in my leg. I started to go out there to whoop her behind, but I thought about it and said to myself, "Let it go because that heifer was crazy!" I'm not a bully. I don't look for fights, and I'm not going to back down from someone either, but I could tell that this heifer had some fight in her too because she was kinda on the "Cock Diesel" side!

One day, Step and I were walking in the neighborhood when Step and another female got into an argument, which ended up them throwing blows. The female who Step was fighting, her boyfriend's sister came walking around the corner and saw them fighting. She thought because Step was getting the best of the fight, she would jump in it. But you know with me standing there, it wasn't happening! So I grabbed the female by her hair, because she had long beautiful hair, and tore her behind up. After the fight was over—well, at least we thought the fight was over—the next thing you know, the female whom I beat up, her boyfriend Tim, along with the female who Step beat up, started walking toward us. And the next thing you know, Tim pulled out a pistol and stuck it to the side of my head and told me, "Bitch, I should blow your brains out!" My life flashed before my eyes, and I just knew that I was dead. I said, "Why, because I whooped your woman's a——. She came like a woman to get a——, so she got a——. She got her a—— whooped like a woman, and you mean to tell me that you, being a man, have to use a gun on a female? Really!"

While this was going on, Step ran and left me, but then she came back running with Bean and his homeboy Chris. Before they got there, Tim put his gun up and was like, "Naw, man, it ain't nothing. My lady ran and told me that your girl and sister had jumped on her." And I said, "It was one-on-one, and she was mad 'cause she got her a—— whooped. That's all it was!" But what made me even madder was that Bean believed Tim when he told him that he didn't pull out a gun on me! I was like, "What really! Oh, so now Step and I are lying on you?"

But Bean was like, "Y'all come on, and let's just go!"

I said to myself, "Either Bean was scared or a pussy." Either way, it pissed me off that he believed Tim over me.

While over at Step's house one day, her oldest sister Sharon was there visiting, and it was just the three of us there. Sharon told us to find her a drinking straw and a pair of scissors. We gave her the straw and scissors, and she told us to come and sit down beside her on the floor next to the glass table. She started cutting the straw in pieces, and she was telling us when we cut the straw, always cut it slant, at an angle. Then she put some white stuff on the table that was cocaine. She took one of the playing cards and started chopping the cocaine up and started separating it in three lines. She took one of the of straws, put it up to her noise, and sniffed the row of cocaine until the line was gone. And she told Step and I to do the same. We did, but we didn't feel anything. And she said, "Just give it some time. Y'all probably just used to having that weed in your system that you can't get a contact." So before she left, she left us some cocaine to do later! Later on that day, Step and I rode to the mall with her mother, and we both went to the bathroom to snort some of the cocaine that her sister Sharon gave us, but again we didn't feel anything. So when we got back home, Step and I decided that we would exchange the rest of the cocaine we had for a bag of weed. When we did, Bean found out, came home, and told us that the guy we exchanged the cocaine for the weed told him what we did. Bean took off his belt and whooped the both of our us like we were his kids and told us that he better not ever hear of us doing something like that again, and we didn't! That was the first and last time Step and I did cocaine. I said that it was a blessing that it didn't have an effect on us, and that was one of the reasons we didn't want to do it.

Bean and I became a serious couple, at least that's what I thought, until one day, while walking in the neighborhood, he drove by me with a dirty female whom I knew that stayed in the neighborhood riding all up under his arm like Oliver Newton John was riding all under John Travolta in *Grease* when they were driving in the sky! Please don't get me started! I was like, "Why in the hell was he with her?" But I should have known that she didn't care who she slept with, especially with all those chilluns she had! Meaning her children. I'm country, and that's the way we say children! But obviously, he didn't care either because that female he was with was dusty and dirty! I was so hurt that he would just passed by me with another female in his car like I was nobody! We got into a big argument that day made up, and that was the end of that conversation.

Step knew there were so many other guys that liked me and wanted to be with me, but I was too in love with Bean, and I dared to get involve with any of them! I must say that Bean was my very first love. I really loved him, and I was getting older to understand what love really felt like, and I had that feeling for him! I loved Step like a baby sister, a little sister that I always wanted and dared for anybody to put their hands on her. Step and I had decided to walk down to another neighborhood that was not far from our neighborhood, and we ran into my cousin Sug, who was hanging out with one of her homegirls, so we spoke to each other.

"What's up, cuz!" and we gave each other a hug. The next thing I knew, Step and Sug started arguing over whose man was who. The guy they were arguing over was Frank. Frank was so fine and sexy that all the girls were crazy about him, including me, but I kept that secret to myself because I knew both my cousin and Step were in love with him. Frank was cool, and I think he also had a little crush on me, but he never said anything. Frank lived in between both of our neighborhoods, and I found myself walking over there a couple of times just to trip. We never did anything other than have a conversation. The boy was so fine, I just wanted to go over there just to look in his face! Step and my cousin started out arguing, but it started to escalate, and the both of them started walking up on each other, and my cousin's homegirl started walking up on Step. I love both Step and my cousin, so I said out loud, "It's going to be one-on-one, and I ain't got nothing to do with it unless, cousin, your home girl jump in, then I'ma jump in!"

My cousin's homegirl looked at me crazy, but she didn't jump in. It was a fair fight, and it was over! I know y'all saying, "Well, who beat the fight?" No one, it was a tie!

Step finally met her someone. A guy named Marcus, and she was falling in love. Marcus was really cool, silly, funny, handsome, and sexy with a beautiful smile! Marcus became a part of the crew, and I remember we all went to Burger King one night, Step, Jeff, Jen—Jeff's twin sister—Marcus, and me. I don't remember why Bean and this guy got into an argument in the parking lot, but the next thing I knew, fists started swinging, and even though Bean didn't need any help, we were like the Musketeers! All for one and one for all! We all started whooping the man's a——, and he took off running, and Bean took off running behind him, and we took off running behind Bean. We were trying to stop Bean and put 'em back in the car before the police came. All I remember me picking up Bean's shoe talking about "my baby shoe," and when we got in the car and pulled off, everybody bust out laughing, talking about that big long a—— shoe. That ain't Bean's shoe. It was the other guy's shoe. The other guy had run so hard that he ran out of his shoe! Bean grabbed the shoe and threw it out the window, and everybody cracked up laughing!

Back in those days, the guys started a crew called the Low Riders—a group of guys whose cars were fixed up with a nice paint job, rims, hydraulics where the cars would sit up high in the front and low in the back or high in the back and low in the front, playing their loud music while driving down the road! Bean's dad had a nice Chevy Caprice Classic that had a very nice paint job. And he gave the car to Bean. Maybe he wanted Bean to fit in with the rest of his friends, I'm not sure, but Bean's car didn't have the rims, the hydraulics, nor the loud music, but it was still one of the baddest cars in the group. And everybody loved it that when they would all get together, driving behind each other in the neighborhood, showing off, Bean would be in the front leading. One day, Step and I was walking in the neighborhood, and Bean passed right by us with another female riding with him. She also was riding so close up under him that she should have been driving! Step and I both turned and looked at each other like, "Wow, that's messed up." We knew the girl, and we knew where she lived, so Step and I started walking fast! By the time Step and I got around the corner, Bean was gone, and the girl had just walked in her house. I was so hurt and feeling like a fool when he got back to the house. We got into a big argument, made up, and I forgave him again like a fool, and that was the end of that conversation! *A fool in love*!

I remember Step and I had an idea about getting our nose pierced. We caught the city bus downtown and got our nose pierced. I was trying to figure out which side I wanted mine pierced on. I chose the right side because that's the side Tupac had his nose pierced, and I promise, that s—— hurt! I didn't tell you that I'm one of Tupac's biggest fans? For life! Everyone that knows me knows that! Step chose the left side. I was fifteen, and she was thirteen. When we got home, Step's mom and Jen liked our nose ring. They liked it so much that they went and got theirs pierced. When my mom saw me, she slapped me so hard that my nose ring flew out of my nose! It hurt so bad. All I saw was stars and flashing lights. It brought tears to my eyes. I almost forgot that she was my mama. I promise you, I almost whooped that a—— that day, but it was just a thought because you know my mama don't play! I only put my nose ring in when I got to school and took it out before I got home.

My mama was good for slapping the taste out of my mouth! I remember her slapping me so hard as soon as I walked in the side door that blood formed in my mouth. I felt like Celie in *The Color Purple* when Mista slapped her! That was the first time that I actually saw stars like how it is in the cartoons. That s—— was real. I actually saw stars! She hit me so hard that she knocked the senses out of me that I forgot who she was! I thought she was a female on the streets who just came up to me and slapped the hell out of me. As soon as she slapped me, my reflexes slapped her back; and before I knew what I did, I came through and I was like, "Oh, Lord!"

I was shaking like a leaf! I told her that I had forgot who she was and maybe because of all the fights that I've had with females in the streets that I didn't know who she was, and she told me, "You better go in your room before I knock your head down your throat!"

I was so mad. When I went to my room, I was crying and wishing that my mom got hit by a bus, but then, I felt bad afterward. I prayed and asked God to forgive me knowing that I loved my mama and would have been heartbroken if anything would have happened to her. The reason my mom slapped me was because she said that I left a little bit of Kool-Aid in the pitcher in the refrigerator because I didn't want to wash the pitcher out. That wasn't true, especially since I was the one washing dishes around the house anyway! I'm a very giving person, and the reason I didn't drink all the Kool-Aid was because I wanted to save some for whoever else that may had wanted some! My mother gave all of us chores to do, only except my sister or brother wasn't doing their chores, and even though I was doing my part, we all still got yelled at. So I decided that I would just do everybody's chores, not because I had to but because I wanted to. I loved my mama, and I knew that she was a hardworking black woman who was trying to provide for her family, and the last thing I wanted for her to do was to come home to clean and cook. I wanted to clean up the whole house, even our parents' room, because when our mom comes home from work, she's tired, and I didn't want her having to do anything but cook us something to eat, and yet that still wasn't good enough because she still came home fussing at me.

"You didn't have to clean up my room. I didn't ask you to clean up my room. I could have cleaned up my own room." My sister and brother didn't do anything but stayed in their rooms all day on the phone and listening to music! My dad told me that my mom and I were just alike, and that's why we always bumped heads! I was always trying to please my mama and get her approval regardless if she knew it or not. But it seems as if nothing I did was ever good enough in her eyes.

I've never cursed at my mother nor disrespected her. The only thing I may have done that she didn't like was defend myself because I was always getting blamed or accused of something. I don't care if there was a fork missing out of the house. I would always be the first to get blamed. One day, my mom was getting on me about something. I can't remember what it was, but I remember her calling me a b———! I was so hurt, a feeling I'll never forget. I said to myself, "What did I do so wrong or so terrible that I had to be called a b——— by my own mother?"

I remember walking through the front door one day, and she just hauled off and slapped me so hard without saying anything. I didn't cry or flinch. I just look my mother straight in her eyes with a serious look and brushed my shoulder off as if, "You can't hurt me any longer. I'm good."

I guess my feelings and heart had gotten numb to her slaps, my mama gave me this look like, "I might have to kill this heifer!" She told me, "Go take your crazy a—— in your room!" To this day, I still don't know what that slap was about, but that was the last slap that I had ever gotten again.

I never felt that real love from my mother the way that I saw other mothers and their daughters together. I would get so envious whenever I saw a mother and daughter together laughing, hugging, or just the love that they showed for each other. It was something I always wanted for my mom and me to have, and because we didn't have that bond, I always prayed for two boys to love and spoil. I don't know why I didn't ever want a girl. Maybe I didn't want for our relationship to be the way my mom and our relationship were, but it's said to be careful for what you pray for because you just might get it.

Step and I were very creative growing up. Even though Step and I both had our ears pierced, one hole in each ear, it wasn't enough. So we decided to pierce our own ears by numbing our ears with ice and using a pierceable ear ring that had a sharp point on the back of it. We would numb our ear front and back with the ice. Then we took the pierceable earring and squeezed it through our ear. I have seven holes on one ear and five on the other. There was nothing to it. As a matter of fact, it was fun. Step and I was always doing something together. I remember us cutting the back of each other's hair with a pair of clippers. We cut different designs in the back of each other's hair, dollar signs, diamond shapes, zigzags, whatever we thought of. We were just very creative, and the guys wanted to know who put the designs in our hair. They were amazed when they found out that it was us, and one of them stated that we should go to barbering school because we did such a great job on each other's hair.

We also started designing our clothes. I remember that we were the first females to come to school with words written out on our jeans. The way we designed it was that we took a rag and dipped it in some bleach and wrote out the words on our jeans. I remember the words on my pants were "unpredictable," "sexy," and some more other words that I can't remember. We would then color the words in with different-colored markers! Step and I were the only two females in the whole school that had those jeans, and all eyes were on us. Females used to ask us where did we get our jeans, but we told them that we designed them ourselves. Of course, they looked at us as if we were lying and probably figured that we didn't want them biting our style. We didn't. If we were smart enough, we should have patent our jeans since we were the first ones to come up with the idea, but we were young and were just having fun! We also were the first females at our school to have our nose pierced, and other females liked that too. Then they started coming to school with their nose pierced.

Bean was my first love, and he always made me laugh. When it was just the both of us together, we were two big kids. We would sometimes pretend that we were Sonny & Cher singing as if we were really on stage. Bean didn't care about. Making jokes about my hair, he would call me Little Burnt Out Edges because my hair was very thin around the edges. He just liked messing with me about that. If I had on a cute outfit, Bean would ask me where I got my outfit from. "Tapp's?"

I would say "Yeap" because he knew my sister had a job working at Tapp's clothing store, and back in those days, Tapp's clothing store was a little upscale department store. Jeff knew I couldn't afford to buy my clothes from Tapp's, but he just wanted to see what I would say. Then, he would just laugh and say, "Yeah, right, with your lying a——!"

Bean was a ladies' man, and I knew that he was seeing other females, but I didn't care because I said to myself, "What I don't know won't hurt me!" until it really did hurt me! I had invited one of my girlfriends from school to spend the weekend with me. Jackie was her name. I felt like Jackie and I were one of a kind. People thought that we were sisters, and we used to make each other laugh so hard in school. This was Jackie's first time spending the weekend with me. We hung out in the neighborhood getting high and drinking with some of the Boys. The next morning, while I was in the shower, Jackie said that she was going outside. So later when I went outside to look for Jackie, she had walked next door to the Boys' house. And when I walked around to the back of the house, I saw Jackie in the backyard, posted up against the house, hard down kissing one of the Boys. I yelled, "Jackie!" and both her and Bean stopped and looked at me in shock! I shook my head and just walked off. She ran behind me, talking about she was sorry. I didn't want to hear that s———. I didn't have anything to say to her. I was so hurt I told my mother what happened, and she told me, "Now you see you have to be careful about the friends you choose."

I stayed home while my mama took Jackie back home before I choked her out because neither one of them wasn't worth me going to prison!

I learned a valuable lesson that day. I didn't know Jackie as well as I thought, especially to invite her over to spend the night. I only knew her from taking a couple of classes together at school. We were class clowns, but now she can be a clown by herself because I stopped dealing with her after that! It was the same as usual. Bean apologized, but I wasn't going to accept his apology so easily this time. I didn't want anything to do with him. I even stayed away from hanging out with Step, but that didn't stop him from hanging next door at the Boys' house looking pitiful and trying to get my attention every day until I gave in two weeks later.

One day, while over at Step's house, we were hanging out in the garage, playing music, dancing, and drinking, just Step, Jen, and myself. We were a little bored, so we decided that we were going to be in a girls gang group of our own called the Ravens, and I don't remember why we choose Raven because Raven was a bird that looked like a black crow. I just remember we got high before we took a lighter, burned the end of a wire hanger, and tattooed the letter *R* on each other's right arm. We were just high and crazy because that's all we did, just burned the letter *R* on each other's arm. And after our high came down, we sat down and didn't think nothing else about being in a female gang. As far as we were concerned, we had our female clique for life, just the three of us, and we didn't have to be in a gang or give ourselves names. We were cool just the way we were. To this day, you can still slightly see that letter *R* on my arm.

Jen had moved to Orangeburg when she was attending South Carolina State College. I don't think she finished, but Step, Bean, and I always had a good time visiting while she was there. Jen was sharing an apartment with a female roommate, and on the weekends Bean, Step, and myself would ride down there just to get away. While they went out partying, Step and I stayed home because as long as we had our cigarettes, beer, and weed, we were good but was tired of coming to a junky apartment with dirty dishes piled up. So while they were out partying, Step and I stayed at the apartment to clean it up. Now Jen and her girlfriend may have been some attractive females who dressed well, but they were some nasty females when it came to keeping their apartment clean.

Bean and I were fighting and arguing all the time about him cheating with different females, it was ridiculous. One day, while we were sitting in the back seat of his car, we got into an argument. Then Bean suddenly grabbed me and pinned me down on the seat with his body weight on top of me. While I was trying to get up telling him to get off me, a car horn blew, and then he put his hand over my mouth. Now I'm really getting mad and trying to figure out what's going on. The horn blew a second time, and I got up with enough strength to pull myself up, but he pinned me back down but not quick enough for me to see who were in the car. Tree, Tonya, and their girlfriend Angie, a pretty Puerto Rican female whom I didn't know very well, but she was driving with no one on the passenger side, and Tree and Tonya were sitting in the back. They pulled up right beside us but couldn't hear us because the window was rolled up. They waited for about a minute, then pulled off. Now, you know I confronted them the next day!

"Tree, Tonya, what's up? You know when y'all came to Bean's house yesterday, we were sitting in his car, but you all didn't see us because we were arguing, and he had me pinned down on the seat. What was up?"

"Oh, nothing. Bean heard us talking about going to the movies, and he told us to come by and pick him up so he could go!"

I wasn't tripping too much because I had to remember that all of them have been friends for years before I even came into the picture, so I took that into consideration but not before thinking that maybe the passenger seat was empty because Bean was going to the movies with Angie.

I remember another day, Bean and I had got into a big argument while I was walking home through the cut. The cut lead you straight to the back of my house. That's the cut the Boys always used to go through to get to their house. So while Bean and I were walking through the cut, arguing, the argument turned into a fistfight, and I was fighting Bean back with all my might, but my might wasn't good enough. I knew that I couldn't beat him so when Bean hit me, he hit me so hard that I decided that I would fall to the ground and play dead. Bean had stopped hitting me, and I didn't know what he was doing because I was lying on the ground, face down with my eyes closed, playing dead when the next thang I knew—pow" Bean had broken off a big branch off the tree and started beating me with it!

"Get your a—— up. You ain't dead!"

I jumped up fast like *The Matrix* and ran through the path with long twigs that was stuck in my hair! The next day, Step was telling me that Bean had told her about me trying to play dead on him and how I ran home with branches sticking out of my hair. We laughed about it, but it wasn't funny when I was getting hit.

I guess my dad heard about the arguments and fights that Bean and I were having because one day, while I was over at Step's house sitting on the porch with Step, my dad pulled up and asked Step if Jeff or her dad was home. Bean wasn't home, but their dad was, and he came out on the porch. My dad told him, "I'm coming to speak to you man to man and a father to a father, but I don't appreciate your son putting his hands on my daughter and that if he was to put his hand on my daughter one more time I'ma tell ya, I don't mind serving time for him, and I mean, what I say!"

Step's dad said, "Mr. Hammonds, I don't blame you for feeling the way you do. I feel the same way because I too have daughters, and I told Jeff about putting his hands on that child!"

That wasn't the only time someone in my family had to confront my relationship with Bean. One day, while over to Step's house, we were all in the front yard playing with each other, and one of Bean's closest friend Chris was there. The same guy who was with him when they confronted Tim for pulling the gun on me. I was standing in the yard talking to Step when Chris came over and saw me wearing a pair of sunglasses and snatched them off my face. He was playing, but I didn't appreciate him just snatching something that was mine off my face, and Bean didn't say a word! So about two or three days later, Step and I was walking down the street from her house when Chris pulled up beside us with Bean on the passenger side. They stopped to talk to us for a minute, and in that moment, I decided to snatch Chris's hat off his head because I wanted him to know how it felt just to snatch something off a person's body.

Chris was so furious that he jumped out of his car and chased me up and down the street, yelling that he was going to kick my a—— when he catches up with me! When he caught me, he got all up in my face pushing me and talking about he should beat my a——, and Bean just stood there and didn't say a word. I went home, and my brother knew that something was wrong with me, so when he asked me, I told him what had happened. My brother had walked me back through the cut, and he walked right up to Chris's face and snatched his hat right off his head and threw it on the ground and told him, "Now you want your hat. There's your hat. Now pick it up! And Jeff what kind of man are you that you would sit up here and let your homeboy get up in your woman's face without saying or doing anything?" Bean and Chris didn't say a word, and I said to myself, "I thought they went for bad. My brother just punked the both of their a——. Now they up here looking stupid!"

I was so proud that my big brother came to my rescue but hurt and disappointed at the same time that Bean didn't defend me. Then my brother turned around to me and said, "And you stupid to be with somebody like that anyway. Now come on here and let's go!"

I felt like Chester the Terrier on the Looney Tunes cartoons, when I was following my brother back home through the path. Chester, the little dog that's always jumping around following after

Spike the Bulldog that wore the hat and kept a toothpick in his mouth. Yeah, Spike is my main man. Spike is my hero!

There was another time when I was leaving from home and walking through the path to go to Step's house. The path was a short-cut to the next streets over, but it wasn't a path of woods. It was just a path, a shortcut between houses instead of walking all the way around to get to the next street over. If you were to turn your head to the right, about eight houses down, you could see one of Bean's homeboys' houses that was facing the path, and I saw his homeboy Bit standing in his doorway as I was walking through the cut earlier that day. He waved to me to say hello, and I did the same and kept walking. Later on that night, when I was walking back through the path going home, I heard someone's voice from behind a tree that I had just passed, "Shannon!"

I stopped and turned around because I thought that it was Bean playing with me. I was like "Who's that?"

And he said, "It's Bean, come here."

I said, "Bean, stop playing."

Then the person said, "Come here."

I started walking toward the tree. The person stuck his arm out from behind the tree, and as I got closer, I noticed the person's arm was dark, and Bean is light-skinned. When I got close to the tree to see who the person was, it was Bit, whom I saw earlier hanging in his doorway. He tried to grab me, but I jumped back before he could grab me, and I ran home like I was in the Olympics!

The next day, I told everybody what happened, and that's when I found out from the Boys that Bit was a pervert and child molester whom the police was investigating, concerning his last relationship where they said that Bit supposedly molested his ex-girlfriend's ten-year-old daughter, and they said that if he would have grabbed me that, he probably would have raped me! I asked them why didn't they tell me about this fool in the beginning! My heart was beating a mile a minute. Just looking at Bit, I said to myself, "I believe he did it. He looks like a pervert!" This goes to show you that there are some very sick people in this world. He knew that I had to come back through the path, and I guess he was waiting for me all that time. Now that's scary and crazy. We young girls have to be more careful about the things we do and more aware of our surroundings. I should have not walked home through that path that time of night, and if I had a real boyfriend, a real man, he should have walked me home that night. But he wasn't home that night as usual to walk me anywhere! A week or two later, I ran into Bit who got word back that he was hiding in the woods trying to rape me, and he was trying to apologize to me telling me that he was only joking with me that night, but I didn't buy it. I've seen and met too many freaks and perverts in my life to know to stay as far away from them as possible, and he was definitely one of them!

I was now in the tenth grade at our new high school WJ Keenan, and Step was in the ninth. Some of the females who I used to fight back in Saxon Homes called the Gucci Girls were attending the same school with us, and we still didn't like each other, so when we saw each other in school, we gave each other that "what's up, whatcha wanna do" look and rolled our eyes at each other. A couple of times, we got into each other's faces, getting ready to fight, but it never happened. The principal told us that he was going to one day put us out in the school field and let us fight it out. He said that was the best way to settle scores back in their days, and we told him, "Yes, let's do that please. Put us out in the field so we could settle this matter!" But he didn't. It's sad that I don't remember much about being in school or my classes, but one particular class, I do remember being in, and it was my fashion designer class. A class full of clowns and I always had a good time in that class. Our teacher Mrs. Cockran was old enough to be our grandmother, and we tried running over her as much as possible, but she wasn't having it. She still couldn't control us. We were too wild at that time. The classroom was full of weed smokers, drug dealers, alcohol drinkers, pimps, and w———! Mrs. Cockran wasn't slow either. If anybody came into the classroom smelling like weed, she would bring them out in a second.

"I don't know who it is up in here smelling like marijuana, but I can smell it, and I don't want to smell it, so I wish you would just leave!" When no one would get up, Mrs. Cockran would walk around sniffing everybody one by one until she found her man or woman and put you out of her classroom. It was so funny.

I started working my very first job in my sophomore year. My cousin asked me if I would catch the city bus with her downtown because she was going to put in an application for McDonald's. I decided to go with her, and while she was sitting there filling out her application, I was just sitting there, watching her. Then I said, "Well, I'm just sitting here. I may as well fill out an application myself." I ended up getting hired, and my cousin didn't. Boy was she mad. The one thing I heard was to never take someone with you when looking for a job because that other person just might get the job and not you! My first day on the job didn't go so well. The training they gave me was a one-hour video tape, and after that, they put me on the register on a busy football game night. The place was packed, and I didn't know what I was doing! I got so frustrated with the cash register, trying to keep up until I started giving food away! The manager saw what I was doing, came over, and took me off the registered and told me to just go and clean the bathroom and dining area. I was so mad and told myself that I did not apply for this job to clean bathrooms. At the end of my shift, I told the manager that when they were ready for me to work the cash register again, to please call me. I never got that call, so I decided to call them. I asked to speak to the manager, and I told him, "I was waiting for someone to call me to come back to work. Now I can come back or just drop y'all uniforms off?"

The manager told me, "You can just drop off your uniforms."

I was like, "Well, I never!"

My little feelings were hurt. I thought I was doing something by telling those people that I could come back to work or bring them their uniforms. I guess they told me! I didn't care because they didn't train me properly anyway, and I didn't take back their uniforms. I used them in Mrs. Cockran's fashion designer class on a project that we all had, where I designed a mini clothing department store where I cut up my uniforms in different barbie dolls clothes. I was very creative! One day, while in Mrs. Cockran's class, there were a group of guys huddled up in a circle over in the corner of the classroom. Me being Miss Nosy, I went over to see what they were doing. They were standing around looking at this small bottle, and I asked them what was in the bottle. This guy name Mike told me to come over and smelled it.

I said, "Smell it?"

It was a small clear bottle that looked like it had water inside and a small white pill at the bottom, so the guy Mike told me to hold one side of my nose and sniff the bottle real hard. I did what he told me and sniffed the bottle really hard. It only took seconds, and everybody in the classroom was bloodshot red. I felt like I was on top of the moon walking on air. All the guys busted out laughing. I was walking in slow motion, and I remember Mrs. Cockran yelling at me telling me to sit down, but I couldn't get to my chair fast enough. I was walking in slow motion. I could barely walk, and she said again, "Sit down right now."

I was telling her but also speaking in a slow voice, "I'm... try- ing... to... sit... down," and because I didn't sit down fast enough, she told me to leave the classroom and go to the principal's office. I found out later that the liquid I sniffed in the bottle was a drug called Rush! I didn't know what it was then, but it's a methamphetamine that include heroin and cocaine!

One day, we had a class fieldtrip in Mrs. Cockran's class where we went to Midland Center, a facility where they have mental patient. The reason Mrs. Cockran chose to have a fieldtrip at a mental insti- tution was still crazy to me. We went there to help the staff give the patients a party. We helped the staff by putting on the patient's party hats, serving their food, interacting, as well as dancing with all the patients. Now I didn't know about anyone else, but I myself was ner- vous as hell, being there with a bunch of mental patients, slobbering out the mouth, looking and walking like zombies. I had to get out of there, so I decided to walk outside and get some fresh air. There were a couple of patients that were outside walking around, and I was just looking at them. I don't know what happened, but the next thing I knew, this patient started walking toward me really fast with his hands out like he was coming to grab me, so I took off running. When I looked back, the patient was on my tail. I put it in top gear and ran across the field like Carl Lewis. When I looked back the second time, the staff had caught up with him and detained him. They were waving to me to let me know that everything was okay and that I could come back. I waved to those people like there was no way I was going back inside. I was so nervous I went to go sit on the bus with another one of my classmates who said that he wasn't going in there to mess with those people, so we smoked a blunt, something I needed for my nerves!

Once we got back to the school, I was still a little shaken up, but what seem so crazy to me was that all the students that was walking around at school was looking just like those patients at the mental institution like they too belonged in a mental facility. I was scared and nervous, looking over my shoulder feeling like I was in *The Twilight Zone!*

There was another day while in Mrs. Cockran's class, Step came to get me. I could tell that something was wrong. She wasn't trying to make a scene. She was waving, telling me through the glass window to come outside, I didn't hesitate at all. I grabbed my books and walked straight out of the classroom with Mrs. Cockran yelling at me, "Come back and sit back down!"

I wasn't hearing Mrs. Cockran. Step was my baby sister, and she was more important to me than a classroom. When I came out, I asked her what was wrong, and she told me that MoMo, one of the Gucci Girls, came up to her to fight her. I asked her, "Where she at!"

We walked outside, and when I saw MoMo, I walked straight up to her in her face and asked her, "You got a problem? If you got a problem with my sister, then you got a problem with me. Don't you ever get up in my sister's face again, or it's going to be me and you, and I know you don't want none of this because you know me from the neighborhood, so you know I ain't about no games!"

She just looked at me with a smirk on her faced, rolled her eyes, and walked off.

Our new high school was a school where the cool and popular kids didn't eat free lunch out of the cafeteria. It just wasn't cool. Even though we didn't have the money like that, I'm sure a lot of us were hungry and wished we were eating free lunch. We just had an image to keep up and were afraid who might see us just in case we did. We always went off campus, or we walked to the food stand that was right behind the school, and boy did they have the best sausage dog ever. Step was spoiled and told her parents that she was tired of catching the school bus because she had girls on the bus that wanted to fight her, so Step's parents brought her a car. It was a sharp '84 baby-blue Maximum, and the year was '88! Do you know how cool it was to drive to school plus in a sharp baby-blue Maximum! Step was in the ninth grade, driving her own car. That's how spoiled she was. Sometimes Step and I didn't make it to school. We sometimes stopped at our girlfriend DeeDee's house where we sat around, getting high, smoking weed, and drinking beer until school was out, and then we went home as if we were in school all day.

Step's parents found out that she and I weren't going to school, and they sometimes took the car away from her. But it didn't do any good because as soon as they gave her back her car, she started skipping school again. Most of the time, I would tell Step to drop me off to school because even if she didn't want to go to school, I knew I had to go because my parents weren't playing that! After Step dropped me off, she didn't hesitate to keep going to hang out in the streets. Step's sister Rosalyn was the third from the oldest, and she was as crazy as crazy could be. Her nickname for Jeff was Hank. Jeff was their baby because he was the baby boy, and there were only two boys in the family, Jeff and his older brother Todd. Todd was locked up in Mississippi. It was said that Todd was in the military, and while in Mississippi, he and a couple of his soldier buddies were up in a hotel, taking turns having sex with a white female who they said was a prostitute. Suddenly her boyfriend, who they said was her pimp, bust into the room, and that's when she hollered rape. During those days, racism was a lot stronger than it is now. They said that the white female was scared being caught in a room full of black men, so since Todd was the last one to get caught with her, he was charged with rape and sentenced to thirty years in prison.

In our neighborhood, they said that they called Todd's gray eyes because of his eyes being gray, and they said that he too was crazy. I think the whole family was crazy, except their dad. He was nice, quiet, and humble who raised his family in church. I guess you know what they say about preacher kids or children who were brought up in the church, they turn out to be the wild kids because they were sheltered from the world, so when they did get out into the world, they become curious. There's nothing wrong with trying to protect your children from the world but also teach them about the good and the bad to basically prepare them for the world, so that when a situation comes their way, they would know how to handle it, instead of finding out the hard way, which, in most cases, they do anyway! So when Step, her sisters, and brothers got old enough, they strayed away from the church to go into the world to do the same things that their parents were trying to keep them from doing. Jeff called Step and I around five or six in the morning to come and pick him up because he was running from the police. He got away and was hiding out in the woods in an abandoned, torn-down trailer.

The first time Jeff went to jail, he just knew that he was going to be there for a while, meaning months maybe years? He had a warrant and a couple of fines. He asked me if I could pay one of the fines for him, so when he goes to bond court, it wouldn't look as bad, and I did. About two to three hours later, Jeff called us, breathing hard, talking about, "Come and pick me up right now from downtown. I'm running that way now!" We jumped off the phone and into the car. When we reached Jeff, he said, "When those people called my name and told me that I was free to go, I thought that they were lying and playing a joke on me, so as soon as they let me out, I ran for my life as fast as I could, just in case they messed up and let me out by mistake!"

I didn't know if it was a mistake of if Jeff got blessed through me. I wonder.

Their oldest sister Sharon, the one who gave us the cocaine, started sneaking around and hanging out with a guy in the neighborhood that was known for selling and using drugs. And he got Sharon hooked on them also. Sharon was Step's oldest sister. She was beautiful, had a nice shape, a beautiful home, beautiful children, and a hard-working military husband that gave her everything that she ever wanted, and the only thing he wanted from Sharon was for her to stay out of the streets while he provided for her and their family. But

Sharon didn't want that. She wanted the drugs, the alcohol, the party life, instead of the boring life she said that she had with her husband. I remember her husband coming over to the house to talk to their mother about Sharon, and I remember how that man cried over their mother's shoulder about Sharon. He said that she was hanging out in the streets and not coming home and that he was just so tired. He loved his wife very much, and he's willing to do anything to keep her, and he just wanted their mother to talk to her for him.

When their mother got a chance to speak with Sharon, she was telling Sharon about how much her husband loved her and that any man that will come and cry on their wife's mother's shoulder about his wife has got to be in love!

Sharon told their mother, "You don't know him like I know him, Mama. That man beats me!"

"Well, maybe he beats your a—— to keep you out of the streets!"

Sharon wasn't listening to any of that. She was far too gone. She was already hooked with the drugs, the other man, and the streets.

The one thing I remember Step's mom telling the both of us was, "The best man to marry is an older man because he'll take care of you!"

But I said to myself, "I don't know if I want to marry a man old enough to be my daddy!"

One day, Sharon's husband came out to the house looking for her, but she wasn't there. But we knew exactly where she was, and after he left, Step, Jeff, Chris, and myself decided to walk around the corner where we knew where Sharon was to get her. And sure enough, she was there getting high. When Jeff went in the yard to get Sharon, she told him that she wasn't going anywhere, and Jeff told her that she was leaving even if he had to drag her home, so the guy who she was getting high with have a very big family. And when I say a *big* family, I mean just that. The house where they were getting high at was the guy's mother's house where family and friends hung out just about every day, and every day was a party.

On this particular day, there was a yard full of family and friends, and the guy told Jeff to leave his yard, but Jeff said that he wasn't going anywhere without his sister. Sharon just kept saying that she wasn't going anywhere.

The man said, "Man, don't you hear her saying that she ain't going. What part don't you understand!"

But Jeff kept trying to make Sharon leave until the guy got upset and started walking up on Jeff, and they started fighting. Then the next thing you know, Step started fighting one of the family members. Then I started fighting one of the family members. Then Chris started fighting one of the family members. The female that he was fighting was looking like she was getting the best of him, and then I jumped in, and we both were toe to toe. Jen, Jeff's twin sister, and their mom came down to break up the fight and told us that if Sharon didn't want to go, then to leave her, and that's what we did.

One day, while over at Step's house, their sister Sharon asked me to ride with her to the store, and I did. On our way back, Sharon decided to ride up the street to the park, and she drove down the dirt road that was next to the park. She said that she needed to pee and couldn't wait until she got home, but instead of her stopping to pee, she pulled out some drugs, crack, and asked me, "How do people smoke crack rock on a can?"

Now I said to myself, "This heifer must really think I'm stupid! She must not know or think that I already know she's smoking crack, so she already knows how to smoke crack on a soda can, stem, or whatever else crackheads do!" She was asking me how do people smoke it on a drinking can while she was preparing to smoke it on the can. She kept asking me, "Do they poke holes in the can like this?"

I was looking at her stupidly and dumbfounded, and I was like, "I don't know."

"Do they bend the can in half like this?"

"I don't know."

"Do they put the ashes in the creases where you bent the can where the holes are at?"

"I... don't... know."

"Do they put the crack rock on top of the ashes where the holes are at and light it with a lighter and smoke it through the hole that you would drink out of?"

I started getting loud. "I don't know." But what I wanted to say was, "But it sure looks like you do!"

After she hit it, she then had the nerve to ask me to hit it. I told her that I didn't want any. She asked me again, "Just try it!"

"I don't want any!"

"There's nothing to it. Just try it!"

"*I told you that I didn't want any. Why are you still trying to give me something I don't want!*"

I got out of the car and started walking home, and she just hollered and told me, "Okay, then don't worry about it, and please don't tell Jeff!" That's because she knew that if I would have walked back home and told Jeff what she tried to make me do, he would have whooped her a———, and because I know how Jeff's temper is, I never mentioned a word of it to him. I was so proud of myself for standing up to Sharon, having a strong mind to say no because if my mind would have been weak, I probably would be on drugs today, if not dead! But as time went on, I knew that it wasn't my strength that kept me from saying yes, but it was the Lord that kept me! But *God!*

Their sister Rosalyn is the third from the oldest, and she too has a long history of drugs. Rosalyn preferred to shoot her drugs up with needles, something I didn't know much about. I just remember one day, Jeff and I were in the kitchen talking, and Rosalyn walked in like it was nothing. She had a spoon in her hand, and she put something in the spoon with a little bit of water. She then started heating the bottom of the spoon with a lighter until it started boiling and bubbling. After that she took a needle and squeezed the liquid into the needle. Then she took a rubber rope or something and tied it around her arm. She then started slapping her arm to get a vein and stuck the needle in her arm to shoot up like it was nothing. I was just sitting there looking at her as if it was a science experiment, but Jeff was mad and was like, "What are you doing? You just don't care who you do that in front of!"

Rosalyn is the reason sometimes Step and I did dumb and crazy stuff. Like, I remember a girl named Kim from our school walked to our neighborhood to fight us. For what reason, I don't remember. I just remembered she walked through a cut from her neighborhood to ours to the front of Step's front yard to talk some real serious trash to us. This girl was really bold and by herself. Step looked at me, and I looked at Step.

Rosalyn said, "Y'all mean to tell me that y'all gonna let this chick come to y'all house talking s——? Beat that b—— a——!"

Step and I beat the clothes off this girl and stripped her down butt naked. Rosalyn said, "Take the b—— and tie her up to the tree!" and we did just what she told us to do. We tied her around the tree while she was naked, and I am so shocked that no one called the police because a couple of cars drove by and blew the horn. After about five minutes, we untied her, threw her in the trunk of Step's car, drove her back to her neighborhood, put her out in the streets, and made her walk home butt naked. Believe it or not, we really did something crazy like that, and God saved us because we coulda went to jail facing thirty years for kidnapping and lynching. I know the Lord was on our side! I guess the only reason Kim didn't tell on us was because she knew she was the one that started the fight with us. She was the one that walked to our neighborhood to our house and the one who had to be crazy!

I consider myself a people person. I make friends, not enemies. Mary was a friend of mine that I met at Keenan. She also stayed in the same neighborhood that the girl Kim lived in. Mary and I became close friends, and we had a couple of classes together. Mary was the baby of four girls, and Mary's mother's name was Mary, who named all of her daughters with the letter *M*. Margaret, Maryee, Marty, and then Mary! Mary's mother was very strict. I felt like her mother treated her like Cinderella. Mary couldn't come out before 12:00 p.m., and she had to be in before 10:00 p.m. Mary couldn't leave the house until she finished shining the silverware. I know because sometimes I helped her, and she had to make sure that the house was dust free and spotless. Mary was her mother and father's little angel that did no wrong! Yeah, when she was around them. But when Mary came out of the house, Mary was a totally different person. Mary drank, smoke weed, and knew a lot of guys from sleeping around with them. I, too, drank, smoke weed, but the only guy for me was Jeff.

One day, Mary had plans for the both of us to go out to the movies, but what I didn't know was that Mary had planned for us to go with two other guys. Those two guys came and picked us up on the corner of Mary's neighborhood, but instead of them taking us to the movies, they took us to a hotel, and that I was not cool with. I told them that I was ready to go home, but they told me that they were not going anywhere because they paid for the room. So while Mary was in the room with one of the guys doing her thang, I stayed in the car with the other guy in the backseat. I was so upset. I told myself that this would never happen again! The other guy who came with us sat in the car to keep me company. He stated that he had much respect for me as a lady for doing what I did by not going into the other room. I was getting older and wiser. I was not a loose goose. I was and still am a daddy's girl, so I respected myself as a daddy's girl. I was not going to be call a sl———, w———, or prostitute because that's the name the guys called you when you slept around with every Dick, Tom, and Harry! That was not me. I may have crushes on guys and nothing more. There's nothing wrong with finding a man attractive. I could look and not touch. Besides, I was too in love with Jeff to even think about another guy.

Mary was quiet, easygoing, softhearted, and very giving, but I didn't know that Mary was dealing with depression. After introducing Mary to the Boys, Mary became a part of the crew, but there was something about Mary that didn't sit good with Jeff, and he told me that he didn't want me hanging out with her anymore. I asked him why, but he didn't tell me anything. The only thing he said was, "I just don't want you hanging out with her." Was it something that Jeff knew about Mary that I should have known, but if so, why not tell me? I just brushed it off and left it alone. While in school, I was missing Mary not being in class for a couple of days, but it was said that Mary had taken a bottle of pills and tried to commit suicide! It was said that her sister found her on the floor, and they rushed her to the emergency room where they pumped her stomach. Mary had taken the bottle of pills, trying to kill herself over a guy that she was in love with, and the news got back to school.

Mary finally recovered and came back to school, but while in class, the kids were all being mean, talking about it as if she wasn't in the classroom. They were making fun of her about it. I'm sure Mary was hurting inside about it, but she didn't want anyone to know it. So while the students were laughing at her, she too began to laugh at herself. I turned and looked at Mary with a shocked look on my face. I couldn't believe that she was sitting up here laughing with these clowns. I was so mad because I didn't think someone trying to take their life was a laughing matter, so before I knew it, I took my right hand and slapped the taste out of Mary's mouth and told her, "Why would you sit up here laughing at yourself about something that was so serious. You almost took your life, these dumb kids don't care anything about you!"

Mary just dropped her head and said, "You're right."

A couple of weeks later, Mary called me up to ask if I wanted to ride to the mall with her. I started to say yes, but then she informed me that she was riding with Sonja, a female who was a friend of ours, but I cut her loose because she talked about Mary like a dog in the classroom when Mary wasn't there. I told Mary about it, but she still considered her a friend. I'm saying to myself, "Why would Mary want to hang out with a person like that? A two-faced person, someone who talked about her grandparents to our classmates, telling them about how Mary's grandparents had us out in their field in the hot heat, picking and shelling peas, something that I didn't mind doing." I'm a country girl, and that was something I was used to, picking and shelling peas with both my grandmothers and mother. She also talked about the way their house looked. Mary's grandparents lived in the country, so it was an old country house, but so what. I too grew up in the country in my family houses, looking the same way, country! Next, she started talking about Mary calling her stupid for trying to kill herself, so then, I got up in Sonja's face. I told her that I wasn't about to let her continue talking about Mary and her grandparents like that, especially when Mary wasn't around to defend herself. Sonja sat down, and there wasn't anything else said after that.

That's the one thing about me. Once I consider you as a friend, *I'm your friend to the end* and will always have your back no matter what. But let my brother tell it, "Shannon, stop calling everybody your friends because you don't have any friends!" But I would tell him that he didn't know what he was talking about because he didn't know my friends! It was a day before New Year's Eve. Mary and I had decided that we were going together to the big New Year's Eve party at this club close by our neighborhood that everyone was talking about. So Mary and I decided that since I was closer to the club, I would get the tickets for us, and Mary would pay me for her ticket when we both met up together that night to go to the New Year's Eve party. Earlier that day, Mary's sister brought her to my house to pick up her ticket. I was wondering to myself why would her sister bring her to pick up her ticket if she and I are going out there together. She could have just gotten her ticket when we meet up.

So I asked Mary, "I thought we were meeting up together at the club?"

"We are. I'm just getting my ticket just in case I'm running late and I didn't want to hold you up." Mary paid me for her ticket, and they left. I didn't think much more about it. We just told each other that we would get up with each other later.

I called Mary to let her know that I was on my way to the club, and she told me that she would meet me there. When I got to the club, I called Mary to let her know that I made it to the club and that I was outside, waiting on her, but she didn't answer. I waited for another thirty minutes, but Mary never showed. I decided to go inside with some more of my girlfriends who were there—Tree, Tonya, Grace, Jody, and a few more! When I got inside the club, Mary was already inside with some of the same females who were picking at her in class, about her trying to kill herself. My eyes gotten wide, and I was shocked and kinda hurt at the same time.

I asked her, "Why didn't you just tell me that you were coming with some of your other homegirls?"

She didn't say a word. She just looked at me like she had an attitude or something, so her homegirls who was with her had some smart words to say, "Because she came with us, she ain't got to tell you nothing!"

I said, "First of all, I wasn't talking to any of y'all. I was talking to Mary!" So they started walking up on me, but what they didn't know was that my girls were standing all around me, so my girls basically moved me out of the way and got all up in Mary and her homegirls' faces.

"Do we have a problem?"

Mary and her girls were outnumbered. They started looking around, like, "Where did all these females come from, like the Mafia!" Yeah, because we roll like that! I looked at Mary, rolled my eyes, and shook my head. I told my girls, "Y'all come on, let's go!" When I looked back at Mary, it seemed to me that she had to be scared of these girls, but oh well, that's what she gets for flipping on me!

I didn't know that my mom was keeping up with me and my cycle. She reminded me that my cycle didn't come on for that month. I wasn't paying it any attention. I was just doing me. She said that she knew how many sanitary napkins, pads for those who don't know, were in the bag, and I should have used some of them by now and that she should know since she was the one buying them for me. She said that sometimes cycles come on late and that she was going to give me another two weeks. After that, she was taking me to the doctor to get a pregnancy test! Two weeks went by, and she took me to the doctor, and sure enough, I was pregnant again! I was pregnant with Jeff's baby. I told Jeff that I was pregnant with his child but that my mother told me that she was taking me to get an abortion. He didn't object. I guess he was just a little shocked about it as I was and maybe just wasn't ready to be a dad, and I wasn't ready to become a mother at the time, so now I'm having my second abortion at the age of sixteen!

My mom knew that Jeff was the dad, and she didn't raise hell about this pregnancy like she did the last. She just took me to the abortion clinic like it was nothing, and I got rid of my child. After my second abortion, I started thinking about the two babies that I was carrying in my stomach and what if I would have kept them, what would they have been, and what would they have looked like, but it was too late now. I had killed both of my babies, something that I had to live with for the rest of my life! Thinking about this made me sick to my stomach and very sad.

I may call a man who's a parent a dad quicker than I would call them a father with no disrespect to anyone, I just know that we only have one Father which art in heaven, and he's the only Father I know other than my dad! Matthew 23:9 (NKJV) says, "Do not call anyone on Earth your Father; for One is your Father, He who is in heaven"

We always had a good time every weekend at the Boys' house. It could just start out with two people standing around talking, and then the next thing you know, it's a cookout with coolers full of beers, a grill full of chicken because we had to feed the alcohol and two card tables to play spades. Whenever someone came, they either brought more beer or chicken to put on the grill. If it wasn't at the Boys' house next door to me, then it was a party somewhere else in the neighborhood. Then if it wasn't in the neighborhood, then we're all ride out to wherever the party was at. It didn't matter where; we were there. I was still friends with the girls in the neighborhood—Tree, Tonya, Step, Tammy, Sam, Tracy and Regina. We were still friends. It's just that everybody had their own clique who they hung out with the most. Tree and Tonya were always the best of friends before I came along, and it was mainly Tree that kept telling me that I needed to be a comedian. I didn't think of myself as being a comedian. I just guess it was me being naturally funny. I never tried to be funny. I was just always a people person. I love people, and I love to make people laugh. Even though Step and I were the best of friends, she was my sister, and Jeff was my man. He was my first love, and even though he and I were a couple, we were still friends.

I spent most of my time with Step than I did with Jeff, but he didn't mind because she was his sister, and he knew that we were friends before he and I became lovers. I thought because Step and I were so close that everything we did was just between the both of us. *Wrong!*

I found out later that Step was taking news to Jeff, telling him everything she and I were doing together. If a guy spoke to me or had a conversation with me, she was telling Jeff about it. I didn't believe it. I just figured he was making her tell him about what I was doing in the streets, which was nothing because, like I said, he was my first love, and I was too in love with him to want to do anything with anyone.

I remember one day, we all rode to the park in the lowrider cars, and we were all having a good time, sitting around drinking, getting high, and cracking jokes. Jeff's car wasn't parked correctly, and he had to move it. I told him that I will move it for him. Now at the park, they had these steel bars that block the cars from driving on the grass, and when I jumped my fast self in his car to move the car in a different space, I hit one of the bars and dented Jeff's car, and all I can remember was Jeff jumping up like a bull and turning red.

"What the hell!"

All I could say was, "Oh hell, I'm drunk!" and laid down on the seat like I had just passed out, but really, I was just that scared and afraid that he was going to do something to me, but he didn't. He was mad as hell, but he didn't do anything to me. He just said that he wouldn't let me drive his car again. We used to talk about that scene and laugh about it.

Jeff and I started hanging out a lot, going to parties, and sometimes we would pick up his cousin Trapp and his friend Jeff who was Jeff's best friend. I remember one day, while at a party, the four of us had gotten into an argument with some guys that were there. The other Jeff was a scary guy who didn't want to fight. He was just like, "Man, let's go!"

So Jeff told him, "Man, shut the hell up with your scared a——!"

Jeff said, "Man, I ain't scared. There's just too many of them guys and only three of us!"

Jeff understood, and he said, "Okay, let's just go." He told his cousin Trapp to drive while Jeff sat in the front, and he and I got in the back. We were pulling off when I suddenly saw a guy standing behind this tree with a gun in his hand, and I said, "Hey, somebody is behind that tree with a gun!" It looked like the same guy who Jeff and Trapp got into an argument with. Right when he started aiming the gun toward us, the police had stopped us leaving the party to check proof for driver's license, and that's when I yelled, "Hey, look behind the tree!"

The police turned around and took off running toward the guy, and sure enough, it was the same guy! If I didn't see that guy behind that tree and the police wasn't out there, I'm sure he would have shot up in our car, and one of us, if not all of us, could have been dead right now!

Step met this guy, and she was telling us that she was falling head over heels for him hard. We didn't meet the guy until later. Guess who the guy was? The same guy who Jeff and Trapp got into the argument with at the party. The same guy who was standing behind the tree about to shoot up our car! He apologized to Jeff, but Jeff half-accepted his apology, and after he left, Jeff told Step that he didn't want her messing with the guy because he didn't trust him. Step still messed around with him anyway for a little while without Jeff knowing about it, but then, she soon learned that he was a ladies' man, and she left him alone after he broke her heart. I will say that he was a nice-looking guy.

Twin Lakes was a lake on the military base, and this was the place to be in the summertime. It was basically a place to show off your cars, motorcycles, loud music, hairdos, and new outfits. It was a place to meet men and women. There were people all over the place with barbecue grills, coolers full of beer, and weed being passed around. Those were the good ole days! Jen, Jeff's twin sister, had a Z28 where you could take the top off, and so did her best friend Kim. Step rode with Jen, and I rode with Kim with our tops off looking fly! Kim was a beautiful girl, and I knew that Jeff had a crush on her, but Kim was cool with me. She treated me like a lil sister and Jeff like a brother. Sometimes he would even flirt with her in my face, but I didn't care about that. I knew Kim didn't want Jeff. She would just laugh at him, look at me, and would tell him, "Boy go and sit down somewhere!"

I'm an animal lover, but my preferences are dogs. Boy dogs, that is! Hanging out at Twin Lakes is one of the reasons I fell in love with Rottweilers. One weekend, while we were hanging out at the lake, I noticed this guy walking around with his Rottweiler. He and his dog were looking good and fit, the workout kind of fit, when all of a sudden, these two guys walked up to this guy and started jumping on him! While this guy was getting sucker-punched, he was more concerned about his dog, because his dog was ready to eat those two guys alive. The closer the dog got to one of the guys, the faster they would move out of the dog's way, and the owner was telling his dog, "Stay! Get back!" He even had to try to hold his dog back, but each time one of the guys would sneak a lick in, his dog would leap up like a lion. But the owner kept detaining his dog because he knew that if his dog would have grab one of those guys, it was over for them. Those guys got some good licks in on that guy, and I was really mad about it. But I guess he said, "I'll rather walk away with some knots on my head than handcuffs on my wrist going to jail for my dog killing somebody!"

It was amazing to me to see how so obedient and loyal his dog was to him. I wanted that for myself, so I promised myself that I too would get a Rottweiler!

We loved fixing each other's hair, and I wanted my hair cut. Since Jen's best friend Kim was a hairstylist, I asked her if she would cut my hair. She did, but the one thing I know now is to be careful and not let any and everybody get into your hair. Now I knew that Kim was a hairstylist, but if I knew the scissors that she used to cut my hair with was so rusty…and black…that you would have thought the scissors was buried for ten years and dug up just to cut my damn hair…I was like, "I know you didn't just cut my hair with those rusty scissors!"

I heard that there was a such thing as stunting someone's hair to where your hair will only grow a certain length, and then after that, it takes a while to grow. And that's just what she did to my hair. She stunted my hair with those rusty scissors. My hair still has a hard time growing to this day! Someone could cut their hair short three times and let it grow back, and my hair would still be trying to catch up from their first hair cut.

Jeff's twin sister, Jen, was very well-known, pretty, popular, and envied by many. People used to call her Goldie because of her blond hair and all the gold that she was wearing around her neck, wrist, and fingers. She also had a nice gold Z28, but Jeff wrecked it one night while driving drunk and drove it into a ditch. I'll never forget it. The next morning, Jen called me to come around to the house. "Shannon, you know Jeff done wrecked my car, but it's not my car anymore. Johnny brought that car from me, and he's pissed. He's on his way over here. Come on around here when you can!" When I got there, Jeff was still in the bed asleep or playing sleep because I doubt that he was asleep with all the fusing and cursing his sister was doing about her car. When Johnny got there…First, let me say that Johnny is a big Debo, the guy who played in the movie *Friday* kind of man.

When Johnny got there, he walked straight in the house without knocking and straight into Jeff's room. I was standing in the hallway looking at Jeff. He had the covers over his head, but Johnny pulled the covers back and slapped Jeff so hard, you could hear the lick outside! If Jeff wasn't asleep, Johnny slapped him back to sleep. It was so funny because after Johnny slapped Jeff, Johnny walked into the living room argued with Jen about the car walked out of the house. Once Johnny got in his car and pulled off, here comes Jeff jumping out of his bed like he was Superman with a knife, like he was going to kill somebody, talking about, "I'll kill his a———!"

I said to myself, "Sit your scary a——— down somewhere. That man been left, and he probably home by now."

Jeff wasn't crazy. He didn't want any of Johnny, and when their sister Rosalyn got there, she cursed all of us out about her Hank. Hank is what she calls Jeff, and Rosalyn was crazy about Jeff. But really all of them was crazy about their brother, but Rosalyn was the craziest about him. She asked us, "Why y'all just let that man walk right in the house like he lives here and let him just walk in Hank's room and slap Hank like he was crazy. Y'all should have gutted his a———!" Now I'm telling you, if Rosalyn was there, which I'm glad she wasn't, she would have gutted Johnny for sure over her Hank. I promise you, she's not the one to play with!

Jen met a new female friend with the same name as hers, and I could tell that whenever this female came to the house, she had eyes for Jeff, but I didn't think too much of it because she was coming to see Jen. One day, Jeff called us to come and pick him up. He said that he was in a car accident where he wrecked his car. So when Step, Jen, and myself got there, we saw Jen's homegirl sitting right up in there with Jeff. I'm looking at the both of them like, "What in the hell are you two doing together!" Step and Jen are looking at me like, "It's about to go down!" Jeff saw the look on my face, and the only thing he could say while in pain was, "Look, I don't have time to talk about this right now because my shoulder is out of place." From the looks of it, his shoulder was messed up pretty bad. Jeff was so skinny like JJ on *Good Times* that the shoulder that was knocked out of place was so swollen, it looked like Arnold Schwarzenegger lifting weights but just on one side. This fool was in so much pain but still had the nerve to look at his shoulder and say, "Boy, if both of my shoulders just look like this, I'll be a bad joker!"

I said to myself, "That's what you get for always doing something you ain't got no business, like cheating on me!"

I can't remember if the accident was a hit-and-run or if he just hit something while trying to do something with the girl Jen while driving. I approached the female Jen not to see if she was okay but to ask her, "What the hell you doing with Jeff?"

She didn't say anything. She just looked at me with a smirk on her face, so I told her in front of everybody, "Now you may have rode with Jeff, but your a—— is walking by yourself!"

I wasn't even driving, nor was it my car, but we got in the car and left her standing right there! I looked at everybody like, "I wish you would say something to me about making that heifer walk home!" Jeff, Jen, and Step knew me, and they knew that time was not the time to mess with me at all! At the same time, I said to myself, "I guess I'm still the fool in love or just a plain fool, and how long was I going to play this fool's game?"

One day, Jeff, Trapp, and I were just riding around in Jeff's car drinking. Trapp was driving, chauffeuring Jeff and me. I was a little intoxicated and fell asleep in the backseat. When I woke up, Jeff and some female who he had just met were flirting outside of the car with each other as if I wasn't even there, again being a fool! There was another time when Step and Jen called me to come around to the house, and when I got there, they told me to go into Jeff's room. Jeff was asleep in the bed, lying on top of the covers with his clothes still on, but there was another female lying right beside him, asleep with her clothes on. And before I knew it, I flipped. I jumped on top of the female with a pillow trying to smother her because I said, "Let me get her first because I could get him anytime!"

She was kicking and screaming, and then Jeff woke up, trying to stop me. Then I started fighting him, and the female jumped out of the bed and ran out of the house. I never saw her again! I had to say to myself, "This was not this female's fault. How would she have known if this man was in a relationship unless he tells her, and I'm sure he didn't. It's not like she already knew me and just didn't care like the female Jen did." So again, ladies, it's not the female's fault, and it's not right for us to jump on that female or any female, for that matter. We shouldn't even jump on the man because he's not even worth fighting. We should be strong enough to walk away, knowing that we're better than that.

We're queens! And we deserve better!

I was now in the eleventh grade and wanted to take up cosmetology, but my guidance counselor told me that I missed my deadline. The cosmetology course was a three-year course, and I should have signed up for it in the tenth grade, so now if I wanted to take up cosmetology, my parents would have to pay for it. I was very disappointed. I found out that Step didn't pass to the tenth grade. She will remain in the ninth grade. Their mother was mad at me as if I was the reason Step didn't pass, but Jeff told their parents, "Don't blame Shannon. It's because you and daddy gave Step that car to drive to school, and y'all knew she wasn't going to school, so if you want to blame anybody, you need to blame yourself for getting her a car. I told y'all it was a bad idea from the jump!"

I spoke up, "Mama, I told Step let's go to school, and sometimes I begged her, but she just dropped me off and went wherever she was going. How can it be my fault? I passed to the next grade. That should tell you something right there."

Step was not dumb. She was an A, B honor roll student in middle school. That's why her parents were so upset with her, but after Step got to high school, her grades dropped. She was no longer interested in going to school. She was more interested in hanging out, getting high, and drinking. I'm not putting Step down because I too liked getting high and drinking, but I knew the cost that I would have had to pay if I didn't go to school. My parents weren't having it, and I would have gotten my head knocked off my shoulders!

Today was my birthday, and it fell on Friday the thirteenth—a birthday I'll never forget. I couldn't wait to get home because I had some plans, but I missed the school bus and had to catch another school bus that put me off at a different bus stop, so I got home a little later than I expected. Then I broke my house key off in the key hole and had a hard time trying to get it out before my mama got home. Needless to say, I didn't get it out. Now I was mad because my plans were to come home celebrate with a drink or something before my mom got home, but instead, I had to wait next door to my neighbor Tammy's house until my mom got home. Once my mom got home and cursed me out for breaking my key off in the keyhole, I just went to my room to get myself together before going outside.

I had decided to use my sister's big hot curling irons to curl my hair. Now my sister was a nice person, and I was never afraid of any female, but my sister, on the other hand, was a different story. She was one I didn't play with. When my sister got home and walked into our room, she caught me using her curling irons, so she came and snatched the curlers from out of my hand, held up my arm, and stuck the hot curlers under my arm and held them there while at the same time yelling at me, "Didn't I tell you to leave my hot curlers alone!" It was the most excruciating pain I ever felt in my life, and all I could do was scream and run out of the house while at the same time hearing my mom screaming at me, "She shoulda tore your a—— up. She done told you about messing with her stuff!"

I always knew that my mom and sister were very close, and my mom always took up for her regardless if she was wrong or right. Like my sister could never do no wrong!

I was next door to Tammy's house, and my mom called over there to tell me to bring my a—— on home. So when I walked in the house, I still had my arm up because the pain and the burn under my arm was so unbearable that I couldn't let it down without it touching my body. When my mom saw me, she was like, "What's wrong with you? Put your arm down!" But I told her, "I can't. Joyce burnt me under my arm with her hot curlers." When I turned around to show my mom my arm, she didn't know how serious the burn on my arm was. It was so severe that my sister took my skin off my arm. The burn could have been a first-degree burn, and when my mom saw how severe the burn was, her eyes opened so wide, like, "Oh my God!"

My mom went straight to the kitchen, came back with a broomstick in her hand, and broke it on my sister's back! I'm sad to say that I felt good about what my mom did to my sister because that was the first time my mom ever took up for me!

The day my life changed was the day when I was in my math class. Now I was never great in math, but it's my favorite subject. I like math because it's a challenge; Timark and I enjoy a challenge. So does a lot of our children. That's why they get bored easily because teachers are not challenging them to keep them busy, and we parents wonder why our children sometimes act out in school. They need to be *challenged*. Now when I got into algebra, you couldn't tell me nothing because I felt like I had moved up from a slow math class to a smarter math class, but it was a lot harder than I thought, and the teacher told me that if I wanted to go back to basic math, I would have to fail my standardized test, so I failed it intentionally, just so I could take an easier math.

MoMo and I were in the same math class. MoMo was a female who was part of the Gucci Girls Gang and one who we fought back in Saxon Homes and the same girl who wanted to fight Step when she came and got me out of my classroom one day. This particular day, MoMo sat across from me, so when I looked up at her, she was looking at me with an evil look on her face and crying, telling me, "I'm going to kill you! I'm going to kill you!"

I just looked at her and said, "Oh yeah, whatever!"

She was so loud that the teacher had to tell her to be quiet or leave his class. I didn't know what was wrong with her, and I didn't care. All I knew was whatever she was talking about went in one ear and out the other.

Step drove her car to school, so that day, when school let out, Step, DeeDee, and myself were about to leave. I ran into a girlfriend of mine whom I grew up with in Saxon Homes.

"Hey, Monique, I didn't know you went to this school," I said.

"Yeah, I just started. I missed my bus. Do you mind giving me a ride home?"

I told Step that Monique and I were cool and that we grew up together and if it was okay if she could give her a ride home. Step agreed, and we first drove to drop DeeDee off, and when we pulled into her neighborhood, we noticed Step's boyfriend Marcus and a bunch of his buddies standing on the corner. We decided to stop and talk with them for a while. While we were all standing there talking, a car pulled up across the street from where we were standing. We noticed that it was MoMo riding with a carload of guys. I said to myself, "She must have been following us." MoMo opened up the car door to get out, but the driver Lamar told her not to, and if she did that, he was going to leave her. Well, she decided to get out anyway with one foot on the ground and the other foot still in the car. Lamar pulled off, dragging MoMo with still one foot on the ground until she jumped out.

MoMo was out there by herself, and she had decided to walk straight over to where I was standing, stared me right in my face, nose to nose, turned her back on me, bent down to do what, I don't know, tie her shoe, get a knife a gun, or whatever. All I remember was her telling me in class, "I'm going to kill you!"

At this time, I said to myself, "This girl must be crazy!"

Before she could stand up, I was throwing blows left to right. She didn't know what hit her. After I got tired of beating her down, Step jumped in, and those two went at it. Then after Step, DeeDee, and her went at it one-on-one. And then at the end, the four of us beat her down—Step, DeeDee, Monique, and myself. After that, we all ran and jumped back in Step's car, and Monique said, "I stabbed her. I stabbed that b—— with a pair of scissors!" Monique was holding a large pair of scissors, and the blood was dripping down the scissors like water! I said to myself, "Why would she stab the girl if all of us were on her. That's crazy." But we were wild, and we all laughed about it and gave each other high-fives, not knowing the seriousness of the crime we just committed.

The next day, which was a Saturday, I was home alone and was just about to get into the shower when the doorbell rang. I went to the door with a towel wrapped around me because I thought it was Jeff, but it wasn't. It was a black man, a black woman, and a white man, all investigators with a warrant for my arrest. They told me to go into the room and put my clothes on. When I tried to close the door behind me to get some privacy, they pushed open the door hard, and the three of them watched me as I was putting on my clothes. I was so embarrassed. I tried to call my dad, but they told me that I couldn't use the phone until I got to the police station. They took me outside and handcuffed me. When I turned my head to see if anyone was looking, I saw Jeff standing beside the tree. He was watching the whole thing.

Mr. Johnson was the black investigator. I remember his name and face because about three weeks earlier, Mr. Johnson came to my house for me to be a witness in a fight that I witness to Rena, the same female Step beat up that time, the guy Tim drew a gun on me well. After that, Rena, Step, and I became friends, but she and Step were mainly closer because Rena lived next door to Step, but I still didn't care to much for her myself. Three weeks earlier, Rena and her boyfriend had gotten into a big fight where Step and I was there, and I guess she pressed charges on him and told them that Step and I witnessed the whole thing because this same investigator came to my house asking questions about it. While he was there getting information from me, he and my mom realized that they once went to school together, and Mr. Johnson told my mother that he remember my mother's brothers beating him up on the basketball court, and they laughed about it. Mr. Johnson was still sore about that because while I was in the backseat of his car with handcuffs on, he and the other black female investigator was in the front seat.

He told me, "Y'all Hollywood Hills people ain't never like us people from Meadow Lakes, and yeah, your mama's brothers may have beat me up on the basketball court, but I am going to see that you and your girlfriends get twenty years, and you think those girls are your friends. Those girls are b——, and so are you!"

I said, "Yeah, well, if I'm a b———, your daughter and your wife's a b———!"

Then the black female investigator, while looking at herself in the mirror, told me, "Y'all people make me sick!"

I said, "Y'all people? What you mean *y'all people*? You must haven't look in the mirror lately with your raccoon wiggy a——— head. Maybe if you take that raggedy wig off your nappy a——— head, then you will see you just like y'all people!"

She had a wig on her head, and I don't know who she thought she was because she was just checking herself out in the mirror like she really had it going on!

Then they asked if I had anything on me.

"Yes, my brass knuckles, but they wasn't in the fight!"

They both looked at each other. I guess they said, "Now when did she get a chance to grab some brass knuckles?"

I was saying to myself, "When you wasn't looking, I was going to jail, and I felt that I needed some protection!"

They took the brass knuckles from me, and we pulled off. When we left my house, we drove first to go and pick up Monique from her house, and they put us both in the back of the same car. When they got us to the police station, they put us in separate rooms. I was in Mr. Johnson's office when his phone on his desk rang. When he picked it up, I could hear my dad's voice screaming at the top of his lungs on the other end of the receiver. "Why in the hell didn't y'all call me about my daughter?"

Mr. Johnson said, "Mr. Hammonds, I didn't know that this was your daughter."

That's when I found out that my dad was a Mason. I didn't know that Masons had that kind of pull. Jeff told my dad what happened once he got home. When they finally had the four of us at the police station questioning us, Step and I didn't snitch on anyone, but DeeDee told the investigators that it was Monique who stabbed MoMo. Monique lied and stated that it was Step who stabbed MoMo, and once we found that out, Step and I started singing like birds.

We didn't want to tell on anyone, but since she wanted to play dirty like that, we had no other choice. The investigators said that they know that it was Monique who did the stabbing because of the simple fact that as soon as they knocked on her door, she opened it and said, "I didn't do it. Step did it." And they were like, "Did what?" Like how do you know what we came here for. We could have been insurance salesmen or anything. She basically told on herself. They charged the four of us with assault and battery with the intent to kill! The worst charge that anyone could ever get other than murder, we just didn't know how serious these charges were. I stayed in jail for one week. That one week felt like one year. I felt a little better because they put Monique and me in the same cell. We found out later what the fight was really about my so-called friend Monique stealing MoMo's jacket, which was a nice spray-painted jacket with her name MoMo on the back of it, and Monique told MoMo that I stole her jacket! I'm saying to myself, "That's the reason why MoMo came to class crying that she was going to kill me?"

I was so upset. I could not believe that we went through all this madness and in jail with intent to kill charges all over a spray-painted jacket—a jacket with the name MoMo sprayed on the back. And my name is Shannon! Now wouldn't you think the person whose name was close to yours would have most likely stolen your jacket?

Our first day in jail, we were supposed to receive condiments like a tooth brush, toothpaste, a wash rag, soap, a comb, and a clean blanket to sleep on, but the COs were mad and said that what we did to MoMo was considered lynching, so they didn't give us anything the whole time we were locked up. I remember looking outside my cell window, and it was around the time the State Fair came to our town. You could see the Ferris wheel going around and around, and all I could say to myself was, "Wow, I'm locked up and won't be able to go to the fair this year because I'm in jail for an attempt to kill charge!" Then I said to myself, "You're more worried about going to the fair when your young and dumb behind need to be thinking about the seriousness of your crime!"

I myself was very uncomfortable, nervous, and scared while Monique, on the other hand, was just walking around in her shorts and bra like she was at home. I found out that she had a record of shoplifting and has been in jail before, so I said to myself, "Well, I guess she is at home. I guess she's used to something like this, but I'm not!"

Monique and I were in a cell together with about five other females, and I remember that it was dinnertime. They had a female inmate on the outside of our cell serving the food trays and a CO standing behind her. After serving everyone their food, the female inmate asked me, "So you don't want nothing to eat!"

I told her, "No."

She said, "Why?"

I said, "Because I'm not going to be here much longer, so I don't want anything to eat." Monique was telling me to still get my tray because she would eat it, so the female inmate told me, "Oh yeah, you ain't going nowhere because you are going to be mine!"

I looked her in her face and told her, "B—, you crazy. Get out of my face. I ain't going to be yours nothing. You have the wrong sister. No, you got the right sister, so you can get out of my face with that!"

I never backed down from anybody, and I wasn't going to start now. Even though she was on the other side of the cell, I was showing off and letting her know that I was not afraid of her and she was not going to do anything to me. I made that very clear!

The female inmate looked at me with a smirk on her face and started shaking her head like, "Yeah, we'll see!" The CO made the inmate walk off, and as soon as she was out of my sight, I broke down and ran to the phone to call my mama! I was so nervous and scared that I could barely dial the number from shaking so bad. When my mama picked up the phone, I was crying like a baby. I told her, "The female inmate who just got finish serving our food told me that she wanted my booty! You have to get me out of here!"

My mama stated, "Your daddy has the money, but he said he has to cash a check before he can get you out."

I told her with a high voice, "A check? I'm tired. Every time I look around, he always talking about he has a check to cash before he can do anything!"

My dad has his own auto body shop that he invested in after he had gotten out of the military, but let my mama tell it, when he went AWOL, and he does pretty well for himself so the checks he's talking about are the checks that his clients pay him with. But any-time whenever we would ask my dad for money, the first thing he would holler is, "Okay, I gotta cash this check."

I told her that I didn't have anything to comb my hair with or wash my face or brush my teeth. It was embarrassing and I was ashamed! When my mom and dad came to my bond hearing, I was looking at my dad, and you could tell that he was stressing really bad because his hair turned gray overnight. He looked like Moses when he came down from the mountain. I was his baby girl, and I was in jail with an attempt to kill charge. They knew how serious the charges were, but I didn't.

After bond court was over, I had to go back to my cell. I was feeling sick and tired, and my throat was hurting as though maybe a roach crawled into my mouth during the night. I didn't have any-thing to eat or drink. I wasn't hungry. I was too concerned about getting out. A female officer walked in our cell and called my name. I jumped up so fast, I almost jumped in her arms. As we were walking out, Monique had the nerve to ask me with a sad look on her face, "Shannon, you think your mom and dad could give my mom some money to help me get out?"

I turned around and looked back at Monique, like, "This girl is really crazy. She's the reason we're in jail and all for a jacket!"

I didn't say anything. I turned back around and told the CO. "Ma'am, let's go!"

I was walking so fast behind the CO, I was stepping on her heels! That was the last time I saw Monique.

I found out that MoMo's lungs almost collapsed. Plus she has sickle cell, so that just added to her injures. We had to wait until she got well before going to court. The day of our trial, we had to go in front of one of the meanest well-known judges in our city. When my mom and I had gotten there, my cousin was also there with his mom to go in front of the same judge, so there were two sets of Hammonds in the courtroom that day. My cousin's mother stated to my mom, "This judge did not like us." And my mom stated, "Well, I hope we go before y'all do!" While we were sitting there, waiting to go into the courtroom, MoMo was sitting across from us with four other females. I'm sure they came to get revenge on me. My mother leaned over and asked me, "Which one of those girls you fought?"

I showed her MoMo, and my mom was like, "You mean to tell me that big girl couldn't beat you, and now she's bringing more girls to fight you. I wish like hell they would try something!"

Oh, Lord, I started getting nervous. I was like, "Please let's not worry about that right now. We will worry about that later." The only thing I could think about at the time was me going to prison; I was not worried about MoMo and her little girlfriends that she brought to court with her.

The judge's secretary came out to inform Ms. MoMo that she would not be allowed to come into the courtroom dressed inappropriately the way she was dressed. She was dressed in short shorts, and the judge's secretary told her, "The judge told me to tell you that before you can come into his courtroom, you will have to change your clothes." But do you think she left to change her clothes? No, she did not. She stayed right there almost an hour had passed, and when they called us into the courtroom, I was thankful that we were called in before my cousins went in the courtroom. MoMo stood up to walk into the courtroom, and the secretary stopped her at the door and told her, "I'm sorry, ma'am, but you were told to go home and change your clothes, and since you didn't, you will not be allowed to go into the courtroom."

MoMo looked at the secretary and rolled her eyes. When we got inside the courtroom, the judge stated to us, "Now let me tell you something, people, my courtroom is not a picnic, and I told that little heifer to go home and change her clothes, and since she didn't do what I told her to do, how do you plea?"

My lawyer stated, "We plead guilty to the fighting, but not guilty to the stabbing."

The judge stated to us, "As far as I'm concerned, I'm throwing the whole thing out because I told that young lady to change her clothes, and she didn't. But let me tell you something, young lady, do you see those two police officers standing outside my door? Ooh yeah, you were going to jail because that young lady's lungs almost collapsed, and she has sickle cell. But let me tell you something else, if that young girl dies within a year, you and your friends will be going to jail for murder!"

My eyes got wider than a crackhead! I knew God was with me that day. The judge threw the case out. He could have postponed it to another date, but he didn't. I wasn't in court five minutes, and I sure didn't ask the judge how much time I was looking at nor did I want to know. I heard that Monique served time for the stabbing, but how much, I didn't know. Step and DeeDee, because they were minors, received six months in DJJ. Monique and I were seventeen, and the oldest, so we were considered as an adult and were going to get tried as an adult.

When I got back to school, the principal wanted to kick me out of school and told me that I would not be able to graduate because of the incident with MoMo, but my mama was not having it. She went straight to the school and told them that her child was going to graduate because the incident didn't happen on the school grounds. It happened in the neighborhood and that the young lady followed her child and started the fight with her child. If they were going to put me out of school for a fight that happened in the neighborhood, then they may as well put out just about every child in the school! They allowed me to stay in school, and I was grateful because if it wasn't for my mother, they would have kicked me out!

About a month later, I was back at school trying to get my life back on track when one day, while walking through the school doors going to class, I bumped right into MoMo walking with some guy. She looked at me with a smirk on her face while biting her lip and shaking her head up and down like, "Yeah, I got you now!"

But the look I gave her, I stepped to her with tears in my eyes. Nose to nose, I told her, "I see you still f——— with me, I'ma tell ya like this. The next time I go to jail, it won't be for nothing. It'll be for killing your a———!" She knew that I meant it. I wiped that smirk right off her face. She stepped off, and I never had any more problems with her again. Jail was something I didn't ever want to experience again. It was one of the worst experiences of my life. I was only defending myself, so I meant just what I said. I'm not going back to jail for nothing like over a spray-painted jacket, especially not over a spray-painted jacket. After that incident Step, DeeDee, and I became closer than ever. Step's mom, Jen, Jeff, and myself visited the both of them every weekend because we were able to visit the both of them at the same time. DJJ wasn't so bad, but it was bad enough. God saved my life. He gave me a second chance to make a change in my life, and I thanked him for it every day!

I'm back in school, finishing up my senior year, and I had enough credits that I didn't have to stay in school all day. I could have left after third block, which was around twelve o'clock. But because I didn't have a car and I thought that I was too good to catch the city bus home, I decided to wait outside up front on my dad to pick me up. But because he was slow most times, when he did pick me up, school was about to let out, and I could have just stayed in school all day. The kids would laugh at me while they were changing classes. "Girl, you still out here? You may as well have stayed in school!"

It was in my senior year when I found out about the man they called Jesus! I was standing outside with two other females whom I didn't know, and they were having a conversation. I don't remember how I ended up in the conversation. All I remember was that I was standing along with them, and they were standing face-to-face with each other, having a great conversation about Jesus. I was a part of the conversation, but I wasn't saying anything. I couldn't say anything because I didn't know what to say. I was ashamed and embarrassed that I didn't know what or who they were talking about, and I said to myself, "I don't know who these girls are talking about, but I'm sure going to make it my business to find out!"

I know it wasn't by coincidence. I was in the midst of those two females having that conversation. Jesus put me there just for that conversation to get my attention!

One day, I was standing outside waiting on my dad to pick me up from school while the other students were changing classes. The next thing I know, a good guy friend of mine named Freeman was getting jumped on by two other guys while others were just standing around watching. I couldn't just stand there. It was two on one. It wasn't a fair fight, so I ran and jumped straight in to help him, and we whooped their butts. But after the fight was over, Freeman took off and didn't even say thank you or nothing. I think he was ashamed that a woman had to help him fight, but I didn't care. A friend was a friend. I saw him some years later at a party, and he acted as if he didn't remember me until I refreshed his memory in front of everybody about when those two guys whooped his a—— at school and I had to help him out. He still acted like he didn't remember and walked off mad. I yelled at him as he was walking away, "What you getting mad about? I was only trying to help you out!" At the same time, the guys were all laughing at him.

Around this time, my parents and I decided that it was time that I find a job. I got a job working as a cashier at a grocery store. I found out that my cousin Cassandra was working there as a cashier, but we didn't tell anyone that we were cousins. We felt it was just for the best. When I started working there, the manager, with his wet Jheri curl looking like "Jerome in the house" off Martin Lawrence, didn't waste any time flirting with me and telling me how good I looked in my jeans and sometimes followed me around the store. I didn't like it, and it made me very uncomfortable. Whenever we finished our shift, we had to go upstairs in the office and count our register. I used to notice that the safe was always open, and I used to wonder to myself if he knew it and if it was a trap! Maybe about two months of working there, I got nosy and went into the safe since it was late and the store was closing. No one was there but the manager, another cashier who was out on the floor, and myself. I decided that I would go into the safe to see what I could see and maybe steal a few twenties. You should have seen me when I tried to open up the safe slowly and quietly. The safe was so loud, it scared me that I jumped. I was so scared, but I had to close it back or got caught and got fired or worse jailed! You couldn't tell me somebody didn't hear that. I'm sure people all outside heard. I assumed the safe was rigged, and I was about to fall into the trap! I was able to push the door back to where it was originally. I was in the clear. I left that safe alone and never touched it again!

I started telling Jeff about my manager flirting with me at work and the things that he was saying about me always looking good in my jeans and did I wear them just for him. Jeff decided to come up there one day just to check on me, and the manager saw us talking on one of the food aisle. He then told me in a nasty tone that I could not have any of my boyfriends on my job while working. Jeff told him that he didn't have anything to do with him coming up in the grocery store and that if he kept coming out of his mouth the wrong way, flirting with his girl, what he was going to do to him. So my manager and Jeff got into a heated argument, and he told Jeff to leave the store or that he was going to call the police, so Jeff just left!

Later that night, when my mom came to pick me up around 12:00 closing time, I saw Jeff sitting in a car with two of his guy friends. I started to walk over to the car, but he just flagged for me to just keep going and not to walk over to the car. I got into my mom's car, and we left. The next day, Jeff said that they just followed my manager around just to scare him up. He said my manager knew that they were following him, but they didn't care. They just wanted him to get the message not to mess with me again. The next day at work was a crazy day. I saw my manager talking to the same two older females, the same two that I knew from back in the day from my old neighborhood. Sometimes when they came through my line, we would talk about us knowing each other from the old neighborhood, and yes, I have given them a couple of free food items before but only a couple.

Now on this particular day, when I noticed them talking with my manager, I guess they didn't think that I was paying them any attention. I noticed them first going through my cousin's line only giving her just their baby food on WIC to ring up, even though they had food items in the buggy as well. They then got out of her line just to get back in my line with the grocery items. I felt like something wasn't right, because why didn't they just do everything while they were in my cousin line? So while I was ringing up their food items, one of the females was taking the food out of the buggy, while the other female was bagging it up as it was coming down the conveyor belt. Then the same female who was taking their groceries out of the buggy started pushing items down to the other female to bag without me even ringing it up. I asked her not to do that because I didn't want to get in any trouble. She wasn't listening. She was just pushing more groceries down without me ringing them up.

So now at this point, I'm pissed, and I had a trick for them, so when they gave me their book of food stamps, I took the whole book of stamps and told them that since they pushed down a lot of groceries, I was putting the whole book of stamps in my register.

They didn't object. They just started putting their grocery bags into their buggy. Then the next thing you know, my manager walked up and started helping the females put their groceries in their buggy. I knew something wasn't right, so now, I'm trying to tell my manager on the sneak side about the females pushing down groceries without me ringing them up but that I did keep their whole book of food stamps and put it in my register. My manager wasn't paying me any attention. He just told me too finish putting their bags in the buggy. Now I'm really pissed! My manager then told me to help take their groceries to their car. As I was walking outside toward their car, I turned around and saw my manager at my register looking at my sales receipt. When I got to their car to help them put their groceries bags in their car, my manager ran out of the store to the car and told the females to hold up for a minute. I tried to explain to my manager again about what happened, but he told me not to worry about it and for me to go to the produce area and stock some produce. About twenty minutes later, I was called up front. When I got there, the police were there, and they told me to put my hands behind my back. I asked them, "For what?" and they told me, "For shoplifting!" I was like, "Shoplifting? What did I steal?" And if that was the case, how come the females who took the groceries didn't get arrested. The police told me that the manager said there was no one else but me!

They took me to the city jail. I was saying to myself, "I can't believe I'm back in jail again!"

I was so upset because I knew the manager set me up, and when I called home to tell my mom what happened, she didn't want to listen. She just said, "Your a—— will sit there this time!" and hung up in my face! The male police officers were very nasty toward me. They were eating a giant bag of popcorn and offered me some, but when I declined, they told me that I wasn't getting any, no way. They just wanted to see if I was hungry! After that, they asked me if I needed a tampon to put on. I asked them, "Why would I need a tampon?" They said they thought that it was just something they thought that I needed, and I told them, no, I did not! About five hours later, my mom and sister came to pick me up, and I was given a court date to be in court. In the car, I was trying to explain to my mother what had happened, but she just didn't want to hear it, and I didn't say anything else!

When I got home, I explained to my dad what had happened and how I knew the manager set me up and how he could ask my cousin Cassandra who was working. He did, and she told him the same thing! The day of court, my cousin came as a witness for me because like I said, they didn't know that we were cousins. So now I have a witness who can tell the truth! When my name and the manager's name was called to face the judge, my manager told his side of the story first. He told the judge that I was giving away groceries to the customers in the store, and when he realized what was going on, he then called the police. Then the judge asked me for my side of the story, and I told the judge exactly what had happened…that I was telling my manager what the females were doing and that they paid me with food stamps, which I took the whole book of stamps and placed them in my register. When my manager walked up, I tried explaining things to him, but he ignored me and told me to take their groceries to their car. And then he came out, told me to go to the produce. After that, I was being handcuffed and taken to jail, just me, myself, and I!

The judge asked my manager, "Why didn't the two females go to jail as well?"

He said because he didn't see where they did anything wrong.

The judge told him, "If she went to jail, then those other girls should have went to jail too, and I have never had a case where someone was giving food stamps. What can she do with food stamps? She took the book of food stamps, tore them out of the book, and once you tear the stamps out of the book, you can't reuse them. So I just don't understand what would Ms. Hammonds be gaining from food stamps?"

And my manager got mad at the judge and asked the judge, "Well, is that all?"

The judge told him, "Yeah, that's all, and if I was you, Ms. Hammonds, I'll sue!" And that's just what I did!

My dad rehired the same lawyer that represented me with my attempt to kill charge, and all he got me back was $1,500. Ain't no telling what he got for handling the case. That was back in 1989. I'm sure false arrest should have been more than that. I saw that same manager years later at the gas station. He was a painter now with the all-white painter clothes, white hat, and the shoes that had paint all over on them. He was looking pretty rough buying a beer and walking because he didn't have a car!

I just shook my head and said to myself, "Wow, God don't like ugly, and karma is something else!"

It was getting close to my high school prom, and I was showing my best friend Tammy next door the dress that my mom and I agreed on getting, and it was a beautiful dress. I showed Jeff the dress and told him that I wanted him to get a nice suit so that we could go together. Jeff told me that he was not going to a prom because he was too old, and I wasn't going either. Jeff was twenty-two years old, and he felt that he was too old or just didn't want to go. Either way, I didn't care. I was going to the prom stag or with some girlfriends until I found out that the same dress my mom and I was going to buy for the prom, my so-called best friend Tammy went and got the same exact dress made! I was so mad, more hurt than anything, that she would stab me in my back this way. Getting the same dress that I showed her that I was getting wasn't cool at all.

After that, I didn't speak to Tammy again, and it didn't seem as if she cared. I was also hurt that I didn't go to my senior prom, something I'll never forget!

A couple of months later, my dad got me a job working at a gas station where they had a food area inside selling sub sandwiches and pizza. A good friend of my dad's wife was the manager there, and she hired me to work for her. My job was easy and fun. All I had to do was make subs sandwiches and pizza for the customers. Mrs. Shirley was the manager, and she was so cool. I felt like I had known her for years. She showed me step by step on making the subs and pizza. She showed me where they kept the food supplies for the pizza and subs inside the cooler, where the store kept all their alcohol. Mrs. Shirley also showed me how to sneak beer out of the cooler by putting it inside the plastic container whenever I went inside the cooler to get my food supplies so that no one would notice.

After that day, I became a pro at making pizza, Subs, and drinking beer. It was the life. If I got hungry, I could fix me a pizza or make me a sub and wash it down with a cold beer that I had in a cup, of course, so no one would notice what I was drinking. When I wasn't busy, I would sit down on the floor in the corner where I was working so that no one would see me and take a nap. Wow, what a job. I remember one day Jeff came by to visit me, and we were sitting at the arcade game. While I was sitting on his lap, my dad walked in unexpectedly and told Jeff and I that we were both wrong. I was on my job, and I didn't have any business sitting on his lap and that he didn't want to see anything like that again! When I first started working at my job, I was weighing around 115 pounds. Three months later, I was 165 pounds. That was the most that I have ever weighed in in my life, which came from all that eating and drinking beer. I was enjoying the weight since I was always slim. Now I had hips and thought I was fine!

Mrs. Shirley worked the morning shift, and she waited on me to relieve her in the afternoon when I got out of school. I couldn't believe that all the cashiers that worked in the gas station were all bisexual, the men and women. So of course, you knew I stayed to myself, just me, my sub, pizza, and beer. I was just fine there by myself. The beer was free and just for me, and I was loving it. I really didn't want to be bothered with them anyway because if I wasn't working, that beer had me passed out sleeping in a corner, and a couple of times, customers had to bam on the counter just to wake me up to serve them!

On this day, as always, I was working and minding my own business when one of the cashiers, a guy, told me that a gentlemen came in and brought him a beer, but he didn't want it nor could he take it home because his man would kill him, so he asked me if I wanted it. I said yes and just told him to leave it on the counter and that I would get it, but I forgot it and left it there sitting overnight. The next morning, when I came in for work, everyone was there. Even the head manager. She was questioning everyone about the beer that was left on the counter. All the cashiers put the beer on me, and I stated that the beer was given to me by another cashier, and yes, I left it on the counter, but it wasn't open, it was only one beer can. Mrs. Shirley was defending me like she was my mother, and I really appreciated her for that. Mrs. Shirley told the head manager, "Look, if y'all going to fire Shannon, you may as well fire me!"

Mrs. Shirley knew those people needed her. They looked at Mrs. Shirley and said, "Okay, you're fired!"

Mrs. Shirley looked at me, and I looked back at Mrs. Shirley with our mouths open, and that's when I saw the real side of Mrs. Shirley. Mrs. Shirley cursed everybody out! "Y'all can keep this job and kiss my a—— while you're at it. I was tired of this job anyway with all these funny a—— people working up in here, and if you ask me, I believe your a—— is gay, too, is what she told to the manager. Now come on, Shannon. Let's get the hell up out of here."

When we walked outside, Mrs. Shirley said, "Come on, and let's go smoke a blunt." After that, Mrs. Shirley and I became very close friends, and we didn't tell my dad what happened. We just told him that they laid everyone off! I later found out that Mrs. Shirley's sister and my dad used to mess around. That's how my dad knew Mrs. Shirley, but I didn't tell my dad that I knew nor my mother. I just knew that as long as I was around, it better not had happened again!

It was three months before graduation, and the only man in my life was Jeff, even though he wasn't faithful I still loved him because he was my first love. Jeff told me one day that his dad asked him if I was pregnant. Jeff said he asked him why he said that. His dad said because he was watching me walk down the street going home one day, and he noticed that my hips were spreading! Plus he said that Jeff must had left his car window down because a cat had kittens in his car, and that was a sign that I may be pregnant. When Jeff told me what his dad had said, I just laughed and told him that I wasn't pregnant. I finally graduated high school, and my mother gave me four options: I would either go to college, cosmetology school, military, or find a job, so I choose cosmetology school. My mom stated that she noticed that when it came to me fixing my own hair, I did a great job, and she thought that I should go to cosmetology school because she knew that I wasn't going to college or into the military and that she and my dad would help pay for my tuition.

I was two months into attending cosmetology school. One morning, my dad was taking me to school, and I started feeling a little upset on my stomach, and the next thing I knew, I vomited up the breakfast I ate in my dad's car. And all I can remember hearing was him yelling, "God d———, Shannon!" We had to turn around to take me back home to change my clothes. A couple of weeks later, Jeff's twin sister Jen asked me if I would ride with her to the free clinic to take a pregnancy test. While I was sitting there waiting on her, I decided to have a pregnancy test done myself. Both Jen and I stepped out of the examiner's room at the same time, we were both pregnant and both came up positive with an STD. I had a feeling that I was pregnant but not a STD and especially while I was pregnant. I was mad as hell, and when I told Jeff about it, the only excuse he could give me was that it was just so easy for him to catch anything since he was never circumcised. I wanted to grab his penis and cut it off myself!

I was feeling sorry for Jeff because he wasn't circumcised. As the Bible states, "A man uncircumcised is unclean and must be circumcised!"

I knew that his family were churchgoing folks, but just because you go to church doesn't mean that you're not still ignorant to the Bible, and ignorant doesn't mean that you're dumb. It just means that you just don't know! Well, years later, I found out that it was I who was ignorant to the fact about not being circumcised! Being circumcised doesn't just mean cutting away the foreskin but circumcised of the heart and flesh. Anything that is not good in your life or good for you like sin should be cut off!

I was eighteen when I graduated high school, and my dad brought me my very first car. He was outside cleaning it up one day when I stepped outside to look at it. He started talking to me in the process, telling me that if I would just give up my child and have an abortion, he would have given me this car.

And I told him, "I thought that the car was already mine. I can always get a car, but I can't get the same child that I have inside of me now." My dad was very upset and disappointed in my decision of having my child. I spoke to Jeff about it, and he came over like a man to speak to both my parents, and he told them, "Shannon got rid of one of my kids. She's not going to get rid of another one. Now if y'all don't want her here, then she can stay with me at my mother's house." The decision was made. I was going to keep my child, and my parents didn't put me out!

I remember standing in Jeff's yard when the spirit of the Lord told me to name my son Mark. Now at the time, I didn't know that I was carrying a son nor did I know that Mark was in the Bible. Maybe if I was reading the Bible, I would have known. I told Jeff that I wanted to name our son Mark, but Jeff stated that Mark was a white boy's name, and he wanted our son's name to be Ty.

I told him, "Ty, that little dirty boy that live next door to you, his name is Ty, and I'm not naming my son Ty." So we decided to put both names together and named our son Timark! I'll never forget that year 1989, not only because I was pregnant, but that was the year hurricane Hugo hit South Carolina. I remember just sitting in the window watching the trees blowing in the wind, not knowing how devastating this tornado really was until the next morning!

I'm about five months pregnant, and something, the Spirit, was telling me to get into the car and ride over to my old neighborhood Saxon Homes. When I pulled up, Jeff and his homeboy Scott were picking up my best friends, and they were all loading up in the car— Tracey, her sister Chris, and their two cousins, Lisa and Val! How in the hell did they even know them?

I jumped out of the car so fast and asked them, "Where in the hell y'all think y'all going?"

And they all said, "We going to the movies."

I said, "How the hell y'all going to some movies, and I didn't know anything about it. And why the hell y'all going to the movies with my man?"

While I was raising hell, all my so-called homegirls was jumping out of the car, and Jeff and Scott followed me back to our neighborhood! I guess my brother was right I didn't have any friends. After that, I stopped hanging with those homegirls from Saxon homes, but I still loved them.

I lost another good friend during my pregnancy. Rachel's parents found out that I was pregnant and told Rachel that they didn't want her hanging out with me anymore. They felt that I was a bad influence on Rachel. It was very hurtful for their parents to think that I was a bad influence on Rachel when Rachel was already having sex. But what could I do. Rachel lived with her parents, and she had to obey their rules, so we had to end our relationship. I guess just because you're eighteen doesn't mean you're grown until you're on your own.

I was around six months pregnant when Step called me and told me that she was hanging out at the club and that the Gucci girls were there and that she was afraid to leave because they were watching her. I told her, "I'm on my way!" When I walked inside the club, I saw Step sitting off to the side like a scared little kitten. The leader of the Gucci Girls, Quincy, who's nobody to play with, if I must say, was there with some more of her squad standing close by as if they were watching Step's every move. I walked over to Step. "Come on, let's go!" I said. She and a couple of her girlfriends followed us toward the door, and Quincy got in our way.

So I stepped to Quincy and told her, "Now let me tell you something. You f—— with my sister, you f—— with me, and if you put your hands on her, me and my baby gonna beat the hell out of you and them. Now think I'm playing!"

Step and I walked straight outside, and as soon as we started walking toward the car, something, the Spirit, told me to turn around. Quincy and her squad were all running out of the club behind us. We ran into Step's cousin Snoop, who asked if we were good. As soon as we turned back around, Quincy and her crew had all shot back into the club. I was wondering what was up with that. When I turned back around, Snoop was behind us, holding up his big pistol. When Quincy and her crew saw it, they took off!

I stayed out there for just a little while, talking with Snoop and a couple of more people that I knew. When I turned around to look for Step, she was gone! When I called Step to see where she was, Step's little scary a——— had left me and was already at home. When I got to the house, Step was sitting at the table, drinking a beer with her mama. I wasn't even mad. We all just laughed about it. She was my baby sister, and I loved her!

On New Year's Eve, Jeff and I was next door to Tammy's house standing in the yard talking with Tammy's mother, just having a friendly conversation, when she decided to pour us both a glass of wine to celebrate the New Year coming in. After drinking the glass of wine, I started having painful cramps, so Jeff's mom told me to go home and take a warm bath. Around three o'clock in the morning, my mother said to me, "Shannon, I think it's time for you to have that baby because you have been getting up all night using the bathroom. Now let me tell you something, you were woman enough to lay down and make that baby, so you better be woman enough to have that baby. And don't go in there screaming and hollering and acting like a fool, and don't ask me to babysit because I'm not. Now get your sister up to take you to the hospital because I'm getting ready to go to work, and I'll see ya when I get off!"

I thought that since I was the baby having my first baby, my mother would have wanted to be there. My sister took me to the hospital, and I was only a couple of centimeters. They wanted me to walk for a little while, so the baby could drop down some more I was miserable. From the time I got to the hospital until the time I had my son, it was one hour and thirty-six minutes. My son was born 1989, at 11:36 a.m., on New Year's Eve. The nurses and doctor all said, "I guess he couldn't wait a little while longer for the New Year's!" The only person who was there with me when I had my son was my sister. Jeff called me while he was at a New Year's party in the neighborhood at one of our girlfriend's houses, and a few of my homegirls all got on the phone.

"Hey, girl, what's up? What you doing?"
I said, "Having a baby, what else!"

I would find out years later that while he was at this party, he slept with one of my best friends, but I'll tell you about that later on, how and when I found out. A *big shocker*!

During those days, after having a baby, the doctor made you stay in the hospital for about four days. Everybody came to see me and the baby, except my dad because he was still disappointed with me. I was his baby girl, and I knew he only wanted the best for me. I guess he felt that I was too young at the time to have a baby. I was eighteen, just a baby myself. On the very last day of my stay in the hospital, Jeff and I were in my room alone when the nurse came in. She was filling out our son's birth certificate, and as soon as she asked us the name of our son, my dad walked through the door, and the nurse said, "So what is the name of your son."

I said, "Timark Modesto Curry."

My dad stated, while standing there, "Since you and Jeff are not married, then your son's name would be your last name. If or when your last name changed, then that's when your son's last name would change."

The nurse looked at Jeff and me, then stated, "This is his and your son, and you can name your son whatever name you want to name your son. Now what is your son's name?"

I said, "Timark Modesto Hammonds, because I gotta go home with him."

My dad was my dad, and I respected what he said.

Even though Jeff was a little upset about the last name, he still stood up to be a father to his son. Jeff found a job working second shift, and before going to work every day, he made sure that he came over to the house to check on Timark and me. I was homebound for those six weeks, and during those days, your parents wouldn't even so much let you go outside to the mailbox! Even though my parents were very much against me having my baby, my mother fell very much in love with Timark that she changed her shift from working in the mornings to working third shift at night so that she could keep my son during the day while I finished up cosmetology school. My mama said that she didn't trust a baby being in a day care, especially when the baby wasn't old enough to talk, and I really appreciated my mother doing that for me.

My cousin Sadarious was staying with us at the time, and because she and I were so very close, I wasn't paying any attention to what she was doing until it became a routine. I started noticing every ten minutes, before Jeff came over to see Timark and me before going to work, my cousin Sadarious would jump in the tub. And as soon as Jeff would walk in the house down the hall passing by the bathroom to come into the living room, my cousin would walk out of the bathroom with a towel wrapped around her, and my mom would say, "Sadarious, I done told you about walking out of that bathroom with a towel around you." Another day came when my cousin jumped in the bathtub ten minutes before Jeff got there, a voice spoke to me, the Spirit, telling me to put my ear to the door to hear what she was doing, which was nothing. I didn't hear any water splashing of her bathing. She was just sitting there. It was like clockwork. As soon as Jeff walked in, here came Ms. Sadarious coming out of the bathroom with just a towel wrapped around her, and I met her face-to-face.

I told her, "That sure was a quick bath, and I sure didn't hear you washing off!"

She just chuckled and said, "What are you talking about?"

I just rolled my eyes and went into the living room to sit with Jeff. Then the heifer got so bold that she came into the living room with a see-through gown. It's in the afternoon. Why are you putting on a gown instead of clothes? Jeff looked at me and said, "Your cousin is dressed very inappropriate in front of me. I don't want to see her in her nightgown. You better watch her." My cousin turned out to be a very loose young lady whom I couldn't trust. She was no longer my favorite cousin. She was just another cousin.

After I was able to start going outside again, I started hanging out sometimes with T, the bootlegger's wife who stayed up the street from me. Plus she had fallen in love with Timark, so I would take him with me sometimes. I used to go up there sometimes on Sundays when I wanted something to drink. She knew that I was in cosmetology school, so she asked me if I knew how to do a Jheri curl, which I did. She asked me if I would one day come over to fix her hair and she would pay me. So one day, Timark and I went over to her house so I could fix her hair. While I was fixing her hair, we were having a good time, drinking and smoking getting high. While the rods were sitting in her hair to process, I asked her if she mind watching Timark for me while I went to the gas station to put some gas in my car.

Now it's not like it was that important for me to put gas in my car. I was just feeling good and wanted to ride out. Before I left, I poured me up a *big* cup of beer for the ride. When I came to a complete stop behind a couple of cars, I decided to turn it up and take a drink. And as soon as I did, something hit me from behind so hard that I hit the steering wheel with the cup. The beer went straight down my nose and into my eyes. I couldn't see. It was burning my eyes and chocking me, and my clothes was soaked with beer! When I came to, the first thing I said to myself was, "Ooh, Lord, I'm going to jail on a Sunday, and my baby is at the bootleggers house. My mama and daddy is going to kill me." Then I said to myself, "My dad's body shop is right there. Maybe I can run there real fast before the police come to change clothes, but I don't have any clothes to change in." So I panicked, open up the door, threw the cup outside because it was evidence, and pulled off! When I looked back, I saw a white man with a homemade motorcycle and pieces of his motorcycle scattered all over the ground, and he was limping across the street with what was left of it.

When I got back to the neighborhood, I went to the park to get Jeff where he was at playing basketball. I jumped out of the car in a panic and told Jeff to get in the car. I told him what had happened. He said, "Well, where is my son?"

I said, "With T, the bootlegger."

He said, "So you left my son at the bootlegger's house?"

I told him yeah because I went to go get some gas. So he told me that I had left the scene of an accident and that I was sure enough going to jail! Jeff and I drove back to the accident, and there were no one there. No police, no one. So I stopped to where I threw the cup out of the door, and I was getting ready to pick it up.

Jeff yelled, "What the hell are you doing! I know you high. You gonna stop to pick the cup up? Put that damn cup down, and let's go!"

I assumed the person who hit me knew that he was in the wrong and was probably happy that I drove off!

After that incident, I learned my lesson about drinking and driving, but that lesson only lasted for about a week if that! Timark was a son I always wanted, a son that I loved with all my heart, a son that brought a breath of fresh air with a beautiful rainbow that shined in the house every day. Timark was spoiled and cried all the time. He cried so much behind me that I couldn't use the bathroom without him there under me. I'm sure I'm not the only mother who have gone through this, and don't we get so mad that when it happens. We tell our child, "It don't make any sense. I can't even use the bathroom without you crying behind me. I hope you smell every drop that comes out, and I mean it. Maybe you'll stop!" They don't care about you being on the toilet. As long as they're with you, they're good.

It was funny how Jen and I both had a baby three months apart, and she too had a boy who was very handsome. Now Jen loved to party. Even after her having her son, she still loved going out. I remember one day Jen asked their mom to watch her son, and Jen got very angry when their mother told her that she was not watching her son so that she could go out, lay up, and bring more babies in her house. Now Jeff's family was very close. I mean, so close to where each of them could tell their mother everything all the way down to them having sex. Their mother didn't mind them sitting around her drinking, smoking cigarettes or weed. That's because their mother drank and smoked with us, the cigarettes, not the weed. Their mother said that she always wanted the relationship with her kids where they could come to her with anything on their minds, and she would prefer them to do what they did around her instead of out in the streets.

Step and I were sitting around drinking with their mom while Jen was still asking their mom if she would watch her son and was getting madder by the minute. But their mom was drinking a beer, being cool, calm, and collected. "I don't see the problem of you watching him while I went out for a little while!"

"Jen, because that's your son. I done raised y'all!"

"Yeah, but what's the big deal of you watching him. It's not like you're going anywhere!"

"Jen, I'm not watching your child. That's your child. Now you need to stay home and watch your own child!"

"That's real f——— up. I just asked you one thing, and you act like that's a problem!"

Their mother told Jen in a very nice and calm voice, "Jen, you're a w———, Jen."

"Why I gotta be a w———!"

"Jen, any woman who go to a hotel with a man and lay up with them is a w———."

"When I go and lay up with those men in a hotel, we just go to have a good time!"

So their mom said, "So you mean to tell me when you go and lay up with those men you don't get any money?"

"No!"

"Well, you'll the damn fool then 'cause ain't no way I'ma go and lay up in a hotel room and don't get any money!"

Boy was I cracking up on the inside, but I held it in. I'm glad I wasn't drinking when she said that part because all of my beer would have been spitted out! Jeff's mom was a trip, and she was no one to mess with!

Jeff and I dated for four years before having our son, and within those four years, it was always infidelity on Jeff's part. I've never cheated on Jeff. I never even thought about it. Jeff was my first love, and I thought after having our son, maybe Jeff would change and start loving me just as much as I loved him. I just wanted him to be faithful, but I started noticing that Jeff stopped coming around the house to see his son and me, like he used to, and he wasn't helping me with our son's milk, Pampers, or anything else that our son needed. Even though I was receiving WIC for my son, the milk didn't last until his next voucher. Baby milk was very expensive, so my dad took it upon himself to spend his money and brought our son cases of milk at a time. I really appreciated my dad doing that for me. Instead of Jeff and me becoming closer, we were growing farther apart. I should have known that Jeff never loved me the way that I loved him, especially since he never took down the picture of his ex-girlfriend off his dresser. I told him that I knew of his ex-girlfriend. She was pretty, but I didn't tell 'em I used to have a crush on her brother when I was younger. Oh, he was a sexy dark chocolate thang!

My mom and I were talking one day, and she asked me about Jeff because she wasn't seeing him coming around to see us like he used to. I told her that it wasn't so great, but she already knew Jeff was a liar and cheater. My mom started telling me that our dad was a rolling stone and wherever he laid his hat was his home. She started telling me about this woman who my dad was messing with while they were together, and when she said this woman's name, she had the same last name of Jeff's ex-girlfriend, the same one whom he had a picture of on his dresser. I told my mom about the picture of Jeff's ex-girlfriend and her name, and my mom said that Jeff's ex was the woman's niece. Wow, it's a small world!

A couple of days later, I was standing outside with my son next door to Tammy's house talking to her mother when I saw Jeff and his ex, the same female who's in the picture on his dresser walking down the street together laughing and pushing his twin sister's baby in a stroller, like they were a couple and the baby in the stroller was their child! I started talking loud enough for him and her to hear me. Now this n—— got some nerve walking by my house pushing his sister's baby in a stroller when he can't push his own son in a stroller or spend time with him! They just glanced over to where I was and kept on walking, talking, and laughing. Tammy's mom looked at me and said, "You better handle that. Go ahead. I got Timark!"

I waited a couple of minutes to give Jeff and his little company time to get around the corner before walking through the cut. I walked in the yard and got straight up in his face. "So you mean to tell me that you can walk your sister's child in a stroller, but you don't have time for your son!"

He said, "You don't tell me what I can and cannot do. That's my business!"

As he and I were arguing, his ex started taking off her earrings.

I said, "Oh, so you wanna take off your earrings. Okay!"

Before you could blink your eye, I walked up the steps, grabbed that heifer by her head, and rammed it straight into the glass picture window on the front porch. Because when you start taking off your earrings, you were inviting me to a fight. Since you initiated the fight, I ended the fight by wearing her behind out!

While I was wearing her behind out, Jeff ran through the cut to tell my mama and daddy that they needed to come and get me because I was at his house beating up on a girl around the corner, and sure enough, my mama came around the corner and got me and told me, "Now what kind of a man is that, that he will come and tell me that you around here beating up on some girl. You just need to stay your butt from around there and leave him alone!" That didn't do any good because Jeff and I ended up back together again. His mom was very angry because I broke her window and told me that I was going to pay to get it fix, but I never did. Two years after having my son, I finished cosmetology school, but I didn't officially receive my cosmetology license until two years after finishing school.

Jen moved out of their parents' house and moved into these apartments not too far from our neighborhood. Jeff and I decided to move out there as well with our son who was now seven months old. I started hearing rumors about Jeff, but before I get into the rumors, let me tell you how the rumors started.

A lot of us were hired to clean up a building that was being renovated for a ten-dollar clothing store. One day, I was taking a break with some of the other female workers, and we just started talking about our kids, boyfriends, where we lived, etc. One of the females in the group were passing around a bunch of her pictures, and I saw an old enemy of mine named Betty whom I grew up with in Saxon Homes. I said, "Oh, I know this female right here. I grew up with her in Saxon Homes. I don't like her, and she don't like me."

The female who was passing around the pictures said, "That's my cousin!"

And I said, "So!"

I was having just a casual conversation with Jeff about the job and how the female who was passing around the pictures didn't like me talking about her cousin Betty with an attitude. Jeff stated that he and Betty used to date back in the day, something I didn't know anything about and wondered who else he may have been with that I knew.

One day, while I was over to Jeff's mom's house, I was standing outside on the front porch when I noticed a car stopping at the Stop sign on the corner. It looked like Jeff on the passenger side and a female who looked like Betty driving. The car turned the corner and went the opposite direction away from the house. I wasn't sure if it was Jeff or not, so I didn't say anything about it.

A couple of weeks later, after we were done cleaning the building, they hired a few of us women for cashiers, and a few of the men for stocking. One day, while at work, a very nice, clean-dressed good-looking gentleman came through my line. After paying for his items, he walked out of the store but turned back around and came back into the store and walked to my counter. I thought that something was wrong with his receipt or items, but he said that he couldn't just leave without introducing himself. He told me that he was very attracted to me when he saw me, and he wanted to know if I was married or had a boyfriend. I told him that I wasn't married, but that I did have a boyfriend. He still wanted to give me his number and told me that if I ever just needed someone to talk to, give him a call. I could tell that he was a little older than myself, and normally, I would have thrown someone's number away. But as fine as this guy was, well dressed, smelled good, and seemed like a nice gentleman, I was definitely keeping his number.

One day, while at home at the apartment, Jeff and I were in our bedroom watching television when he decided to get down on one knee and asked me to marry him. I was excited, and I said yes, but I didn't take him seriously because he proposed to me without a ring. I thought that we had come a long way as a couple especially now since we were living together. Plus Jeff didn't mind paying majority of the bills. He may have had a dirty job working on the back of the garbage truck, but the one thing that I loved about him when it came to Jeff cleaning as a man, he could clean up a house just as good as any woman, if not better. We would take turns each week. He would clean the kitchen and front room while I tackled our bedroom and the bathroom, and the next following week, we would switch up. I had my girlfriend Tree laughing about my mom stopping by to get a beer. I would be in the back room while she was in the kitchen in my refrigerator. "Okay, Shannon, I'm gone. I got a beer!"

When I looked into my refrigerator, I said to myself, "Well, she musta had a beer in her hand and two in her pocketbook because I know how many beers I had!"

I was so in love with Jeff and so naïve at the same time. I received another sexually transmitted disease, but Jeff said that it was only bacteria and not an STD. But we both had to take medicine. I was so dumb. Our arguments and fighting never stopped, and my neighbor Tracy who lived underneath us was a lifesaver. She was our babysitter. Every time Jeff and I got into an argument, she always came upstairs, knocked on the door, and would tell us, "Give me my baby!" We would let her in, and she would take Timark downstairs to her apartment until things cooled off. Then I would go back to get him. I would never forget her for that.

I was hearing rumors in the street that Betty was pregnant by Jeff, and I questioned him about it. He just denied it and said that it wasn't true. Weeks later, I was told again that Betty was pregnant, and Jeff was the father. I questioned Jeff again. "Wow, there's people out here still telling me that Betty is pregnant, and it's your baby!"

He stated, "Well, you know people trying to start trouble, but it ain't true."

One day, Jeff and I decided to go over to Jen's apartment just to hang out. Jeff knocked on the door and walked in. Jeff said, "Coming in!" Jen was walking from out of her bedroom with a female walking behind her whom I didn't know, and behind that female was another female walking with a big belly. It was Betty. She was pregnant, and the only thing I could do was shake my head and sit down in disbelief. I was so disgusted and hurt.

Betty got up in Jeff's face and started cursing him out, like, "Every time I talk to you, you keep telling me that you coming to see me and you never do! You keep telling lies that you gonna leave this b—— and be with me but every time I look around, you still with this black b——. And then you talking about you always with your motherf—— son!"

And that's when I stood up and got up in Betty's face. "Now you can call me all the black b—— in the world, I don't care, but if you ever say anything else about my son!" I put my finger right in her face. "Then I'ma beat you and this child's a——!"

Jeff grabbed me by the arm and said, "Let's go!"

On our way walking out the door and down the steps, Betty came behind Jeff yelling, screaming, and cursing him out. Then she started pushing Jeff in the back of his head. When we got down to the bottom of the steps, Jeff turned around, grabbed Betty by the arm, slammed her to the ground, and started beating or her like she was a man. Jeff has a very mean and quick temper. Betty's girlfriend looked at me, and I looked back at her, and we both jumped in to help Betty. We basically had to fight him off her! I've known Betty for a long time. Regardless if she and I didn't like each other, she was a woman and pregnant. I was not about to stand by and let any of that go down!

Betty left with her girlfriend; she was crying hysterically. That night, while Jeff and I were asleep, the phone rang. I picked it up, and it was his mother. She told me to tell Jeff that Betty was in the hospital, and she almost lost her baby, but she had it. It's a boy, and she named him Jeffrey Denzel Curry Junior. I leaned over to wake Jeff up, and I said, "Jeffrey, you gotta go!"

The next day, Jeff was hanging out at his mom's house, and I packed up all his clothes to drop them off. When I got there, Jeff was in the house, and I was taking his bags of clothes out of the car and sitting them on the porch. Jeff came outside, yelling, "What the hell are you doing?"

I knew how Jeff's temper could be, so I started walking fast to get back into the car. Once I got inside, I tried to drive off quickly, but the car that I was driving was a LeBaron. It was stalling to drive up the hill. When Jeff saw his bags of clothes sitting on the porch, he started running behind the car. He caught up with me, grabbing my door from the inside, trying to open it because my window was down. The only thing I remember was me running over something until I heard him scream. Then I knew it was his foot!

My mom stopped by that same day, something she normally did to check on Timark and me as well as get her a beer. Jeff came in, raising hell about me putting his clothes out, and he didn't care about my mom being there. He was just calling me all kinds of b——, and my mama stated, "As long as your daddy and I have been together, he has never called me out of my name!"

Jeff kept talking about beating my a——, but he wouldn't have to because he would get his mama to beat my a——. And that's when my mama said to Jeff, "Well, you forgot she got a mama too, and I'll go and get my gun for your a——, but I don't need a gun for you, boy. I'll whoop your a—— my damn self because you ain't nothing! Shannon, put this man out of your house right now, and I mean it!"

I asked my mama, "So me putting him out, how will I pay my bills?"

My mama stated, "I'll help you pay your bills. Put him out right now, or I will disown you as a child!"

I knew my mother meant just what she said. I turned around and looked at Jeff. "Jeffrey you gotta go!" Because I know where my bread and butter comes from!

When I called the police to put Jeff out, my mother and I were standing outside, and the police told the both of us, "Well, we really can't put him out because you're common law married. In the state of South Carolina, after spending one night together, you are considered common law married."

So my mother leaned in and told the police, "Well, don't tell him that." They said since he was willing to leave, they would just stay there until he left! The next following week, when my light bill came, I called my mom to see if she would help me pay it like she said she would. She told me, "Child, I can't help you pay your bills and mine too. You may as well come on back home!"

I said, "Well, ain't this something. I done put this man out for nothing." I knew my mother and I didn't get along very well, so I made sure I paid my bills.

Every day, I walked in the apartment. I was so depressed. I felt like I couldn't breathe; I had to hit play on my tape player to hear this particular song every day I walked through the door to get my mind back on track! It really hurt me when I found out that Jeff's mother and family started saying that Timark was not Jeff's son and that I had him taking care of another's man child, which was not true! Timark was Jeff's son, and he damn sure wasn't taking care of him. The only thing that Jeff ever gave our son was a used jacket his sister Jen gave him from her son and a bike that he found on the side of the road while working on the back of the trash truck. The only reason I think they were saying that Timark wasn't Jeff's son was because I started seeing an old ex-boyfriend of mine whose sister was staying out there in the same apartment complex, and he was staying with her at the time.

My ex LO was the same guy I used to date back in the day when I was a Fila Female! That was so long ago when I dated LO and the last time we were intimate, so it was impossible that my son was his. I remember one day going to the medicine cabinet and grabbing a razor blade. I looked at my wrist, and I started crying hysterically, looking ugly. I was ready to slit my wrist and kill myself, and at that moment, I looked at myself in the mirror and said out loud, "Child, you crazy. You better put that razor down talking about you ready to kill yourself." At that moment, I stopped crying and had to laugh at myself. I called myself a good actress and that I needed to be on TV!

Now the song that saved me when I was going through my depression with Jeff, the song that I played every single day when I walked through the door, was "Smile" by Guy! "Every time I see you... you're wearing the same ole frown...lift up your pretty hair... show the world that you're not down...baby please smile... smile... just for a little while!"

I love that song. The job at the clothing store didn't last no more than a month or two, and I got another job working at a cleaners pressing shirts. I didn't work there no more than two to three months because the white man I worked for was a very nasty redneck who thought he had workers working on the plantation! I called him one morning to inform him that I had just gotten in from taking my son to the emergency room and that I needed to stay home that day to take care of him. The first thing that came out of his mouth was, "Well, my shirts ain't gonna get pressed you staying home." And I told him, "You're right. Just have my check ready. I'll be there to get it!"

When I got there, he wanted to apologize, and I accepted his apology, but I still got my check and left because when it comes to my child, you can take this job and shove it. I ain't working here no more!

My cousin knew that I had some experience working in the cleaners as a shirt presser, something they needed at the cleaners where she worked. Also her husband was a manager, and he decided to give me the job! Working at that cleaners was so fun. I met so many good people while working there, customers and coworkers. My coworkers told me that if I wanted to drink my beer, all I had to do was bring a personal cooler to keep my beer inside and a cup with a plastic top on it. I didn't have to worry about anyone telling on me since everyone who worked in the back with me drank, especially Mrs. Peril. Mrs. Peril was the oldest out of all of us and have worked there the longest. Mrs. Peril was nice, didn't bother nobody, did her job, and drank her beer, and boy could she drink!

Shirley was a trip and loved flirting with every man that came through the door. I remember her flirting with the janitor one day, and she was all over him, telling him how good he smelled and that she ain't never smelled that kind of cologne that he was wearing. She told the janitor, "Man you smell good. What's that cologne you're wearing?"

He said, "That ain't nothing but some Pine Sol. I just got finished cleaning out the bathrooms!"

Shirley just walked off, and the janitor said, "Yeah, I know she loves to flirt with every man she sees. She won't get my money. I bet I fixed her that time!"

I was laughing my butt off on the inside. I said to myself, "That's what she gets for trying to flirt with every man she sees!"

All of us became close like family, but Mary and I became the closest of friends. She took to me like a daughter. After work, I sometimes took Mary home, and I would sit over there for a little while. We would smoke a joint and drink a couple of beers. One day, while on the job, my cousin who also worked there asked me, since I was on my lunch break, if I would go with her husband's brother to her house because she was sending him there to pick up something for her. Since she was busy, she wanted me to go with him just to watch him just in case he wanted to get more than what she was sending him to get. I went alone even though I didn't want to go. While he was in the back, getting whatever it was he was supposed to get, I was sitting at the kitchen table eating my lunch when he called me, "Shannon!"

"What!" I said.

"Come here!"

I said, "What!"

"Come here!"

I was saying to myself, "What do he want because even though he was fine, he was married, and I was just a little on the aggravated side and ready to go."

I started walking down the hallway, yelling, "Where you at?"

He was like, "Come in the room." The light was off, and when I turned on the lights, he was standing up with a pose looking like Dexter! Dexter was the guy Eddie Murphy was talking about on his standup comedy *Delirious*. He was talking about Dexter with the long penis thrown over his shoulder while walking on the beach with your woman. That was him. I kid you not. That man's penis was so big and so long hanging down to almost his knees, and the first thang that came out of my mouth was, "Child, I don't want none of that. You ain't gonna kill me now, let's go 'cause I'm ready!"

I walked out of the room! I said to myself, "Now his wife just had twins from him. I guess she had to get used to that."

He took me back to the job, and I didn't say a word to anyone. I just went to his wife's baby shower last week, and she was really nice and cute. Some men, the nerve of them! One day, my cousin Trina's husband hired a new lady to work on the presser to press the pants, and she was on the crazy side and out for money. The reason I say this is because she told us that she didn't have much feeling in her right arm, and she was only working there for about three weeks. Mary and I saw with our own eyes that she laid her right arm on the pants presser and closed the presser on her arm. She screamed and yelled, and Mary ran over and popped the handle on the presser to come up, and when it did, all of her skin was on the presser. You could see her flesh down to the white meat. Doctor's care was right next door, so we all rushed her over there. I guess she figured that since she didn't have much feeling in her arm, it wouldn't bother her as much. Plus she was next door to the emergency care, so she didn't have to go far.

I don't know what happened with her after that. I just remember them saying that since she was the one who closed the pants presser on her arm, she may not get anything! Now my bills at my apartment were starting to get a little too much for me to handle by myself, so I decided to moved back home with my parents but to at least stay until the end of the month. One day, I was at the apartment with my best friend Barbara, someone I grew up with. I was close with her whole family, and my uncle was best friends with her oldest brother who at the time was serving a life sentence for killing a principal. The story I got was that her brother was working at this school as a janitor and got a ride home from the principal one day. When the principal turned and asked him if he would perform a sexual act on him, he flipped out and killed the man on the spot. Some people said that he tried to rob the guy. I still don't know the true story behind it. I remember one day before her brother went to prison, I was hanging out with Barbara and her family over at her mom's house; and her oldest brother, the same brother who went to prison for killing that principal, offered me a drink. I thought he was going to hand me a can of beer, but instead he gave me a glass and poured me up a half glass of what I thought was a wine cooler. I looked inside my glass, looked back up at him with my glass still tilted, and said, "That's all?"

He said, "That's all you need, believe you me!"

I still felt as though he was being stingy with his drink. Why offer me something if you really didn't want to share. I started drinking the drink, but he told me not to drink it too fast and to take my time because that was not the kind of drink I wanted to drink fast. It wasn't much to drink, and it kinda tasted like medicine. It was called Cisco.

That was the only drink that I had that day, and I was feeling good when I left Barbara's house. No, let's just say I was drunk off that lil drink her brother gave me, and as a matter of fact, I was still drunk for three days! I found out later that drink Cisco her brother gave me was killing people, and they had to take it off the shelf! No wonder I was still drunk for three days! Jeff and his cousin Trapp came to the apartment to get the rest of his things, mainly his waterbed. I guess he was drinking because he took the waterbed a part before taking the water out of it, which caused the bag to burst, and it flooded the apartment. While we were waiting on the maintenance guy to bring the water vac, Jeff and I had gotten into a heated argument. We were standing face-to-face when Jeff had decided to take his's dad heavy-duty Black & Decker screw driver gun that he brought over with him to take down his bed with and hit me in the back of my head so hard, it knocked me down to my knees! I struggled to get off the floor and sat on the chair. When I felt the back of my head, my hand was covered with blood! Barbara and Trapp both looked at him with their mouths wide open as if this man was crazy, and the Holy Spirit told me, "If you get up, you'll gonna have to kill him, or he's going to kill you, and it's not worth it!"

I sat there looking at Jeff with hatred and vengeance in my eyes. Then he and his cousin left, and I never told my family what happened.

I didn't even call the police. I guess I still had feelings for him! I moved back home with my parents, which I really didn't want to do because my mother and I still didn't have that mother and daughter bond that I always wanted. I didn't get the love or conversations that I needed or wanted with her. I knew my dad loved me, but there's nothing more precious than the relationship between a mother and daughter because they share the same similarities. A female couldn't express herself to her dad the way she could to her mom, especially when it came to personal things that needed to be discussed with their mother. I never had that with my mom growing up, so the one person that I turned to was always my grandmother, Mama. Mama was the only one who I could talk to about anything. I loved her. She wasn't just my grandmother; she was my best friend.

I still had the number of that nice-looking guy named Randy who came through my line that day at the clothing store. A couple of days later, I decided to give Randy a call and invited him to come over to visit me. Randy and I had a very nice and long conversation. While sitting outside, we talked about his ex-wife and children. I told him a little bit about what was going on in my life with my son and his dad. Since we kicked it off pretty good, we mainly kept in touch over the phone. Nothing serious because we both were going through a transitioning in our lives.

Timark was two years old when my parents moved out of Hollywood Hills, and they brought their very first home. It was the Fourth of July, and my girlfriend Barbara and I decided to ride out to the Hills just to see if the Boys were cooking out. I happened to drive by Jeff's mom's house, and the door was open. I looked inside the glass door and saw Jeff and Betty standing beside each other dressed alike with his and hers outfit on.

I said to Barbara, "Wow, did you see that? Jeff and Betty dressed alike, and he haven't done anything for my son!"

Barbara stated, "I didn't see anything."

I wanted her to see their outfits, so I decided to go back around in a circle so that I could drive by their house again. When I came back around the corner, everybody was outside on the porch except Jeff and his mom but everyone else was standing on the porch—Step, Jen, Rosalyn, and Betty as if they were waiting for me to drive back by.

I pulled over in the yard and got out to speak just because I wasn't with Jeff anymore. I knew that I was still cool with my sisters. I said, "What's up, Step, Jen, and Rosalyn!"

But what came out of their mouth was the most hurtful thing. They started calling me all kind of black b——, telling me they would whoop my a——, to get out of their yard, and everything. I was like, "*What!*"

I was hurt, and I looked at them in amazement. "What? Really? So y'all flipping on me for her? As much as I loved y'all like sisters and been down for y'all since day one. It's cool though!" They knew me, and I knew them, and they knew I was not the one to mess with, so I offered them one by one to come off the porch, and I will beat each one of them down one by one! Do you think that they were bad enough to do it? They each looked at each other scared as if "Who's going first?"

So they all started coming off the porch together. I told them as I was walking back to my car, "It's all good. I'll catch y'all one by one. I can't beat all of y'all by myself!"

I was getting back into my car. The door was locked, and the windows were all rolled up. Barbara was in the car like a scared little mouse, balled up in the corner of the car. I started banging on the window, telling her, "How you gonna lock me out of my own car! Open the door!" When I got back in the car, it was so hot. I started rolling down my window while asking her, "Why in the hell did you lock me out of my car?"

She said, "I'm pregnant. I can't get into no fight and lose my baby!"

I told her that I understood, but why lock me out of my own car and have me to get jumped on by four females. As I was cranking up my car to pull off, Barbara shouted, "Shannon, watch out!" Betty came around my car reached into my window, and we started fighting! It was the Fourth of July, and the beers I've been drinking and the weed I've been smoking had me feeling pretty good, so as I was fighting Betty through my window while my car was running. I told Barbara, "When I tell you to put this car in drive, put it in drive!"

I grabbed a hold of Betty with both hands and shouted, "Put in drive!"

I hit the accelerator in high speed and was dragging Betty up the street. Step, Jen, and Rosalyn started running behind the car after her. My plans were to get Betty away from the rest of them, so I could have my one-on-one time with her and give her what she needed, but I was unable to drive the car while trying to hold on to Betty at the same time. I was hoping Barbara would have taken over the steering wheel, but she was too scared in her seat to move.

My car turned into someone's yard and toward their house, so I grabbed hold of the steering wheel with one hand while still trying to hold on to Betty with the other. I wasn't able to hold on to her with only one hand, so I let her go and drove out of the yard. As I was driving out of the neighborhood, I felt something dripping down my arm. When I turned on the inside car lights, I noticed my right pinky finger was almost cut off. It was cut down to the bone! I had a cut on my right arm, a very bad cut on my left arm down to the white meat, and a smaller cut under my left arm! All I could say was, "She cut me! That b——— cut me!"

She cut me with a box cutter, and the reason I couldn't feel it was because I was intoxicated. When I reached my cousin Lulu's house where my sister and her husband were living at the time, I ran into the house, and they were having a Fourth of July party, but let me tell you about my sister. My sister is very laid-back, quiet, and don't bother nobody. But as soon as my sister saw me walking in the house bleeding, she looked at me like, "What happened?" and all I said was "Step and Jen!"

My sister never cared for them anyway. She turned around and started walking toward their room.

My sister had on a skirt, and as she was walking, she was taking off her skirt in front of everybody and changed into her shorts, T-shirt, and tennis shoes! She and I was ready to ride until her husband told her that she didn't have anything to do with that and to let the police handle it! Yes, I can understand the best thing to do is call the police, but you don't tell my sister that she didn't have nothing to do with her little sister almost getting killed because I'm sure if it was his sister, he would have been the first one out the door!

My sister's husband and I are both Aquarius. Our birthdays are on the same day, and yes, we both bump heads, but I still love him! The police came and took the incident report. My sister took me to the emergency room where I received about twenty-five stitches in all, but the worst cut was my pinky finger. She just about cut it off, and this is what Betty was telling me as she was fighting me: "Every time you see these cuts on you, it's going to remind you of me!"

At the hospital, while the doctors were stitching me up, they stated to me that the young lady Betty who I was fighting was over in another room getting her knees worked on because she stated that I dragged her with my car. At that moment, I said to myself, "Yes, so

I did get her a———. I may not have gotten her like she gotten me or the way I wanted to, but at least I got her a—— too."

I told them with my best acting skills and a sad look on my face that I didn't do anything to her but tried to defend myself, and she was cutting me through my window as I was driving off! Betty had to pay all my hospital bills and pay me restitution of about $800. I stated to myself, "If I could press charges against Betty, why didn't I press them against Jeff when he hit me upside my head with that electric screw driver!" I felt stupid that I didn't, and every time I look at these cuts on my arm, I do think about Betty! My mom told me, "I never told you to go out there to fight anyone, but what this girl did to you, I don't care how long it takes. You better get her back!"

I was really hurt on how the Currys flipped on me, but I was even more hurt that my baby sister Step didn't have my back after all we've been through! She was my sister, and there wasn't nothing in this world that I wouldn't have done for her. I would have fought for her to the end. I loved her as if she was my blood sister, and I thought that we would be friends forever! A piece of me died that day. A piece of me that would never be the same, and I still hurt about it till this day! When people saw me, they would ask me about my sister, and I would say, "Who? Step? Oh, she wasn't my sister. She used to be my best friend" And they would say, "Used to be? She's not anymore because when you saw one, you saw the other one!" That's just how tight we were. Salt and Pepper, that's what people called us, and no one could believe that we were no longer friends, especially me!

Some months later, I received a phone call, and it was Jeff. He was begging for us to get back together. He was telling me how sorry he was and how much he loved me and wanted us to be a family again. He asked me if I would meet him at this chicken spot so we could talk. I told Jeff that it was late, but he begged me to come, so I told him that I would. I guess I still had feelings for Jeff. Even after all he had taken me through, he was still my son's father. I was driving up to the spot when I noticed Jeff through the glass, just sitting at a table waiting on me. It was as if he was the only person in the restaurant. I parked my car, and I sat there for a minute just to look at him, but he didn't see me. Jeff didn't look like himself. He looked tired as

173

though something was wrong. He looked as if he were spaced out on some drugs or something. I walked inside and sat down in front of him. Jeff didn't even sound or acted like himself. This was not the Jeff I knew nor the Jeff I used to be in love with.

We talk for little bit, and I told him that all I wanted from him was to spend time with his son. To me, that was more important than money. It was late, so I asked Jeff where was he staying, and he tried to lie that he was staying with his mama. But I knew he was staying with Betty in Saxon Homes. I asked him if he wanted me to drop him off somewhere, but he stated that he didn't have anywhere to go. I dropped him off in Saxon Homes anyway. I used to be so in love with Jeff, and I knew when I dropped him off in Saxon Homes at Betty's house, I was getting over Jeff. The hurt and pain that I endured with Jeff was just too painful for me to go back to.

One day, I had a dream about Jeff's dad, and in the dream, Timark and I was in a church sitting in a chair in the aisle. Timark was sitting on my lap because all the seats were filled. Jeff's dad started walking toward us without his cane, a cane he always used to walk with because of an accident he had while in the military. Once he got to us, he stood in front of us, looked me straight in my eyes, and said, "Take care of your son." That was the end of the dream! Wasn't that something! I took that dream to say that Jeff's dad was letting me know to take care of my son because I wasn't going to get any help from Jeff and to bring my son up in the church!

During this time, Jeff and I wasn't communicating at all, but he called me one day to ask me for a favor. He told me that he was working at a Fishing and Tackle plant right around the corner from my parents' new house, and he wanted to know, since he was still at work and wasn't able to get off in time, if I could go to the Temp Service to pick up his last check and give it to his cousin Trapp. I asked him why was this his last check. He said because the job was only temporary, but they would find him something else. I told him I would pick up the check, and I didn't even ask him how much money would he give me for our son. The reason I didn't was because my dad told me that I shouldn't have to ask a man to take care of his responsibilities. I wanted to put child support on Jeff because I didn't bring my son into this world by myself, so I shouldn't have to take care of him by myself. I didn't understand my dad. He hated Jeff with a passion, and yet he told me not to put child support on him.

Trapp and I went to the Temporary Service to pick up Jeff's check, and while we were there, we both decided to put in an application for a job. Trapp got hired to work at the same Fishing and Tackle plant where Jeff was working, and they hired me to work at a uniform cleaning company. I asked them why they didn't hire me for the same job at the Fishing and Tackle plant since the plant was right around the corner from where I lived. The lady stated that the job at the Fishing and Tackle plant was only temporary compared to the uniform job where they were sending me was a permanent job. I told her that I really appreciated that, but I would prefer to take the job at the Fishing and Tackle plant since it was right around the corner from my house. Wasn't that a blessing! Trapp and I only went to pick up Jeff's check and ended up with a job!

Trapp didn't have a car, so I decided to pick him up every day for work since we both were on the same shift. Neither one of us had any money and wouldn't get our first check for another two weeks, so we both decided that we would take turns bringing something from home to feed the both of us because we both stayed with our parents. One morning, I drove to pick Trapp up, and he was outside talking with a guy that I knew from back in the day who was originally from New York but been living here all of his life but still acted like he was still in New York with his New York accent. Once I pulled up, he noticed me and started putting his rap on, but I wasn't even trying to hear it, calling me "gurl."

"What's up, gurl? When you gonna let me take you out?"

I guess that's the way they say it in New York. I told him, "The only thing I need for you to do was get out in the street and direct traffic!"

I had to back out of Trapp's driveway, and I wasn't able to see because of this big bush that was in the way. New Yorker got in the middle of the street, started waving his hand for me to come out, and as I was backing out, he said, "Come on out, it ain't nothing coming but a car." And as I was pulling out, thinking he was playing, there really was a car coming. I had to shoot back into the driveway fast! He walked off laughing, but I knew he was being funny because I shot him down. When Trapp and I pulled off, we busted out laughing because it really was funny.

Each day, Trapp and I both took turns bringing something from home so we could both eat. It may not have been much, but it had to do. One day, when I was picking Trapp up, he came outside with one of his mom's big bowling ball bags, and I asked him where he think he was going with that big bowling ball bag and what was in it. He said it was our food. I said to myself, "Trapp must have a lot to eat in there!"

When lunch time came, we meet each other in the break area as always, and Trapp put the big bowling ball bag on the table, opened it up, and pulled out one can of Vienna sausage and one pack of saltine crackers! I cracked up and almost fell on the floor from laughing so hard, but Trapp didn't find it funny.

I said, "I know damn well you ain't bring that big a——— bag with just one can of Vienna sausage and a pack of crackers."

He said, "Yep, because I was tired of coming to work with not much to eat, and I got tired of people looking at us, so I wanted them to think we had a lot to eat."

I busted out laughing again and told him, "You crazy because they still see that we ain't got nothing to eat!"

And we ate the hell out of that one can of Vienna sausage and pack of crackers like it was steak and potatoes because we were hungry!

After two weeks of working at Shakespeare, the company hired us both on permanently, Trapp on second and me on first. Trapp didn't have a car to get to work, so he turned the job down! When I got hired, the minimum wages were about $4.75, but my pay was $7.75, so making that kind of money just fresh out of high school was nice, and I made sure I dressed my son in the best named clothes OshKosh B'gosh.

After some months working at the plant, I was told over the intercom that I had a phone call. When I answered the call, it was Jeff. He was telling me how so sorry he was about us breaking up and that he wanted me to know that it's true about what they say, you don't miss your water until your well run dry.

I told him, "Yeah, and your well will never get full with me again!" I hung up the phone! I felt as though Jeff didn't want to be in his son's life as much as he wanted to be in mine because he didn't ask about his son. I think he just mostly was missing me, and I didn't want a relationship with him. I wanted him to have that relationship with his son—a son who needed his dad!

I started hanging out with Lamar. Lamar was the driver of the car that MoMo got out of in the neighborhood when we fought her. Lamar told me that he told MoMo not to get out of the car, but she did anyway, and that's why he drove off. Lamar told me that he lived in that same neighborhood, and he was just riding with his homegirl MoMo and a few other guys when MoMo saw us and told him to follow the car that we were in. But he didn't know that was going to take place. Lamar said that when he went to visit MoMo in the hospital, she was grabbing for him, and he figured she was trying to hug him. But she really was trying to stop him from stepping on her oxygen tube because she couldn't breathe! Lamar and I laughed about it. I forgave him, and he and I became close like brothers and sisters. We both started hanging out at parties, bars, shooting pool, or just riding around singing ole school songs like Curtis Mayfield, Al Green, Marvin Gay, and many, many more. We didn't have a radio in the car, so he and I was the radio, and boy did we sang our butts off!

One day, I had Tonya and Tony riding in the backseat all lov-ey-dovey. I was driving as if I were their chauffeur. I'm a *big* Tupac fan, so I kept playing one of my favorite Tupac songs over and over, and each time the song ended, I played it over again. Tonya and Tony told me that they were tired of hearing that same Tupac song! Who did they think they were riding in my car and talking about they were tired of listening to Tupac. They were about to get tired of walking because I was about to put them out! I started fussing about the brakes on my car, and Tonya and Tony asked me what was wrong with my brakes. I told them that I just get tired because every time I take my car to get brake shoes put on, three months down the road,

I need more brake shoes. Now if he can't fix my brake shoes right, I could just take them to somebody else!

They said, "Well, who are you taking your car to?"

I said, "My daddy! His sign is going to say GOING OUT OF BUSINESS. Let 'em keep playing about my car!"

Tonya and Tony burst out laughing. They thought that was the funniest thing. They were cracking up in the back seat, all on the floor, on top of each other. I didn't think it was funny at all. I was mad.

Tree called Tonya and me up one day and told us that she had someone that she wanted us to meet. She said that it was a female coworker of hers named Grace and that Grace wanted to meet us and was inviting us over to her house for drinks. When Tonya and I got there, this female's apartment was laid out like in a magazine. Grace was a little older than us and very pretty. She was a Filipino. She was a good person; we all clicked with her instantly as if we had known her for years! She was now a part of the crew. Eventually, we started calling ourselves the Waiting to Exhale Crew! Tre was Savannah, Whitney Houston (even though I thought that I should have been Whitney Houston since I'm one of her biggest fans!). Grace was Bernadine, Angela Bassett. Tonya was Robin, Lela Rochon. And I was Gloria, Loretta Devine.

I told them, "Why am I Gloria?"

They said, "Because you're ghetto just like her with that big butt and the only one who have a son!"

I looked at them heifers and rolled my eyes!

Lamar came to be cool with all of us. We went to a football game together one day—Tre, Tonya, Lamar, and myself. After the game was over, we just sat in the car, drinking beer and tripping. Lamar and I were in the backseat, and the next thing you know, Lamar was sneaking out of the back door, and we were like, "Where the hell are you going?"

Lamar said, "I see those police sitting across the street looking at us drinking in this car!"

We said, "Well, damn, and you wasn't going to say anything to us!"

He said, "Hell, somebody gotta tell the story!"

He wasn't playing. He was really sneaking out the car. That's how dirty he was, but we all just laughed about it. We wasn't crazy. We sat there until the police left.

I meet a young guy at work by the name of Kevin. He was tall, light-skinned, and kinda cute. Kevin said that he wanted to ask me a question, and I told him to ask me.

Kevin took off his hat and said, "Do you think that my head is too big? Be honest."

I said, "No."

I really didn't want to hurt his feelings. This boy's head was so big that he had a head like ET. I just couldn't tell 'em the truth, but big as his head was, he knew he had a big jug a—— head. Why put the pressure on me! Why ask a question when you already know the answer. I guess he believed me. I'm not sure. After that, we became cool at work but nothing serious.

Kevin asked me one day at work if I ever wanted a gold cap. I told him yeah, but looking at him, I should had turned it down seeing that he didn't have one in his mouth. I told him that I knew of a dentist in a trailer who put real gold in your mouth. Nothing fake. But it would cost about $250 to $300. He still said that it was cool! If I knew that real gold would mess up a person's grill, I would have never gotten it! Everybody knew about Mr. JD, the dentist who was working out of his trailer especially all the drug dealers. We went about a week later, and I got one gold cap on my front tooth, and I thought I was the s——! I had the gold cap in for about three years when it came out one day while at work. I was hungry and broke, and I found a piece of candy named Mary Jane in the draw, which was probably there for about a year. I was chewing on it, and it felt like it pulled my whole tooth out! I kept my mouth open and didn't chew anymore because I didn't want to swallow my real tooth. All I could say was, "Uh-oh, my tooth done came out." And my coworkers were like, "Let me see." They said that my real tooth was still in. It was the gold cap that had come off. I was so relieved that my tooth didn't come out, so I went back to JD to put my gold cap back in.

My girlfriend Barbara called me up one day and told me that she wanted to introduce me to her son's father's cousin, Jermaine. I told her that I would, and when I did, I fell head over heels. He was nice, sweet, cute, and sexy with a nice body and smile. He was also a hustler, a drug dealer, and in love with someone else. But Jermaine and I still hit it off. Both Jermaine and his cousin Brian stayed with their grandmother, which was our hangout spot. I was so crazy about Jermaine that I would hang out with Barbara and Brian for hours, waiting until Jermaine came home. Once he did, the party was on! We had a ball, drinking, smoking, playing music, dancing, laughing, just having a good time.

The one thing that Jermaine and I enjoyed the most was having sex. We both had a serious connection with each other, and I did something that I didn't do with any other guy, and that was to bring my son around. I started bringing Timark around, but the one thing I didn't do was have my son around too long because I didn't want him around that kind of environment. He was three years old and still didn't know his dad.

I met another one of Jermaine and Brian's cousin. His name was Troy, and he too was nice-looking. He had a nice sharp box haircut with a blond streak in the middle of it, and he put you in the mind of the rapper Kwamé. Even though he was cute, I still only had eyes for Jermaine. Brian also was a drug dealer, and he came to Barbara and me, asking us if we wanted to make some money. He said she and I could put our money in together and get a package. He said that he would sell the package for us and we'll split the money up between the both of us. Barbara and I both agreed and came up with about $250 together. Brian brought us back $500, and we split the money up between the both of us! We put the $500 back in the pot, and Brian brought us back $1,000! We put the $1,000 back in, and Brian brought us back $2,000! We just couldn't believe that we were making that kind of money, not within the same day, but each time we put back in the pot. Brian would bring us back the money, and Barbara and I would split it between the both of us.

I remember Brian bringing us back $5,400 that was $2,700 split between Barbara and me. I didn't want to put all of my money back in the pot, but Brian convinced us that he was used to selling big boy weight, and the only reason he was selling our small stuff was just to help us out, and this was the kind of money we needed to step our game up—to bring in some real money, over $10,000! We both gave Brian our $2,700 apiece, and Brian never came back! A couple of days later, Barbara's brother who's also a good friend of mine told me that both Barbara's and Brian's big fat a—— were lying up in the hotel with my money, and they were eating and shopping for new clothes and shoes!

I called both my cousin, Kevin and Vincent, who were brothers, and we waited on Brian to come home, but he never did. I never forgave Barbara or Brian for stabbing me in the back like that. She was supposed to be my best friend, but I should have known she was not to be trusted when she set up the convenient store where she was working to get robbed. She lost her job, better than losing her life and going to jail. Not only that, I should have known Barbara was not to be trusted when she took me to one of her friends' house and introduced me to one of her girlfriends' brother, who took my her-ringbone gold necklace off my neck and didn't give it back! Barbara sat there and didn't say a word. I believe she was in on it as well. Jermaine told me that he was sorry that Brian and Barbara did me the way that they did, but he did not want to lose friendship with me, and I told him that we wouldn't, that we will always be friends. But since he was still in love with someone else, I thought that it will be best that I just moved on with my life, and I did. But he and I always stayed in contact.

Years later, Brian got picked up by the Feds and is now facing life in prison without parole for something Jermaine wouldn't tell me about. He just said that Brian did something unimaginable, some-thing I wouldn't even believe. Years later, I saw Barbara in the grocery store riding on one of those mobile carts, looking really bad! Both she and Brian were both big people, but she was overweight, dirty-look-ing, bad, and sick! She kept telling me that I looked good, but too bad I couldn't say the same thing about her.

As it is said in Deuteronomy 32:35 (NKJV), "Vengeance is Mine, and recompense; Their foot shall slip in due time; For the day of their calamity is at hand, And the things to come hasten upon them." But at the same time, I had to also remember what the Bible says about your enemies. Proverbs 24:17–20 (NKJV) states, "Do not rejoice when your enemy falls, And do not let your heart be glad when he stumbles; Lest the LORD see it, and it displease Him, And He turn away His wrath from him."

Yes, God would turn his wrath away from them and back on you! I tried to hold a nice and pleasant conversation with her, but it wasn't the same. It would never be the same. I'll forgive, but I would never forget!

I've been working at Shakespeare for about two years now, and I've became very close with an older white lady named Jody. Jody was in love with a guy named James who also worked out there. I knew that Jody and James lived together, but what I couldn't understand was when she stated that she lets James hold on to her check because she was trying to watch her figure and she didn't want to eat too much. So he only gave her two dollars a day, enough for a pack of crackers and coffee while smoking her cigarettes.

I said to myself, "Watch her figure? She only weighs about ninety-five pounds, if that!" Jody and I had worked together as partners for a while, so we had time to bond and talk to each other about our personal life, and we became very close. Jody was offered a floor manager position, and she took it. And after she took the position Jody, changed for the worst. Our job duty was that two people operated the machine while the other two people sat down to pack the product. Then the next day, we would switch. On this particular day, I had to run the machine by myself because my partner wasn't there, and Jody and her partner sat down packing all day. The next day, Jody and her partner had to run the machine, while I sat down and packed. But Jody told me that she was tired and that she didn't feel like running the machine that day. I told her that I didn't care that she was tired. I was tired yesterday, but I still operated it. I wasn't going to run today. I was going to sit down all day and pack like she did the day before! Jody grabbed me by my arm to get me to listen to her because I turned my head and didn't want to hear it.

I told her, "Child, if you don't take your hands off me!"

She then went and got our supervisor, Mr. Mike, and he called us both into his office.

Mr. Mike said to me that Jody told him that I wouldn't run the machine, and I told him, "No, I wasn't going to run the machine today because I ran the machine yesterday all by myself while Jody sat down all day. Now she's tired!" Then he commenced to tell me a story with his prejudiced self talking about, "See sometimes we gotta do things that we don't want to do, just like my mother worked all the way until my daddy died and worked up until she died working for her boss man, doing things she wasn't supposed to do and all she got was peanuts!"

I told Mr. Mike, "Yeah, my people worked all the way up until they died too working for their boss man doing things they weren't supposed to do, and all they got was a whip on their backs so at least your mama got peanuts!"

He turned pink and said, "Well, Jody wrote you up."

I said, "Well, if Jody wrote me up, then you may as well write Jody up for grabbing my arm."

He asked Jody if it was true, and she said, "Yeah, but I was only trying to get her to listen to me." So he asked her if she wanted to tear up the write-up, and she said yes!

Later on that year, my grandfather died, my father's dad, and I put in a request to go to his funeral and was denied by my supervisor, Mr. Mike. Mike told me that I would get written up if I went to my own grandfather's funeral. Of course I went anyway, especially after I told my dad what he said. My dad went off, "Well, let him write you up because that's your granddaddy, and if it was not for him, I wouldn't be here, and you wouldn't have been here. So let him write you up. I will pay you myself for missing that day!"

Well, I went to my grandfather's funeral, and I tell you, my grandfather had one of the biggest funerals that I have ever seen in my life. My brother-in-law said the same thing. My grandfather's funeral cars were line up behind each other one for about twenty miles long. And one thing about a funeral in the country, those country folks knew how to feed ya! Back at the church while everyone was standing around eating and talking to one another, one of my relatives pointed at these two young boys standing close by and said, "Those two boys over there are your brothers."

I heard them, but I didn't think anything of it other than they didn't know what they were talking about because I knew my brother, and I only had one.

After my grandfather's funeral, my supervisor Mr. Mike wrote me up just like he said he would. And a couple of days after that, my supervisor was released from his position as our supervisor. They didn't fire him. They only gave him another position in the company, and everyone who had gotten write-up records were wiped clean. Now how about that! After that, Sabrina and I had gotten really close. Sabrina is the older sister of my friend Monica, the one who ran away and came to our house. I saw Monica from time to time when she was over at her mom's because by now, she had moved out with a daughter of her own. Sabrina was working at the Fishing and Tackle plant years before I was even hired. She and I started hanging out mostly over to her house, and that's when I met their oldest and only brother Roy with his fine self! Roy was married, and the one thing I always respected about a married man was his wife. I wouldn't want anyone disrespecting me and my husband because what goes around comes around!

Some of the times that I was over at Sabrina's house drinking, her brother Roy would sometimes stop by. I remember one day, I had just gotten over there, and he and his wife were pulling up. It was on a Sunday, and I had just stopped at the bootlegger's house to get some beer for Sabrina and me. And as soon as I stepped out of my car, the brown paper bag tore, and all the beer cans started rolling down the street. Roy came over to help me, and I found out later from Roy that his wife was very upset that he helped me, and she told him, "Yeah, I know that you probably f—— that black b—— since you like dark women anyway!" Roy was fine and all, but I never thought about messing with him until his wife said what she said, so I said to myself, "Well, since I'm a black b—— and she thinks I'm f—— him, then I will!"

Roy also worked at the Fishing and Tackle plant, and when he told me that he and his wife were having problems in their marriage,

Roy and I became close, so close that we started messing around. Roy and I were always attracted to each other. We just never said anything because I was his sister's homegirl, and he was married. I told Roy that I only messed with him that one time because of what his wife had said about me and that I didn't mess with married men. He told me that he and his wife were planning on divorcing. I told him that I'll believe it when I see it! Roy would stop by my mom's house to visit me before he went to work, and sometimes he would want me to ride off with him for a little while before he went in, but his car was a two-seater Corvette, and I would tell him that his car didn't have enough room for my son to ride. When he said, "Oh, let his little bad a—— stay home!" that really pissed me off, and I almost slapped the taste out of his mouth!

One night while hanging out at this club, things got really heated between Roy and me. I was sitting there hanging out and talking to my homegirl Tonya when Roy walked up and sat between Tonya and myself. You could tell that he had been drinking, so he sat there for about five minutes. He decided to lean over and whisper to me, "Your homegirl Tonya got some big a—— titties!"

Before I knew it, I threw my drink in his face. Then he threw his drink on me. Then I threw a bottle at him, and he picked up a bottle and threw it at me. Then he picked up a chair like he was going to throw it at me, and I picked up a chair and swung it at him. We were going at it until the club security put us both out. We were outside pushing each other. Tonya was holding me, and my boy Feet was holding him. After that, the club just put everybody out. We both looked at each other and said, "Damn, we done closed the club down!" Roy called his sister Sabrina to come up to the club to fight me, and she came, but she didn't do anything. She just said, "I ain't got nothing to do with it because y'all be back together tomorrow!" I called my homeboy Lamar, and he said the same thing! We all looked at each other, laughed about it, and left! Roy and I left together. Drunk, that's what we both were, drunk! Roy and I didn't mess around much longer after that because I kept telling him that I was very uncomfortable about messing with a married man, but he kept reassuring me that he and his wife were definitely getting a divorce. When they did, he found another lover and told me, "See, I told you that I was getting a divorce, but you couldn't wait!" I was a little upset because I figured if he really cared about me, then he would have come for me, but he didn't, so life goes on!

After Roy and I stopped messing around, Mary and I started back hanging out on the weekend going to clubs. Mary is my home-girl who tried to kill herself in high school. I remember one day while at this club, I was checking out this cute guy who put you in the mind of Gerald Lervert. He was playing pool, and he saw me checking him out, so he asked me if I played pool. I told him some, so he asked me to play a game with him, and we had a good time. He said that his name was James, and after the club was over, he asked me where was I headed, and I told him to take my homegirl home. He wanted to know if we could get up after that, and I told him yes. He told me that he would stay there and wait until I got back. When I got back, James told me to follow him. I followed him to a hotel where he rented a room. We talked and had sex. I woke up around four o'clock in the morning knowing I had to get home to Timark, so I left James a note that said, "I had a good time, but I'm sorry that I rushed off. I have a son at home that I needed to get back to so just call me when you get up."

I left my phone number on the note for him to call me.

James told me when he woke up and noticed me gone. He thought for sure that I robbed him for everything he had and the first thang he did was check his pants pocket. He said, "Oh, okay, my money still in my pocket." He said when he read the note that I left him, he was like, "Aw, this girl is all right!" His nickname was Winnie, and I wondered why they called him Winnie because he was on the big side but short, cute, and sexy. A couple of days later, Winnie and his homeboy Pop picked me and Mary up. We rode off just to hang out together. While we were riding, Winnie and Pop was talking about a couple of their homeboys, and Mary kept butting in saying that she knew them. They then started asking us about other guys, and Mary knew them all! They then asked me if I knew any of the guys that Mary knew, and I told them, "No, I don't get out like that." The next thing you know, they were dropping Mary back off at home. I thought that they were going to drop me off next, but they told me, "We can hang out with you, but your girl we can't do because all those guys we named gets around. Her knowing them lets us know that she gets around too!"

Winnie, his homeboy Pop, and I became real close. I found out later that Winnie was a drug dealer, but Winnie treated me so nice. I guess that's all that mattered at the time. Winnie always took me out to eat, and I didn't have to pay for anything. And afterward, he always rented a room where we would go to drink, get high, and make love. Winnie was always buying his and hers shirt. I remember one of my favorite shirts he brought me, I wore the colors out! It was a white T-shirt with a black hand holding a gun that said, "I don't dial 911!" Yeah, I was a gangster! I always had a good time with Winnie, and I had starting falling for him. Wherever there was a party, we were there! When there was something going on at Twin Lakes, we were there! We always did something together, but I told him that it seemed like every time we did something, it never involved my son Timark.

I told Winnie that I always had a good time with him, but I didn't like the fact that every place we went didn't involve my son. So one day, we decided to bring Timark along with us. I used to like to drink white liquor. Tom Collins was my drink. So Winnie and I got a room, and we brought Timark with us. I had just made me a drink of Tom Collins while Winnie was drinking his beer. Winnie and I were talking, and the next thing you know, Timark's little a——— had started doing backflips in the bed. My son was four years old, and I ain't never seen him do no back flips ever! He was all hyper and wouldn't sit down, and I was trying to hold him down and keep him calm. But he started crying because he didn't want me holding him, and he didn't want to sit down. I was wondering what was wrong with my baby. I happened to look at my cup and realized that Timark had drank my whole cup of Tom Collins! Winnie thought that it was funny, but I was scared. Timark was running around the room, jumping off the bed until he tired himself out and passed out! That was the last time I made a drink around my son. I didn't say that was the last time I drank, just the last time around him.

I started staying home more with Timark instead of hanging out with Winnie because I started feeling guilty leaving Timark home while I was out in the streets partying, so Winnie would stop by my mom's house often to see me, and I remember while he was in the front room, watching TV, my mom was in the kitchen cooking, and she asked me in a loud voice, "Aren't you tired of seeing him?"

I said, "No."

Then she said, "Well, you might not be, but I am!"

I know Winnie heard her. It was so embarrassing!

I really liked Winnie, but the one thing Winnie loved to do was eat! Winnie was a big eater, and I remember the times we would go out to a buffet, Winnie would eat a big plate of food, sit back, rub his stomach, wait about five minutes, go back, and get another plate, and another, and sometimes two more big platters after that! One day, Winnie and I was going into our hotel room, and we saw his daddy coming out with another woman! Winnie's parents were still married, and Winnie was so upset, he told me that he should have gone up to his daddy and asked him what the hell did he think he was doing cheating on his mama like that! He left it alone, but I know it was still on his mind just by the way he was acting, but eventually, he started being himself. We had a good time like we normally did, which was drinking and getting high.

Now I will say Winnie may have been a big guy, and his nickname may have been Winnie. But he wasn't a big fellow in his "shoe size," if you know what I mean. Now I've been intimate with a few guys, and I had a son but Winnie was the first person to have ever given me an orgasm before I knew what an orgasm was! Winnie might have been good in bed, but his stomach had started getting in the way. I was trying to tell him to lie back from the dinner table some because whenever we was making love, I felt his stomach before I felt his penis. It was like I was on a roller-coaster ride at the fair. Bump, bump, bump, bump, bump, bump! Stomach, penis, stomach, penis, stomach, penis. It just didn't feel good, and I was trying to tell him in a nice way. "Winnie, baby, you need to start sitting back from the kitchen table, or do some sit ups or something."

I should have told him why, but I didn't. Winnie just loved to eat!

One day, while Winnie and I were together. We had Timark with us, and we were going over to one of Winnie's friends' children's birthday party. Timark was sitting in the backseat behind Winnie, but he wasn't in his seatbelt. He kept getting out of his seat and pulling on Winnie's headrest. Winnie turned around and screamed at Timark, telling him to sit down, but Timark still got up out of his seat and pulled back on Winnie's headrest. Winnie turned around again and cursed my baby out! "I told your little bad a——— to sit your a——— down some damn where!"

I stopped the car. "Oh, I know you ain't talking to my baby like that. You done lost your mind. Now get out!"

I put Winnie out of my car even though I didn't know where we were, and we were a long way from home. I didn't give a damn. I told Timark to climb in the front seat to put his seatbelt on, and we pulled off! A couple of days later, I met this cute guy in the club. Years prior, I was checking out this guy at the club house party that we went to years ago, the one where I hide the two sawed-off rifles under my trench coat, and there was a guy there that I kept my eyes on. He was just so cool and good-looking and by himself. When I saw this guy in the club, I thought for sure this was the same guy at the house party or if not his brother because he sure favored the guy, but it wasn't him. My next-door neighbor Boosie whom I used to live next door to in the Hills were there at the club. Boosie is the sister to Tammy, my so-called best friend who backstabbed me with our prom dresses. Boosie and I was just standing around talking when I showed her the cute guy who were sitting down on the other side of the club, and it looked like he was looking at me.

Boosie said, "Who? That's my cousin Nuscey. He ain't got no teeth!"

I thought that she was saying it as a joke. I said, "What!"

"Yeah, child, that's my cousin. He all right, but he missing his front teeth!"

I said to myself, "Well, damn!"

While still hanging out in the club, Nuscey decided to walk up to me. He spoke and asked me my name. I spoke back to him and told him that my name was Shannon. Nuscey sat down beside me, but I couldn't tell if he had teeth missing in the front of his mouth or not because when he talked, his head was kind of slanted down. Nuscey and I talked for the rest of that night, and he asked me for my number so that he could call me to make sure that I made it home safe. I found out later that he didn't have a home telephone. He was talking to me in the cold at a payphone. I just could not believe that this guy stood out there for hours in the cold talking to me on the phone. I was a little impressed yet still young and naïve. He even sang me a song, and he had a nice voice. Nuscey did something no other man have ever done. Stand in the cold to talk to me and sang me a song over the phone! But it was cold and late, so I told tell him to please go home and get out of the cold, and we will talk tomorrow!

Winnie was sweet and all. I just got tired of us always doing something that didn't involve my son. And each time I would bring it up, he would always say, "Well, there's no kids where we're going." Nuscey and I became very close, and he one day asked me if I knew of anyone who sold weed that he could buy from, and the only person I knew that sold weight was Winnie. I called Winnie up and made it seem like I knew someone who I was real cool with, and he wanted to spend some money. So Winnie told me that it was cool to bring him, so I took Nuscey down to Winnie's house to buy the weed. Even though I knew it was wrong, I just liked Nuscey like that. When we got to Winnie's house, Winnie was sitting on his porch, and I got out of the car while Nuscey stayed inside the car. I knew it was wrong for bringing Nuscey to Winnie's house, knowing that Nuscey was someone more than just a friend, and I think Winnie knew it because he asked me to give him a kiss. I wouldn't, and he asked again. I denied him a second time, and then he asked me if that was my man in the car. and I told him no, that wasn't my man. So he said, "Well, why you won't give me a kiss."

I said, "Because I'm still mad with you."

And he was like, "Yeah, right. That's your man."

I told him it wasn't, and I walked off. Winnie was still sitting on the porch watching us as we pulled off, and I really felt bad. I gave Nuscey the weed that he wanted, and that was the last time I spoke to Winnie! Winnie and I dated for about a total of six months.

My mother was so in love with Timark that she even asked me if she could adopt my son, but I told her no because I loved my son, and I wanted my son. She even tried to teach Timark to call her mama and me Shannon until Mrs. Brenda, his day care provider at the day care, taught him that his grandmother was called his grandmama and I was called mama because she didn't like that. Even when she first told me not to ask her to babysit, I didn't because I felt that my son was my responsibility, not my mother's.

She, one day, asked me, "Why you ain't never ask me to babysit?"

"Because you told me not to."

I guess my mom saw that even though I was young, I was still a good mother to my son, and I owe that all to her. I don't know what changed my mother's mind about her babysitting Timark, but she was the one telling me to go out and that she would keep Timark for me. It didn't matter how much I went out, my mother cared for Timark as one of her own.

Timark was about three years old, and he never liked his pacifier. It was his bottle that I found hard trying to wean him off. I would throw his bottle away and give him a cup, but he was not having it. One night, while everyone was asleep, I took Timark's bottle and hid it because now, he's drinking whole milk so he could drink whole milk out of his cup. Timark woke me up by hitting me very hard, telling me in his heavy man's voice, "Mama, where's my baba. I can't find my baba!" He's all up under the bed and everything so I told him, "Since you're old enough to tell me you need your baba, you should be old enough to get off the baba. Now lay your a——down somewhere!"

About a year later, I had decided to go out to the club Purple Rain where I saw my cousin Squeaky and some of her friends sitting at a table getting tore up. That's when my cousin brought to my attention that Betty was there on the dance floor and that this was my chance to get her back from what she had did to me when she cut me. So my cousin gave me a beer bottle and told me to go over and bust Betty up side her head with it, and I was on my way to do it with the beer bottle in my hand until God sent this man to stop me. He grabbed me around my shoulders and told me, "I overheard those girls pushing you up to go over to hit that young lady on the dance floor but let me show you something." Betty turned around. She was pregnant again, and she flaunted it in my face like she knew that I was there watching her, and I said to myself, "Well damn!"

The guy told me, "Now see, that women is pregnant, and if you would have jumped on her, then you were going to be the one in jail not them!" He was right! I left the situation alone, for now, and thanked the Lord for stopping me because I may not have been here to tell my story!

Even though we didn't live in Hollywood Hills anymore. I still went out there as if I did because all of my close friends still lived out there, and by now, my girlfriend Tonya and her boyfriend Tony had a daughter together. Tonya and Tony were a funny-looking couple that put you in the mind of Betty and Barney on *The Flintstones* because she was a lot taller than him. One thing I would say about Tonya, she was tough, another female D Bo on "Friday." She was nothing to play with. She and Tony was always arguing, and she used to always beat on him and boss him around, and it seemed as though he never wanted to fight her back until one day. Tony just got tired of Tonya jumping on him. Tony went to her a——, and he must have knocked her senseless because when she got up off the ground, looking all cross-eyed, talking about, "Y'all ain't had to double teamed me!"

I said, "Oh no, that man whooped your a—— by himself. We told you to leave that man alone!" Boy did we all laugh about that night, and we still laughing about it till this day!

That wasn't the only time Tonya and Tony got into a fight. I remember one day while out in the Hills over at Tonya's house where she lived with her mother and sisters. Tonya got into a big argument with Regina, one of our girlfriends who was pregnant at the time. Tonya was mad that Regina repeated something to Tony that she told Regina in confidence, and Tony and Tonya got into a big argument about it. Tonya was so heated that she took Regina, who was pregnant, by both of her legs, lifted her off the ground, and had her literally dangling over a tree stump, yelling and telling her that she would kill her. Remember, I told you that Tonya was a big girl more like an Amazon, someone you didn't want to mess with. So everyone was yelling at Tonya, telling her to put Regina down. Mrs. Thompson, Tonya's mom, was so upset with Tonya. She told her that she was going to call the police on her if she didn't put Regina down! Tonya finally put Regina down, but then she turned her anger on her mom, and that's when all hell broke loose!

Mrs. Thompson went in the house to get her gun, and we locked Tonya outside. Tonya started banging on the door to let her in, and I told Mrs. Thompson, "Mrs. Thompson, you don't have to use your gun. I got this," and I yelled through the locked small glass door window and told Tonya, "Ain't nobody letting you up in here. You acting all crazy. You better calm your a—— down before you come up in here!" But Tonya wasn't listening to me. She just kept yelling and banging on the door, "Let me up in here before I f—— somebody up!"

I was telling her, "You ain't going to do nothing!" And as soon as I turned my back on the door to walk away, I turned back around, and my heart dropped. Somehow, Tonya got into the house and rushed in like Debo on *Friday*, and I hugged Tonya like Chris Tucker who played Smokey did Depo. I hugged her real tight and told her, "Girl, calm down. It's gonna be all right!" Tonya broke loose from my hug and went yelling at her older sister who was sitting down. Tonya's sister looked up at her and just told her real calm, "Girl, you better get out of my face, girl!"

I just remember telling myself that the whole family was crazy! We still laugh about that incident to this day with my scared a—— talking all that s—— and didn't do nothing. I said to myself, "That's a silverback. You better leave that crazy child alone!"

There was another time when we all went to a cookout, and this guy was trying to ask Tonya if she wanted to dance, but she just told him no. I guess the guy was just feeling good with his alcohol because he wouldn't take no for an answer, so he asked Tonya again, and she still told him no. After the second no, the guy decided to grab Tonya by the arm, and when he did, Tonya hit the guy with one punch knocking him out cold! We found out that the guy was our girlfriend's uncle, the one who was having the cookout! We left the cookout quick, fast, and a hurry! If you ask me, the whole family is crazy, and I love them all. I remember Tonya's baby sister Felicia was going to braid my hair, and I had to meet her at her house. So we both met up at her house, and she told me to sit down while she got herself together. The next thang I heard was, "Oh hell no, I know this b—— didn't. You just wait, I'm about to call this b—— right now! Trina, b——, I know damn well you didn't make my last pack of Kool-Aid!"

I said to myself, "I know damn well this b—— didn't just call this girl up to curse her out over a pack of Kool-Aid. Wow!" I just laughed to myself and shook my head.

One day, while I was out and about, I met this guy who said that he was a truck driver. He was very handsome and sexy. He told me that he was around thirty years old, and I believed him. He would call me while he was on the road, and he one time brought me back a souvenir, which I thought was nice. We talked on the phone for about two to three weeks before I had decided to tell him where I lived. He decided to stop by one day, and I introduced him to my mom when she came outside to walk to her car. She walked past us, and this guy was like mesmerized by her beauty that his eyes followed her.

He asked me, "You said that's your mother."

I said, "Yes, why?"

He said, "Nothing, I just think she's a beautiful woman."

When he left, I told my mother what he said about her, thinking that what he said was a compliment, but my mother explained to me, "When you have a male friend, and if he's looking at your mother the way he looked at me, then you need to get rid of him!"

Not long after that, I went over to Tonya's house, and it was a young girl who looked familiar, but I know that I've never met her before. I told her that she looked like someone I knew, but I just couldn't put my hands on who it was. She asked me if I ever met her dad because everyone always said that my dad and I look alike.

I asked her, "Who is your dad?"

When she told me who her dad was, he was the same truck driver that I had met. "Your dad told me that he was only thirty years old."

She said, "I know. He tells everybody that. My dad is in his forties and he be trying to get me to hook him up with my girlfriends." Wow, your dad is up in age with my parents. I couldn't believe that this man lied to me like this. When I told him about it, he just laughed like it was nothing. After that, I didn't want anything else to do with him. This was one of the reasons I said that I would never date a truck driver again.

One day, I ran into an old classmate I always had a crush on. Tom Cat was his nick name, and he was some sexy, cute, and quiet. Tom Cat and I started conversating on the phone as well as him coming to visit me while I was staying at my mom's house. The day he came over really kind of pissed me off because my sister was never the kind that sat in with me and my company. She was always in the room, doing her own thing until the day Tom Cat came over, and she sat her a——— downstairs where we were. It wasn't like where we were sitting my mom couldn't see us or anything. Hell, I had already had a son who was three years old, so I kind of consider myself grown and didn't need a chaperone. I felt as though my sister was being fast, looking up in Tom Cat's face because she kept looking up in his face, and he kept looking up in hers. I always felt my sister was a lot better looking than me, but why would she be in my company's face instead of being in her room like she normally does. I didn't think that any of my male friends were her type. I guess she liked what she saw.

One night, I picked Tom Cat up, and we had decided to go to the park in the hills and park on the grass! We both got in the backseat and smoked a blunt, and the next thang you know, I was feeling good. I started taking off all of my clothes and started kissing Tom Cat. Then the next thang you know, we heard a tap on the window. It was the police. He had his flashlight and shined it right on my naked body. I was so embarrassed because I was the only one with all my clothes off like a fool. The police told Tom Cat, "You mean to tell me you couldn't take this young lady to a hotel?" As he was talking to Tom Cat, I was putting my clothes back on. I was so scared because I thought that we were going to jail, but he let us go. I was so relieved. Nothing ever happened with Tom Cat or myself after that. I guess I was too embarrassed to face him.

Timark was so in love with my best friend Tree, and she got her first job working at a fast-food drive-through burger restaurant. Tree only worked there for about three weeks because she really didn't like it there, and our other best friend Tonya, who wasn't working and living on food stamps, convinced her to quit her job and hang out with her. She did. One day, Timark and I were passing by Tree's old job, and he was so excited with his little baby voice, "Mama, let's stop by and see Tree where she works."

And I told him, "That b—— don't have a job."

And what he said was so cute and so funny. "Mama, don't say that."

"Well, I'm sorry, but she don't."

Timark was always so friendly even with strangers. Everybody loved him because he was just so cute! One day, while he and I were in the grocery store, I let his hand go for just a second to pay for my groceries. I looked back down to grab his hand, and he was gone! I panicked and started looking everywhere for him, and I saw an older black woman with my son by the hand walking out of the store's sliding doors!

I yelled, "That's my son." I ran over to get Timark, and she looked down at Timark and said, "Oh, I thought this was my grandson!"

She just walked straight out the door. If she thought that my son was her grandson, she sure didn't turn around to go back in the store to see where her real grandson was! I believe that lady was trying to kidnap my son! After that incident, I started keeping a very close eye on my son.

There was a time when I really appreciated this white woman for stepping in one day. I did one of the stupidest things that I could have ever done. I left Timark locked in the car with the windows cracked. I pulled to the door of the store because I knew that I was going to run in and out, and when I came out, there was this white lady standing next to my car. She said, "Don't you *ever* leave your child in the car by himself again. I started to call the police, but I didn't. I wanted to see whose child this was and how long they were going to leave him in the car like this!"

"Yes, ma'am!"

I apologized for my actions and thanked the lady for watching out for my son and told her nothing like this will ever happen again, and it didn't! I was so nervous and said to myself, "She was right. I should have never left my son in the car by himself because anything could have happened, and I could have gone to jail for child abuse and neglect! To be honest, this lady saved my son's life and mine! Thank you, Lord!

Timark was around four years old when Mary and I started back communicating on the phone. Mary is the one who tried to commit suicide in high school. Mary and I had started back going out, and there was this one particular club that we liked going out to. Trapp, Jeff's cousin, was also hanging out there as well. I didn't blame Trapp for what Jeff did to me when they both came to the apartment to get Jeff's things, and Jeff hit me upside my head with that electric screwdriver. Trapp was only there to help Jeff get the rest of his things. On this particular Saturday, the club was having a pajama party where you could wear your pajamas in the club. Now Mary and I was going to the pajama party, but we definitely were not going to wear our pajamas up in a club, no way! This Saturday, Trapp didn't show up, and one of the females who we always saw out there. I mean, you couldn't help but notice her because she was on crutches and she could barely walk.

I was saying to myself when I first saw her, "Who would come out to a club with crutches?"

The young girl asked me if my cousin Trapp was coming out to the club, and by then, I did consider Trapp as my cousin since he and Jeff were first cousins, and we all were really close. Well, at least Trapp and I were still close at the time. I told her that I didn't know, and she wanted to know if I could give her, her sister, and their cousin a ride home. I was like, "Yeah, I guess. Just meet me out front outside by two o'clock." They said okay, and we went our separate ways! Back then, I was still a cigarette smoker, not a big smoker, but I still smoked.

I was sitting on this wall inside of the club. When I was about to light my cigarette, this guy I didn't know walked right up to me. His

197

beard was braided in two long braids about eight inches long with hair beads on them. He grabbed not only the cigarette out of my mouth but my lips too as he was grabbing the cigarette out of my mouth and balled it up in his hand. He told me, "You don't need that cigarette!" Now that was one of the most disrespectful things that you could ever do to a person you just don't know! You done put your nasty dirty hands not only on my cigarette but on my lips. I flipped! The next thang I knew, I took my lighter that was in my hand, and I lit both of his braided beards on fire! We all know that hair burns fast and the fire on his beard was burning fast like gas was on it!

Mary was scared, trying to knock the fire out with her hand. I jumped off the brick wall and walked away, mad! I started to sing, "The beard, the beard, the beard is on fire." We don't need no water; let the motherf—— burn! I didn't give a damn. You don't put your nasty a—— hands on my mouth, and you don't know me! So when two o'clock came, the girls were outside like I told them to be. When we got to the car, I got in first. I was about to unlock the door for Mary with my right hand. She was getting in the front seat on the passenger side. I was sitting up, and I leaned over to pull up the door latch with my right hand, but I heard a voice in my head telling me to lay down! I guess I didn't lay down fast enough because I promise, you there was a hand on my left shoulder that laid me down so gracefully on the seat, in a slow motion. While lying down on the seat, I lifted my left arm over my head to unlock the door for Mary, and there were gunshots. *Pow! Pow! Pow!* The next thing I know, everybody started jumping in the car. We were all screaming for our lives! People were running everywhere! I felt like I was in a movie, and I was going to die because people were shooting everywhere! When the shooting stopped, I was cranking up my car to pull off, and Mary shouted, "Shannon, you can't go anywhere!"

I said, "Why?"

She said and pointed, "Because there's a body lying on the ground in front of your car!"

I was like, "Oh my god!"

We were all crying. I looked over toward the club, and the big security guard was sitting in a chair. He was yelling and kicking his left leg. He started taking off his pants because he had gotten shot in his thigh, and you could see the bullet hole with blood running down his leg! When I looked back at the females in my car, I noticed that my window was shattered. This was my very first car, a Chrysler LeBaron! Once we heard the police sirens, we all felt a lot better. People started running, and we got out of the car since we couldn't go anywhere. Mary and I was so shaken up that we were walking together basically holding each other up. We were glued to each other. As we were walking, we noticed these guys watching us. Why I don't know. We just knew that they were following us. Each way we turned, they turned until we finally got to a policeman. When we looked around to tell them that someone was following us, they were gone!

The police talked to everyone who was involved in the shooting as well as anyone whose cars was hit by any bullets during the incident and asked that everyone get escorted down to the police station to make a police report as well as statements. They put most of us in one room where we all sat at a big round table with one phone to pass around. They told everyone to call our parents and let them know that we were okay and to get some insurance information about our cars. While everyone was taking turns calling their parents about the incident, you could hear some of their parents on the other end of the receiver were very concerned about their loved ones, and some were on their way to the police station. Now when it was my turn to get the phone to call home to inform my parents about what just took place, my sister answered the phone and said, "Hello!"

I said, "Joyce, where is Bonnie?"

She said, "We already know what happened because Kevin called already!"

I didn't know that my cousin was there, so I guess he saw what happened and called my mom and dad and told them what happened.

When my dad got on the phone, the first thing he said to me was, "Now, now, now, let me tell you one thing, now...I don't want no police at my door!"

I said, "Well, the police wants us to get some insurance information about our car."

My dad said, "You don't have nothing but liability on that car!"

Click! My dad hung up in my face! I said to myself, "I know this n—— didn't just hang up in my face!"

I was so hurt. Here I am at the police station where I was almost killed in a shootout, and my family just act as if they didn't give a damn about me, talking about he don't want no police at his door because they done move from *Good Times* living in Hollywood Hills to moving on up like the Jeffersons, and now they too good to where they don't want no police at their door. But I bet when my mama threw that lye on his a——, I bet he wished the police was at the door then! I was so embarrassed. I know these people sitting at the table heard my dad hang up in my face because it was loud, and it seemed as Tupac would sing "All Eyez on Me!"

So I pretended as if my dad was still on the phone. "Well, okay I'm fine. And I'll just talk to you all when I get home. Okay, I love you too!" The police told everyone to bring their cars back the next day because it was just too dark for them to see anything.

Driving back home, Mary and I were nervous and shaken up. It was so cold that night I don't know if Mary and I were shaking from the incident or from the cold air that was coming in from my shattered back window that were breaking at each moment. When we arrived at Mary's house, which, by this time, she was living with her boyfriend Frank's parents. I was not ready to drive home by myself because I was still shaken up, so I stayed with Mary for about an hour. Frank was the same guy who Step and my cousin Sug was fighting over a while back. When I got home, it was about eight o'clock in the morning. My mom was in the kitchen cooking breakfast, something she normally does, and when I started walking toward my room, she said, "There's no need to sneak into the house now!"

I looked at her with a crazy look on my face like, "What?" I said, "Why would I be sneaking into the house when I called y'all from the police station!"

On my way to my room, I had to pass by my parents' room, and my dad was sitting up in the bed watching TV. My dad didn't even look at me. He stared at the television the whole time. He stated to me, "Now, now, now, now, Shannon," with his stuttering a——. He continued, "Now, now, now, now, I'm not arguing and not fussing, but don't let daylight catch you again!"

At that moment, I'm saying to myself, "Don't let daylight catch me again? Don't I have a four-year-old son sleeping in the room?"

I said, "I was at Mary's house." And my dad yelled at the top of his lungs. If he was a cartoon character, you would have seen fire shooting out of his head! I said to myself, "I thought that he just said that he wasn't yelling or arguing."

He said, "I don't wanna hear it! And by the way, did you take a can of tuna out of the house? Your mama said that she was missing a can of tuna!" He then hollered at my mom in the kitchen. "E, did you find that can of tuna?"

"No!"

I flipped!

I said, "*A can of tuna? A can of tuna! I was about to get killed, and y'all worried about a can of tuna!*"

My dad screamed, "Go to your room!"

I couldn't believe that my parents were worrying about a can of tuna, but it wasn't a can of tuna. It was a can of pink salmon, like that was any better! My dad loved him some pink salmon, and my mama is the kind of person that noticed if anything was missing out of her house, even a pair of silverware. When I woke up later that morning, I wanted to see what my parents were talking about, so I went and looked inside the cabinet. Do you know there were eight more cans of pink salmons in the cabinet! I couldn't believe it!

When I went back to the police station later that day so they could take pictures of my car, the police stated to me, "You are very lucky. God was with you!"

I asked him, "Why did you say that?"

He said, "Because the bullet that went through your back window stopped right here at your inspection sticker. If you were sitting up, the bullet would have went straight through you, and you would have been dead!"

I knew right then and there that the hand that laid me down was my one and only guardian angel!

When I got back home and showed my mama the same thing the police showed me at the police station, she then realized with a serious expression on her face and her hands over her mouth how serious this incident was and how I really could have died that night! I told my mama, "I was so mad with you and Bonnie last night that if I had a gun, I wouldn't have shot y'all. I just would have pistol-whipped the hell out of the both of ya!"

My mama just laughed, but I didn't think that it was funny at all because I meant every word of it! I was driving home one day when I saw that same guy about three weeks later walking in the neighborhood. The same guy at the club who got mad at me for smoking a cigarette, and he grabbed my cigarette and my lips and balled my cigarette up in my face, and I set his two eight-inch braided-down beards on fire. I saw him, but he didn't see me. Now his beard was an inch and a half braided down. I got scared and I hauled a———!

Now Mary and my cousin Trapp are both messing around, and one day the three of us were all out, joy-riding with me driving, and the both of them in the backseat all hugged up like I was driving Mr. and Mrs. Daisey around. Instead I was the *Dukes of Hazzard* because I'm a fast driver. We were just having a good time, drinking, smoking, tripping until I went over the railroad tracks too fast and made the whole axle come from up under the car! When we got out of the car, you would have thought we were riding in *The Flintstones* car with the bottom out. The car was sitting on the ground, and we were in the middle of the road! I was scared, but I knew I had to call my dad, and luckily his shop was just around the corner. Trapp and I thought my dad was going to come and curse me out, but instead my dad came, fixed my car the way it was in about thirty to forty-five minutes, and left. Trapp and I looked at each other and said, "Damn, he good!" We were back on the road again!

Later on that day, Trapp called Jeff and asked him if he wanted to hang out with us. Since we were just going to hang out at the park, we could swing by and pick him up. I guess Trapp didn't want me to feel like a third wheel so we picked Jeff up and headed to the park. Jeff and I hit it off pretty good, and our conversation was nice until

I saw a picture of his son on his key chain, and I asked him, "Oh, is this your son?"

He was proud to say, "Yeah, this is my son Jeff!"

I said, "Oh, so you're proud to claim Betty's son but you denied mine!" And the next thing you know, my hand went back to West Africa, and I slapped the taste out of his mouth. I jumped down off the playground that we were on, and I ran. I was running to my car with Jeff chasing behind me. I was able to get to my car with my bat in the trunk. I was able to get to it, and when I swung it to try to knock his head off, I swung it so hard that it flew right out of my hand. Jeff ran to go and pick it up. As soon as he was about to swing and hit me with it, Trapp body-slammed him to the ground and told him, "Man, I sat up there and watched you hit this girl in the back of her head with a screw driver and didn't do anything. I'll be damned if I let you hit her this time!"

Jeff said, "So you, my people, and you gonna take up for her, then I'ma beat your a—— then!"

But Trapp was a lot bigger and stronger and whooped Jeff's behind that he started crying, and I started to make him walk back home, but Trapp said, "No, because we got him from the house, let's take him back to the house."

Trapp sat in the back with Jeff to watch him, and Mary sat up front with me. When we pulled in front of the house to let Jeff out, his mom, Step, and Jen were on the porch. Jeff's mom was yelling at Trapp telling him that he's no longer welcome to her house, and Trapp was like, "So you gonna flip on me like that, Auntie." And she cursed us all out and told us to get from in front of her house before she calls the police, and Trapp told them, "Well, to hell with y'all too!" and we pulled off.

Some months later, Jeff's dad called me and asked me if I could come over to their house to talk to Jeff and get Jeff to leave before he kill 'em. He said that Jeff was over there drunk and that he put his fist through Jen's car window because they wouldn't let him in. Even though Jeff and I weren't together, I guess Jeff's dad felt he didn't have anyone else he could call that could talk some sense into Jeff, other than me and the police. I guess he didn't want to call the police. When I got there, Jeff was sitting on the back porch, crying like a baby with snot running down his nose with his hand all busted up bleeding from the glass window he broke out talking about, "All I wanted to do was get in the house to get a pair of drawls!"

All I could do was shake my head and talk to him about leaving, and I dropped him off somewhere I don't remember. A couple of months later, Jeff called me up and asked me if I still loved blue crabs.

I told him, "Yes, why?"

He said that they were having a seafood party at his sister-in-law's house, and he wanted to know if I could come. I told him yes. I fell in love with blue crabs ever since I was fourteen years old. My auntie's husband who's retired from the army turned me on to blue crabs. He's a fisherman, and he also used to catch blue crabs so whenever I visited them, they always had blue crabs because my auntie and my cousins loved them also. My uncle stopped fishing, crab-fishing, or any other kind of fishing. I was told that the story was they all were watching my uncle fish off a bridge, my grandma, both of my aunties, and my cousins. My uncle was fishing when he threw the net over the bridge, and it pulled him over as well. I didn't know that my uncle didn't know how to swim. The water was flowing rapidly, and my auntie said that all she could see was my uncle going under, and she knew that he wasn't going to make it because neither one of them knew how to swim either. They said it was a blessing when a white guy who was out there ran over and jumped in the water to save my uncle. After that my uncle never went fishing again.

Jeff nor his family knew anything about blue crabs until they met me. One day, Jeff's aunt decided to buy them some crabs not knowing how to eat them, and I wasn't there to show them. They said that Jeff's aunt had eaten so much of the wrong thing inside the crab that they had to rush her to the emergency room where they pumped her stomach! She was eating what they called, inside of the crab, the Dead Man, and I was told that it was poisonous and eating too much of it could kill you. I'm just glad that they were okay. I felt bad because I wish I could have been there to show them exactly how to eat the crabs properly.

I picked Jeff and Step up, and we drove over to their brother's wife's house where we had blue crabs, crab legs, shrimp, fish, beer, wine, weed. Ooh, we had a ball. It was like old times. It was getting late, and we all decided that we would spend the night. Jeff decided that he would sleep with me, but I told him, "We are not going to have sex."

He said, "Why?"

I told him that it was that time of the month, and it was. I'm glad that we didn't have sex because I'm sure that some of those old feelings would have come back, and I didn't want any of that again. I used to be so in love with Jeff and suffered a lot of hurt and pain in the process. I would never want to go through that again with him or anyone!

Some months went by, and I hadn't heard from Jeff, so I assumed that he and Betty were back together and doing well. I decided to give Jeff a call and ask him about not only my child support but him spending time with our son, and he had the nerve to inform me, "You don't need to call me and aggravate me because I'm moving up in the world!"

I told him, "You ain't moved nowhere but from the bottom of Saxon Homes to the top!"

I guess Jeff didn't know that I heard that he and Betty had moved from the bottom of the hood to the top of the hood, talking about he's moving up in the world. Yeah, right, what a joke and a jacka———!

Nuscey had decided to invite me over to his mother's house where he lived, but I didn't want to go there alone, so I took Lamar with me and a twelve pack of beer. Nuscey and his mom lived in a duplex apartment building, and as soon when Lamar saw where they lived, he was like the Addams family house! I just looked at Lamar and shook my head. Their apartment was an unusual duplex, and it really did look like something that could have been on *The Addams Family* show. Nuscey came to the door, and I introduced him to Lamar. Lamar and I followed Nuscey back upstairs to their apartment. Once we got inside, Nuscey walked to the back room, and Lamar asked me for a beer. When he opened it, he was about to sit his beer can on the glass table, but the only problem was there wasn't a glass to sit it on. It was just an open table. Lamar was like, "What kind of bulls——— is this to have a glass table in the house with no glass in it? Just for decoration?"

I knew how Lamar was, and I had just met Nuscey and was kind of liking him, so I didn't want Lamar making any jokes about him or his house. I told Nuscey that we wasn't going to stay long. I just wanted to know where he lived and that I would be back another day.

The next time I went over to Nuscey's house, I was by myself, and this time, I met his mother, Carolyn. She was lying on the sofa, and she looked up at me and said, "Who this older woman in my house?"

I was only two years older than her son, so I know I didn't look that much older than him. I introduced myself to her, and out of fear, I offered her some candy, which was a box of chocolate whoppers, and she said, "How did you know that these were my favorite candies?"

I told her, "I didn't. They're mine as well."

One night, Nuscey and I went out to a club, and wow, all eyes from a group of females were on us. In the group was an old girlfriend of mine, Marilyn, whom I went to school with when we were younger, and we were very close growing up. I walked over to give her a hug, but Marilyn just pushed me off her and started calling me all kind of b———, and I'm wondering what was wrong because she and I were very close like the best of friends. She stated to me that she and Nuscey were dating, and I said to her, "I didn't know that he was dating anyone. He didn't tell me anything, so if anything, you should be mad with him and not me!"

I walked over to where Nuscey were standing, and I told him what Marilyn had just stated to me. He said that they were dating but not anymore, that they had broken up. Then he said, "As a matter of fact, let's just go!"

As we were leaving, Marilyn gave me a look as though she could kill me, but like I said, I didn't know they were dating, and I probably would have never dated him if I did.

Nuscey said he and Marilyn used to live together, and after they had broken up, he moved back to his mother's house. There was another time when I was hanging out with Nuscey at his mom's house, and this day, it snowed. I told him that I needed to leave before the snow got thick on the road, but when I went to get in the car, my doors were stuck from the snow and cold. I knew Nuscey knew how to get inside the door. He just didn't tell me. I ended up spending the night and the next morning he told me to pour cold water down the window to break up the ice. After that, I was able to open the door. I said to myself, "He should have done that yesterday," but I guess that was just his way of making me spend the night. While I was there, Nuscey showed me a picture of a beautiful little girl. He said that she was his daughter but that his mom and sister didn't think that the little girl was his.

I told him, "Yes, that's your daughter!"

He said, "You think so?"

I told him, "I know so because she looks just like you!"

How could anyone look at that beautiful little girl and not know that she was his daughter. After Nuscey and I spoke about his daughter, it was like his feelings for me changed. They got stronger. Maybe that was something he always wanting to hear, and for a woman, someone he liked, to confirm that his daughter was his daughter was something some females would have denied to say.

Another time when I was over visiting Nuscey, he asked me if I wanted to make some extra money, and I asked him, "What do you mean?"

He said, "Well, if you had to put some of your money in, would you do it?"

"Well, how much money do I have to put in?"

"How much can you afford?"

"Forty dollars!"

"Okay. Well, let me get the $40, and I'll be back."

I stayed there and watched television until Nuscey came back, and he came back with drugs, crack cocaine. He said that we could turn the $40 worth of drugs that he brought into $120. After turning my $40 into $120, I was sold. Nuscey and I became partners in crime!

After Nuscey and I officially became a couple, I decided to buy us both beepers, and the beepers were so big, you would have thought that they were TV remote controls. We both were so proud of our beepers that one day, at this party, I told him that I was going to use the people's house phone to call him just so his beeper could go off, and everyone there would think that he was important and for him to do the same for me. It was crazy, but we did it like two fools! I finally met Nuscey's three sisters. He was the oldest and only boy of four. I met his mother's three brothers—Bo Hop, Noland, and Jeff—and her three sisters—Bird, Bebop, and Catherine. I also met Noland and Jeff's girlfriends, Lisa and Gloria, which I found out later that they both didn't care for me because they both had crushes on Nuscey. After a while, just hanging out over there with them drinking, smoking, and playing cards (spades), they all took a liking to me, and the four of us became the Budweiser Crew—Carolyn, Gloria, Lisa, and myself because that's all we drank!

Lisa became pregnant, so now it was just the three of us drinking. One Sunday, the four of us decided to ride off to the bootlegger to get more beer. I was the only one who had a car at the time, so everyone rode with me. I was driving and drinking while everyone else was riding and drinking except Lisa. The only bootlegger I knew of was in my old neighborhood Hollywood Hills. Once I turned into the neighborhood, the police put the blue lights on us and pulled us over. When he asked us to step out of the car, he found three open beer cans! He then asked us who the beer cans belonged too. Carolyn said that she had one, Gloria said that she had one, and Lisa said that she was pregnant.

So the policeman said, "Okay, so there's four people and three beer cans and two confessions and one said she was pregnant, so the driver must have had one."

I said, "No!" Because if I would have said yes, that I was drinking knowing I was driving, he was going to take me to jail. The officer told us that he was going to give us a chance to figure out who beer can it was.

Carolyn asked Lisa, "Would you just say that the beer can was yours get the ticket, and Shannon would give you the money for the ticket, and that way, she wouldn't go to jail!"

Lisa said, "No, I don't want no ticket, and then when it's time to pay, I gotta pay it."

I told her, "Lisa I will pay the ticket for you. That's not a problem. I just don't want to go to jail."

Lisa was still talking about, "No, I don't know."

Carolyn threatened her, "B——, if you don't say that's your beer, I will beat your a——!"

I guess Lisa knew that Carolyn wasn't playing because when the police came back and asked us who did the other beer can belong to, Lisa said, "It's mine!" The police wrote all four of us tickets close to $200 apiece! I thanked Lisa and gave her the money for her ticket and said to myself, "If she pays it, she pays it, and if not, I ain't got nothing else to do with it because I did my part!"

Nuscey didn't work at all. His only job was selling drugs, which he wasn't very good at, and I wasn't any better because I would give him money to try to get back on his feet whenever he got low. Nuscey and I were dating for about six months when his sister Marilyn and I talked about getting a place together, and I agreed, knowing that Nuscey would move in with us!

Marilyn and I had found a house not far from where my parents lived. My first home, even though we were renting. It was a three-bedroom house, and Timark had his own room, of course! Nuscey wasn't working, so Marilyn and I had to split the bills, and whatever Nuscey brought to the table was used to make ends meet. I'm an animal lover, and my favorite are dogs. Lamar's sister in-law's dog had puppies, cocker spaniel, and she gave me one of them at the age of four weeks old. An all-black male cocker spaniel. He was beautiful, and I feel in love with him instantly! I had to have a boy dog because female dogs and I just don't get along. They have attitudes just like regular females, and this was one of the reasons I never wanted any girls, having to deal with their attitudes and sure didn't want to be bothered fixing their hair. I named my dog Kirby from the movie *Boomerang* with Eddie Murphy when he paid someone for their dog collar and started calling out to a make-believe dog named Kirby just to get the female's attention who was walking by with her dog! That was one of my favorite parts of the movie. Kirby acted as if he was human in the way he would lay on the floor stretch out and don't let Marilyn lay on the floor sleeping with her beautiful long hair. Kirby would lay on top of it like he was lying on a mink rug. Nuscey and I would snicker knowing that if she knew, she was going to be pissed off! When Marilyn did wake up, realizing that Kirby was on her hair, she would scream, "Kirby, get off me!" Kirby would jump up, and she would chase him all through the house. It was so funny!

During this time, I met a young female named Shay while still working at Shakespeare. Shay was from Michigan, and she and I had click instantly. I told Shay, "Shay was my nickname."

She said, "Oh really?"

"Yeah, it was a nickname that I gave to myself, but I didn't keep it because no one was calling me by that name, so I stopped saying it."

When I told her that I was going up front to the canteen, I asked if she needed me to bring her back anything. She said, "Yes, bring me back a pop."

I was like, "A pop, what's that?"

She said, "A soda pop. That's how we say it in Michigan."

When Shay saw one of our palmetto bugs (water bugs, cockroaches) crawling on the floor, she screamed so loud. "What the hell is that?"

I said, "What, a water bug? Everybody knows what a water bug looks like!"

She said, "We don't have nothing like that in Michigan!"

Shay and I became close friends, so close that she even wanted to spend the night over at the house. I told her that I was too old to do sleepovers. Plus I don't have women sleeping over where my man lay his head.

Nuscey one day warned me about Shay, telling me that she was looking at him in a flirtatious way and that he didn't care for her and for me to watch her. I thought that he was just talking until one day

I wanted my car windows tinted, and Shay told me that her broth-er-in-law tinted windows and she would ask him for me. Shay told me that her brother-in-law agreed to tint my windows, and I went over there a couple of days later. While I was over at the apartment, I found out that Shay's brother-in-law was in the military, and he was stationed at Fort Jackson this was the reason Shay and her family were here.

While Shay's brother-in-law was tinting my windows, Shay had informed me that her brother-in-law had a crush on me!

I said, "Why would he have a crush on me if he's married to your sister?"

Shay told me that her brother-in-law and sister were about to get a divorce, but it didn't look like they were getting a divorce to me. Nuscey was right. Shay was trying to hook me up with her broth-er-in-law so that she could get with Nuscey! What a dirty b——! I stopped being cool with her after that. I realized that Marilyn was kinda on the hot mama side. She had a nice-looking boyfriend who was a gentleman, and I felt who was good to her and for her. One day, Nuscey noticed a guy sneaking in her back window, but why would she want to sneak a man through the window? We're not her parents, and her business was her business until things started getting out of hand. One day, she brought another guy home with her, dif-ferent from the one who was sneaking in her window. And as soon as she got in the door, she went straight to the bathroom. I went in after she came out, and I noticed that this heifer's period was on because she rinsed out her nasty panties, which she didn't rinse out good, and threw them over the shower curtains to dry. Nasty heifer!

After I came out of the restroom, the gentlemen went in after me and came out looking at me like I was crazy. I wanted to tell him that those panties weren't mine but the nasty b—— that you're with! Then if that wasn't crazy enough, Nuscey and I came home, and Nuscey came to me, "Baby, before you get mad, let me show you something." This heifer done left a used condom on our kitchen table!

I said, "Now that done did it. You wait until that hooker gets here!"

When Marilyn walked in the door, she had just come from McDonald's, and Nuscey started telling her how nasty of a sl—— she was, bringing different men up in house and then leaving her nasty condoms on the table and what if Timark would have picked it up! She was like she didn't want to hear that BS, so Nuscey took her food and threw it on the floor, and she ran out of the house crying.

I asked him, "Why did you throw her food on the floor? S—— I was hungry, and I could have eaten it!"

I ran outside after Marilyn trying to calm her down. She was walking and fussing, telling me that she was moving out. It was either her or Nuscey. I told her that she didn't have to go anywhere. If anybody had to go anywhere, Nuscey would have to go because he wasn't working, and she and I were the only ones paying the bills. Marilyn calmed down and came back to the house with me, and everything was back cool for the moment.

Nuscey is a jokester, and I remember one day while walking out of the house to get into the car, Timark and me, Nuscey was hiding behind a bunch of bushes. When we got close to the car, he jumped out from out of the bushes and scared me so bad that I took off running! But what he was laughing about was that he said, "You let my son's hand go, and then you ran. You left my son. That's sad!"

I told him, "I didn't mean to do it, but like my boy Lamar said, somebody had to tell the store!"

My family are dog lovers, especially my mom, so when I asked her to watch Kirby for me a couple of times, she didn't mind. One day, when I came to pick Kirby up, my mother was crying hysterically. She said, "I told you that I don't like getting close to dogs. I get too attached and fall in love, and now look what done happened!"

She said that she let Kirby out to use the bathroom, and he ran across the street. A car came by and killed him. I was hurt and upset but not at my mom. I was mostly hurt that I too had falling in love with Kirby and was going to miss him!

I loved my mother, and I know that she loves me, but at one time or another in my life, I wasn't sure. My mother and I never got along, and my dad would say the reason being was that she and I were two of a kind. I couldn't step foot in my parents' house without the first thing coming out of my mom's mouth, "Did you take…" Before she could get whatever she thought that I took out of her mouth, I was turning right back around and walking out the door. I got tired of that. She was always accusing me of taking something when I didn't even live there anymore, so what makes her think I took anything out of her house. Then she'll find out later that it was my dad. It was always my dad, but she always accused me first. I was always getting mad at my mom, but that didn't stop me from still going over there.

One day, while over there, my mom made me so mad that I stormed out of the house, and as I was leaving, I decided to leave through the glass sliding door. While walking out, I tried slamming the sliding door as hard as I could, but it didn't slam because my baby Timark's hand was caught in the middle, stopping it! When I looked back, Timark started screaming. I just knew that I broke his hand, but it was just his fingers! I rushed him to the emergency room where they couldn't really do much because it wasn't broken. The doctor told me to give him Tylenol for the pain and said that he was going to lose his nail. I still feel so very bad for what I did to my baby! I messed up one of his fingernails, which eventually one day came off.

It was on a Saturday when Tree sister's Elaine was having a party over at her house where she invited all the girls and their men to come, but of course, I went by myself. When I got there, she had a nice crowd of people and all the chairs were taken up except the one that Angie and her boyfriend were sitting at. So I had decided to sit with them. Y'all remember Angie? Angie was the one who were driving the car that time when they came to pick up Jeff to take him to the movies with them. Angie, Tree, and Tonya. Angie's boyfriend was sitting in between the both of us, and as soon as I sat down, Angie's man was all in my face flirting and acting as if Angie wasn't even there, but Angie was ignoring him.

I started feeling very uncomfortable sitting by Angie's man and me ignoring him didn't do any good, so I got up and went into the kitchen where some of the girls were and, I asked them, "What's up with Angie and her man?" They were like, "Girl, he's been acting like that all night with everybody here and, Angie ain't saying a word!"

"Well, he's being rude and very disrespectful I don't like it!"

Tree was saying she didn't like it either, and she always told Angie that she could do better. Angie was a very beautiful young lady who was an American Indian, and to be honest, I was always a little jealous of Angie because she was so pretty, thinking that was one of the reasons Jeff wanted to go to the movies with her, but that didn't stop me from being her friend. When it came to friendship, I'm more loyal to my girlfriends than I was to a man even if they weren't loyal to me. The way that I view things was that a man came a dime of dozen, but a true friend was going to be there when that man came and left!

Angie's boyfriend was very nice looking, and this was my first time meeting him. He was a tall, slim black guy whom I heard was treating Angie badly! About a couple of months or so after the party, Tree called me and said that someone found Angie's car in the neighborhood but no sign of Angie! Tree and Tonya decided to go out looking for Angie since the police stated that Angie's car had dirt on her tires. There were a couple of dirt roads in the neighborhood, so Tree and Tonya figured that her car had to be on a dirt road, so they went out looking for her, but they didn't find anything! The next day, Angie's body was found by the mailman truck driver! The driver of the mail truck said that he was driving down the dirt road and saw something as he was driving by and thought that it was a body, but he wasn't for sure, so he went back. Sure enough, it was a body. The body had been severely beaten and unable to be identified due to being left out in the rain for several days. They had to identify the body by dental records, and it was proven to be Angie's body!

The dirt road was right across the street from where Tree and Tonya were looking the day before, and they said that they were planning on looking over there that same day! Maybe it wasn't meant for them to find Angie that way. The story that was told to me was that Angie's boyfriend was on drugs, hard drugs, crack, and someone saw Angie and her boyfriend leaving out of the neighborhood driving her car when they said that they stopped in the middle of the street, and Angie got out of the driver's side to get in on the passenger side while her boyfriend got in the driver's seat, and they left out of the neighborhood! After that, he took Angie to the ATM where he had her to withdraw all her money. Then he took her to a sleazy motel across the street from the ATM, where he had a couple of his guy friends taking turns raping her, and after that, he took her on the dirt road where he killed her with blows to her head with a metal pipe or a hard object! After that, he went home wearing the same bloody clothes and shoes, and that's where the police found the objects in his house, in the closet, still covered with Angie's blood on them! I was so hurt and upset and couldn't stop crying when I found out. I told Tree and Tonya to be sure they came and picked me up because I wanted to go to the funeral because I didn't know where the service was going to be held. I got off work early and called Tree to make sure she remembered to pick me up, and she assured me she would. I sat on the porch and waited on Tree for hours, and she never showed. I cried like a baby! I was so hurt and angry because I couldn't see my friend's farewell. Angie left behind her only beautiful daughter who was about five years old at the time. Angie is gone but never forgotten. She knows I still love her because I did, and I do!

When it came around for court, Angie's family were all in the courtroom, and they said that her youngest brother jumped over the courtroom wall just to get to his sister's killer and almost got to him when three bailiffs got a hold of him quick before he could touch him as if they knew that was going to happen. Angie's brother screamed out and told Angie's boyfriend that he was going to kill him, and the judge told him, "Please don't go to jail, son, for this scum bag, and I know you love your sister, but he is not worth going to prison for!"

Marilyn decided that she was moving out, and I told her that since I couldn't pay all the bills by myself, eventually I too would be leaving, especially since Nuscey and I were having problems about him cheating on me with other women. Some nights, Nuscey came home, and sometimes he didn't. I just figured he was out hustling late at night and the area where he was hustling in was where his mom moved to, so I figured he just went to his mom's house to sleep. But what I found out was that he was hustling, but afterward, he was going to lay up at another female's house in that same area! I confronted Nuscey about it, but as usual, he denied it.

Marilyn finally moved out, and Nuscey never came back home. It had been almost two months. Vib, a crackhead who lived in the same area where Nuscey was hustling, told me that Nuscey had moved in with the same female I questioned him about. The female stayed across the fence from Vib, and Vib told me that the female was from New York and that she was a very pretty girl, but Vib said that she believed the female was sometimes smoking crack. Vib also said that she sees Nuscey running in and out of the female's house, and when she sees him, she asked him about me, but he just tells her that I'm good. Vib called him a dirty snake! I told Vib that I didn't care anymore, and that he could stay where he lay!

My parents lived just around the corner from us, so Timark started spending a lot of nights over there. One day, while I was out and about, I ran into this guy whom I had a very big crush on back in the day. I mean, I was heads over heels with this guy, and I knew that he liked me too, so since Marilyn was gone, Timark was at my parents, and Nuscey wasn't staying there anymore, I decided I'll just get even and invite this guy over! When we got there, we first just sat on the couch, watching television, and then we sat a little closer to each other. After that, we started kissing, and my clothes came off. He only took off his pants, and we had sex on the floor. Not ten minutes after we put our clothes back on, Nuscey kicked in the door! I found out that some guy came there looking for Marilyn and saw us in the window and went and told Nuscey. I wasn't scared because this guy that I was with had a gun, and he was known for not caring about putting a cap in your a———, but Nuscey got all up in his face and told him, "Now she might have brought you over here, but you walking back to wherever you came from!"

The guy left with the same guy who brought Nuscey over there. They didn't know each other I guess he just needed a ride back home since it was late. Nuscey and I started arguing, and he said, "So you had sex with that man in our house?"

"No, I didn't have sex with anyone, and how was this your house when you don't stay here half the time and you're staying with some other woman!"

So he grabbed me by my arm, put me in my car, and drove us over to his mom's house. Nuscey told his mom what was going on and that he was going to kill me and the guy, but his mom told him to calm down take me back home and for the both of us to talk about it. But I was too scared to go back to the house with him. When we got in the car, Nuscey told me that we were going back home to have sex and that he was going to see if I really had sex with this guy or not. Now I'm really nervous. After we got back home, Nuscey made me have sex with him, and he couldn't tell if I had sex like he thought he would! I guess it's not true what they say that a man could tell if their woman had just got finished having sex with another man, unless the other man was just smaller than your man, which he was.

Nuscey may have his faults, but I knew that he cared for Timark and I, and he really showed us how much. One day, I ran into Step and Jen at the store, and by now, Step had a son who was about a year old, and the three of us talked for a little while. Jen told me to bring Timark by the house for Christmas because they were going to have him some gifts. I told them that I would be there because I too wanted to give both of their sons something. On Christmas Eve, Nuscey, Timark, and I drove over to Jeff's mom's house, and Timark and I only got out. Now mind you, my son Timark last saw his dad when he was only one year old, and now he's almost five. He never received anything from any of them except what his dad gave him when we were living together in Hillandale apartment, which was a training wheel bike that he found off the trash pile when he was working for the trash company and a hand-me-down jacket that his twin sister gave him that was of her son's.

Timark and I brought with us two presents both for Step and Jen's son gifts that Nuscey and I brought together. When we had gotten inside to give them the gifts, Jen nor Step had a gift for my son, and when my son walked over to his grandmother, my baby said in his little sweet voice, "Grandma, where is my present?"

Mrs. Tiny said, "Grandma ain't got that, baby, Nothing." It hurt me so bad because she could have given my baby a dollar or something. Jeff was not there, so we gave them their gifts, and Timark and I just left. When we got back in the car, I told Nuscey what had happened, and he jumped out of the car mad and told me to go right back in there to get his baby's gifts back, but I told him not to worry about it and to let them keep them.

Grace's house became our hangout house, and I remember all of us over there, Tonya, Tony, Tree, Lamar, and me. We were all sitting around the table doing our thing. Smoking weed and cigarettes. Drinking wine and liquor. Not everyone smoked cigarettes and not everyone smoked weed, but we all drank! Tony brought up a situation about Tonya, telling Tonya that he remembers seeing her and another guy holding hands in the rain walking down the street. When he said that, Lamar and I instantly looked at each other like clockwork, and at the same time, we started singing Oran Juice Jones's song "In the Rain." "I saw you and him walking in the rain...you were holding hands and I'll never be the same!"

Everybody broke out laughing except Tony. He didn't find it funny at all. As a matter of fact, he was mad as hell, but we didn't care, not even Tonya. We just kept laughing!

At the end of the month, Nuscey and I moved out of the house, and I moved back home with my parents, and Nuscey moved back home with his mom or wherever he laid his hat was his home! Nuscey and I were a couple, and he was still selling drugs and still seeing other women! Nuscey didn't have to sell drugs. He had a talent in drywall, and he was very good at it. His dad taught him how to hang sheetrock when he was fourteen years old. Nuscey had his sheetrock tools, and his dad always complimented him on how good he was at hanging sheetrock, but that didn't faze him. He still preferred to live the street life, making that fast money instead of working for it. My mother and I at the time weren't getting along but when was we ever. I used to tell Nuscey about how my mom used to treat me, but he didn't believe it until he started seeing it for himself, and he didn't like it one bit. He said to me one day, "I know you used to tell me how your mom's treated you and all, but I used to think that you were joking, but I see how nasty and different she treats you from your brother and sister!"

"Yeah, I told you!"

"That's messed up!"

I told Nuscey that I didn't want to stay there in my parents' house anymore, so about three months later, Nuscey and I found a duplex apartment where we lived right next door to his auntie and cousin. Which was in the same neighborhood where I grew up as a child, the same street when I was a little girl going to school and I flew out of the car when our mama turned the corner because I wanted to sit by the door and rolled across the street balled up in my fur (squirrel) coat and into a ditch where I jumped up crying about the fifteen cents I had in my hand!

It was a very nice two-bedroom apartment where Timark had his own room. I used to enjoy living next door to Nuscey's auntie and his cousin Tara! I would go over there where we would drink our beer and smoke our weed. One day, Tara had some moonshine, and that was the first time I had ever taste moonshine, a peach flavor. It was good and sweet, and Tara told me to be careful drinking it because it would sneak up on you, but I told her not to worry about me because I got it. She said, "Oh you do? Well, walk backward down the stairs."

I was at the top of the stairs in our apartment talking to her, and I told her, "Oh, okay, watch me!"

I started walking down the stairs backward all crazy like a soldier in war. Tara burst out laughing. "You drunk as hell!" And I was! We both fell out laughing!

One morning, while Nuscey and I was still in the bed, we started making love. As soon as we had finished, an excruciating pain came over me, a pain I've never felt in my life, a pain where I felt as though I wanted to die, a pain that if you were to touch me, it would only make it worse. So I just laid on the floor, balled up, crying like crazy for about three minutes, and just like that, it was over! I felt as if nothing was ever wrong with me, the pain was gone, and I was feeling good again. I told Nuscey that I was pregnant. He thought that I was crazy, but I told him that I knew that I was pregnant. Plus I had missed two of my birth control pills. Later on that day, we all went to the zoo and Nuscey's Uncle Neno. They call him Neno from off New Jack City because he was another Neno Brown drug dealer except one thing. Neno Brown accepted only money. Neno accepted food stamps and whatever else they gave up to buy crack!

Lisa, Neno's girlfriend, was there also. Lisa is one of the Budweiser Crew, the same one who was pregnant when I got pulled over by the police. Neno's medication was weed, something he said he had to have every day. When Neno lit the blunt, he passed it to me, but I told them that I was good, and they couldn't believe that I was passing up the blunt. I told them that I was pregnant, and they said, "Whaaat!"

I told them that I just knew. It was time for my yearly annual, and when I went to the doctor, the first thing they asked me was, "Do you think that you're pregnant?"

I said, "No, I don't think so."

They said, "Are you sure, or you just don't know?"

I said, "I don't know."

So they told me to urinate in a cup, and when they came back with the results, they told me the pregnancy test came back positive. I was really shocked because even though I felt as if I was pregnant, I really wasn't ready for another child. I was only twenty-two years old with one child already. I loved Nuscey, but I wasn't in love with Nuscey because I knew that he wasn't faithful and still messing around with other women. Nuscey was over at his mom's house sitting on the porch when I got there, and the first thing I said was, "I need some money."

"How much?"

"About $300."

Nuscey sat up out of his chair, looked at me, sat back down turned his head, and said, "You ain't getting rid of my child!"

"What make you think I need money for something like that?"

Nuscey looked at me. "Girl, who you think you fooling? You better go and sit down somewhere!"

I told Nuscey, "I'm not ready for another baby!"

"Well, you better get ready. You ain't getting rid of my baby. I want my baby!"

I looked at Nuscey, rolled my eyes, and walked off.

When Nuscey's family found out that I was pregnant, his sister Noby started spreading rumors that I was pregnant by Timark's dad, Jeff, and I was telling Nuscey how could I be pregnant by that man when I haven't been with him in five years. That was the very last time we were ever together. I was so hurt because here it was Jeff's family said that I had Jeff taking care of another man's child. Now Nuscey's sister is telling people that I was pregnant by Jeff. When was the drama ever going to end! Timark was four years old when I kept begging and begging Jeff just to spend some time with his son. I told him that time was more important than money any day and that his son needed to know who his dad was, but Jeff was more in love with the streets and the women in it, so I decided to put him on child support. When the time came for us to go to court while sitting in the courthouse in a room, Jeff had to take a blood test, and there were two other women in the room with us, a black and a white female.

The white female asked Jeff, "Do you know if he's your son?"

And I looked at him, and he said, "Yes, I know he's mine!"

Then the black female said, "Are you sure he's your son? You better make sure!"

Then the white lady who asked Jeff if he thought that Timark was his son said, "I think he's your son because he looks like you."

I was so pissed off by what the other lady said, talking about, "Are you sure?"

Hell, I thought she was on my side! So I said, "No, I want him to take the blood test so I can prove to him and his mama that my son was his son and not somebody else!"

The test results never came in the mail, so I had to call up to the courthouse, and they told me that they sent the test results to my address in Hollywood Hills, where we didn't live anymore, but she gave me the results over the phone. She said, "The blood test came back 99.9 percent. He got more of his daddy's blood than he have of yours!"

When we went to family court, the judge asked Jeff where he worked, and Jeff tried to get smart with the judge and told the judge, "I don't work. I'm in school getting my cosmetology license!"

I guess he thought that since he told the judge he didn't work, he wouldn't have to pay any child support. The judge told him, "Well, since you are getting your cosmetology license, you plan on making some good money, so your child support will be $70 a week!"

221

I said to myself, "That's what he gets for trying to be smart."

One day, while at home in our new apartment by myself, the doorbell rang. When I opened the door, there were three females with about five children with them, and one was in a stroller. The one female I recognized was my cousin, but she didn't remember me because we both were a lot younger when growing up.

She asked me, "Is Nuscey home?"

I said, "No, he's not, and why are you here?"

"Because Nuscey said that he wanted to see my daughter."

"See your daughter for what?"

"Because he said he wanted to see her!"

I told her that she and I were cousins, but I know that she didn't remember me because we were a lot younger, and we didn't see much of each other back then. She said that I kinda looked familiar. I told her who my mother was, and she knew my mother, and I told her that my mother was her dad's second cousin. I told her to wait at the door and to give me just a minute to call Nuscey. I called over to Nuscey's mama's house, and in a very loud and sarcastic voice, I asked his mom, "Is Nuscey there!" His mama gave him the phone. "This female who's my cousin is over here standing in the door and she came to see you. She said that you told her to bring her little girl over here so you could see her!" While Nuscey and I were arguing on the phone, because to be honest, I was about ready to jump on my cousin and her little homegirls for coming to my house disrespecting me, but when I turned around, they all started walking off, and I just slammed my door behind them!

Nuscey claimed that he knew my cousin, and he saw her one day at the store where she told him that she had a daughter, and he said the only reason he told her that he wanted to see her daughter was because my cousin was claiming that Nuscey could have been the father of her daughter, which would have shown him cheating on me with my cousin because the little girl was just a toddler. I never found out if Nuscey was the father of my cousin's daughter or not, and to be honest, I don't believe she even knew who the daddy was since she was on her fifth child! I let it go as always and went on with life.

One day, Nuscey and I decided to go to the flea market just to look around, and Nuscey saw a man who was selling snakes, so he decided that he wanted one.

"What are you going to do with a snake?" I asked. I contested it, but he bought the snake anyway! Even though these snake's fangs were removed so they couldn't bite, I told Nuscey, "I'm afraid of snakes and I'm pregnant!"

I told Nuscey that I heard of snakes killing newborn babies because the snake smelled milk around the baby's mouth and suffocated the baby by wrapping himself around the baby's mouth! I told Nuscey that if he brought that snake, it wasn't coming in the house around me, and it was sleeping outside. Nuscey brought the snake, and it stayed outside in a cage that he brought for it.

The next day, Nuscey decided to take the snake over to his mom's house to show the snake off to his family and everyone in the neighborhood while walking down the street. Nuscey was acting like this was his pet snake Sam whom he had for years! Nuscey had the snake around his neck while he was pimping with his walk, not knowing the snake was wrapping himself around Nuscey's neck! Nuscey started feeling the snake getting tight around his neck, and then he panicked and was yelling for someone to get the snake from around his neck! Each person he went to asking them to get the snake off him ran. No one wanted to touch the snake. Everyone was looking at him like he was crazy and laughing at him at the same time until finally his cousin D Hop came and helped him take the snake from around his neck. I said to myself, "That's what he gets from trying to show off in front of everyone!"

Nuscey decided to take the snake back to the flea market to get his money back, but the man who sold him the snake stated that he would take the snake back, but he couldn't refund Nuscey back his money, and Nuscey was furious! "Why I can't get my money back, man? This snake tried to kill me!"

The man said, "Because the snake has a cold."

Nuscey and I looked at each other and simultaneously said, "Got a cold?"

"Yes, if you look, you can see bubbles coming out of the snake's nose." And sure enough, bubbles were coming out of the snake's nose. I said to myself, "I guess he got a cold from sleeping outside?" Nuscey was mad because he was out of fifty bucks, but there was nothing he could do, so we just left.

I moved out of the apartment after two months of living there. For one, I was tired of paying most of the bills, and I was just tired of Nuscey's lies, so I decided to move back home. I didn't want to, but I had to do what I had to do! I never told my parents that I was even pregnant because I never would have heard the last of that! While living there with my parents and older brother, we both had to pay my parents something for living there. My payment was $25 a week, plus I was putting food in the house with my food stamps while my brother was only paying $25 every other week. I thought it was unfair, and I spoke to my parents about it, and they brought to my attention that it was two of us there, my son and me. I felt like it was still unfair that my brother only had to pay $50 a month whereas I was paying $100 a month plus putting food in the house, not just for my son and I, but for everyone. After about a month living back at home, Nuscey begged for me to come back to the apartment. He said that he would do more with helping me with the bills, keeping the house clean, and staying home more. I agreed and went back like a dummy, the good times only lasted for two weeks, and I found myself moving back home again!

After a couple of weeks living back home, a friend of the family who was a realtor asked me if I was interested in buying a home. I wasn't because I just didn't think that I could afford buying a home. Then he told me, "Why would you want to pay rent for someone else's home when you can pay for your own?" which made sense. He also asked me if I ever heard of Hud Homes, and I told him no, so he explained it to me that Hud Homes were homes brought "as is" and that if I was interested, I would have to put down $500 to secure the home but most homes had a waiting list. If the person or persons before me decided that they wanted that home, then I could either get my money back or just put the $500 back down on another house. I found a house that I liked and put down the $500 that I borrowed from my brother. The house was nice on the outside, but it needed a lot of repairs once we were able to go inside. I had decided that I didn't want the house, and the only way I was able to receive my money back was to wait to see if the two people who were in front of me wanted the house or wait until it was my turn to choose whether or not if I wanted it.

The two persons who was ahead of me turned the house down as well, and when it came my turn, I was able to receive my $500 back, which I gave back to my brother. So now I've been back at my parents' house for about two months, and Nuscey knew how much my mother and I bumped heads. Since I was now pregnant with his child, he was just ready for me to get out of there, but where would I go? He knew I wasn't moving in with his mother and sisters. I was still thinking about having an abortion when I was just mentioning it to Ms. Helen on my job while still working at Shakespeare. Ms. Helen begged me to have my child, and she would take care of it! I knew that she was serious, so I told Ms. Helen, "Ms. Helen if I'm going to carry my child for nine months, then I'm going to keep my child." Ms. Helen knew I was very serious about having an abortion. I really want to thank Ms. Helen for stepping in and helping me to keep another one of the greatest gifts that God gave me! I remember Ms. Helen telling me a funny story about her granddaughter who was two years old at the time. Ms. Helen said that she was keeping her granddaughter on this particular day for her daughter who had to work. Ms. Helen said that she was sitting on the bed talking on the telephone when the next thing she knew, someone had knocked her upside her head. She said that she grabbed her head and instantly thought that someone had broken into her house and had knocked her upside her head when it was really her granddaughter. She said that her daughter buys her granddaughter the glass baby bottles instead of the plastic ones, and the granddaughter was trying to get her attention to put something in her bottle, but Ms. Helen wasn't paying her any attention because she was on the phone. Ms. Helen said that she almost forgot that her granddaughter was two years old! Meaning her reflex almost made Ms. Helen punch her granddaughter! I thought that it was hilarious.

One day, I got a call while at work, and it was the realtor, Mr. Gary. He called me to tell me that he had the perfect house for me and that he wanted to meet me over there after work, which wasn't far from the job. I was a little hesitant because I just didn't want to be disappointed again, but I decided to meet him over to the house, and once I got there, it looked nice on the outside, small but nice. We walked inside, and it was still nice, but I was still undecided about it until we walked through the kitchen that led to about four steps that lead down to the living room area that was just so romantic and cozy with three big bay windows and a big fireplace, something I always wanted. I fell in love! I told Mr. Gary, "I want it!" During this time, the interest rate for houses was at a 4 percent rate.

Mr. Gary told me, "Yes, this was a nice house but because the interest rate was at its lowest, you and your fiancé could put both of your incomes together and get a bigger home!"

I looked directly into Mr. Gary's eyes, and I told him, "My boyfriend and our relationship is always on the ups and down, more down than up, so I would rather get something that I could afford myself just in case!"

It was settled. I decided that I would get the house and put the down payment down with my money that I had saved up in the bank along with my income taxes.

I was so excited about the house. I told my family, and they too were excited for me, stating that it was a big step for me. A couple of weeks later, my mother asked me to ride to the store with her. She then turned to me and asked, "Shannon, are you pregnant?"

I told her no, and she got loud with me, "You telling a d—— lie because I saw the papers you got from the clinic in you drawer!"

"Why are you in my drawer?"

"Shannon, how are you going to take care of another child plus you talking about buying a house!"

I told her, "Don't worry about it because I got money saved up in the bank."

She said, "I know and you gonna give me $300!"

I said, "What I'm giving you $300 for?"

She said, "Because I said so!"

I said to myself, "What kind of s—— is this!"

First, she said how you gonna take care of a child plus buy a house and then takes my money from me. That's why I made this song up just about her! "Mothers, how many of us have them. Mothers, the ones we can depend on. I have a mother, and she don't love me 'cause all she wants is my EBT. She's a beautiful woman, and you just won't believe, but when she comes from church, she just curses at me. I want to believe I didn't come from thee. But we look so damn alike, she just can't deny me!"

Now here's a week later. I'm riding with my dad, and he's telling me how so very proud he was of me and that a lot of girls my age, which was twenty-three at the time as well as people older than me, weren't thinking about buying a house or even had a house. He pulled over, and we were sitting in the parking lot at the bank, and my dad was just really going on and on about how proud he was of me and how God has blessed me to get this house and how this and how that and how he needs to borrow $300! I mean really? Ever since I told them that I was buying my first house, they must really think I got some money. I couldn't wait to move out before I had to give them all my money! Nuscey and I were going back and forth to the house, giving it the extra cleaning it needed before moving our things in, and it was very tiresome for the both of us, but I didn't mind because I was ready to leave my parents' house. Nuscey was tired and getting aggravated. One day, while we were at the house cleaning up, he just shouted, "S——, now I'm tired and hungry, and I'm ready to go. We can finish this s—— another time!"

I said, "Okay, let's go then!"

As we were walking out the front door to go and get into the car, this noisy young female who was pretty and lived across the street was walking by and asked us if we were moving in, and we told her yes. So we all introduced ourselves to each other, and after that she and Nuscey took over the conversation. Now I'm sitting there trying to be nice and patient while this female and Nuscey was talking about any and everything, but I just couldn't understand it. Here it was that Nuscey just got finished cursing me out about how hungry and tired he was and how he was so ready to go, but yet here he was, just laughing and flirting with this female and carrying on right in my face as if I'm not even here.

So I'm looking at the both of them and saying to myself, "Now I'm going to see how long this conversation is going to last because I didn't want to be rude." So I waited and waited and waited for about thirty minutes for the conversation to end until I had to end it myself. I told him, "Damn, I thought you said that you were ready to go, talking about you so damn hungry and tired and so ready to go, but yet here you are with this female flirting and s——— all up in my face, like I ain't even here!" The next thang I know, that female was getting the hell up out of my yard, and Nuscey was jumping in the car. I didn't have any more problems like that.

Nuscey, Timark, and I moved into our house March of 1994. God had blessed me to buy my first house at the age of twenty-three! Not long after moving in, we found a snake. Well, I saw a snake while we were outside cleaning up the backyard, and the snake was wrapped around a fig tree! Nuscey ran in the house and grabbed his shotgun and shot the head off the snake! I didn't know if he was that good or just lucky. Our next-door neighbor, an older white man who was about in his late sixties, early seventies, walked over to the fence. He started yelling, telling us, "You can't shoot your rifle here in the city. The police will be coming out soon!"

Nuscey yelled back, telling him, "Well, there was a snake in my yard, and I got my family over here to protect. I was not about to let a snake bite one of us, so I shot his head off!"

Mr. Hoyte said, "Well, it ain't going to die until the sun goes down!"

He was right. That snake's body was still moving until the sun went down. Mr. Hoyte turned out to be a very nice neighbor who always worked in his yard. Mr. Hoyte had a beautiful Korean wife, a nice manicured yard that he kept up with a huge fig and muscadine tree, and six Beagle hunting dogs that he loved.

On my job, a memo went out that our work schedule was going to change. If that person had a child, then it was optional. You could keep your schedule the same unless you wanted to change it. The very next day, when I got to work, my schedule was changed, and I spoke to our floor manager Ms. Reese about it as well as our supervisor Stanley and told them both that my schedule was changed without my consent and that I have a four-year-old son that they knew about. I was not able to work the schedule that they changed me to work. My floor manager Ms. Reese stated to me right in front of our supervisor "Well, your son can't stay there by hisself until someone gets home?"

I couldn't believe what just came out of this heifer's mouth! Did she just say what I thought she said? I went off! "Are you crazy talking about leaving my four-year-old son home alone by his self so that he could turn on the stove, burn down the house, while he's inside, and kill his self, and the only thang you all will do is put someone else in my place to work, so no I ain't leavin' my child home by his self!"

She said, "Well, mine stayed in the house by themselves."

Before she could finish, I put my hand up in her face, giving her the stop motion, and I was like "Well, those are your kids!"

I just could not believe that my supervisor, Stanley, didn't say one word about that. They changed my schedule back to where it was originally, and a couple of weeks later, my supervisor, Stanley, came to me to apologize because he and his wife had just had their first child. He said that he wanted to apologize about what was said to me about leaving my son in the house by his self. He said now, since he has his first son and he loved him so much, he wouldn't dare leave his child alone by his self, and I told him, "But why did it have to take for you to have a child of your own? That's just common sense to care for someone else's child as your own!"

It was just crazy, and I was done with my job after that. Even after Nuscey and I moved into our (my) house, I still had problems with him cheating and sometimes not coming home. One day, after work, Nuscey came home with basically brand-new furniture. He said that he and his dad was together when he saw this guy. I don't know if this guy was a drug dealer, a football player, or what, but all I remember was Nuscey telling me that he was giving away all of his furniture because he said that he was getting new furniture, and he gave Nuscey a very nice brand-new-looking mahogany wood twin bed set that came with new mattresses and the dresser to match! He said that he could have gotten more stuff, but his dad said he didn't have time to take him back. Boy was that a blessing. Even though Timark had his own bed, he could have a use for another one!

Nuscey could sometimes make me happy by the things he did for us, his family, but a lot of times, Nuscey was just a ladies' man who loved women, and I should have listened to his sister Marilyn when I first met her. She told me, "Oh, you're dating my brother? He's a w———!"

I was thinking that she was only joking. I would have never thought that he would have taken it as far as to flirt with my best friends Tree and Tonya right in my face! We were all at a New Year's party, and I was about two months pregnant. Even though I was a big drinker and a smoker, both cigarettes and weed, I dare not do any of those things while I was pregnant. While we were all sitting at a table, Nuscey was feeling pretty good, and he had decided to play around with Tree and Tonya by playing with their New Year's hats. He started pulling on their hats and making them pop on top of their heads, and my girlfriends already knew how I was and knew I didn't play. So they looked at me all crazy, like, "What is Nuscey doing?"

And before you knew it, I cursed him out. "What in the hell are you doing? You just don't have no kind of respect for me playing with my friends all in my face!"

Nuscey and I never went a day without an argument, and one day, he decided to move out to go and live with his baby sister's brother who lived up the street from the house in a trailer park and decided to take one of the twin beds with him. I was about five months pregnant at this time and unable to work. The doctors put me on an early maternity leave at five months due to my job duties of me constantly lifting boxes over my head, which could have caused my umbilical cord to wrap around my baby's head and suffocate him or her. I didn't know what I was having at the time. By this time, the grass was getting tall, and I needed Nuscey to come and cut it. So I drove up the street to where he was staying. When I knocked on the door, some young female answered the door, and I just walked in.

There were two older gentlemen sitting on the couch, and Nuscey walked out of the restroom being nasty, asking me why I just come walking up in there. I told him that I didn't just walk up in the house, that this female let me in. Nuscey started messing with the TV, and I walked over to the young female where she was sitting down. I got up in her face, and I asked her, "Who are you here with?"

She didn't say anything, I pointed at the first gentlemen, and she shook her head no. So I pointed at the other gentlemen, and she shook her head no. So when I pointed at Nuscey, she said, "Yes."

"Oh so you here with him!" I said.

That's when Nuscey started yelling, talking about, "You coming over here starting s——!"

I told him, "I ain't starting nothing. I want to see who this b—— was here to see, and she said you, and here it is. I'm at home pregnant with your child, grass needing cutting and you up here sleeping around with this b——!"

Nuscey told me to leave, and I told him that "I'm not going anywhere. If anyone was going to leave, it was going to be this b—— right here!"

So Nuscey told everyone in the house, "Let's just get up out of here!"

They all got up to go and get in the car that one of the guys who was there was driving, and as soon as they got into the car, that's when the female started getting tough, jumping all around and acting all crazy in the car, yelling calling me all kind of b——, and talking about what she would do to me, so I told her, "Well, get out of the car then!" But Nuscey wouldn't let her out, and they started driving off. That's when I shouted and told them that I got their license plate number and that I was going to call it in to the police and tell them that there was drugs in the car! The driver looked back at me like, "This b—— is crazy!"

I jumped in my car and got right behind them, of course. Now one thing you will know about me. I'm what they call a race car driver. I always wanted to be one ever since my dad was one back in his day. Nuscey and the person driving was really trying to lose me, and they did at one point, but my nose senses was like a hound or just that crazy woman intuition, and something told me to make this turn and that turn and aha! I got 'em!

I caught back up with them and the place they went to was about twenty miles from the house, so when they stopped, I stopped. And when the female jumped out of the car, I jumped out of my car and ran up to her and slapped her like Angela Bassett slapped the white woman on *Waiting to Exhale*. The female ran into an apartment where she and her mom came to the front door, staring at me, and I had my blade out, waving it in the air, telling them that I wish they would come out. And that's when Nuscey ran up to me, took my knife, threw it over the fence, and told me to go home!

Nuscey got back in the car and left. I couldn't believe that this n—— threw my knife away, leaving me unprotected and left me standing there by myself where this female and her mama could have come outside and jump on me. So I did the next best thang; I got back in my car and left. A couple of days later, Nuscey called me up telling me that I had that girl scared, and she really thought that I was going to cut her up! I asked him how did he know that, and he said, "Oh, because I called her back to check on her, and she told me."

My heart sank. He called her to check on her. What about me? I'm the one who's pregnant and carrying his child!

Nuscey and I got back together, and it wasn't long after that he started back hanging out and not coming home. Sometimes he would ask if he could use my car to go out, and I would let him. I guess I was one of those women the comedienne Sommore was talking about when you let your man drive your car and you know he ain't got no license! Nuscey was never the kind of man that had my back, his own woman. One day, this guy who's friends with Nuscey, he and I had some words one day, and I couldn't remember exactly what it was about. I just remember the guy getting in my face calling me a b——, and I told Nuscey about it. A couple of days later, Nuscey had the same guy riding with him in my car, and I stopped him in his tracks, and I said, "You mean to tell me even after I told you this guy called me a b——, you still got him riding in my car!"

Nuscey looked at me and said, "He said he didn't say that!"

"And you're going to believe him over me?" I was so hurt. "Here, this man sitting up here in my car, and I'm telling you he called me a b———, and you believed him over me! I want the both of ya to get the hell out of my car!" They got out. I took my keys and pulled off!

One day, while over to Nuscey's mom's house, I was leaving out of the neighborhood when these two young girls stopped me. "Hey, ma'am, did you let Nuscey hold your car the other night?"

"Yes, why?"

"Because we saw him with your car at this club sitting in your car with another woman sitting in the passenger seat with her foot hanging out of the window, and we told him that we were going to tell you!"

Now I didn't even know these young girls, but I sure appreciated them telling me this. My first mind told me to go over to his auntie's house who lives just around the corner from us. She's a bootlegger, and that's where he's been hanging out lately. I drove over there, and sure enough, he was there sitting on the porch with another female, and when I pulled up, I jumped out of the car.

I asked him "Is this the b——— you had in my car?" He acted like he didn't hear me, so I asked him again, "Is this the b——— you had in my car when you went to the club with my car and she had her foot hanging all out of my window?"

He said, "Yeah, this the b——— I had in your car, and what?" Nuscey held his hand out to the female to grab her hand and told her, "Come on, baby. Let's go!"

I was already hurt when he told me, "Yeah, this the women I had in your car!" but he really hurt me when he reached out to grab her hand and told her, "Come on, baby. Let's go!"

They started walking down the street, what they did that for, I got in my car with his aunt standing outside looking at me, and I guess the look I gave his aunt, she already knew what I was about to do. I was driving off, and she yelled to me, "Shannon, don't do it. He ain't worth it!" The aunt knew I was going to run the both of them over! I pressed my foot on the gas almost running Nuscey over, but he jumped out of the way while pushing the girl over. I just kept going, and I went home to cry my eyes out. It was three o'clock in the morning when I woke up, and I had an evil spirit in me telling me to go back to the aunt's house where he was and kill 'em! The evil spirit told me how to do it and all. The evil spirit told me to get a gas can and pour the gas around the house, on the house, and light it on fire, and if Nuscey tried to run out of the house, dash the gas on him! Then I said to myself, "Because I care about his aunt, the only way I would do it is if Nuscey's Aunt Louise's car wasn't home. I know that she likes going out of town to gamble, so if her car was not there, I'll do it!"

Then something said, "But what if her husband Willba was home?" I knew that Nuscey and Willba was tight and liked hanging out together. I said to myself, "Well, Willba gonna be a burnt-up a—— too then!"

It was three o'clock in the morning, and I even made a song about it! "It was three o'clock in the morning where you gonna be, outside in the woods…with a gas can and a lighter…'bout to set… my baby…daddy… on fire…!"

Because that's where I was, hiding in the woods, and sure enough, Nuscey's Aunt Louise's car was in the yard, and the Lord told me just like this, "He's not even worth it. You got two boys to take care of!"

I went back home! I said to myself, "God told me that I had two sons to take care of when I didn't even know the sex of my child that I was carrying! God saved my life that night and Nuscey's life too! I became a stronger woman after that.

Even though I was about seven months pregnant, I still got out to cut my grass and did whatever I had to do without depending on anyone, especially Nuscey! Nuscey wasn't there. He went with me to the doctor's office one time for a checkup, and one of my questions for the doctor was, "Why was I having such a bad odor under just my right arm when I've never had a smell under my arms before?"

The doctor said, "Well, do you put deodorant under your arms?"

Nuscey started to chuckle which made me go into defense mode "Yes, I put deodorant under my arm!"

The doctor said, "Let me finish. Do you use an antiperspirant deodorant because if so, you would need to find a non-antiperspirant deodorant. They are hard to find, but they are out there. It is because your body is changing because you are pregnant."

While the doctor was listening to my stomach, he asked us if we knew the sex of our baby, and we told him no. He also asked us if we had any more children at home, and I said, "Yes, a son."

He said, "Well, tell your son to get ready for his baby brother!"

I asked him how could he be so sure it was a boy. He said, "Because the heartbeat was very strong, and boys have the stronger heartbeat."

I said to myself God told me that I was having another boy! Wow!

It was the summertime, and my due date to deliver my baby was in July, and it was June. I was miserable and nothing I did to try to stay cool worked. During my last month, someone told me that if I wanted to have my baby early, for me to take some castor oil. Someone also told me to walk, so I did. I walked for a long time. I walked so long that my dad came looking for me and picked me up. I wasn't looking at the time. I had walked about three hours straight. Not only because I was just ready to have this baby. I was still hurt by Nuscey, and I just had a lot on my mind. Once I got home, I took a big spoon of castor oil, which was very nasty, and the three steps that led to the living room, I kept bouncing and sliding down the steps. No one told me to do that. That was just something I thought of doing just to hurry up and have this baby!

About three hours later, I felt some hard contractions, so I called my brother to come and pick Timark up and take him back home with him because I was going to drive myself to the hospital to have my baby! My brother came and got Timark, and I drove myself to the hospital doing about seventy miles per hour and saying to myself, "Now where's the police when you need one!" No one stopped me, and no one was there while I was having my baby. I decided to have my baby naturally, without having an epidural, because I had my first son naturally. Thirty minutes later after entering the hospital, my baby didn't wait on the doctor. The nurse delivered my baby, a son. And I heard them call, "Code blue! Code blue!" because he was blue and wasn't breathing! The doctor said that my son had a bowel movement inside of me, which got into his nose and mouth, and that's the reason he wasn't breathing when he was born. I didn't tell the doctor what I did, and I blamed myself for taking the castor oil.

I was so scared and nervous. Five minutes later, Nuscey walked through the door with Willba! He said something told him to call to the house to check on me, and that's when he called my parents' house and my brother Skeet told him that I went to the hospital to have the baby. While Nuscey and I were in the hospital, our families came up with some names for our son. My brother Skeet told me to name him Shaquille, which was close to my name, and his sister Noby told us to name his middle name Dajohn.

I asked Nuscey what did he want our son's last name to be, and he said, "Hammonds."

I asked him, "Why don't you want his last name to be your last name?"

He said, "Well, I figured you gave Timark's last name your last name. I figured you would do the same with this one."

I told him, "You sure knew right!" And rolled my eyes! I said to myself, "Unless he thinks me giving my son my last name would make it harder for me to put child support on him or something?"

So our son's name is Shaquille Dajohn Hammonds, and I'm proud that they carry my daddy's last name, and so are they! It was so funny with both my sister and my pregnancy. When I conceived my first son, my sister and her husband a year later conceived their first daughter! Five years later, I conceived my second son, and a year later, my sister and her husband conceived their second daughter. My sister's husband was in the Navy, and four years later, he called me up and asked me "Sister in-law, are you pregnant!"

I said, "Hell no, why do you ask!"

He said, "Because your sister is pregnant, and usually it seemed every time you got pregnant, your sister got pregnant!"

I told him, "Well, y'all on y'all on this time. I'm done!"

They finally got their boy that they were trying to get. CJ is his name, but his nickname for me is my Stankle Butt. I love my Stankle Butt that I would beat the hell out of my own kids if they bothered him, and Stankle Butt would always run to me when they did because he knew that I always had his back.

After leaving the hospital, the first thing that I had to do was go to the clinic to get my baby's WIC paperwork so I could get him some baby formula from the store, and while Nuscey was sitting in the car with Shaquille waiting on me, I found out later that he took my baby to Saxon Homes to show the same female my baby, the one he walked off with at his auntie's house, the same one who I was going to run over his a—— for being with. He took my baby over there so that she could see my baby how crazy was that. What if that woman was crazy enough to do something to my baby. I chewed him out when he told me about it later! I can say before having my son that I loved Nuscey, but now after having our son, I was in love with Nuscey, very much in love!

Six weeks after having my baby, I returned back to work and was told by the supervisor that if I did a great job and worked hard, she would consider moving me up to a better position, which meant a higher pay. I worked my butt off for about three months straight, only for my supervisor to give the same position that she promised me to a new female who had just gotten hired and was only there for no more than three to six months. We were in a meeting when Thelma told us that she was giving the position to the new female worker. I had tears in my eyes, and I was about to break down and cry. I said to myself Miss Thelma knew that I needed that extra money knowing that I just brought my house and knowing that I had another mouth to feed. My coworker Elaine, an older woman, walked up to me, looked me straight into my eyes, and told me, "Don't you let these people up in here see you cry. You're going to be all right. Now get yourself together and hold your head up high!"

I'll never forget what Elaine told me, and I appreciate her being there for me.

It seemed as though Nuscey feelings for me changed as well. He still wasn't working, but I could count on him to take care of the boys while I was at work. Nuscey smoked weed every day, and he must had been high this day or just in a rush because he was always late picking me up in my car. On this particular day, picking me up,

Nuscey got out of the car to run into the building to get me with the car still running, windows rolled up, and Shaquille three months old in his car seat with the doors locked! My baby was in there, crying his eyes out, and everyone was getting off work and started looking hysterically. It took him about ten minutes to get the door open, which seemed about two hours! My coworkers chewed him out about leaving my baby in the car like that!

Timark was now five years old and had started calling Nuscey daddy. I told him that Nuscey was not his daddy and to call him Nuscey, which hurt Nuscey's feelings. Nuscey said, "If my son wants to call me daddy, then let him!" That made me feel good inside since Timark didn't have his real daddy to call daddy. He was just a sperm donor to me!

After I had Shaquille, I decided on using an IUD for my birth control, instead of the pills. This IUD was a shot that you would get every three months. The nurse stated that after I got the shot, I would have a light menstrual period, but she didn't say that my menstrual period would stay on for the whole three months, and this made Nuscey mad; we weren't able to be sexually active because of my cycle being on every day! Nuscey couldn't deal with the situation, so he left us again! He told me, "Call me when your period goes off!" Now what kind of mess was that! It was just my boys and I alone again, but I still had to do what I had to do—*live*! I love my boys. They are my world other than Jesus, and that's the reason I have no respect for this female who lived across the street from me, and please don't get it twisted, because I ain't no better than the next woman, but I am because when it comes to my children, I'm going to protect them because that's my job as a mother. So when I see a section 8 female who's not working and don't have anything to do but keep a clean house and take care of her kids instead of allowing your two daughter, ages four and five, to leave out of the house by themselves at six in the morning to catch the school bus while you're getting back in your bed instead of making sure that they're getting on the bus, I had to do something! Since their mama didn't do it some mornings, I made sure that her daughters got on the bus safely because it takes a village! See, it's women like that that really need to think about having children, if they are not seriously ready to have children. I'm not perfect, but I would have stood out there with my children making sure they got on the bus safely through rain, sleet, and snow until high school. Now peace out.

I decided to enroll Shaquille in the same day care that Timark attended when he was younger. Shaquille went there for only two weeks before I took him out. Mrs. Brenda, the owner, was charging me fifty-five dollars a week. That Friday, I paid Mrs. Brenda sixty dollars because I didn't have any change, and neither did she. I just told her that I'll get my five dollars on Monday when I bring Shaquille back. When Monday came, I needed my five dollars because I didn't have any gas or money, and Mrs. Brenda told me that she didn't owe me anything and that she told me that my day care fee was sixty dollars, not fifty-five! I told Mrs. Brenda that's not what she told me. The fee was fifty-five dollars, and she said, "No, it was sixty."

So I told her, "Well, my son will not be coming back. You just lost a child over five dollars!"

My mom stepped in and decided to change her work hours. Instead of her working her morning shift that she worked for years, she changed her hours and started working third shift just so I could work in the mornings while she kept my boys for me. Plus she wanted me to be home with them at night. She said that she didn't believe in putting a baby in day care so young because they weren't able to tell you if someone had done something to them! Wow, I really appreciated my mom sacrificing her time for my boys and me.

One day, I went to pick Shaquille up from my mom's house, and she said to me in a mean and nasty voice, "Shannon, you ain't feeding this boy. You just dropping him off and getting in the streets with your friends!"

"What are you talking about? I do feed Shaquille every time before I bring him over here. Shaquille just can eat!"

She said, "No, you don't feed him. This boy act like he be starved out every time you bring him over here."

I just told her, "Look, I feed my child before I bring him. Shaquille is just greedy!"

So a couple of days of my mom keeping Shaquille, she said, "Shannon, this boy is greedy and can eat. He act like he be starved out after you done fed him."

I said, "See I told you, but you didn't believe me. Shaquille can eat!"

My mother said, "Yeah, I see I had to put cereal in his bottle, and he still acted like he was starved out!" My mama stopped feeding Shaquille baby food and took him straight to the table. I only remember him eating baby food only twice when he was a baby, and I also have a picture she took of him in his walker eating a pork chop!

Even though we lived in district 1 area and my parents lived in district 2, which had the best schools, I had decided to use my parents' address so that Timark could attend the district 2 school. The teachers all loved Timark and praised me on how well I dressed him and on how well his clothes were so nicely ironed and cleaned. I stated, "Don't all the kids come to school with their clothes ironed and cleaned?"

Timark's teacher said, "Child, if you would only see how these parents send their child to school like they got their child school clothes straight out of the clothes basket or the dirty clothes and put the clothes right on them!" Wow, I just couldn't see myself being that lazy sending my child to school looking any kind of way. I felt really bad for the children whose parents were sending their child to school looking any kind of way because it wasn't the children's fault. I blame the parents, but the children were the ones who always suffered.

Nuscey and I was doing good for a while, but it didn't last long, Nuscey started staying out again, and things started getting worse. I remember being over at his mother's house because that was the hangout for everyone. Plus that was the side of town that he sold his drugs at. One day, I saw Nuscey coming down the street, and I went walking up to meet him. There were these two females walking down. As I was walking up and when they passed by me, I politely said, "Hello" and the both of them looked at me and rolled their eyes as if I did something to them. I said, "Well, f—— you then!"

Nuscey got in my face and said that I was coming down there starting trouble and threw a drink that he had in his hand in my face!

I went back inside his mother's house, and she asked me what had happened to me. I told her that Nuscey just threw his drink in my face. She ran outside and cursed him out! She was about to jump on him, but a couple of us were holding her back. It was nice to see his mother taking up for me that day. I remember being so upset when I got home, I called my best friend Tonya crying and all upset, but she didn't answer, so I left a very upsetting message on her voice mail for her to please call me back! I never got that call back until about ten to eleven years later! I never called her either, so there goes one of my best friends I grew up with, gone!

Nuscey and I was off again, and I went to visit Mary, an old friend that I used to work with at Burnette's Cleaners, but she wasn't home. While I was sitting there waiting on Mary to come home, I was listening to Mary's daughter, Joann, and her girlfriend both talking about catching the bus up to Staten Island, New York, to go to their auntie's house for Christmas and to pick up some Christmas presents for the family. Now New York was a place that I always wanted to visit, and I made this known in their conversation. Mary's nephew was there also, who's dating Joann's girlfriend. He asked me, "If I were to give you the money to take them instead of them catching the bus, would you?"

He told me that he would give me $300, the amount that it would cost for them both to catch the bus, fill up my gas tank all the way there, plus give me some money to put in my pocket for food, and they would do the same thing on our way coming back! I was saying to myself, "Wow, that sounds like a plan, and I sure could use the money!"

It was December, and Shaquille was five months old at the time. I wasn't going to take him with me, so I went to Nuscey's mom's house to tell her my plans and see if she would watch Shaquille for me. She said that she would, but that I needed to take Nuscey with me and not go there by myself. I told her that I haven't seen Nuscey. As soon as I said, that Nuscey walked through the door. Now I would have gone there by myself only because I was still mad with Nuscey, but I didn't want to go there by myself especially traveling so many miles away from home. Nuscey agreed to go with me after his mom told him about it, but I was unsure if I wanted him to because he had lipstick all over his shirt collar and a passion mark on his neck. But because I was going to a place I've never been before so many miles away from home, I decided to take him with me anyway. He then had the nerve to tell me that if I would have gone without him, he would have beat my a—— when I got back home! I looked at him like he was crazy, sucked my teeth, rolled my eyes, and contemplated on slapping the hell out of him from coming in my face with a passion mark on his neck.

We left out for New York two days later. I picked up Joann, her girlfriend, and their uncle, someone who they just put in my car because I sure didn't know he was going. They gave me $500 in all, enough for me to take them up there, fill up my gas tank, plus buy *me* something to eat, and I said to myself, "Since Nuscey got that passion mark on his neck, he better have his own money!"

We drove for twelve hours, and Nuscey helped me drive even though he didn't have a license. We stopped twice to fill up and to eat. When we got to New York, Nuscey and I were so excited that I forgot all about the hickey on his neck! Nuscey told me that he came to New York once with his oldest daughter's mother, and it was so long ago that he had forgotten what it still looked like. We went straight to Joann's auntie's apartment building that put you in the mind of the apartments on *Good Times*. I hit the button on the elevator and was about to step on until Nuscey pulled me back because the elevator was out of service! I was like, "Oh my god, what if a child was trying to get on this elevator and kill themselves?" Joanne and her uncle were like, "Oh, believe me, these kids in the building knows not to get on this elevator!" Once inside, Nuscey and I introduced ourselves to everyone, and they told us to make ourselves at home. Even though we were sitting inside, it was still cold as hell inside their apartment. They had their heat furnace blowing high, but the window was wide-open, letting all the heat out. I'm saying to myself, "What's the need to have the heat blowing if you gonna have the window open. Maybe that's just the way they do it here in New York?"

Their apartment and furniture weren't in any good condition, and they had a roof leak with a little bucket that was barely catching the water because most of it was on the floor. Joann's girlfriend that rode with us started arguing with another female that was there. The argument that they were having was about Joann's cousin who we left back in Columbia, the same guy that gave me the money for bringing Joann them here. The problem was that both Joann's girlfriend and the female here in New York were both messing with the same guy, and the next thang you know, the fight was on! I mean, they were fighting like cats and dogs. Nuscey and I were just watching and getting out of the way because we didn't know these people! After the fight was over, basically, after Joann's homegirl got her a——whooped, Joann's uncle asked if we wanted to go and get something to eat, and the only ones were hungry was Nuscey and myself. So the uncle took us around the corner to the main strip. We had a choice from Chinese, seafood, burgers, or hoagie. He asked us if we ever tried a hoagie.

I said, "What's a hoagie?" and he took us into this store where this guy was making a sandwich that looked just like a sub. I said, "Oh, a sub sandwich!"

He said, "This ain't no sub sandwich, and don't let them hear you called it a sub, baby. This is something you ain't never had in South Carolina!" So Nuscey and I got a hoagie a piece, and he was right. I'm still talking about that hoagie to this day, and no, it's something I ain't never had in South Carolina!

After we got back to the apartment, it was getting late, and the female who beat up Joann's girlfriend asked Nuscey and I if we wanted to stay in her apartment since it was kind of crowded in Joann's auntie's apartment, and we agreed. I'm glad we did because her apartment was much better and nicer. She told us that she knew that we probably would have preferred staying there where it was much nicer and more comfortable, and we told her that we appreciate it because we did big time. The next day, Nuscey and I met their two cousins, Country and Big Time, two big cocky dudes who were brothers. Both of them were cool, and the first thang they asked us was if we smoked weed. They told us that there were different kinds of flavors of weed like chocolate, vanilla, purple, high tide, etc. There were just so many different types to choose from. They informed us that nothing went on during the day, that most people were sleep during the day and party all night. We went over to Big Time's apartment. He stayed in a high-rise apartment building that was so tall, we were frightened by just looking down.

We were having a good time sightseeing, but we only stayed in Staten Island. We went to the grocery store, and everything they got, they paid for with food stamps! Beer and cigarettes! We even paid for our Chinese food with food stamps! Nuscey and I both said, "Y'all got it good here. We couldn't dare pay for beer, cigarettes, and Chinese food with food stamps back at home!"

"That's because the people here don't care because they're going to turn those stamps in for cash anyway!"

The next day, Sunday, we were back over to Joann's auntie's house where they were getting all the Christmas packages together, and I was telling them that I was going to leave that day because I had a five-month-old baby that I had to get back to. Country told me that I wasn't able to leave so soon like that because the people there in New York always knew who the visitors were and that they pay attention to stuff like that.

I was like "What that got to do with me?"

He said, "What that got to do with you? You can't just come here and turn around and go back home. They look at stuff like that!"

That's when Nuscey said, "Baby, I knew something was going on."

I said, "Going on like what?"

Then Country said, "Don't you know that these Christmas packages boxes has weed in them!"

I said, "No, I didn't. All I knew was that Joann and y'all cousin back in South Carolina told me that they was going to give me $300 to bring them here, money to fill up my car, and money to eat with. He gave me five hundred, and he told me that I would get the same when I got here!"

Country said, "Oh, he did, did he!"

So Country called the cousin and asked him why did he tell me that I was going to get my money when I got there in New York when he was supposed to be the one to give me all my money up front coming and going! Both of them started arguing back and forth on the phone until Country just hung up in his face. I told them that I didn't know anything about no drugs, weed, or anything else going back in my car, and that nothing was going back in my car because I wasn't doing it!

Country got upset and got all up in my face talking in his New York accent! "So you mean to tell me you ain't taking the packages back because you thought that you were going to get your money when you got here?"

I said, "No, I ain't taking no packages back in my car period for nobody. Plus I ain't getting my money so hell no, I ain't doing it!"

I'm looking at Nuscey's lil punk a—— letting this dude get all up in my face, and then Nuscey said, "Well, Shannon, I knew that the money was just too good, and drugs had to be involved."

"Well, if you knew it, why you didn't tell me?"

"Because I thought you knew!"

"Don't you think if I knew, I would have said something?"

So Country was like, "So you ain't taking the packages back?"

I told him, "As far as I'm concerned, ain't nobody going back in my car, but me and my baby daddy. Now how about that!"

Here goes Nuscey scary a—— again taking up for the people in the house talking about, "Well, Shannon, we did bring them up here, so just suck it up and do what you said that you were going to do, and you will just know the next time."

I told him, "Well, why don't I just leave your a—— here with them, and y'all can find a way back home!"

Country's brother Big Time was the coolest, and I really liked him better than Country, so Big Time pulled me to the side. He apologized to me for being misled about the deal, and he told me because I made a deal, it's always good to do what I said I would do and that the next time to just get all of my money up front, but I told him, "There won't be a next time!"

He promised me that when we got back home, he would make sure that I was compensated for taking the packages back home! He told me not to worry. They sprayed all the packages, and there were a lot of packages, with a spray that even the police dogs couldn't detect. And they wrapped the boxes well with Christmas wrap since it was in December and a couple of weeks before Christmas! On our way back home, I was nervous as hell and decided that no one was going to help me drive back but me. Joann's uncle stayed back in New York, and I noticed that each time Nuscey would talk to both Joann and her homegirl, they would have a conversation with laughs and giggles. And each time I would say something, they wouldn't say anything, just grunt, rolled their eyes, and acted like they had an attitude. So I told them, "Y'all practically flirting in my face with my baby daddy because every time he say something to y'all, it's all conversation and laughs, and when I say something, y'all act like y'all got an attitude sucking your teeth, grunting, and rolling your eyes at me up here in my car!"

Joann and her homegirl started mouthing off and talking junk up in my car. I guess they didn't know me very well because those that do will tell you that I will put your a—— out of my house and my car quick, fast, and in a hurry! Joann and her homegirl was talking big noise, so I told her homegirl, "Oh, I see you all billy bad a——, but when that girl was whooping your a——, Joann wasn't your friend. She was laughing at you. Now y'all get out of my car and call somebody to come and get ya!"

I pulled over, got out, and open the door for them. "Now get to steppin'!" and put their a—— out on the side of the road. When I told Nuscey to give them their Christmas packages, they acted like they were about to cry until Nuscey told me not to put them out because I got them from Columbia, so I needed to take them back to Columbia.

Once they got back into the car, nobody said nothing for about an hour or two. I decided to break the ice, and I told Joann how much her mom and I were close, and I'm sure that she would be very upset with the both of us if she knew that this was going on. Joann apologized for her actions and said that she understood. We both forgave each other, and I drove all the way back home by myself nonstop. I wouldn't give that wheel up for nothing. I drove about ten to eleven hours straight, and everyone kept telling me that I was falling asleep, so I told them to stay up and keep me from falling asleep because no one was driving this car because no one had a license but me! I drove until I couldn't drive anymore. When I saw the south of the border, I said, "We're home!" pulled over and passed out! Nuscey pulled me over to the passenger seat and drove us the rest of the way. When we got to our destination to drop Joann and her homegirl off, her cousin was there waiting on us, and he told us that Country and his brother Big Time told him to compensate me for bringing the packages back. They gave me a couple ounces of weed's street value was about five to seven hundred dollars. I was just glad to be back home with my baby, and I thank the Lord for allowing us to make it back safe, and I promised myself that I would never do anything like that again!

Once we gotten back to pick up Shaquille, Nuscey decided that he was going back home with us. The next day, after leaving Nuscey's mom's house on our way going home, we saw a baby Rottweiler walking in the streets, and we're both dog lovers, and Rottweilers are both our favorite. When we stopped at the Stop sign, we opened up the back door and whistled at the dog, not knowing what he would have done and the damn dog jumped in the back seat with Timark and Shaquille in his car seat. Everyone started screaming because we didn't know exactly what the dog was going to do, but to our amazement, he didn't do anything. He sat there as though he was a part of the family. We all laughed and drove off. When we got home with our new dog, we named him JB! Nuscey was still selling drugs, but I was the breadwinner because the little bit of money that he came home with to help with the bills was nothing, and I stress to him all the time about finding a job with the trade he had with dry wall! The family life lasted a couple of months, and our relationship was off again. It was a routine that I was used to, either me putting Nuscey out or him just leaving on his own!

During this time, I decided that I too would start selling drugs. I've bought this house, I have two children, and I needed the extra money. I went to Nuscey's Uncle Neno and told him that I wanted to buy some crack to make some money and that I needed him to show me how to cut it up, and he did. He showed me what a nickel, dime, twenty, thirty, fifty, and a slab, which was a hundred piece looked like which was the size and shape of your pinky finger, maybe just a little smaller. Now I knew a little about selling drugs because of what I saw from Nuscey. Plus I knew mostly everyone that he knew so one day, while over to his mother's house with his mother and Gloria. Gloria is Nuscey's other uncle's girlfriend and one of the Budweiser Crew. I asked Nuscey's mother and Gloria if they would watch Shaquille for me while I made a run and told them that I would be right back. I was gone for about three to four hours. When I got back, I had money stuff all down in both of my socks because I was too scared to put the money in my pockets. When I counted my money, I had about seven or eight hundred dollars! I only spent about $150 to $200! After that night, I was hooked.

Some of my customers knew that I worked during the day, so most of them waited until I got off. The rest just went somewhere else. I made my rounds before I picked my boys up from my mom's house, and if I was at home, when I got a phone call, no matter what time it was, as long as it was twenty dollars or more, I would leave my boys in the house asleep by themselves at different times at night just to go and make my drug runs. One day, I got careless with Shaquille in the car. Shaquille was in the front seat in his car seat, and I stopped by the house to get something. I jumped out of the car and left some of the drugs on the front seat. When I came back, it looked like Shaquille had a piece of crack on the side of his mouth! I freaked out. I opened my son's mouth praying that he didn't get ahold of my drugs. I just knew that he did, and I just didn't know what to do or what was going to happen next. I didn't want my son dying over me being careless, and I just knew I was going to jail. I was scared and nervous that I didn't want to call anyone, so I waited for about ten to fifteen minutes to see how my child would react but nothing happened. I still feel that my child ate some of my drugs because some of it I couldn't find, but God was with him and me!

My hangout spot for selling my drugs was in the neighborhood where Nuscey's mom lived because everyone around there knew Nuscey, and they knew that I was Nuscey's baby mother and knew that I too had dope for sale. When Nuscey saw me standing at the boarder house on the corner, he got up in my face, "What's this I hear about you selling drugs!"

"Well, I gotta do what I gotta do, because you're not there to help me take care of our son nor the bills!"

He then told me, "You ain't got no business being out here on this street corner, talking about selling drugs!"

"I can take care of myself!"

We both were arguing back and forth nose to nose until he kissed me and we both embraced each other in a passionate kiss. I guess we just missed each other. We left and went back to his mother's house to get Shaquille, and we went home. The relationship was good again for a little while. Nuscey's mom's house was our hangout spot. I would sit around with the ladies, drinking beer with the Budweiser Crew, Nuscey's mom, Lisa, Gloria, and myself! We all had gotten very close with each other, we were now family. The four of us would sit out on the porch drinking beer, smoking weed, playing our music, and just having a good time while watching Nuscey walk up, down and around the neighborhood selling drugs. We knew that Shaquille was a daddy's boy. Shaquille would cry nonstop. Even I couldn't get him to stop crying. Nuscey's mom would holler off the porch to someone walking by "If you see my son tell him I said I need him to come here and put his son to sleep!"

As soon as Nuscey walked through the door and grab his son, that boy would stop crying every time, and we all would just look at each other and shake our heads with a laugh.

One day, Gloria and I rode over to Neno's and Lisa's house looking for some weed. Neno was one of those smooth-talking, smooth-acting kinda guys who loved his weed. It was his breakfast, lunch, and dinner. He said he just had to have it, and he couldn't do without it. The one thing I could say about Neno is that he made sure that he provided for his family and you too, if you needed it. Neno was generous and knew how to have a good time, cooking out and having parties for family and friends. When Gloria and I got to Neno's house, he told us that all he had was the joint that he had in his hand, which looked like a blunt. Neno didn't smoke his weed in cigar wraps like we did. He said that he wasn't wasting his weed by putting it in a cigar wrap because it didn't take all that to get high. Neno rolled his weed using 1.5 top sheet rolling paper, sticking about four to six sheets together to make him a fat joint because he said that the cigar paper hurts his throat. Neno broke the joint, and gave Gloria and me half of it, and we left. Gloria and I smoked the joint together over to Nuscey's mom's house, and afterward, I got Shaquille and we went home.

When I pulled up in the driveway, I was high as a kite. I was so high that my heart started beating faster than it ever beaten before, and I felt higher than I ever felt before. I was saying to myself, "What in the world did Neno give us? Was he trying to kill us? What was in that weed?"

Here I was with my baby sitting in my driveway, and I'm feeling and thinking as though I was about to die. I didn't want my son here in his car seat alone in the car if I died on him! So I called Nuscey on the cell phone, and I was breathing very hard and talking very slow. "Hey, Nuscey. This is Shannon…I'm sitting in the car in the driveway with Shaquille, and Gloria and I stopped by Neno's house… And he gave us a piece of joint, and we both smoked it. And now I'm about to die!"

He said, "What!"

I said, "Yeah…Neno gave us a piece of joint, and I'm about to die, and I need for you to come and get Shaquille!"

Nuscey said, "You ain't about to die. You just done smoked some good weed!" And he cracked up laughing! About two to three minutes later my high came down, and I was so relieved. I told myself that I would never smoke anything else! Well, anything else that was already rolled, and that was a lie too!

While Lisa was in the hospital recuperating from delivering her and Neno's daughter. she said that Neno called her up because he and another one of his partners were together and that he needed to know how to spell "Applied."

Lisa said, "A-P-P-L-I-E-D. Applied. What are you applying for a job?"

He said, "No, I need to know how to spell *applied* to write on these paper tags to put on the back of this car!"

When Lisa called me about that, I cracked up!

Nuscey and I was on our off again relationship, and this time, it really bothered me because this was the time that he was missing out of his son's life, the time when he started walking. Those were the most precious times for any parent too see, but he didn't care because he loved the streets more! Everyone in Nuscey's family loved Shaquille, and some of the people in his family and in the neighborhood called Shaquille little BoHop, especially Nuscey's grandmother. BoHop was Nuscey's uncle, his mom's brother, and he was so funny. I remember him telling me one day that he was cheating on his wife with another woman, and his wife busted him with the woman hanging out in the streets one day. When his wife jumped on the woman, he helped his wife jump on the woman because he said that he had to go back home with his wife!

To be honest, my son did look every spitting image of his uncle BoHop. Shaquille looked more like the uncle than he did his daddy. People started calling my son Little BoHop so much that it scared me as if this could have been this man's baby when I knew I didn't even lay down with the man! At first, Nuscey didn't say anything about them calling his son Little BoHop but then he had gotten tired and mad and started telling everyone that his son was not Little BoHop, that he was Little Nuscey, and that he was his son and not BoHop's! Nuscey's mom had to tell him how much he too looked like his Uncle BoHop when he was a baby. Most people stopped calling Shaquille Little BoHop, and the ones that didn't care about Nuscey's feelings just kept on calling Shaquille little BoHop, especially his grandmother! I liked BoHop. He was a big, bright-skinned man. Big, tall, and solid. He loved Shaquille, Timark, and me as his family, and he showed me just how much when Nuscey and I got into an argument, and it was about to turn into a fistfight, so I just decided to get Shaquille and leave.

But let me first tell you about Shaquille. My brother gave him the right name Shaquille, Lil Shaq as most people call him. He was seven pounds and eight ounces when he was born, but he didn't wear the newborn pampers long, probably right after I brought him home from the hospital. I had to buy him larger size baby clothes because his thighs were so chunky, and he could eat. The boy was just plain greedy. Heavy D is what some of our family members called him. He was only a year old, and when he slept, he was deadweight. I had to get someone to help me put him in the car in his car seat. If I had to do it by myself, when it was time to bend down, I would have to rock with hm back and forth to actually throw him in his car seat because the pain in my back from just bending down to put him in the car seat was just excruciating. On this day, Nuscey and I had gotten into an argument, and it was like clockwork. Nuscey's sister, Lit, was there, and as soon as she saw me getting ready to put Shaquille in the car, she went to grabbing both his legs, and I would carry him by his arms as if he was a grown man who was passed out.

After getting in the car, I was still arguing with Nuscey so I said what I had to say, and as I was driving off, when I looked back, Nuscey had a gun, shooting it in the air. The next thing I saw was his uncle BoHop taking him down, but what I also found out later was that his sister Lit fell and broke her leg because she was running to Nuscey to stop him from shooting the gun. I also found out that his uncle BoHop whooped his behind that day. His uncle told me, "Yeah, I put blows to his head because I told him that he was crazy to shoot a gun regardless where he was shooting it at. He didn't have any business shooting a gun, period, and his baby was in the car. That was stupid. Now what would have happened if you or his son gotten hurt, he would have been hurt and in jail!"

Nuscey was, as my mama would say it, a big bucket of water and would get mad and cry over anything.

I used to tell Nuscey all the time that a man who fights a woman is not a man, and he damn sure ain't going to fight a man. I remember one day while over to his mama's house, he got upset with someone in the cut (a pathway in the woods) over some drugs or money. I can't remember. But what I do remember him running in his mama's house, crying and going in the room to get that same gun, and he ran back outside. His mama and I went running after him wondering what was going on. He ran back into the cut and starting shooting. All you heard was someone yelling in the woods, "Nuscey, cut all that noise out! You ain't going to shoot nobody!" Nuscey's mom looked at me, and I looked at her, and we both burst out laughing and went back into the house. Nuscey was a ladies' man, and I know when he wasn't with me, he was selling drugs or with another woman. I'm just a fool I knew I was a fool when his mama told me, "I couldn't date a man cuter than me." So she's trying to say that her son is cuter than me? See that's what's wrong with his punk a_____ now. Thinking he's the s——!

I really tried to get along with Nuscey's family, but I realized that I was just being used from the use of my services as a hairstylist and cab driver and doing both for *free*! I decided to cancel all services completely. I started going to the Budweiser Crew parties that they invited me to, but it always seemed that somebody was accusing their husband of looking at me. Then the rolling of the eyes came. I didn't know why they kept inviting me if they were going to feel like that and then get into an argument with their husband at the party. I don't know why my foolish self kept going back, so they weren't a fool by themselves. I remember Lisa and Noland had a nice gathering, and when I say gathering, I mean family and close friends. It was always like that, and it was always nice. On this particular day, a lot of us were standing in the yard when Jeff, Nuscey's crazy uncle who they call Dunk, pulled up riding in the car with Nuscey's Great-aunt Louis and her husband's Willba. Yes, the same couple who house I wanted to burn Nuscey up in and Willba too. It's not that I wanted to burn Willba up. It's just sometimes people are at the wrong place at the wrong time! When Dunk got out of the car, he went into the house and left Louis and Willba waiting for him in the car. When they felt that Dunk was taking a long time, they began to blow the horn for Dunk, and when Dunk came outside, he came outside eating a piece of chicken and told Louis and Willba, "Y'all can go head. I'm straight!"

Willba got out of the car, begging Jeff to get back in the car. "Come on, man, you said that you were leaving with us." But Jeff refused to go back with them, and they got very upset, mainly Louis. She told Willba with her fast and country, I mean, deep in the country voice, "Come on, Willba. Let's go. Get back in the car. If he doesn't want to come, don't worry about it!"

I found out that Jeff was a crackhead, and so was Willba. Nuscey's great-aunt knows this about her husband because she has been with Willba for about fifteen years and they have a child together, so she knows he smoke crack. She sometimes took him to get it so he can come back to the house and do it instead of him going to get it himself and not coming back for days, which he still did. Louis made Willba get back in the car, and Nuscey's great-aunt is a short heavyweight, meaning stout and heavyweight in boxing, who don't play no games kind of women. She told Jeff, "That's all right, Jeff. I know you. You suck dicks for a dollar!" When she jumped in her car, she burned wheels going down the road yelling back out the window telling Jeff, "I'm going to get you, Jeffrey!"

Everyone was on the ground rolling! This was also around Christmas time when Nuscey came and asked me if I had some money because he wanted to flip it to make some extra money for our boys and his daughter's Christmas. I decided to use my boys' Christmas money that I was saving for them for their presents, and I didn't see Nuscey or my money! I wasn't able to really get my boys anything. I was so mad with him but mostly with myself for doing something so foolish like that, but it was a lesson that was taught at a price. But thank the Lord the money was for their wants and not their needs. Thank God he was with us!

Nuscey and I wasn't the only one going through some rough times. Lisa and her husband, Neno, were also. Lisa called me up and told me that Neno walked in the room where she was and told her just like Angelia Bassett's husband told her on *Waiting to Exhale* that he had another woman and that he was leaving her for her. The only thing she couldn't do was set his car on fire because he didn't have one, so she said the only thing she could do was cry! I told her she was good because I would have set his clothes on fire with him in them.

A couple of weeks later, Lisa and I pulled into the parking lot of the grocery store, and we saw Neno and the other woman and her children getting out of her car to go inside the store. These were grown children who had children. Come to find out, I knew this woman and knew her very well. She used to date my son Timark's dad's first cousin! The first thang Lisa said was, "There go that sorry mother—— right there, and he with his other woman. Now ain't that something. He pushing a grocery buggy when hell, he wouldn't even go with me to the store!"

I didn't want to tell Lisa that I knew the woman. Lisa walked up to Neno and started cursing him out, and the woman said, "Well, if you were doing what you were supposed to do as a woman, then maybe he wouldn't be with me!" When she said that, Lisa got up in her face, and then the women's son got up in Lisa's face. I went into my trunk and got my crowbar and went up in his face telling him, "If you don't sit your a—— down, I will knock you out!"

Since this woman knew me, she just told her son to go into the store, and she told me, "Well, you better get her then!"

I told her, "No, I'm not because she was talking to her husband, and you where the one who jumped in it!"

When I said that, she just walked in the store, and Neno turned around and started walking right behind her. Lisa just started crying, and I told her not to worry about it because every dog has their day! Lisa told me that she really appreciated me being there for her. I told her not to worry about it because we were family, and I wasn't about to let nobody do anything to her. After that, Lisa and I became real close, so close we were always partners at a spade card game and were always about to fight each other because one of us always accused the other person for not paying attention for losing the game!

That wasn't the only time I had to take up for Lisa. I remember Nuscey's mama and Gloria was talking about Lisa like a dog. Lisa was not there to defend herself, and I told the both of them that they were wrong as two left shoes to act like they really like Lisa and now talking about her like a dog and about what they would do to her when they saw her. I told them they were not going to talk about Lisa while I was there and that I wouldn't let them jump on her if I was around because I felt that if they talked about Lisa like that, then I knew they would talk about me, and I felt that Lisa would have done the same for me!

Not long after Neno left Lisa for that other woman, Lisa asked if I would help her sell some crack since her husband Neno was mostly paying the bills in the house, so she really needed the money. I told Lisa that I would help her out, but I first had to put down some ground rules. I told Lisa the way we would sell the drugs was that we would take turns. The first sale would be mine and the next sale hers, and it didn't matter what that person brought, my sales were mine and hers were hers, especially since everyone that came to us was my regular people anyway! So when the first person came, I took the sale, and the next sale was Lisa's. I really didn't have to show her how much she needed to give because she learned that best from her husband. Her only problem was getting the customers. I didn't ask Lisa how much the person had wanted or anything because that was not my business. I just knew it had to be good because she had a smile on her face. Things went as planned, and the next sale was mine, then the next one was hers. I guess Lisa didn't like her last sale because as soon as the next sale came around, which was my sale, Lisa came barging over to where we were talking about, "What he buying? I wanna know what he buying?"

I told Lisa, "That ain't none of your business because like I said, your sale is your sale and my sale is my sale!"

So she started getting all loud talking about, "No, that ain't right. You getting all the big sells!"

I told her, "Look, what you get on your sale is your business and what I get on mine is my business. I can't help it if somebody come to you wanting something for $5, and then somebody come to me wanting $20. That was just your sale!"

She was still mad and arguing about what wasn't fair, so I told her like this, "Don't even worry about it. I'm going to take your a—— back home before you get me locked up, and you ain't gotta never ever worry about me trying to help your a—— again, I promise ya!"

I said to myself, "This woman is crazy as hell, almost knocked the man's stuff out of his hand talking about what he buying. What the hell. Now where they do that at?"

Shaquille was now two years old, and the one thing that I loved about him is that he was so affectionate. Timark wasn't. He was just a big cry baby, cried all the time, but not Shaquille. He's always hugging and kissing me, telling me he loves me with his little chunky self. My mama always said, "Shaquille's your baby." She only said that because she knew how affectionate Shaquille was. I love my boys the same so how can I not love my firstborn the same as my baby boy. Shaquille was still sleeping with me, and one morning when I woke up, I just sat there for a minute watching him. When he woke up and looked at me, the first thang that he said was "Boo!"

I said to myself, "Boo!" What does he mean "boo." Something told me to go and look in the mirror, and when I did, I looked like the boy on *Mask*! My face was all swollen. I was looking bad, and I was afraid to go out, but I had to go to the doctor, and they told me that I had an allergic reaction to the medication that I was taking.

Nuscey gave me a bacterial infection, and I had an allergic reaction to it, or I said to myself, "Maybe I shouldn't have eaten those blue crabs. Maybe they were the reason for the reaction?"

Timark was now eight years old, and my mother called me up because Timark had spent the night over there. My mother told me to pack up all of Timark's things because she was taking him to live with her because she said that Timark woke up in the middle of the night crying, saying that his daddy was fighting his mama, and she said that Nuscey was not Timark's father and that he didn't need to be around all that mess that Nuscey and I had going on. She came and picked up my son things, and I didn't have a problem with that, knowing that my son was only about five minutes away. Plus the school district that my parents lived in were better. Even though Shaquille had a bassinet to sleep in, I allowed him to sleep in the bed with Nuscey and I. Most times, it was just me and Shaquille because I considered my relationship with Nuscey an "if relationship." If he was coming home, if we were going to get into an argument or a fight, or if he was out messing around with another woman. It was always a if, and we were always more off than on, but that was my fault for letting him come back. My dad told me, one day, he said, "Shannon, I know you're doing the best that you can to have a family, but you can't make a man love you or stay with you!"

Ever since we were young, my dad always enjoyed buying us fireworks, so therefore, my dad brought some for Timark. One day while in the backyard at my parents' house, Timark was in the backyard shooting fireworks, and some of them were sky rockets. Timark said that he thought that the sky rocket stem went out, but it didn't. When Timark picked up the rocket, it exploded in his hand and messed his hand up pretty bad that my cousin who was there rushed him to the ER. I would like to very much thank my cousin for taking my son to the ER and not treating it the way my mama would have by giving him some ice in a rag and telling him, "Now go and sit your a—— down somewhere!" But we all know that when it comes to grandkids, the grandparents are going to give them all the love in the world. I think they do it because maybe they feel a little guilty with the way they raised and whooped our a——, but we came out fine. That's what's wrong with our children today. We are a whole lot more lenient on our children than our parents were on us because what we thought was child abuse growing up really wasn't. It was just discipline. We would yell, "I'm going to call 911!" Our parents didn't care nothing about that. They would tell you, "Go ahead. As a matter of fact, I'll call 'em for 'ya and tell 'em that I done whooped your a—— and that they can come and pick you up!" Proverbs 13:24 (NLT) says, "Those who spare the rod of discipline hate their children. Those who love their children care enough to discipline them."

Nuscey and I are off again, and I ran into my old friend Randy. The guy that I met when I was working at the clothing store after Timark's dad and I split up. We haven't seen each other in about five years, so we had a lot to catch up on. He told me that he was single and raising two of his children on his own. He told me that he still thought about me, and he asked me when I will be able to come and visit him. We found out that we both stayed close by each other. One day, my cousin was over at my house visiting and I asked her if she mind watching Shaquille for a little while, while I went to go and visit a friend. She told me to go head and enjoy myself, that she had Shaquille for me.

Once I gotten to Randy's house, he and I sat on the sofa watching television and started catching up from where we left off. He told me that his two young children were asleep in their beds. It had started getting late, and I told him that I was getting ready to go, but I would like to use his restroom before I left. When I came out of the restroom, Randy was butt naked sitting on the sofa! I told him that it wasn't that kind of party, and I started walking toward the door. And it was locked. Randy came and stood behind me with his naked body pressed up against me, telling me that I didn't have to go, and I told him that I did and I didn't come over for that. At that moment, I was getting really nervous because he was trying to stop me from opening up the door. I thought that he was going to rape me, but he didn't. He let me out, and I thanked God again for getting me out of that mess, and I promise myself that I would never go over to another man's house late at night again!

Nuscey and I was what you called a part-time drug dealer. When I had the drugs to sell, I would sell them, and when I didn't, I just didn't. Drugs was something I really didn't want to do at the time. I just did it to make ends meet, so I had decided to get a second job while still working at Shakespeare. I found a second job as a security guard (flashlight cop). I was working inside of a building where they made forklifts. It was a very nice and comfortable building. My hours were from 10:00 p.m. to 6:00 a.m. and at Shakespeare from 7:00 a.m. to 3:00 p.m. Since my mother worked at night, I would take my boys over to Mama's house, and she would watch them while I was at work. My job duties at the second job were to make a walk around the inside and the outside of the building on every hour, and afterward, I had to check in (call in). "Hello, this is Shannon Hammonds calling in. I have done my walk around, and everything is good!" Then around 5:00 a.m., I had to go outside and raise the American flag before I got off at six o'clock. Well, doing my duties as a security guard lasted good for about two days only because I was working at Shakespeare for eight hours, and here for another eight hours. It was just too much for me to keep up with, and I found myself dozing off while sitting at my desk.

I was the only one there, so I tried lying my head on the desk to get a couple minutes of sleep, but the desk was very uncomfortable. So on the fourth day, I decided to bring a pillow to lay my head on. The pillow was too comfortable that I started sleeping longer than I expected. So on the fifth day, I decided to bring a radio with an alarm on it to wake me up. It started getting cold, and I found one of the employees' small space heaters along with some snacks that they left in their desk. I started snooping around and found a lot more snacks in another desk as well. I was hungry! On the sixth day, I decided to bring me a blanket to wrap myself up with. And on the seventh day, I found a very nice cozy room that had a very cozy sofa, and I just made myself at home. I was like my heavenly Father; I rested on the seventh day.

I had my pillow, my blanket, my heater, and my alarm clock to wake me up every hour on the hour so that I could call in with a very vibrant voice, "Hello, this is Shannon Hammonds reporting in. I did my walkthrough, and everything is good. You all have a good night!" Child, I ain't walk around nothing. My walking around every hour on the hour was over. I was tired and sleepy and had to go to work that morning, and plus that place was kind of scary as hell. What could I have done if someone really broke into the place? Blind them with the flashlight and call the police! One day, I had a close call. Something told me to get up, and when I lifted my head up, a car head lights were shining in my face. Someone who had a key to get into the gate was coming in. Now I was scared, so I had to hurry up and grab all my stuff. Put the heater back, run out to my car, and put up all of my things before they came in and back to my station to put on my best act ever, like I was there all the time.

Well, whoever it was did what he had to do and then left. I said to myself, "What a close call!"

I went back to my car, got my things and the heater, and laid back down to sleep, and the only thing I made sure I did every morning was go outside to raise the American flag! After a month of working there, everyone was laid off because the company installed cameras! So Nuscey decided that he wanted to come back home, and I let him come back because if I wasn't putting him out, he was leaving on his own, and I felt that all boys needed a dad in their lives.

A funny thing happened while I was at work at Shakespeare, I was told that I had to go to doctor's care and take a drug test. I was saying to myself, "A drug test? They wanted me to go to doctor's care and take a drug test?" I needed to stop by the house and get Nuscey and Shaquille. Shaquille is about two years old, and while I had them with me riding to the doctor's care, Nuscey had Shaquille's zipper down with his wee-wee out pointing into a cup, hoping that he will pee in the cup, so I can give it to the doctor for my drug test.

We pulled into the doctor's care parking lot, and Shaquille still hadn't done anything. Now I'm getting mad like, it's Shaquille's fault that he won't pee. I decided to go inside to let them know that I was there because the job had informed them that I was on my way. The doctor asked me if I needed to drink anything so that I could use the restroom, and I told him yes. They gave me a bottle of water. I took it and went back outside to see if Shaquille peed into the cup, and still he had not. Just then, a lady in her car had pulled up beside us, and I told Nuscey to ask the lady if she would do it for me and that we would pay her. I went back inside and told the doctor that I was still drinking the water to be able to use the restroom. I went back outside to the car to see if the lady had agreed to give us her pee.

I asked Nuscey, "What did the lady say?"

Nuscey said, "Man, that lady cursed my a——— out!"

Nuscey zipped Shaquille pants up and was mad at me for me asking him to ask the lady to pee in a cup for me. I was just desperate because my job was now on the line.

I just sucked it up and went inside to take the drug test. I said to myself, "Whatever happens just happens."

While I was sitting there waiting to take the drug test, I overheard the doctor talking on the phone with someone, and he was saying, "A person who smokes weed every other weekend would likely pass a drug test than a person who smokes it every day!"

I said to myself, "Now I smoke weed, but I don't smoke it every day. Maybe I have a chance of passing, but I better be on the safe side and try to alter it or something." So on my way to the restroom, I grabbed some salt and put some salt and a little bit of water with my pee. I must had passed because I still had my job! I was so addicted to weed plenty of times. I couldn't wait to get off work or think of different things to do or say to get off early just to go home and smoke because I loved weed just that much!

One time, I got into an accident on the job. I thank the Lord that it wasn't my fault, and I didn't have to take a drug test. I was just only told to go see their doctor so he could check out my shoulder. The incident wasn't too serious, just a bump on my shoulder because the guy who was driving the forklift had the lifted up halfway in the air with nothing on it. He wasn't paying any attention that I was behind him, and when he turned around with the fork lift, the lift pushed me to the side, almost knocking me down. I went to their doctor the same day, and he had prescribed me some pain relievers. The bottle said to take two. I can't remember the amount of dosages, but I do remember that when I took the medication, I was like a crackhead at the job. Not that I know what a crackhead feels like, I will just say that I was looking like a crackhead. I was so messed up. I showed them the medicine bottle, and they confirmed with the doctor that the dosage he gave me was too strong for my system. They allowed for Sabrina to take me home that day, and I sent Nuscey back to pick up my car. This is one of the reasons I don't like taking medicine because Jesus is my doctor! He writes out all of my prescriptions, and He gives me all of my medicine in the room.

My job at Shakespeare started having random drug testing, and it seemed to me like each time they were doing a drug test, my name kept coming up! So now instead of them sending a person to doctor's care to take the drug test, the job brought the people to the job to take the test. So here I am again back in the hot seat, but now I can't leave to do anything, and my job is on the line. On my way to take the test, I passed by a file cabinet that had all kind of stuff on it, and there was a clear white plastic solution bottle that had something in it. I didn't care whatever was in it. It was going to be mixed in with my urine specimen. I guess I passed because nothing came back. God was with me again!

About a month or two later, we were out for our Thanksgiving holiday break. And during that whole break, my cousin Trapp and I got tore up every day. When we got back to work the next day, they called me up again for a drug test. I was like, "What the hell. Now this is crazy!"

I don't remember what I did to alter the test. I just know that I passed my third drug test, and I knew that God was trying to tell me something. God was trying to tell me that I either leave that weed alone and keep my job or keep smoking and lose my job.

I knew that I wasn't ready to stop smoking weed because I felt like it was my medicine to keep me going every day. One day, I was talking with Sabrina, Monica's sister, on the job. She was our forklift driver and my home girl. I was telling her about how funny it was that each time when it was time to do a random drug test, my name always came up. Sabrina told me, "Well, it could have been when I was sitting around Thelma one day at lunch." Ms. Thelma was our supervisor, but she and Sabrina was cool with each other. That's why Sabrina only referred to Ms. Thelma as Thelma, but to everyone else, it was Ms. Thelma. Sabrina was telling me that one day while she and Ms. Thelma was sitting down together, eating lunch, Ms. Thelma asked her, "Does Shannon smoke?"

"What, weed?"

"Yeah."

"Yeah, Shannon get plenty messed up!"

I told her, "Why didn't you tell her you get plenty messed up with me!"

She just looked at me stupid.

"That's why my name kept coming up because you done ran your mouth!"

I made up my mind that I was not going to let myself get fired from smoking weed and have that on my record, so it was time for me to find another job. I had decided that I would just get the job to lay me off, and I would just apply for unemployment, food stamps, and sell my condiments on the side, and smoke my weed at the same time since this job was trying to catch me with drugs in my system. I talked to my head supervisor Stanley, and I told him that since I was still on light duty because of the incident from the forklift and working part time after coming off worker comp, I told Stanley that I couldn't afford getting paid light-duty pay since we were getting paid by production. I told Stanley that I thought that it would be best for me to just get laid off. I told him that I didn't mind getting laid off and receiving my food stamps and Medicaid for my boys even though I was getting Medicaid already. I was just ready to get away from that job before they fired me and have on my record that I was fired from using drugs. It would be hard getting another job with that on my record, so I would take that chance instead of getting a bad record! Plus they didn't mind for two reasons, one they didn't care about you wanting them to lay you off, so you could receive food stamps and Medicaid because they were glad to lay your dumb a—— off thinking that's all you wanted. Plus they didn't want a lawsuit. I'm not crazy. That's why they kept me on light duty. I said to myself, "You made those people feel that you would just settle for some food stamps and Medicaid instead of a steady paycheck!" But it was me and my flesh wanting that high freely without having to stop for anyone or waiting to get off just to get it. I let a good job go! That weed had me hooked!

A couple of weeks after leaving my job, Nuscey and I had gotten into an argument because the bills were due and the money was low, and I'm looking at him like, "Where's your half of the bills?" And then he tells me, "You're the one who was stupid to want to buy this house!"

I said, "What are you talking about? How's that stupid? A house is an investment!"

The lights were due, and there were little canned goods in the cabinet and only ice trays in the freezer, but that didn't stop Nuscey for still leaving us. Another lesson learned to make me stronger!

One day, I was talking to Nuscey's dad, and he told me something that always stayed in the back of my mind. He said, "I've never not want you and my son together because I think that you're good for my son, but if you and my son never make it, please get as far away from those people as possible!"

I didn't understand it then, but I do now! Nuscey's dad's wife cursed Nuscey's dad out. She said, "Why would you tell that girl that when you know your son ain't s———. What you need to be telling her is to get as far away from him now!"

I heard them, but I wasn't really listening because I was still in love!

I started collecting my unemployment, food stamps, and started back selling drugs on the side. I told my mom that my job had laid me off and asked her if she could keep my boys while I went out looking for work (selling drugs, that is). My mom didn't mind. She loved my boys like crazy, especially Timark because he was the oldest grandchild. I was buying my drugs from Noland, and I would sell them only to the people that I knew. I found out after hanging in the streets who were really on drugs like the Boys, family members, and close friends who were like family members. I was shocked. I left my boys over at my mom while I was doing my thang. Selling drugs was easy, and the money was addictive! I made my rounds, but the people were complaining that I was dragging them with the weight. They said that I wasn't giving them enough with the amount of money they were spending. I told them that they were crazy and that they were just trying to get over on me.

I had to go and re-up on my drugs with Noland, and I was telling him what my customers were telling me, talking about I was dragging them with the weight. Noland asked me to show him how much I was giving them for the amount they were paying me, and when I did, Noland burst out laughing!

He said, "Man, you are dragging those people, and I'm surprised that they still brought it. They must want that dope bad!"

I felt bad after that and told myself that I had to do better! Around six or seven o'clock in the evening, I would go back to pick up my boys from my mom's house to take them home so that Timark could get ready for school! My cell phone was always going off all times of night, and I would leave my boys locked up in the house asleep at all times of night just to make a sale until I got tired of just coming out for anything. So I told everyone, "Do not call me unless it was twenty dollars or more." I was only gone for about ten to fifteen minutes from the house, but still I didn't like leaving my boys home alone while I went out to sell drugs! A lot of times late at night, I would just sit over at the crack house because normally, when they buy a twenty piece from you, that was just the tester. They will call you right back for some more, and it was like as soon as I walked in the house, I had to turn right back around. So I just decided to sit and wait for them to smoke the first twenty-dollar piece, which only took about ten minutes. After that, they were ready for some more!

I just couldn't believe the people that I knew all this time were smoking crack like that especially the Boys, my family members, and my close friend's family members. I guess they were what you called functional crackheads. Someone who did drugs but kept their life-style of living up like their jobs and paying their bills. I could only shake my head and say to myself, "How can I judge them when I'm selling them the crack. I guess if they didn't buy it from me, then they would just buy it from someone else!"

I wasn't addicted to selling drugs. I was addicted to making the money. It was easy money, and I was making some very good money in a day, enough to pay all my bills and have plenty in my pocket!

Smoke was a cousin of one of the Boys, and Smoke was from New York. Everyone in the hills knew Smoke because he was crazy, cool, and fun to be with. One day, Smoke asked me to do him a favor. He told me that he would pay me to take him to North Carolina and bring him back. I needed the extra money since I wasn't working, so I agreed, and I strapped Shaquille down in the car seat, and we headed out. When we got there about an hour and a half later, we went into this apartment and met this guy that Smoke knew. He told me to just make myself at home and that they would be back. When they left, the only ones there were Shaquille and me. I went snooping in the kitchen where I saw three big-size coolers, and each one of the coolers were full up to the rim with compressed weed. I said to myself, "So you mean to tell me this is the reason he asked me to bring him up here with all this weed, and he was only offering to give me this pissy a—— little money." I got mad and decided to peel some weed off the top of each of the coolers, but then, I got scared for the safety of my son and me. I said to myself, "I'm sure they had already weighed the weed up, and I didn't want no s—— from nobody." So I put the weed back and said to myself that I was going to get some more money from Smoke.

I laid back down and went back to sleep with Shaquille until they came back. When they walked through the door, Smoke grabbed a cooler, and I looked at him crazy, and he knew why. He just looked back at me and said, "Bring your crazy a—— on so we can go back home!"

I told him, "Not until I get some more money!"

He gave me some more money, and then we left. I told him that he not only got me risking my life but my son's life and that my son needed to get paid too because I know that he was using the both of us to make it seem as though we were riding like one big happy family! It's sad to say that obviously I loved weed more than my son. Even though at first I didn't know that we were going for weed, but I wasn't crazy. I knew we were going for a drug run because that's what Smoke does. He's a drug dealer, and after I found out that it was weed, I could have just left. But because it was weed, something that I loved and obviously more than my son, I stayed.

Weed would make me do crazy things like going to buy a bag from the weed man, and when you get there, he's smoking on a blunt and then passes it to you for you to smoke. I guess they do that to show you that they got some good weed, but all they did was get me high. When they asked me what do I need, I would just say, "I'm good!" Hell, I was I was already high, so why do I need to spend my money to get an extra high? "I'm good!" is what I'll say to myself until the high comes down.

Little do I know the next time I go back to them, they are going to get me back when they say, "Oh, I ain't got nothing right now. Holler back at me later!" Don't let you get the weed man that brag on their weed talking about "I got that fire!"

"You got that fire!"

"I got that fire!"

Now you all excited driving home running red lights and Stop signs to smoke some of that fire! I started singing my song, "I got that fire…that fire…oh yeah, I got that fire that fire oh yeah." Get home rolled it up, light it up, and smoke it, and you realize that the only fire you got was from that lighter you use when you lit it up because the weed was garbage! Made me so mad that I didn't want to buy nothing else…Well, just from him! If you do go back, you'll know that they knew that their weed wasn't any good because they give you more to compensate you from the last bad batch just to keep you coming back. Ain't nothing but a hustle.

That's why it didn't pay to be high on this day. The day I was in this clothing store and on my way out the door, my girl Sam was all quick and fast, rushing up on me. I mean, we were nose to nose. Now remember Sam, my cross-eyed homegirl back in the day with the two big safety pins in her hair holding up a piece of weave. Yeah, Sam. She came in all cross-eyed, nose to nose, caught me off guard. She scared me, made me jump. "Girl, when you gonna do my hair like that!"

I almost screamed because at that quick moment, all I saw was a face with some eyes that was crosse-eyed like hell! It was so funny. I guess you had to be there.

Nuscey and I was always, I mean *always*, off and on, more off than on. And I just couldn't keep up with it! Shaquille is about three years old, and my cousin Squeaky and her homegirl rode to the grocery store with me. After we were getting back into the car, my cousin and I both laid our eyes on one of the sexiest fine, tall, good-looking black man that you could ever lay your eyes on. And right when I was getting ready to say something to him, my cousin beat me to the punch.

"Hey you, chocolate, come here for a minute."

I was like, "Damn, Squeaky, I was about to call him over. Don't you have a man?"

She laughed. He walked over to my cousin's side of the window, and he bent down to talk to her, but then she told him, "Oh, my cousin wanted to holler at you," and I exhaled! When he walked over to my side, I stepped outside of my car and introduced myself. He did the same and told me that his name was Juicy. Juicy told me that he was just up here visiting some friends, and I asked him what he was doing later. I wanted to invite him to go with me to a party. Even though the party was Lisa's party, I didn't care because I was sure that Nuscey would be there with another woman!

The next day, I picked Juicy up, and we went to the party that was held at a hotel. It was nice, and we were having a good time, but I think after Juicy realized that the party was my ex people's party. He was ready to go, and he asked me to take him back home. On my way taking Juicy back to where I picked him up from, we talked for a little bit just about when the next time he and I could possibly see each other again. I was telling him that before I take him home, I needed to stop by my parents' house to pick up my son Shaquille. When I pulled into my parents' driveway, the first thing Juicy asked me was where I lived. Was it in an apartment or a house? I told him that I lived in a house, and he asked me to take him to my house. After I put Shaquille to bed, Juicy and I smoked a blunt or two, and he was pretty cool. He basically told me that Juicy was his nickname and he was on the run from the police. He said that in the process of him running from the police he had gotten shot. He showed me on his hand where the bullet went straight through. When Juicy was finished telling me his story, I was like, "Well, okay, let me drop you back off!"

About a week later, even though I was kind of uncertain about Juicy, I really liked him, and I wanted to see what he was up to, so I went back to the apartments to where I picked him up from, and they told me that they haven't seen Juicy in about three days.

I don't know what made me drive over to these other apartments. I just remember Juicy telling me that he was hanging out over there, but out of the few apartments that were out there, I went to the right apartment door. A young black couple came to the door, and I told them who I were and I met Juicy. I was concerned about him and if they hear from him again, give him my address. About a month later, I received a letter from Juicy. He was locked up in a correctional institution, and he wanted me to come and see him. Which I did. I went and visited Juicy finding out that Juicy was a country man who was from the country. He was smart, intelligent, and hardworking. He was the kind of man that taught you things like the world geography. Juicy was very supportive and had your back. If there was something you wanted to do, he always pushed you to do it and would tell you that you can do anything, instead of procrastinating.

I was visiting Juicy so much and so excited about going to see him that I almost lost my driver's license. I got stopped three times by the police in three months for speeding! I took Timark and Shaquille with me once to visit Juicy because he asked me if I would bring them, and I did. The more I visited Juicy, the closer we became. About six months of going to visit, Juicy he told me that he had a plan that could help me as well as him, and the plan was that I would receive checks in the mail in different inmate's names. He said that he wanted me to cash the checks, and I could get what I needed out of the money and to just put him something up, so when he gets home, he will have some money to help him get on his feet. The checks started coming every week in different amounts, from seventy to a hundred and fifty dollars a check! Juicy told me that if anyone was to call me and question me about the checks, just to tell them that I was getting paid for having phone sex services, but no one ever called.

The checks came for about a month, and the amount of money in total for all the checks were about seven to eight hundred dollars. I used about three hundred dollars of the money, and I was really shocked and impressed how Juicy was not only handling his business, but he was also helping me while he was locked up. About a month or two later, Juicy wanted me to do him another favor. Juicy wanted me to buy a couple of cans or bags of tobacco and drop them off to his cousin in Camden. He said that his cousin would know what to do with it, and I did what he asked me with no questions asked. Not to long after that, Juicy wanted me to do him another favor. He said that he was the kind of man that didn't like asking anyone for anything and that he would always do what he had to do for his self no matter what. He definitely didn't want to ask me for any money because he knew that I had two boys to take care of as well as bills to pay. Juicy told me to not flip out about what he wanted me to do. He said that he would not ask me or put me in harm's way if he thought that it would and that he knew what CO was going to be working on certain days, so everything would be okay. Juicy wanted me to bring some weed on the inside! Wow! When he asked me to do it, I was very hesitant, but he ensured me that if I do it the correct way, I didn't have anything to worry about. Looking back at all the other things Juicy have done since he's been back there made me feel comfortable that he knew what he was doing. Plus I really cared about him, and he has helped me while he has been back there.

Juicy gave me the instructions on the amount of weed to buy plus the way to dress it up so that when I gave it to him, he was able to do whatever it was he was going to do with it. I did exactly what he told me to do, which was leave the weed in its plastic bag and fold it up good and tight. Then he wanted me to wrap the plastic bag with black electric tape and to put grease all over it. Then put it inside another plastic bag and put it inside of my panties when I walk through because they don't search women down there. Plus the metal detector won't pick it up! I did what Juicy asked me to do, and it worked. I got inside, and when he sat at the table with me, he told me to wait for about fifteen minutes and to go to the restroom. Before I come out, I had to have it wrapped in some toilet paper like I was blowing my nose. Once I sat back down at the table, he told me that in a minute, we were both going to play it off and lean over the table to kiss. And when we did, I slipped him the toilet paper that I had the weed wrapped inside. Once I gave it to him, I asked him what was he going to do with it, and he told me that twenty minutes before our visit was up, he would go to the bathroom and put it up his butt, and that's usually when the visit is over.

Once visitation is over, the security guard would check each one of them by looking in their mouths and ask them to drop their pants and to bend over and cough, but because he knew which CO was working that day, he knew that he wouldn't get check. Plus he said that he would wait until I had gotten out before he walked through the search door. I told him to call me if everything went smoothly, and if he didn't, then I knew something went wrong. Later on that night, I received a phone call from Juicy. Everything went smoothly, and he thanked me. About a month later, Juicy asked me if I could do the same thing again that I did for him last month, and sure enough, I did it with no hesitation. And again everything went well.

Juicy had three boys by two baby mothers that he wanted me to meet once he had gotten out. Juicy and I wrote each other the whole entire time he was locked up, and I went to visit him twice a month.

I had decided to put my cosmetology license to work, so I got my first job at Lilly's House of Beauty and was supposed to be working under Mrs. Lilly herself. She was training me since this was my very first time in a hair salon, but I never got a chance to do anything because Mrs. Lilly was an older woman, and most of her clients were older women who was used to Mrs. Lilly shampooing their hair. If Mrs. Lilly didn't shampoo their hair, then it was her other daughter who was a bus driver. Whenever she stopped by, Mrs. Lilly would get her to shampoo her clients if she was too busy. I met Mr. T, who was a lot older than most of us there. He was also a hairstylist who worked in the salon. Mr. T reminded me of the real Mr. T, and I think that's how he got the nickname Mr. T, just without all the jewelry, and the fact that he liked men instead of women. It was so funny one day when we weren't busy at the shop, I had decided to sit up front where Mr. T and another female stylist were talking. I decided to jump into their conversation when Mr. T looked at me and told me with a straight face, "Baby, you and your lil ABC conversation need to go somewhere and don't you have kids and bills because you need to go and find a job because you ain't making no money around here. You see, Mrs. Lilly ain't got you doing nothing but watching her."

Mr. T was right even though he hurt my feelings telling me that my conversation was an ABC conversation. I cursed him out in my mind, but he was still right because I did have kids and bills, and I wasn't making any money, so yes, I left and went back to the streets!

A couple of weeks later, I started putting in applications and got a job with the temporary service working, a plant job that package seasonings and boy did I load up on some seasonings and still have some to this day! While working there for just a short period of time, almost three months, I really enjoyed working there except when we had to put on this all-white paper material jumpsuit every day. The women there were so country. I thought that I was country, but those women there were deep in the country. The way they talked, dressed, and put on their makeup! Now some of these women were still using their lipstick for their eyeshadow and blush looking like clowns. One woman cut off her eyebrows just to draw them back on looking like Ronald McDonald with all that makeup on their faces. I sure wanted to tell them, but like I said, those big women were from the country and probably strong as an ox. While I was working there, we found out that this lady's son hung himself in his closet. The workers there said that the mother stated that her son was in high school and that he was taking Ritalin medication. When she woke up that morning, she went into her son's room, and he was gone. She thought that it was strange that he had left to go to school early, so something told her to look into the closet to see what he took with him, and that's when she found him. Everyone there was so upset about the accident, even me, even though I didn't know her. We were so sorry for the mother for the loss of her child!

After that, I started getting bored working there and faked a fall, which ended up in me getting workers comp. I decided to get a job working in the hair salon again at Simply Art. It was okay. I just never like to work with a bunch of females because they always kept something going on either the coworkers or the female customers! I was working under the owner as her assistant, and one of her female clients said that she knew my baby daddy Nuscey from a while back. The way she was talking about him, it was like he used to like her or something, but when I got finished putting her in her place, she was like, "Don't nobody want your baby daddy because he ain't got no teeth in the front no way!"

I was like, "Oh no, this b——— ain't trying to make jokes about my baby daddy because even though we ain't together, I'll be damned if I let anybody talk about him because he's still my baby daddy!"

One day, I was waxing a female's eyebrow, and I took half of her eyebrow off by mistake, and she just got real stupid, showing everybody in the shop talking about I done f——— up her eyebrow and that she wasn't paying me. I told her, "Yes, you are paying me because your eyebrow is just like the hair on your head…It'll grow back. Now pay me my money!" Shorty got nasty talking about she ain't paying me s——— and that I would have to take it up with her sister. Her sister was the same female who I just got finished getting into an argument with about her knowing Nuscey, so when the sister walked up. I really let the Read Street, Saxon Homes, and the Hollywood Hills come out. I told them both, "I don't give a d—— about you or your sister because the both of you can get your a—— whooped, you wanna talking about your sister like what she supposed to do to me! I don't give a d—— about you, your sister, nor your eyebrows because they are just like the hair on your head…It'll grow back!"

I walked off because I was done with the conversation. Both of the sisters looked at me crazy and went the other way. I was hemmed up in a corner, so I needed to act crazy to get them out of my face! Now I may play crazy, but I ain't crazy, at least not that I know of, but let all of my friends tell you that I am and that I just haven't gone to the doctor to get diagnosis and put on medicine. I didn't work at the hair salon long because the workers and the female customers were all full of drama. I told myself, "I would rather go back to the streets selling drugs before I work up in here again!"

One day, I had decided to ride out to my old neighborhood, the Hills, since Tonya and Tree's mom still lived out there. When I pulled in front of Tonya's house, Jeff was sitting on the porch in a chair with my home girl Grace sitting on his lap with her arms around him. When Grace saw me, she had a shocked look on her face. I didn't get out of my car, and I didn't say anything. I just drove off and pretended as if I didn't care. I didn't care about Jeff. I was hurt because it was Grace who was sitting on his lap, my so-called home girl. Even if Jeff and I were not together, he is still my son's dad, and for you to call yourself my home girl and to do that was very disrespectful. I don't remember if I ever got an apology from her or not.

I'm proud to say that I'm a very tough and proud black woman, and I got it from my mama. That's the one thing about my mother. She does not play. I remember one day when I was still working for Mary, I was without a car during this time, and I was ready to get off. I called my mom and told her that I was ready to be picked up when Mary sent me to this restaurant to pick up an order that she had placed. I agreed because it was just only a skip and a hop from the shop, and I told Mary that if my mama come, tell her that I went to get your order of food and for her stay right here. While I was at the restaurant picking up Mary's order, I turned around and my mom was marching into the restaurant. I said to myself, "Oh hell, why didn't Mary tell her what I said." As soon as she walked in, she said in a loud voice, "You told me that you were ready now. When I get back to this car and you ain't ready, I'm going to leave you!" and she really meant it. I looked at her while she was going back to the car saying to myself, "If you don't get your a——— back in the car. Coming up in here embarrassing me like that!"

I turned around all calm with a smile on my face as the white cashier looked at me like, "Damn, she really told you." The only thing that I could do was shake my head, shrugged my shoulders, and sound all proper to the cashier, "Mothers!"

I grabbed my food and hated to get in the car where I knew that she really was going to curse me out. It made it worse when I told her that I had to drop Mary's food off. I asked Mary why didn't she tell my mother what I said. She said, "Because I was scared so I pointed down to the restaurant where you was." When I got back into the car and we pulled off, I told my mom that I had forgotten my purse. Boy was she really mad and told me, "You don't have enough brain to last until sun down!"

I one day stopped over to my parents' house, but no one was home. I noticed that my mom's kitchen was all messed up with dishes, pots, and pans all in the sink that looked like my dad did a good job of messing it up from last night. I knew that my mom was still at work, and I didn't want her coming home having to clean up this mess, so I decided to wash up all the dishes, wiped off the stove and the countertops, and sweep the floor. When my mom walked in, I had just gotten finish. I really thought that she would be happy that I cleaned up the kitchen for her even though I didn't stay there. My mom walked in the house and got on me bad about not washing out one ashtray that my daddy smoked out of. She told me, "Well, if you're going to clean up, then you need to clean everything!"

I couldn't believe it. Here I am doing something that I didn't have to do. It is said that it's not important what a person does but what they didn't have to do. I'm still doing things for my mother, things I did as a child just to get a little bit of encouragement or a praise…Well, not really a praise, but something even though a person may do something that they were supposed to do or they just did it out of the kindness of their heart. There is nothing wrong by telling them thank you for doing a great job! I promise you, it will go a long way especially for a child when they just want to please you for something that they are doing right! That's the same way with our heavenly Father—all he wants is for us to just say "Thank you," which is nothing!

Another day I was at my parents' house, and I caught myself getting mad at my mom by something she said that pissed me off, so I stormed out of the door. I slammed her glass door behind me. As I started strutting myself to my car, the spirit told me, "Turn around, turn around, turn around!" As soon as I turned around, my mom was walking up to me fast with a stick in her hand talking about, "Who in the hell you think you are coming up in here and slamming my door!" I threw my arm up to block my mom from hitting me, and she clucked me one time across my shin bone. I jumped so fast in my car and got the hell on!

One day, Lamar stopped by my house, and he brought Mike with him. I found out that day that they were both first cousins. Mike was the same guy who gave me the bottle of rush to smell in high school. He was always a prankster. I remember one day while in class, he and I were talking and he had this scared look on his face. He told me, "What's that in your mouth?"

I was like, "What?"

He said, "You got something in your mouth. Open your mouth and let me see!"

When I opened my mouth, he threw paper in it, and he and I just burst out laughing. Mike was always crazy and funny, and to be honest, I always had a thing for him in high school only because he was cute and crazy, crazy funny. I remember us getting together one day. Mike came and picked me up, and we stopped and parked behind this elementary school and had sex. It was crazy and a long time ago.

That day, when he and Lamar stopped by my house, he was all leaning in my chair like he was the coolest thing in the house. This was the first time that I saw him in about seven years, and the first thang that came out of his mouth to his cousin Lamar was, "Oh, she just wants me for my money!"

I told him, "What money? I don't know what you got and don't care!"

Not to long after that, Mike and I started seeing each other. Plus he too was a drug dealer, someone who I could buy some weight from to sell when I needed it. Mike and I were two fools together, and he really took to my boys. The spot that Mike worked at was about five minutes from my house, and after taking Timark to school and dropping Shaquille off at my mom's, I would go home and cook Mike some breakfast and take it to him around the corner to where he was working. Mike thought me bringing him breakfast was the most wonderful thang that any woman has ever done for him. I told him that I knew that he was probably hungry from working all night especially when I took him some fish and grits. I love me some fish with bones, and if I still had some fish left over from the night before, I would heat that grease up real hot on the stove and drop that fish in that hot grease for about thirty seconds on each side. You would have thought that I had just brought it from Mista Brown's!

Mike was a sweetheart and wanted to help me sell my drugs, so he turned me on to Lamar's brother, Tyrone, so he could help me. One place Tyrone took me to was their Uncle Jesse's spot, a crack house down the hill from where Mike was at. A crack house is just what it is, a house where people smoked crack, and there were people running in and out smoking crack and some who just stayed there smoking their crack. Tyrone and I started hanging out there every day, and I did very well making my money. Plus I enjoyed hanging out over there because their uncle, whom everyone called Unk, was a trip. Unk too was a crackhead, and it was his place where I was selling my drugs. One day, Unk told me after everyone had left, "I'm tired of these crackhead b—— stealing my dope when I turn my back as good as I am to them, but I got something for their a—— when they come back!"

Unk had some moth balls that he cut up in about three to four little pieces that looked like crack, and he placed one real piece of dope with it on the table. When the two female crackheads came back, they sat down next to Unk on the sofa. Unk sat up, grabbed the real piece of crack, and smoked it, and he gave the two women a hit of it as well. After they were finished smoking that piece, Unk got up and walked over to the bar and winked at me. I saw one of the females take a piece of the moth ball that she thought was dope and told Unk that she and her friend would be back. Unk just said, "All right, baby. I'll just see ya when you get back!"

About twenty minutes later, the two females came back mad as hell and told Unk, "You trying to kill me with that s—— you had!"

Unk said, "No, b——, you trying to kill your got d___ self for stealing my s——!"

I cracked up. Even though those crack places were very dangerous to be in, I still had a lot of laughs at the people who was smoking the dope!

My buddy Mike was living a dangerous life, and still is, if I must say! Mike was to me always a target, and even though I was crazy about him (puppy love), I had to turn down having a relationship with him because of those reasons and the safety of my boys. But Mike and I always remained good friends. Mike was very nice to my boys, and I remember one year him buying them some Christmas toys. Mike is good people, and he comes from a good family, a good crazy family, but they are all still good people. I knew that Mike was crazy when he came to my house, wanting me to take some stables out of his head from when he got shot about a month and a half earlier. He said that they were driving him crazy, and he didn't want to have to sit up in a hospital to get them taking out! I told Mike, "I know you don't expect for me to take them out, and if something happened to you, I'm not going to be responsible. I'll put you on my front porch and tell the people that I found you like that!" Mike just looked at me and laughed.

When Nuscey and I went our separate ways again, my buddy Mike and I had hooked up; I was always crazy about Mike. Plus he was fun to hang out with. Mike grew fond of my boys, which I always greatly appreciated; he became my supplier. Mike once asked me if he and I could become a serious couple and live together.

I told Mike, "Mike, you know I like you a lot, but I love my kids and my life, and you are like a marked man. People are trying to kill you, and I'm not trying to risk my boys and my life because we could all be riding together and someone could start shooting up in your car trying to kill you and hit one of us. So no, sir, sorry!"

Plus I believe Mike was already staying with a classmate of ours anyway. I really didn't take him seriously. Mike was crazy. I mean, really. He had a little mental issues going on with him the whole family did, but he was a good person and very funny but don't get on his bad side! I remember one day, I had some company over. My two buddies I grew up with in Hollywood Hills stopped by to see me, and they had a guy friend with them and his brother. Well, this guy's brother was let's say mentally challenged. Two of my friends that I grew up with from the Hills had gotten on drugs but that was them and I wasn't judging them because they still looked good, not as good as they used to, but they were still taking care of themselves, and Mike knew them. When Mike called me, he heard some voices in the background, and he wanted to know who was over here. Mike sometimes likes to be Mr. Drama King, so he said, "Who is that I hear? I'm on my way over there right now!" And he hung up the phone. I didn't pay Mike any attention because Mike and I wasn't a couple. We were just friends with benefits, and plus all of us go way back anyway.

When Mike got there, I opened the door, and he just barged his way inside, and he walked down to my den where everybody was sitting at. He just stood there checking everybody out, and everybody was checking him out like, "Who is he supposed to be!" Their homeboy brother who was mentally challenged was in the bathroom, and when he came out, Mike and I were both back in the front room face-to-face. I was cursing him out, telling him that he didn't have any business coming over here, like he lived here, worrying about who's in my house because he didn't pay any bills up in here and that I could have anybody I wanted to have in my house.

Mike was telling me, "I was just coming over here to check on you and those boys!"

I told Mike, "I'm good. I didn't need you to come over here!"

As we were both talking over one another, the mentally challenged brother came out of the bathroom and interrupted us with his mentally challenged voice and said, "Shannon, you got my lighter?"

Mike just stared and looked at the boy like, "Now where in the hell did he come from?"

I told him, "No, I don't have your lighter."

He told me, "You do have my lighter!"

I told him, "Baby, I don't have your lighter. Your lighter must be downstairs."

So he walked off in his mentally challenged walk still telling me, "You do have my lighter."

As he was walking off, Mike was still watching this boy with a disgusted look on his face, and then Mike turned to me and said out loud, "You just have all kind of mother—— at your house!" When Mike said that, I put him out of my house. Even though it was a struggle, I managed to put him out before my buddies and their friend came up to where we were because the mentally challenged boy heard what Mike had said about him and told his brother, and the brother was ready to go after Mike. I had to tell the guy, "Baby, that ain't what you want. Let that fool go." This guy didn't know Mike, and I sure didn't want him getting hurt because that's what would have happened, I promise ya!

Later on, Mike got busted and was sentenced to about ten years in prison, but I think he did about seven. While he was in prison, I would sometimes stop by his sister's Rat house to ask her how Mike was doing. On this particular day, when I stopped by and got out of the car, I noticed Rat and a couple of people sitting in her front yard. As I started walking up to the house, a female jumped up out of her chair as if she was the lady of the house. When Rat approached me, she said in a low voice, "That's Mike's wife." My heart dropped. I was crushed because I didn't know that Mike was even married. I said, "Well, she may as well just sit her a—— down somewhere because I was with him first."

Rat looked at me like I was crazy! Rat said, "No, ma'am, that's his wife, and she comes first!"

"You're right, Rat. She does come first. I don't know what I'm talking about. Just tell Mike that I stopped by to see how he was doing."

Rat said out loud, "Okay, girl. I'll holler at you later!"

As I was walking off, I assumed she wanted Mike's wife to think that I came over to see her.

Timark was now seven years old, and I had decided to take him to see his dad. The last time Timark saw his dad, he was four years old. That's when Nuscey and I took him over there for Christmas, and no one had anything for my baby. Yeah, that was the last time. When we got there, Jeff's mom and his twin sister told me that Jeff was around the corner, so I let Timark stay there and play with his cousin, his dad twin sister's son who's three months older than Timark. When I drove around the corner to one of the Boys' house, I saw Jeff standing in their yard. I told him that I brought Timark out here to see him and that he was at his mom's house.

He asked me, "Well, how long are you going to be out here?"

I said, "Not long."

He said, "Well, can I call y'all later?"

I said, "Call us later? You haven't seen your son in three years, and you want to call us later!"

I got in the car, went and picked Timark up, brought him back around to see his daddy, and told him, "I said I was bringing Timark out here to see you. Now I have done my part."

Jeff spent ten minutes with our son. After that, my son didn't see his dad again until his dad went to prison some years later.

About six or seven months had passed, I found out that this plant in Ridgeway about forty-five minutes from where I live, were taking applications for a distribution plant. So I had decided to go and put in an application, and boy there were a lot of other people who thought of doing the same thing. Once you put in the application, you were told that you would get a call if hired, and I got a call. The plant first had to get cleaned up and organized, and we were told that we would be giving different job position. You had the runners and the machine packers, and I was chosen to be a machine packer, which was just fine with me! The runners went and got the clothes that were on the shipping ticket and brought them to the machine packer who would scan the items, then pack them in the correct packing boxes, print out a label for the box, and push the boxes down on the conveyor belt. There were about seven of us who were machine packers, and one of my coworkers BaBa, who worked right in front of me, and I became very close like sisters. BaBa was about eight years older than I, but you couldn't tell it because BaBa looked good for her age, and she was always getting compliments about how good she looked.

BaBa and I had started going out eating lunch together, and she started putting me down on the whos and the whats around town. Mostly everyone at the job knew of each other from family to friends, so everyone there were close. After work, a lot of us started hanging out going to one of the guys who worked at the job house to get high (smoking weed) and drinking beer. Sometimes we ended up at a car and bike show, which they had often. I was really enjoying myself! The plant where I worked was a distribution plant that distribute men clothes like Perry Ellis. Very expensive clothes, mainly slacks, that had the price tags ranging from $55 to $150 or more. They had other clothes like shirts, jackets, coats, belts, etc. It didn't take me long before I started getting the sizes of my family and started bringing them back pants by sneaking them out in my lunch bag.

I was getting so good that I started sneaking the items out on every break taking them to my car. BaBa was not a smoker like myself because a lot of times on our lunch break, we would ride off to go get something to eat, and I would roll up a blunt. She would decline until one day, she had decided to hit the blunt a couple of times. Once we had gotten back to work, we had to log back in on our computers with our password. Baba was on her computer for about ten minutes. Then she turned around to me and said, "Black." Black is the nickname that my son Timark's dad gave me because he was very light in his complexion, and I'm dark brown, so the name just stuck as my drug dealer street name, but my cousin Trapp calls me Chip, short for chocolate chip! Anyway Ba was like "Black, I can't get into my computer. I've been sitting up here this whole time trying to figure out my password. I done put in cat, dog, rat, etc. and I just don't know what my password is."

I said, "Your name Ba. Just your name!"

Baba and I laughed so hard for about another ten minutes! I told her you better not smoke no more weed with me because you can't handle it too well!

It was the summer of '97 when I had decided to stop smoking cigarettes cold turkey! I wasn't a big smoker. I started when I was fourteen. I smoked one cigarette before work and one after I got off and a few more on the weekends when I drink. One day, I got sick as a dog after smoking a cigarette. I was so sick that I wanted to go to the ER, but I was too sick to move. I stayed in bed for two days. After the second day, I started feeling better, and I decided to fire up another cigarette and had gotten sick all over again. I didn't want not one more cigarette after that. Plus I was thinking about my son Timark also who told me to stop because he couldn't breathe whenever I smoked around him.

Shaquille is now three years old, and since I was working and sometimes going out at night to make my drug run, I asked my cousin Regina, who was fifteen years old and out of school for the summer break, if she would come down and watch Shaquille for me with pay, and she did. One day, on a hot day while over at my cousin Squeaky's house, I was on my way, leaving to go home, and I noticed this young female and her baby who was in a crib, crying hysterically. Their things were out on the porch, and I just couldn't for the life of me pass them by without asking if they were okay. I noticed a young female and a male standing in the doorway, and she told me that her cousin put both she and her child out in the heat to allow her best friend and her boyfriend to move in. I assumed she was the cousin who was standing in the door, and she rolled her eyes at the female. I told the female to get all of her stuff, and she and her baby could come with me to my home until she could figure some things out. We both packed all of her and her baby things into my car and left. I fell in love with her son the moment I saw him and held him in my arms. He was no more than four or five months old. She said that her name was Angel, and the very next day, while I went to work, I called home to check on everyone. And my cousin said that she was home with both Shaquille and Angel's baby. She said that Angel said that she was going out to look for a job and still didn't make it back by the time I got in for work, which was about 4:30. I started getting worried, and then Angel walked in about 6:30 that evening, stating that she went down to the unemployment office. The next day, Angel left out again, and this time, she didn't make it back to the house at all. Now I'm pissed because this girl is running in and out of my house, leaving her baby with strangers and don't even call to check in on her baby or nothing.

When I went to work the next day, I told my cousin to be sure to call me when Angel calls. Angel came in later that evening after I had gotten home from work, and I asked her where she was. Angel stated that she stayed the night with her godfather, and I told her, "Well, then, if you stayed the night with your godfather, then you must have somewhere to go." Angel stated that she didn't because her godfather's wife didn't like her. On the third day, Angel stayed at the house and didn't go anywhere. When I got in from work, she was on the house phone talking to someone. They were having an argument about something, so then Angel puts me on the phone talking about, "Tell him that it ain't nothing wrong with me!"

I'm like, "Nothing wrong with you like what?"

Angel said, "This is my godfather. Somebody told him that I had AIDS. Tell him I don't have AIDS!"

"Well, I don't know nothing about what you're talking about."

So I just gave her back the phone, and they finished their conversation. Then she hung the phone up! On the fourth day, Angel stayed out again and left her baby with us, and this time, I was ready for Angel to leave. I fell in love with her baby boy, and I didn't want to put him out because I didn't want him to suffer for his mama's trifling a———. Later on that evening, Angel got dropped off by her so-called godfather, which I don't think that he was. I think that he was someone that Angel was having sex with, and he probably heard about her having HIV and wanted to confront her about it.

On the fifth day, my cousin Regina called me at work and told me that she was going through Angel's things, and she ran across her diary. My cousin told me that she read that Angel had HIV, and my heart dropped. You would not believe what my cousin and I read! In Angel's diary, she wrote about her having sex with this guy named Jo at the hotel, and after she had sex with Jo, she had sex with a guy named Paul, and the next day, she had sex with three different guys, and neither one knew that she had sex with the other one. And then we read about her being HIV positive. In her diary, all she talked about was all the men she slept with even after the fact when she knew that she was HIV positive. Even her baby's daddy who was in jail also was HIV positive and they were not sure if her son was HIV positive or not. They were running tests. As soon as I read her diary, I was so afraid for our lives, my son's, my cousin's, and myself.

I asked my cousin, "Did she cut herself while she was here? Do you know if she was bleeding or anything?"

I was just so afraid because I left her here alone with my son and cousin. My cousin stated that she didn't cut herself and that we needed to get her out of here. I told my cousin, "Oh, don't worry. We are about to pack up her stuff right now!"

I decided to call the Health Department and report her. I told the Health Department what I read in her diary, and they stated to me, "In order for us to do anything, she would have to sleep with a man and give it to him, and that man would have to sleep with you and give it to you."

I said, "You mean to tell me that I would have to get AIDS before you all could do anything?"

"Yes!"

"That's manslaughter!"

I hung up the phone and couldn't believe what I just heard. My cousin and I packed up Angel's things, and when she got there I, just expressed to her how I just didn't appreciate her running in and out of my home, and she leaving us to babysit her child and how I felt that she should leave. Angel didn't say anything. She gathered her things and called someone to pick her and her son up. When she left, I really felt sorry for her but mostly sorry for her son and the people she infected! About a week later, my cousin Squeaky called me and said, "Child, you better get that girl out of your house. She has AIDS, and that's why her cousin put her out!"

I told Squeaky, "I know and I've already put her out!"

My cousin Regina was still staying with me watching Shaquille for the summer. She decided that she wanted to get her hair in braids and the only person that I knew that did a good job was my cousin Trapp son's mother. When my cousin Regina, Shaquille, and I got there to my cousin's son's mother's house, it wasn't fifteen minutes when Shaquille and I walked outside to get something out of my car. I saw one of Nuscey's women, whom he used to mess with, walking toward me, talking a lot of junk. She was with another female, and they were both coming in my direction, so while I was in my trunk, I started talking out loud pretending I had a gun. I said out loud, "I know what I wish this b——— would come over here and try something because bullets don't have no eyes. Plus I got my son with me too. Oh, she wants to try something with me knowing I have my son!" That was the real reason I was upset. Because you want to fight me with my child and my child could have gotten hurt in the process. Even though I didn't have a gun, I had my hand on my crowbar ready to go up side her head, but she didn't know it, so she kept on walking.

That's not the only time that I got very heated when my son Shaquille was around and could have gotten hurt. On this particular day, Shaquille was around five years old, and he and I both went inside this bills payment center to pay a bill, and as I was walking through the door, there was a line at the door. Because the door was so heavy, it kind of pushed me inside, and I bumped up next to this guy. Before I could say excuse me, this guy pushed me so hard off him that I fell back on the door.

I said to him, "I said excuse me!"

He said, "Well, you didn't say it fast enough!"

I looked him up and down and noticed that he had on work boots. I thought that maybe I stepped on his nice shoes or something. I got mad and said, "Well, you must have woke up on the wrong side of the bed!"

He said, "No, I woke up on the right side of the bed, and I bet if I slap the f—— out of you, then you will know!"

Right at that moment, Shaquille walked right up to him and put his hand on the man stomach and said, "What's up, man?" The guy grabbed Shaquille by his hand and slung Shaquille's hand off him talking about, "Get off me, homeboy!"

What he did that for! Before I knew it, I grabbed that man by his shirt and had him pinned up in the window by his throat, and I told this man, "If you ever put your hands on my child again, I will kill you!" This man didn't say or do anything. He was probably more shocked than anything.

You would have thought that the men who were inside paying their bill would have said something to this guy, but they were only worrying about paying their bill, so they could get up out of there. The cashier behind the counter told us that she was going to call security. I told her, "Yes, please call security, the police, the coroner, and the ambulance because I'm about to hurt somebody up in here!"

After I took his place in line, I paid my bill and waited in my car. I told Shaquille to lay down because I didn't want the man to see us. I waited until he came out so that I could follow him and find out where he lived and bring Nuscey back to deal with him. When he came out of the building, he jumped right on the back of his bike. Not a motorcycle, but a riding bike, and I said to myself, "This n—— is crazy. He done jumped on a bike. Now I know I'm about to run his a—— over!" and I meant just that if it was not for this guy sitting in his truck when I was pulling off. This guy was not even on the inside to know what had happened. He was waiting on someone, but the look he gave me when I pulled off was a look that said, "Please don't do anything stupid!" I followed the guy for about five minutes, and I believe he knew that I was following him or he was just crazy because he was riding from side to side in the middle of a four-lane road. I looked at him, shook my head, and turned around. I told Nuscey about it, and believe you me, he and his family were ready. But I'm glad that I didn't take it any further because I know that it would have been worse than it was. That's the one thing I don't play with! Please don't put your hands on my boys!

Shaquille and I went into Sprint, trying to get my very first cell phone. While the store associate was filling out my paperwork, Shaquille was not being his self or maybe he was and just really getting on my nerves. I had to tell him to sit down every second while this guy was asking me question.

"What's your first and last name?"

"Sit down, Shaquille!"

"What's your address?"

"Don't do that, Shaquille!"

"What's your social security number?"

"Come here, Shaquille!"

"Because of your credit, it will be one thousand dollars to put down."

"Come on. Let's go, Shaquille!"

We walked in and walked right out. I couldn't believe it. Did he say one thousand dollars just to put down on a phone. I said to myself, "I'll keep stopping to use a payphone before I pay a thousand dollars for a phone!"

Shaquille was so active and so big at his age that Nuscey's family mainly his cousin Tara started calling him Tubby. One day, this guy saw us both and told me that Shaquille was my moneymaker, and since he already had the size of a football player, that's where he was going to make it. So I had decided to put Shaquille into soccer because someone told me that putting him into soccer would help get his choreography together. So that's what I did. I put Shaquille into soccer, which was a bad idea because while Shaquille was on the field instead of him running after the ball like the rest of the players, Shaquille was on the field putting on a dance show and a very good dancer at that. All the parents just laughed. When the time came for him to kick the ball, he was kicking it but in the opposite direction and scored a goal for the other team. I was so embarrassed, and no, I didn't keep him in soccer long. Shame on me.

Since I was still in the pharmaceutical business and our mom's big fiftieth birthday was coming up, I wanted to give her a surprise birthday party all by myself, so I called my mom's sisters up and asked them if they would help me plan my mom's birthday party.

All I wanted my aunties to do was just do all the cooking, and I'll do the rest. I brought all the food and everything to prepare it with as well as all the table accessories and the alcohol. I spent a lot of money for our mom's birthday party, and I didn't ask nor did I want any money from my sister or brother. I wanted to do it all by myself, and I did, and I was very proud of myself. The party turned out to be very nice with my mom's and dad's family there, some of Nuscey's family, and some of my friends from the Hills were there also. I got my boy Toddrick to DJ for me and my boy Feet to do the cooking on the grill. The funniest thing that tickled me that night was when Nuscey's grandmother came up to me and said, "Shannon, I see ain't nobody riding my mule."

I knew just what she was talking about. Nuscey's grandmother used to love to take her a drink and her drink was gin which she called her mule. So when she said that ain't nobody riding my mule, I looked at the bottle of gin and saw that it wasn't open, and I looked back at her and told her, "Ride that sucka!" Boy did that make her laugh, and she always told me that tickled her every time she thought about what I said!

I asked Toddrick for a special request song so that my mom and I could dance off. I asked for him to play Gerald Lavert "Wind beneath My Wings." He didn't have the Gerald Lavert version. He had the original singer Bette Midler's, which was even more beautiful, and I went over to my mother and hugged her. We grabbed each other's hands and danced together through the whole song. It was so beautiful, and everyone was watching us, and I guess they too thought that was beautiful for mother and daughter to be dancing together, especially the ones who knew how my mother and I always bumped heads. After the song was over, my mom said, "Okay, y'all make sure my house is clean up because I'm about to go to work."

We all were like, "You about to go to work, but this is your birthday party!"

"Well, I didn't know nothing about no birthday party, and I'm scheduled to go to work at eleven, so now I'm about to get ready for work. Good night y'all!"

I shook my head, and we all still partied until about twelve o'clock. You know how your people are. The party must go on!

Our supervisor Lindsey was very cool especially with Baba and me. He would allow Baba and I to go back in the warehouse if there was no work and find us a hiding spot to go to sleep, and sometimes he would come back there just to check on us. Now where do they do that at! I had started getting just a little too greedy with my stealing. I noticed how the guys were filling up boxes of clothes and leaving it in the back or outside, and they would come back later on that night and pick it up. Well, I too got up a bunch of stuff and loaded up a box, and the guys in the back were so cool about it. They put it on the outside so that I would come back later on that night and pick it up, and that's what I did with my two boys. Late that night, about one or two in the morning, I got them up and put them in the car with me. When I parked on the side, they were watching me getting this big box that I could hardly carry and put it in the back seat. Wow, I was so amazed at how easy that was. The clothes that I got, I told my uncle, who was more like our brother, about them, and he told me that he was talking to some of the guys on his job about them. They wanted to buy them, so my dumb self was selling the pants for $20, and they were going like hotcakes. I bet my uncle sold them for more than that. My uncle was putting in orders like crazy, and I told him that when I get them, I would let him know, so I got another box up, a bigger one than the first one.

I guess the guy was too nervous to put that one out, so I put it out myself. I guess I didn't hide the box good enough because someone found the box, but no one knew who it was. I was scared that someone was going to tell on me, but they didn't, and you would have thought that the incident would have taught me a lesson. But it didn't.

The next day, I made up another box and put it out and came back late that night and got it and didn't get caught! After that, the company started putting cameras all around and a security guard at the front door. He was checking your bags as you were leaving out, but he still didn't check them thoroughly. He just wanted for you to open up your bag so that he could look inside. A lot of times we would hide the clothes under our food that we didn't finish eating, and we didn't worry about food getting on the clothes since they were in plastic. We even ripped the liner in our jackets so we could fold up the pants and put them in the back of our jackets without falling out as we walked past the security guard!

I told Baba about my friend Juicy whom I was still going to see in jail every now and then, and she said, "Well, you must like him a lot. You still going to see him." I told her that I did like Juicy a lot, but I had to focus on my boys and me first. She said, "Yeah, because he can't do nothing for you or your boys locked up!"

After working there for some months, our supervisor Lindsey was still showing Baba and I more than just favoritism. He was showing us some attention by telling us, "Y'all sure look good today in y'all jeans" or "You sure are fitting those jeans and they are hugging you very well." One day, he went overboard talking about, "What hotel you and your man going to tonight?" I was like, "What do you mean what hotel me and my boyfriend are going to tonight? What makes you think that I need to go to a hotel?" He just said, "I don't know. I just figure you take your man to a hotel to make him feel special." I was saying to myself, "Now where did that come from?"

Lindsey had started making me very uncomfortable with all the sexual comments that he was making toward me, and I was telling my cousin about it. She said, "What you need is a tape recorder and record his a—— when he's saying those things to you" So as time went on, Lindsey's sexual comments kind of stopped, and then he started getting a little on the controlling side. Sometimes, as the computer operators, we had to sometimes help with getting our order, and if we had stopped to talk with one of the guys, Lindsey would wrap his arm around our arm and walk us back to our computer. At first, we kind of laughed about it until he was getting just a little too much out of hand. Even the other workers would notice it. "Man, Lindsey don't never want you and Baba talking to us. That's crazy." A couple of weeks went by, and there was probably about three to four computers up from my computer where I was talking to one of our male coworkers who was in my department. We weren't busy or had anything to do, so while we were talking by his station, he was telling me, "Man, what's up with Lindsey?"

I said, "What do you mean?"

He said, "Lindsey is crazy. He be up here talking to me about you talking about, 'I know you wanna f——Shannon, don't you. I know you want to take her to the hotel and just spank the s—— out of her,' and 'Don't she be looking good in her jeans.'"

Then Lindsey walked up to me and wrapped his arm around my arm and told me, "Get back to your computer."

I unwrapped my arm from around his arm and told him, "We don't have any work to do."

He said, "Well, get back to your computer anyway."

I said, "What's your problem? I'm still in my same department talking to my coworker because we don't have anything to do, and we ain't doing nothing wrong. Why are you bothering me!"

So Lindsey walked off, and I went back to my station. About ten minutes later, Lindsey walked back up and talked to the same guy that I just got finish talking to and walked off, and the guy was like, "What's wrong with Lindsey? He said that he was going to get you fired."

I said, "Well, if he was going to get me fired, then I'ma get him fired for sexual harassment!"

I was part of a union, so I decided to call the head union rep and told him what was going on, and he told me that they would be there at the job to speak with me. While I was waiting on the union rep to get there, everyone at the job heard what was going on, and most of the men there were telling me not to get Lindsey in trouble and that I should just ignore Lindsey. I said why should I if he's talking about getting me fired, well, then, I'ma get him fired. Then they were like, "Well, you and Lindsey need to talk because Lindsey is a good dude." I was like, "Well, what about me?"

I figured my coworkers didn't care about me like they did Lindsey because all those people from that town stuck together, and I was not from around there. So what, it doesn't make it right by what he did either! Before the union rep got there, our head supervisor, an old white man, called me in his office, and he was very upset. He told me, "Now let me tell you something, we didn't have this kind of mess going on until people from another town came here to start trouble!"

I told him, "I didn't come here to start trouble I was sexually harassed by Lindsey, so therefore, the trouble came to me." He told me that he has been knowing Lindsey for a long time, and he knows that Lindsey is a very good person and he knows that Lindsey wouldn't dare do anything like this and that I just need to go back from wherever I came.

I told him that he just knew Lindsey from working with him and that he didn't know what kind of person Lindsey was behind closed doors! Five minutes later, about eight people from the union came to talk to me, and I told them my story. Plus I told them that I had a witness to back my story up.

I asked them to get my coworker, the same guy who was telling me all the things Lindsey said about me, and they claimed that he left because he had a doctor's appointment. I told them that it was a lie, and that the guy didn't have a doctor's appointment but that Lindsey sent him away because he knew what I knew and if it was true, have the guy come back with a doctor's excuse! After I told my side of the story, I was told that I was no longer an employee of that company and that I needed to get my stuff and leave until further notice.

I was so hurt and couldn't believe what had just happened. I was the victim, and I was treated as if I was the person in the wrong! In the union group, there was only one black guy, and he walked me to my car. He told me, "Those people just fired you, and if what you're saying is true, then you have a big law suit!"

I drove home and told my mom what had happened, and the only thing she said was, "Ahh, that's just a man for you. They do stuff like that. Just don't pay it any attention."

I said to myself, "Just don't pay it any attention? See, she must still be living in the ole days because sexual harassment is a very serious matter."

The next day, I got a call from the union for me to come to the plant in Winnsboro to talk with them.

When I got there, I went to the restroom, and there was other woman who worked there in the restroom. They asked me if I was the one who had accused Lindsey of sexual harassment at the other plant. I told them I was, and they told me, "Child, Lindsey been doing stuff like that for a long time and that he even said something to me out of the way!" Once I got into the big room where they were holding the conference, all the union people were there, our head supervisor, Lindsey, a man, and a woman. They all sat there and listened to my story about all the things that Lindsey were saying to me. I even told them how our head supervisor talked to me before they got there and how I was so very upset because I was the victim!

After the meeting was over, the same white man and lady walked me outside of the conference room and sat me down and told me, "We believe what you just told us because we know when a person is lying and when they are telling the truth. We know that you are telling the truth" When we walked back in, they told me that they were giving me my job back, but instead of me working in Ridgeway, I would have to work at the plant in Winnsboro. I told them that I wasn't able to make it all the way to Winnsboro. The head supervisor from my old job said, "So you mean to tell me we are giving you back your job, and you don't want to take it!"

I told him, "No, I'm not able to work in Winnsboro because my car can barely make it to Ridgeway. Winnsboro which was another fifteen to twenty minutes from the other plant!"

I ask the union guy if there was anything else that I could have done, and he said no because they gave me my job back, and it was my decision not to take it! I was at that job for a year, and I left and didn't look back. I told myself, "Damn, I wish I had caller ID at that time because I would have never answered the phone, and I would have talked to a lawyer," Years later, I hated that I didn't talk to a lawyer because I probably still could have done something, but I didn't. About a year later, Nuscey's uncle Noland invited Nuscey and I with him and his family down to Beaufort, SC to the beach, where their family lived, and we had a great time. While we were on the beach, I ran into Lindsey and his family; we just looked at each other, waved, and kept it moving!

I told myself, "Shannon, you know you can really meet some characters." Just like this guy I met that looked just like Tupac and everyone who knows me knows I'm in love with Tupac! When I met him, I was going to the chiropractor, and we started a conversation and exchanged phone numbers. We were just friends, and my mind kept telling me not to get close to this guy. I don't know why. He was a gentleman, and he took me—let me stop lying—he rode with me to some of my doctor's appointments, and he seemed really cool, but something just kept telling me, "Don't get close with this guy." He told me that he was down here from Florida living with his sister and that a couple of months earlier, he had lost his wife in a car accident, and I really felt sorry for him. I still didn't want to get close to him, and he knew it until he one day went to jail for about three months. He wrote me all the time while he was there, and he had a very beautiful handwriting for a man. A week later, when he got out, I had decided to give in and give him a chance, but when I got to his sister's house, she had informed me that he had gone back home to his wife!

I said, "Went back home to his wife? He told me that his wife was dead and that she died in a car accident!"

She said, "Now why would Junior say that, and I'm going to call her and tell her what he said!"

I told her, "If I had her number, I'll call her and tell her what he said myself!"

Wow, so that's why something kept telling me not to get close with him, and I didn't. We just kissed one time, and I'm happy I listened. Thank you, Lord!

This was around the time that I faked a slip and fall! I talked it over with Lamar's girlfriend Simp, and she was scared about doing it, but I told her that it would be easy. Just have her son to go down the escalators with some ice cream and drop it on the floor. I'm going to wait a few minutes, walk—I mean, slip off—the ice cream down the escalators, and everything went as planned, that's why I was going to the chiropractor, and the day came when I had a meeting with some lawyers the store hired to represent them. My lawyer wasn't present because she had just got into some trouble herself. I wanted it to look good, so I had one of my guy buddies to drive me there and go with me inside as my driver. After speaking with the lawyers, we left, and once we got back into the car, my buddy looked at me and told me,

"You know what, you just put on your best act ever. I promise you, you deserve an award!"

I knew I put on my best act ever because I went in, acting like I could barely walk or sit down, because of my back, and when it was all over, *I still didn't get a damn thing.* See, God don't like *ugly!* Not long after, that my homeboy Lamar's girlfriend Simp left him. Simp was a good woman, someone who had love for Lamar, but she got tired of being called out of her name. "Aw, b——," that was his name for her, and she got tired of it, and I didn't blame her. Let's give a shout out to those women who have enough respect for themselves to know when enough is enough and it's time to let it go!

During these times was one of my lowest times in my life. I wasn't doing so well since I wasn't working, and my cousin Kevin and his brother Vincent introduced me to one of their friends named Shawn, only because I ran into my cousins one day, and Shawn was with them. Well, there came a time when I bumped back into Shawn again and he and I both exchanged phone numbers. We kept in touch with each other after that. I would give it about a month later that we had decided to one day meet up. I had invited Shawn to my home, and he and I got into a discussion about me needing a bill paid. He said that he could help me pay the bill, and all I had to do was give him some. Now I've never had sex for money because to me, that's like prostituting your body, but because I really needed my mortgage paid, I had agreed to do it. But where I messed up was I should have gotten the money first because this big, fat one minute of a man told me that he was going to get the money and bring it back and never did.

I'm ashamed that I did that now, but I wasn't then because I called my cousin Kevin up, and I told him what had happened. I wanted to know where the fat bast—— lived. My cousin took me out to his place because he really didn't know who he was messing with. Me, my cousin, and two more of his friends were ready with ski masks. We were ready to beat him down and take all his money, but when we got there, I changed my mind because I knew that if we would have gotten caught, we would have done some serious time in prison. I saw his fat a—— after that, and he thought that what he did to me was funny, but I couldn't blame him but only myself. I promise myself that I would never do anything else like that again, and I didn't, but it still ain't no better having sex for free.

Even though Timark's dad and I wasn't together. I still wasn't close with his family like I used to be, but I still consider them as family, so I asked Jeff's twin sister Jen if she would braid my hair. She said yes. When I got there, I was introduced to Jeff's wife. I never knew that he had gotten married. When Jeff got there later, Jen was just finishing up my hair, and I left. About a couple of days later, Jeff called me and told me that he and his wife had got into a big fight because she said that he didn't introduce us, and I told him that I had already been introduced to her, but I guess she wanted Jeff to acknowledge her. During income tax time that next year, I had received a check in the mail from Jeff for twenty-four hundred dollars, and boy did I put it to good use. Jeff called me up and asked me if I had received a child support check in the mail and how much was it. I asked him why, but he said that he had already known that I got it and that he knew that it was for twenty-four hundred dollars. I told him yes, I did, and he told me that his wife left him because of it. He said that because they filed taxes together, that child support took her check, and she told him about it, and he was like, "Well, what do you want me to do about it" and because of that, she got mad and put him out. He said that he went and stayed at his mom's house for about two weeks, and when he went back home, his wife, who was now the ex-wife, had packed up everything and left the apartment empty. I told him, "Well, I guess when you leave him, that's how you leave him!"

Shaquille is about three going on four years old, and Nuscey woke me up one morning and told me to go into Shaquille's room to see him. Shaquille was not afraid of the dark. Shaquille would get up in the middle of the night and go into the refrigerator. This night, Shaquille ate the rest of the fried chicken and a bag of oranges and had s—— up his self. The whole bed was messed up, and I was so mad. I told Nuscey, "Let his a—— lay in it!"

I let him sleep in his mess for about another ten or fifteen minutes before we got him up. Since we now know that Shaquille would get up in the middle of the night, we put some duct tape on the refrigerator to keep his fat a—— out of it. Shaquille was so greedy that while he was eating his breakfast, he asked me, "Mama, what are we eating for lunch?"

I told him, "Boy, you ain't finish eating your breakfast yet, and you are worrying about what you are going to eat for lunch. If you ask for anything else to eat, I'll kill ya!"

Nuscey moved in with his cousin Connie who lived right across the street from his mom while we were still going through our ups and downs. We just decided to give each other a break from living together. Maybe that's the problem, he said. One day, Nuscey asked if Shaquille could spend the night with him over at his cousin Connie's house, and I agreed even though I didn't want to. I still thought that Shaquille needed to be around his dad. I wasn't used to Shaquille not being home with me, and I was missing him so bad that I decided to get up early the next morning to go and pick my baby up. When I pulled up in the yard, I noticed a child was standing in the window, and it was Shaquille. He was crying, and you could tell that he was crying for a long time because mucus was running all down his face, and I was wondering to myself if he's crying hysterically like this for a while. Where is everybody? I started knocking on the door and knocking, and no one answered. I decided to walk around to Nuscey's room window to see if he was asleep or even home, and the curtains were open. When I looked inside, Nuscey and another woman was asleep in the bed together, and I really got to banging on the window, and they both woke up. I yelled and told him, "Here my baby is crying in the window, and here you are laying up with another woman. Open up the door so I can get my baby!" They both jumped up, and Nuscey opened up the door while the female stayed in the room. I was cursing him out telling him how messed up it was that he asked to spend time with our son, but he wasn't because he was too busy laying up in the room with another woman and that he didn't have to worry about Shaquille spending the night no more!

I went home and called Nuscey's sister Noby and was telling her what had happened, and she was like, "Yeah, I wouldn't have let that go down. I would have beat his a—— and the female a——!"

I told her, "You are right. I should have beat her a——— and his too!"

I told her that I was going back over there, and I dropped Shaquille off at my parents' house. When I got back over there, Nuscey's cousin Connie said that Nuscey and the female whose name was Tameka walked around to her house. I said, "To her house? Where does she live?"

Connie said, "Well, I don't know exactly which house. I just know around the corner up there behind the store."

I drove around the corner, and there were about three houses behind the store, and I must have smelled him because I went to the right house. I knocked on the door, and another female answered the door. I asked her if Tameka lived here, and she said she did but that she was asleep. I pushed my way into the house like I was the Mafia. This female looked at me like I was crazy!

I've never been inside this woman's house, but I guess I smelled the room Nuscey was in. I went to the room door and banged on the door. The next thing I heard was Tameka saying, "I know that ain't you, Shannon, in my house!"

I said, "Yeah, it sure is, and I wanna know if Nuscey's in there!"

She yelled, "Nuscey is not here!" She walked out of her bedroom, tying up her house coat and closing the door behind her, telling me while walking toward the phone, "Shannon, I don't appreciate you coming up in my house like this!" When she bent over, I thought for sure she was getting ready to pick up the phone to call the police, and at that moment, I started getting nervous. Instead she went into her purse and pulled out her pack of cigarettes and lit her one up. At that moment, I was back to Ms. Billy Bad A———! I told her, "First of all, you don't let no one walk up in your house at no time talking s——— to you in your own house! You smoking a cigarette trying to talk to me. See, if I were you, I would have whooped my a——— all through your house and then called the police to come and get my a——— up out of here, so, b———, you ain't bad. Just tell Nuscey I'm looking for him!"

I walked out, saying to myself, "Girl, you are crazy as hell for real!"

I didn't put child support on Timark's dad until Timark was four. Now I see that it's the same for Shaquille's dad. Shaquille is four years old, and I decided to put child support on Nuscey as well. It's not that I planned it that way. I gave both dads the same opportunity of time to spend with their sons. I was always big on time than money because money can't buy love, and I felt that my boys needed their dads' love more than money, and it seemed that my boys weren't getting anything from either! My dad, on the other hand, was telling me not to go down to the court house to put child support on my kid's dad, and I was confused. Why not? He said that I shouldn't have to make a man take care of their child, and he's right. I shouldn't, but I didn't make these kids by myself, and I wasn't about to take care of them by myself. So my dad's little advice went in one ear and out of the other. So down to the court house I went.

The next day, while I was over to Nuscey's mom's house with the Budweiser Crew, Gloria stated to me that she heard what I did about going into people's houses, and I better stop acting like I'm Ms. Billy Bad A—— before somebody whooped my a——. I told her, "Well, when it happens, it just will happen, and I did what I did and what!"

She started mouthing off to me talking about if it was her, what she would have done to me, and I told her that if it was her, she wouldn't have done nothing either. Just talk s——, like she's doing now! So she said you going up in people's houses, what if I got up in your car like that, and I told her, "Oh, you don't even wanna get up in there because I promise, you wouldn't want to get back in it!" Gloria called herself getting in my car on the passenger side, and I jumped in the driver's seat and took her for a ride of her life! Now remember I said that I always wanted to be a race car driver plus my dad was one. And I have a lead foot, and people used to tell me that I drove like a bat out of hell. So when Gloria caught herself being funny and jumped in my car and said that she wasn't getting out, I drove like a bat out of hell, like I was on a race track. She was yelling and screaming to let her out of the car, and I didn't until I got back to the house fifteen minutes later. When I pulled back up to the house, Gloria jumped out of the car and said, "Yeah, you are right. You ain't got to never worry about me jumping in your car again!" Nuscey's mama and Lisa just laughed.

This wasn't the only time Gloria and I had gotten into it. Everybody knew that one day, Gloria and I would one day bump heads because she and I always had smart words to say to each other. That's because I found out that she and Lisa both have crushes on Nuscey even while they were dating Nuscey's uncles. I heard that every female that Nuscey dated, Gloria didn't like and always had a problem with them. So one day, Nuscey's mom's ex-husband ran into the three of us: Carolyn, Lisa, and me. He had decided to buy Carolyn a case of beer, so we had decided that we would go over to Gloria's house to hang out. We sat over there, drinking beer and eating some dip called hot pussy with some Ritz crackers. It's a dip that's mixed with sardines, hot sauce, and I can't remember what else, but it was really good! We didn't finish drinking all the beer. There was probably about a six-pack left, and I took the rest of the beer with us. When we got to Carolyn's house to drop her off, I walked her inside and left Lisa waiting for me in the car. When I walked into the house, Morgan, Carolyn's husband, told me that Gloria had been calling for me, and that she had called about six times within the last five minutes. Morgan couldn't finish getting the sentence out of his mouth when the phone rang, and it was Gloria on the other end. Morgan handed me the phone.

When I got on the phone, Gloria started cursing me out like there was no tomorrow. "B———, you ain't had no damn business taking that beer from over here, and when I see you, I'm going to beat your a——— because you ain't brought nothing to be taking nothing from over here!" When I hung up the phone, I said, "Oh, I'm going to beat this b——— a———!"

Carolyn said, "No, Shannon, don't go back over there. It ain't worth it!"

I said, "Okay."

When I got back into the car and told Lisa what had happened, she said, "Let's go back over there." So we drove back over to Gloria's house who lived in the projects. And once I got there, I jumped out of the car with the six-pack in a plastic bag, ran up in Gloria's house (she was a lot bigger than me), and told her with me swinging the beer in the plastic bag like a slingshot, "Oh, you want some beer. I'm about to give you some beer!"

I went straight to her a—— hitting her with the beer upside her head! We fought in her house about ten minutes with her husband and her daughter watching us, and I heard her daughter screaming, "Get her, Mama! Beat her!"

I tore that a—— up. Then I stopped and started walking outside toward the car with Lisa still sitting in the car the whole time. Gloria came outside for some more, so I went to her a—— again, and as we were fighting, I had on a jean jumper with suspenders that wouldn't stay up on my shoulders, and I was trying to keep them from falling down, and Gloria, who was a lot bigger than me, started charging toward me, so I did the next best thing.

I took my jumper off, and I had on just my underwear, a long T-shirt, and my tennis shoes. We started fighting again, and the next thing I knew, she had me bent over the top of a bench on my back, and Lord knows I have a bad back, so when my back started hurting, I said to myself, "Oh s——, this b— got my back hurting!" Because I was in so much pain, I must have turned into the Incredible Hulk because I got the strength to come up and get this big silverback of a woman off me, and I slammed her to the ground, and I started wearing her out. The next thing I know, I was flipping over backward! Her brother came and flipped me off her until I was dizzy, and I said, "Wow, you couldn't let your sister fight her own battle!"

The only thing he said was, "I was breaking it up!"

"How in the hell you breaking something up, and you done flipped me over on my head. Really? But it's all good!"

I put back on my clothes with half of the projects people watching us for the last thirty minutes I got back in my car where Lisa was sitting the whole time and didn't move! All she did was get the story for news 19, 10, 25, and 57! I heard Gloria got mad at her husband because he told everybody that I whooped that a——! I didn't have any more problems out of Gloria, and as a matter of fact, she told me one day, "I know one thang. Your a—— can fight!"

The one thing that I was taught by my mother was to take care of my family regardless if she was just talking about my boys and I at the time. She told me that once I became a mother, my life changed. I couldn't go out to clubs or hang out with my friends like I used to. My job was to now go to work come home and take care of my family. I'm glad that I was raised in a household with a mother who raised me as a mother should. She told me to raise my sons in a way a respectable mother should and to "make sure you don't wear all those short shorts around them either."

I wore shorts, but they wasn't no Daisy Duke, so I raised my boys the best that I could being a single mother, and it really made me proud. My sister and I were both over to my parents, and she and I got into a discussion about something.

I remember her saying, "You got two kids by two different daddies and ain't with neither one of them."

I'm saying to myself, "Why? Because you have a husband, and you both are raising y'all's three children together?" I wanted to say something, but my mom beat me to it, which made me proud! My mom was never the one who would take up for me, but she did this very day.

She told my sister, "Wait a minute now, she might not be with neither one of them, but she take care of her kids and don't ask nobody for nothing!"

My sister just looked and I could tell that she felt bad about what she said after our mama shut her down.

My brother-in-law called me up one day and asked me, "Sister-in-law, are you pregnant? Hell no!"

I asked him, "Why you ask me that?"

He said, "Because every time you got pregnant, we got pregnant. You were first pregnant with Timark, and a year later, we had Kiara. Then five years later, you were pregnant with Shaquille, and a year later, we had Cara. Now your sister is pregnant again."

I told him, "Well, y'all are on y'all own this time because I'm not pregnant!"

My sister one day asked me if Nuscey and I were together, and I asked her why. She said because she was at the ob-gyn doctor's office getting a checkup, and she saw Nuscey in there with another woman. She was pregnant also! The news my sister gave me hit me like a ton of bricks. I was so hurt. No one told me that Nuscey had someone pregnant, and I sure was going to find out. I knew that Nuscey and I was always off and on, but I still felt as though we were a couple regardless. I went to Nuscey's cousin Connie's house where he was staying from time to time anytime he and I would break up. Connie told me that Nuscey was staying up at Tameka's house, the same female who was with him when my baby was in the window crying.

I drove around the corner to the female Tameka's house, and instead of me getting out, Nuscey saw me pull up. He came outside, and I asked him, "My sister told me that you were at the doctor's office while she was there with a pregnant female and I wanted to know if it was true."

He didn't answer. He just said for me to go home and that he would call me, but I needed to know now. "Did you have someone pregnant?" I asked. Tamekia came outside with her big belly getting on Nuscey telling him that she was not going to have him disrespecting her in front of her house, and Nuscey just left me sitting there in my car like I was nothing or nobody. I kept trying to talk to him, but he went in the house, but that didn't stop me. I started blowing the horn for him to come out, but he didn't. I was so hurt and felt so alone. I went home, but later on that night, I came back out and parked my car a little ways from Tameka's house, and I sneaked in her backyard just to see if I could look through a window to see what they were doing. Then I said to myself, "Shannon what is wrong with you? You are a stalker, and you love this man this much that you would be in somebody's backyard trying to look into their window. Now something is really wrong with you!"

After that, I accepted that Nuscey had gone on with his life and that I should do the same! I should have known that Nuscey's mother was against me when she told me one day, "I couldn't date a man that looked better than me."

I asked her what she meant by that, and she said that Nuscey was a pretty boy. She didn't date pretty boys; she only like to date hard-looking dudes. I'm saying to myself, "What makes her think that Nuscey is better looking than me!" If that wasn't enough, she had the nerve to call me up and invite me to Tameka's baby shower, and I told her, "You got the nerve to invite me to a baby shower knowing that I'm still in love with your son. Plus you all didn't give me no baby shower!"

She said, "Because we all was drinking back then."

I told her, "You still drinking now, so what's the difference!"

I hung up in her face! I couldn't believe that she just didn't give a damn about my feelings, that she would call me up just to invite me to another woman's baby shower! I was so hurt, but I knew that life went on. I had to go with it. I found out that my uncle and auntie helped my cousin get a job at a plant where they worked, and I asked if they would help me also. But my aunt told me, "Child, you don't want no job out there because those women are something!"

I told my aunt, "Believe you me, I know how women are at the workplace."

And she told me, "Girl, I bet you ain't never seen no women like these before!"

I told her that I didn't think that it could be that bad, but little did I know. My uncle talked for me and got me hired on with them at the plant. I was on the ninety-day trial where you couldn't be late or miss any days. When I first got there, the women asked me if I was my Uncle Greg's niece, and I told them yes, and the drama began. The women started treating me nasty by rolling their eyes and wouldn't even speak. One white girl was real cool even though I mistaken her to be pregnant by asking her how many months she was, and she said none because she wasn't pregnant. It was so embarrassing.

The same white female came to work crying hysterically one day because she had a breast reduction. She said that she asked her boyfriend to pick out the breast size that he would like without her even looking at them. The breasts were so small. She said that she and her boyfriend broke up after that; she was so very hurt. She told me that she knew that she shouldn't have let him pick out the size of her breast because she and her boyfriend were mad at each other that day. So instead of her breast being a nice medium size, they were in the teeny-weeny titty committee. Another female that worked with us had a very bad limp when she walked. She said when she was younger, she was in a really bad car accident that caused the back of her heel to get cut off. This same female and I had almost gotten into a fight with each other and had to get called to the office. I found out that she really didn't have anything against me. It was just that she was just following up with the rest of the women there. I told her that she was just too old to follow the crowd and for her to judge me for me and not for what other people say about me, so we hugged and was cool after that.

I really think that her little disability was the reason she wanted to try and fit in with the rest of the women there. One day at work, I was talking to a coworker who lived in my old neighborhood, and as we were talking, a guy walked up to him and asked him where was the new girl in the department that he heard that was sexing all the men in the department and he too wanted to get in on the action. I turned around and looked him in his face and said, "Well, I guess that new girl would be me, and I ain't sexing no one!" The guy was embarrassed and walked off. I worked the morning shift, so as we were leaving, you had the afternoon shift coming in. There was a female on the afternoon shift who also wanted to fight me. She sent messages that when she caught up with me, she was going to whoop my a———, and I didn't even know who this female was until one day. I was getting off and the female approached me. I was like, "B———, you don't even know me and you want to fight me for what?"

I found out that someone told her that I was messing with her man, whoever he was. Our supervisor heard about what was going on and moved me to a different department, and everything started going downhill. I got to work late one day in those ninety days because I was home getting high that morning. One day, I went to work drinking and driving, and my cup of beer wasted all over me. When I got to work, I went straight to the bathroom at work to wash out my pants, and everybody thought that I had peed on myself. I told them that I wasted something on my pants when a guy coworker told me that I smelled like beer. I was like, "Oh s———, I'm busted!" That same guy and I rode to his house a couple of times after that on our lunch break, smoked some weed, got high, and went back to work. Not long after that, I was late for a second time. One day, while getting off work, this guy was showing off in front of some coworkers and talking smack to me, so I started talking smack back at him. He threw some soda in my face and ran because he knew that I was ready to whoop his a——! A month and a half later, I was late again and was terminated. So much for that!

Eventually, Nuscey and I had gotten back together, and he had started working from time to time doing dry walls. Sometimes he worked, and sometimes he didn't. I started noticing Nuscey sleeping with his sawed-off rifle beside the bed that he slept on, and I questioned him about it. I ask him why were he sleeping with a rifle beside the bed. He told me, "Baby, when you and those boys leave out in the morning, I wake up, and it looks like there's a man standing in the doorway watching me!"

I was like, "What are you talking about?"

And he said, "I'm telling you, every time you and the kids leave in the morning, I could be sleep. When I wake up, I notice a figure of a man standing in the doorway watching me, so I'll jump up and he's gone!"

I told Nuscey that he had better put away his sawed-off rifle because I didn't want one of my boys getting up during the middle of the night, and he messed around and hurt one of them.

Nuscey stopped sleeping with the rifle for about a week, and the next thang I know, he had knives and a hammer on the side of the bed! I'm like, "What the hell is going on now!"

He said, "Baby, I'm telling you every morning when you and the kids leave, there's a figure of a man in all black with a hat on his head watching me!"

I figure that what Nuscey was telling me was just an excuse to leave us again. Then I said to myself, "Well, maybe that man who was standing in the doorway trying to tell you that when we leave for work and school, your a—— should have been getting up leaving for work or school or something!"

I really thought that Nuscey was up to his old tricks trying to start something so that he could go to one of his women. One day, Nuscey was in the kitchen. I'll never forget it was like yesterday.

Nuscey was in the kitchen, and I kept hearing him asking me something, but I couldn't understand him because I was in the back room. When I walked out of the room toward the kitchen to see what he was talking about, he was in the kitchen with his back turned to me looking toward our down den. When I walked up on him, he said, "Baby, what are you cooking tonight?" But I'm wondering who was he talking to because I've been in the back room the whole entire time. I said, "What did you say?"

I started looking downstairs where he was looking, and at that quick moment, I saw the tail end of a lady's peach gown walking into our wash room. It was a beautiful peach gown, and you could tell that the gown was made back in the 1800s. Nuscey turned and faced me with a look on his face like, "What the hell was that?"

He said, "Baby, that was you! That was you down there!"

I said, "No, baby, I was in the room, but I saw what you were talking about!"

We both grabbed each other and started crying on each other's shoulders. I told him, "I believe you. I really believe you now!"

Nuscey was telling me the truth, but let me just say that whoever they were, they still never bothered me or my boys, so maybe he was the one who brought them here or maybe they just didn't want him here because they knew that he wasn't good for me. I don't know.

One day, I had taken Nuscey to work; and on our way to his job, we had decided to take a couple hits off a blunt before we got there. I didn't think that it was a big deal. I made a left turn even though I knew because of the sign I wasn't supposed to make a left turn between those hours but it wasn't any traffic, but little did I know that there was a police officer sitting across the street. After I made the turn, he got behind me, and I panicked because we had just got finish smoking weed. Nuscey told me to throw the blunt out, which I didn't, and he had to tell me again. "Girl, throw that blunt out the window. You can get some more weed!"

I threw the blunt out of the window, and the police stopped me and gave me a three hundred and something dollar ticket for making and illegal turn. After I dropped Nuscey off, I went back and found that blunt. Nuscey said, "You was crazy enough to go back and get the blunt."

I told him, "I sure did. After that big ticket I, really needed something to smoke!"

When I went to court, the judge was giving me a day in jail or pay the fine. I told the judge, "I'll take the day in jail." I was not about to pay almost four hundred dollars for a ticket, so I called my mom and told her what had happened. She told me that she would help me pay the ticket. When the day came for me to turn myself in to do the day in jail, I called my mom and asked her if she still was going to help me pay my ticket. My mom said, "No, because I thought you said you were going to do the day in jail."

I was so mad about what my mom said that I hung up in her face. When I got down to the police station, I was crying as I was walking to go in. I'll never forget it. There was this police officer who saw me crying and was looking at me in a strange way. I guess he wanted to make sure that I wasn't going to do something crazy, so he asked me, "Ma'am, are you okay?"

I was telling him in my crying voice, "I'm just turning myself in to do a day in jail!" He asked me if I had any children, and I told him, "Yes, I have two young sons," so he told me that he would talk to the judge for me about giving me community service which the judge agreed. I'm very thankful to that police officer, but hell, I would have come out better doing the day in jail! I think the judge gave me about twenty-five hours of community service at Mothers Against Drunk Drivers. I said to myself, "Now ain't this something. I'm a mother, and I drive drunk so I really don't belong here!"

So now Juicy has gotten out of jail, and I wanted to be there to pick him up, but I had to work and couldn't get off. Once he called me to let me know that he was home, I told him that I was going to make sure that I came down after I had gotten off work. He gave me the direction to where he lived, but I had gotten lost, and my phone didn't work because I was too far out in the country, and it was getting dark. I didn't know where I was going, so I told myself that I would just stop and ask someone to see if they could help me. I had noticed a figure of a person down the road, and as soon as I was about to pull up on the side to ask the person for directions, I noticed that it was an older white man, and he had an axe in his hand, chopping wood.

I'ma tell you that I'm not prejudiced, but here I am in a place deep in the country, a place I've never been before in my life. I just didn't know what kind of person he was, so as soon as I pulled off the road to ask him a question and I saw that ax, I said, "Hell no," and I hauled a——! Yeah, I got the hell up out of there and just prayed that God was going to make sure that I got to where I was going, and I did. At the end, it really wasn't hard. I just got confused about which road to yield off from. After getting to Juicy's house late that night, seeing him and holding each other, my feelings for him had gotten stronger. I stayed for about an hour or two because I had to get back to get Shaquille, and I told Juicy I would call him as soon as I got home. After my first visit, I went and visited Juicy as much as possible, and a lot of times he would ask me to bring Timark and Shaquille with me when I came. I really didn't want to because I still had feeling for Nuscey. and I knew he wouldn't have appreciated me taking his son to see another man. But I took them both anyway. and Juicy and his whole family welcomed my boys and me in like family.

I always had so much fun when I went down to see Juicy. His family and friends started looking at us like a couple. They said that we really looked good together, that we could go for brothers and sisters. Juicy was another person who loved weed. That's what we always did when we were together—smoked weed, hung out with his family and friends, drinking, and playing cards because Juicy wasn't working. He said finding a job there was very scarce. Juicy went back to doing what he knew best—selling drugs!

I must admit I had started getting good in doing what I was doing with my pharmaceutical job, and I started letting my regular customer get some of their medicine on credit especially the Boys. Feet was one of my biggest customers, and I had needed to go by his house to pick up my money, so I called him to let him know that I was on my way to pick that up. When Shaquille and I got there, I put Shaquille in the back seat while Feet and I were in the front. I was asking Feet about my money, which he said he didn't have. I asked him again, "Feet, where is my money because I need my money. You owe me about a hundred dollars. I need my money." But all he could say was "I ain't got it, cat." And all I kept saying was, "Feet, I need my money. I'm not playing with you. I need my money." And at this point, I started getting very loud and very upset about my money. Shaquille got up out of his seat belt and slapped Feet on the side of his face with his toy water gun and kept it on his face, telling Feet, "Give my mama her money, Feet. Give my mama her money!"

I told my baby, "Sit down, Shaquille. Don't worry about it. I got it." My son was serious about Feet giving me my money; he was just about five or six years old. A couple of days later, I heard from some of the Boys that Feet told them what had happened with him and I and how Shaquille got up in his face with a water gun about my money. The Boys said that Feet told them that if I hadn't made Shaquille sit down, he was about to dust me and my son's a—— off, basically a beatdown! We all laughed about it later.

Shaquille was around five years old when I had him a birthday party at the park. It was a nice birthday party. Mostly his family from his dad's side was there, and even though his dad and I were still going through our ups and downs, I still loved him and hoped that he will at least come to his son's birthday party. He did show up with another female walking hand in hand, and boy was I hurt and was about to turn the party out, but I didn't because it was my son's birthday. I didn't have to because I had so much love from Nuscey's family that they ran him and the other woman off. The two of them jumped in their car and burned rubber!

At the age of nine, my mom had decided to let Timark live with her and my dad. She said the reason was because Timark was over there spending the night the week prior, and he woke up in his sleep screaming and crying and telling my mom that his dad and mom was fighting, meaning Nuscey and I, because Nuscey and I were always arguing and fighting, more arguing than fighting, but that didn't make it any better. My mom said that Nuscey was not Timark's dad and that he didn't need to be around that. So I had agreed with my mom because I wanted my son to go to a better school than the district that we were in.

My cousin Trapp and I were very close, and from time to time, he would stop over to see how the boys and I were doing. I remember one day he came over with one of his home boys, and my cousin Trapp had decided to go around to the store. He had left his friend behind until he got back, so while I was in the kitchen, his friend had asked me if he could use the restroom. When he came out, he told me that I had a good son who was very protective of his mother, and I asked him why would he say that. He said, "Because when I came out of the bathroom, your son was standing beside the door and asked me if I was leaving too!"

Shaquille knew that Trapp came with his friend and knew that his friend should have left with him. My boys have always been my protectors, and that's the way it should always be with any boys and their mother—to not let any harm come to their mother.

I had also wasted something on my bathroom sink that I didn't know about until my cousin's homeboy was being funny and said, "Oh, yeah you waste your package on the sink."

I was wondering what he was talking about, so I went into the bathroom, and it was Shaquille's baby powders. I told him that he wasn't funny. My cousin Trapp came over again one day and asked me if he could stay with me until he got on his feet, but I told him that I didn't know because it ain't no telling how long that would be. I told him that I would let him stay here for a minute. So now my cousin Trapp was here living with me and sleeping in my son Shaquille's room. I felt a little comfortable knowing that someone was here with my son and me! Juicy came up maybe once or twice to visit, and he, Trapp and I would sit around the house smoking weed and play bones (dominoes).

For some reason, Juicy was smoking blunts like they were cigarettes, and that was turning me off. I mean yes, I too smoked weed but not like that he was smoking blunts back-to-back. And I asked him, "Why are you smoking weed like that because you can't get any higher. You are only wasting the weed." Juicy even turned my cousin Trapp off, and after his ride came and picked him up, my cousin was telling me that Juicy was cool, but there was something about him that he didn't agree with. After that, I just called Juicy every now and then.

My cousin Trapp had started getting very comfortable at the house because some mornings, I would wake up to him having different females sleeping in my house! One morning, I woke up, and he had this older female just leaving out of the room; she spoke and left. Another time, he had this female who had her child with her. I didn't see the mama at first, just that the child who seemed to be about three years old. The child was crying. I opened up the door and took her out of the room to make her something to eat. When Trapp and her mama came out, it was my cousin. The same female that came to the apartment to see Nuscey with her homegirls. When she saw me, she was like "Cousin!" and I was fake just like her, so I said, "Hey, cousin!" Trapp said, "Cousin!"

I told him, "Yeah, she's my cousin on my mom's side, and that her dad and my mom was first cousins." We explained to her that my son Timark's dad was Trapp's first cousin. I said to myself, "Ain't that something. That heifer up in my house. I should have beat her a—— since she was by herself!"

After Trapp took my cousin and her baby home, I told him that he couldn't be bringing all kinds of women up in my house because for one, he ain't helping to pay no bills, and for two, I'll be damned that you're sexing up in my house when I ain't even having no sex! After that, my cousin Trapp came to me and said, "Cuz, I'm tired of looking for a job and can't find one and staying broke. Why don't we come up with some money together and buy some dope [crack rock] or either buy some cocaine, and I could cook it up. By doing that, we can get more for our money that we can flip and make some more money and keep flipping the money until we come up." Trapp didn't have any money, so I decided to put $100 of my money in it, and Trapp and I went and brought just the straight cocaine. We brought it back home, and Trapp cooked it up.

I can't exactly remember how he did it I just remember him having a small pot on the stove with boiling water and the cocaine and baking soda. After he was done, he mixed the cocaine up with the baking soda and whatever else and cooked it in the water. Out came a solid piece of cookie, is what they called it because that's what the dope puts you in the mind of—a cookie. But the cookie was very thin. I think he put too much baking soda with it, but anyway, he and I went out over to the side of town where I knew people from selling crack the first time I sold crack, which was in Nuscey's territory!

Trapp and I went to sell our dope, and the people were buying it like girl's scout cookies. After we had finished selling it the same day, we had decided to go to Noland with the money we made and buy some more that we could flip. After that, my cousin told me that he knew of someone named Boss Hog whom he could call, and we could buy some dope from him. Boss Hog was even better than Noland. I had learned that it came to the weight of dope that a person gives you is what determines the amount of money that you make back plus your profit. So now Trapp and I were only buying from whoever had the best deal, and if they were out, then I guess we had no other choice but to get what we could get.

Nuscey and I got back together even after he and Tameka had their daughter who was about one years old. I guess the love between us was still strong because I still had child support on him, and he had a baby on me. Even though we weren't together in a relationship when he got her pregnant, we were still together. My mom felt that I was a fool to take a man back who had a baby on me, and Nuscey's uncle felt that he was a fool to still be living with me knowing that I still had child support on him. But we didn't care what anybody said about us. We were young and in love. I guess that's what it was even though the arguing, fighting, and breaking up never stopped. I remember another time when Nuscey had decided to pack up all his stuff again, and I just had to tell him, "Look, I'm tired of you using up my trash bags to pack up your s———. From now own, you need to start bringing some with you because you and I know that either I'm going to put you out or you are going to leave, so just start being prepared!"

When he packed all of his stuff in my car, I was mad. I was so mad that I had decided that I would stab his stereo speakers that was hanging out of my trunk with a knife since he loved his music and his speakers so much. As Nuscey was getting in the car, I decided to walk around the back of the car to stab a hole in his speakers, and he wouldn't know until he plugged them up wherever he was going, so I took my knife. When I jabbed the knife into the speakers, it made so much noise. I was like, "Oh s———!" Nuscey was like, "What the hell was that!"

I looked at him with a dumb look on my face, and when he walked around to the back of the car, he noticed that I had just put a hole in his speaker, and he came running after me, and I took off running around the car.

I took off running up the street to my neighbor's house, and I called 911. You know what the police never showed up. I could see our house, and Nuscey was in the doorway. You could tell that he too was stabbing something. It was the big giant teddy bear that I loved so much that he won for me at the fair, and you know what, I cried over that big teddy bear. It was the size of a twin bed, if not bigger! Since the police never came, I told my neighbor that I was going back home. My neighbor didn't want me to, but I told him that I would be okay. Nuscey and I had cooled down and was plotting on how he should have beat me up since the police didn't show up. I could have sued them for not showing up. You know we were broke always thinking about a lawsuit. I mean, a master plan.

I ran into my cousin's Trapp homeboy, Jab, the one who he was sharing the house with. Jab told me that my cousin Trapp set him up! Jab said that Trapp was the only one who knew that he had just gotten a big package. Jab said that once he got his package, he put it up in the house and left. About an hour later, Trapp called him breathing hard talking about, "Man, come back to the house. Somebody done broke in the house!" Jab said when he got there, his package, money, and jewelry was all gone, but my cousin Trapp still had his jewelry, watches, and rings all still nicely set on his dresser! Jab said he told Trapp, "Well, why all my s——— gone but your s——— still on the dresser!"

Trapp said, "I guess they didn't have time to get mine!"

Jab said that he started to shoot that n——— in the face, but instead, he told Trapp, "N———, you can keep the rest of my s———

whatever is left!" Jab said that he left everything right there with Trapp, and he never looked back!

Around this time was when Timark's dad went to jail for strong-armed robbery and was sentenced to eighteen years in prison. I heard that the bootlegger John in my old neighborhood, the same one whose wife kept Timark for me when he was just a baby, died, and her husband and Jeff were both dating two sisters. I knew of one of the sisters named Betty. She was the one that the bootlegger dated, but I've never met her sister, the one Jeff was dating who was in the car with him when he got caught. I started working at a really good laidback job at a plant packing albuterol, and I loved it. While I was working there, I saw one of the females my cousin Trapp had laid up with at my house. She was trying to figure out where she knew me from, and when I told her, she was so embarrassed because she was the one who was trying to sneak out before I got up that morning, but I busted her anyway. There were four of us women sitting down, one in front of the other, packing the albuterol as they came around on the convey belt. The female that I was sitting in front of asked me if they called me Black. I looked at her because I didn't know her, so how did she know me and especially by that name. I looked at her really good again, and she kind of put me in the mind of the boot-legger's girlfriend. So I asked her if she had a sister named Betty, and she said, "Yes, that's my sister."

I asked her, "How do you know me?" And she told me that Jeff used to talk about me all the time, so I said, "Well, why would he be talking about me to you?" She said, "He used to talk about how he used to do stuff to make you mad, and I would ask him, 'Well, why would you do it' and he said because he liked making you mad, that you were funny when you were mad." I was like, "Ain't that some s——."

She started telling me what had happened the night Jeff went to jail. She told me that they were both on their way back from Orangeburg from seeing her mother. Jeff asked her to stop at the gas station. She said when he ran out of the gas station, he was bleeding, and he told her to just drive. She panicked and drove off. Once they had gotten back to Columbia, he told her to just drop him off at the hospital, and she did what he asked her to do. I learned that Jeff had went into the gas station with a knife and told the sales clerk who was a State Trooper's wife to give him the money out of the register. Instead she got out the rifle, and she and Jeff started tussling with the gun, and as he took off to run out of the store, she shot him once in the hand and once in the side. The shot in the side made him having to wear a colostomy bag temporarily. I heard that even though the police knew that someone had dropped Jeff off at the hospital, he still wouldn't give them a name.

Every day at work, this female would talk to me telling me her business like she and I were the best of friends, and I would just listen. One day, she started telling me about this married man she met at the bootlegger's house and how she was so in love with him and how he was married and that he wanted a child, but his wife couldn't have any and that she would be the one to give him one. Every day she would tell me about this guy and that they would meet over at the bootlegger's house and how she couldn't wait until he left his wife so that they could be together. It was just sickening. I mean Jeff hadn't even been in jail six months, and here she was talking about she was in love with another man. I didn't work at the job long because in order to get on permanent, you had to work all shifts, and I was the type of mother that always wanted a morning job so that I could be home at night with my boys to help them with their homework, so I quit my job and had to get back on food stamps. My case worker got nasty talking about, "Why did you quit your job!" like she was paying me out of her pocket or something!

A couple of weeks later, I got a phone call late one night from Betty, the bootlegger's girlfriend, and how did she get my number. I don't know. But she told me that the police came and picked her sister up and that she needed for me to testify against Jeff, stating that her sister didn't know or have anything to do with the incident and that her sister had a son to take care of. I told her, "First of all, I wasn't there, and I don't know what went on, but just because your sister told me some stuff about what happened doesn't mean anything. I don't even know your sister like that, so why would I go against my baby daddy for her?" She got mad and hung up the phone. They gave her sister ten years in prison for driving the car. I found out that one of Jeff's homeboy saw the sister and her new man all hugged up together at the bootlegger's house and told Jeff, but I blame her dumb a—— because if something like that would have happened to me, I would have made sure that Jeff had money on his books and cigarettes to smoke. As I look back on all that, I thought to myself that the female could have easily been me because I was just so in love with Jeff back then, and I thank the Lord for saving me.

I later found out that my cousin Trapp and my cousin Tonya, the same one that he had in my house and the same one who claimed Nuscey was her daughter's dad, had moved in together, and he had deep feelings for her. A couple of months after them living together, my cousin Trapp called me and told me that he had needed for me to hurt my cousin Tonya really bad before he killed her. He told me that Tonya had set him up to get robbed. He stated that he had just got a big package and off that big package. He had about sixteen thousand dollars and that he noticed that Tonya was trying to get him and her to go off somewhere together, but he said that he didn't want to go. But she had insisted, so they did, and Trapp said when they got back, the back door was open. Somebody had been in the house and had stolen all his money.

I asked him, "Well, how did you know that it was her?" He said because he knew that she was talking to her best friend before they left, and she was telling her friend that they were about to leave and that she would call her back. Trapp said that he had got one of his Jamaican friends to leave a real nasty message on Tonya's best friend's phone, and when he did, Tonya's best friend and her boyfriend told Trapp everything about how Tonya set it up for them, that she would leave the back door unlocked so that they could come in the house and make it seem like someone had broken into the house and stole his money. But Trapp said that he knew something was fishy because Tonya was the only person that knew where he hid his money. I told Trapp that I would do it, but because she knows me and I'm her cousin, I'm not trying to go to jail. I've told him just like I've told my other male cousin: stop telling your women all your money business. I thought that Trapp was lying about the amount of money that

Tonya had stolen from him until years later when I ran into her and she told me out of her own mouth the same amount of money that Trapp said she stole from him. She wanted me to tell Trapp how so, so sorry she was for doing what she did to him and that she was still in love with him and if he could ever forgive her. When I told Trapp what she wanted me to tell him, Trapp said, "Tell that b—— not to put my name in her mouth because I still want to kill that girl for what she did to me!" Tonya is now strung out on drugs! I thought about karma coming back to bite Trapp for when he claimed someone broke in their house and stole his boy Jab's money, hopefully Trapp thought the same way too! Karma is a b——, so be careful of what you do to people because it just may come back to bite you!

During this time, Nuscey's mom and her family got put out again and needed a place to stay, and even though Nuscey and I wasn't together, I still allowed for his family to move in with Shaquille and me. It was his mother, her husband, Nuscey's two sisters, Nuscey's oldest daughter, JuJu, and two of his cousins, which after about three days, Nuscey's mom sent his daughter and two cousins home. So now it's six of us living in my home, and I was a little uncomfortable because Nuscey's mom's husband used to walk around in his old man shorts, which was tight and didn't nobody want to see his old man's balls through his shorts. Nuscey's mom would get home before I did, and you would think that she would have cooked for her family, but they were waiting on me talking about, "I don't go into another woman's kitchen." But as soon as I got finished cooking, she was the first one in there fixing her husband a plate. They stayed for about six months until I put them out. Well, I really told her that her husband had to go but she and the girls could stay because I felt that as long as he had a place to stay, he was not trying to find them a place. They only gave me eighty dollars the whole time they were there. Nuscey's mother understood and decided to leave with her husband. They moved with her mother and accused her mother of liking her husband. Now you know she had some kind of nerve not having a place to stay and accusing her mother of wanting her husband who was walking around in them same nasty shorts and her stepdad, her mom's husband, was there as well. So why would her mom want him?

A couple of months after that, I had to quit my job because the job at the albuterol plant was making us work mandatory shifts. We had to be able to work all shifts, and I knew that I was unable to work all shifts, so I quit. After I quit, I came into some very hard times, and I felt that if I didn't do something, I could lose my home. I thought of an idea that would help me. I had decided to ask my mom if I could move in with her for a couple of months until I get back on my feet. I would cut everything off and just pay on my mortgage, but when I asked my mom, she said, "Well, Shannon, you know that you and I don't get along. Now I can help you as much as I can, but you cannot come back here." So I had decided to go to Nuscey's mom with the same question—if I could just stay there for a couple of months until I get back on my feet. What she told me was, "Well, did you try to call and set up some payment arrangements with the people you pay your bills to?" I told her yes, but that's not going to help. I need to cut everything off and just pay on my mortgage until I catch up. Nuscey's mom told me, "No, I can't help you." I said to myself, "What I guess she forgot that I helped her and her family out a couple of months ago when they had nowhere else to go!"

I was very, very hurt by the rejection from my mom and Nuscey's mom, but those rejections only made me stronger! So now I'm not working anymore at the albuterol plant, and I had to go back down to the social service department to get an increase in my food stamps, and my case worker had the nerve to tell me that I should have stayed where I was, but like I told her, "First of all, those people wanted me to work all shift, and I'm unable to work all shifts because of my boys I wouldn't have been able to pay anyone to watch them, and why are you worrying about it you act like you paying me out of your pocket!"

So I got the increase in my food stamps!

One day, Nuscey stopped over at the house, and he said that he had come by to get Shaquille to take him to get some shoes, and we were standing outside in the front yard talking when my dad had pulled up. My dad said that he was stopping by to check on us, and he looked over at Nuscey and asked me, "Well, what do he want now?"

I told my dad, "Well, he said that he came over to take Shaquille to get him some shoes." My dad went off on Nuscey and let me tell you when my dad gets to stuttering, then you know he's mad. "Now, now, now, let me tell you something now, you might run in and out of Shannon's life, but you ain't going to run in and out of my grandchild's life talking about you coming to take him to get some shoes. Where have you been all this time!"

Nuscey told him, "Man, I be in my son's life. That be your daughter acting like I can't sometimes see my son. Now I just got paid, and I came by to pick my son up to take him to get some shoes!"

My dad told him, "Well, you can just take that three-dollar check and get the hell on because Shaquille don't need nothing from you because whatever he need, his grandmama and me will provide!"

Nuscey told my dad, "Look I'll just go and get my gun!"

Ooh, then my dad really got hot. He got so hot until he started jumping around. My dad said, "Ooh, you want to talk about guns. Well, I tell you what, you go get your gun, and I'll go and get mine, and we'll see who shoot what!"

Nuscey got the hell on and ain't never come back until weeks later! I don't know what made him talk about guns. I guess he was scared of my dad and was trying to play hard poor little thang!

I'm back to the streets doing what I need to do to make ends meet, and this time, I started pushing more weight instead of me buying pieces. I was buying them by the whole because my clientele was increasing, and people loved what I had and loved the amount that I was giving them, so they started spending more money. So as long as they were happy, I was happy. I made sure that I had numbers codes for different places if someone wanted to meet me, and I made sure that I changed them up every day just in case. I was driving for so long over the years with my knees because I had to use my hands to cut up the dope on my way to sell it that it became a habit. I would drive with my knees instead of my hands that people who rode in the car with me would make me put my hands back on the wheel.

One day, while over at my parents' house, I had just come from getting a new package and on my way walking out of the door. My daddy screamed from the top of his lungs. I knew right then I must have dropped my package, and I started patting myself looking for it. I walked back to the room, and my dad told me, "You better take this s—— back to wherever the hell you got it from!"

My mom said that she saw it on the floor, and she picked it up, a small Ziplock bag that she thought was a real rock and a razor along with it, something she thought that my son Timark had playing with. So she gave it to my dad who knew what it was. I took the bag and hightailed out the door! The next day, my mom asked me where did I get that mess from, and I told her my friend Mike that she met since I wasn't working was a drug dealer, and I was giving him $250 that he was flipping for me and bringing me back five hundred dollars, but he got mad at me and told me to sell my stuff myself. So my mom told me to just give it back to him and just leave that mess alone. Little did they know I was in too deep to turn back now!

Tree, Tonya, and Grace were my sisters, and we were all tight. I remember one morning waking up and opening up my front door. I'm a country girl, and I love hanging my clothes on the line to dry. Someone had taken all my clothes off the line and had spread them all over my car. They hung my panties and socks on my car antenna and left a piece of paper on my windshield saying, "I know what you did last summer!"

I was, for one, embarrassed, afraid, and mad that someone would take my clothes and put them all over my car. About thirty minutes later, my phone rang, and it was my girls Tree, Tonya, and Grace. They were all on the phone calling me to see what I was up to. I was telling them what someone did to my clothes putting them on my car, and they couldn't hold in their laugh. They just all busted out laughing. I knew that it was them, so I laughed about it as well. Later, we all decided to give each other names. Tree's nickname was still Tre. Tonya was Silbal. Grace was Wonder Woman because of her many jobs and her different names. And I was called Ghetto Girl. Wow, so why does my name have to be Ghetto Girl? Something I really didn't like, but I accepted it and told them, "Well, I'll be ghetto, but I still handle my business."

We were all close, but I always felt that the three of them were a lot closer with each other than they were with me. I guess it was true when the three of them called me up to tell me that they were the Chicken Girls.

I was like, "What do you mean y'all name is the Chicken Girls?"

They said because they were working at this club selling food and that they wanted me to come to the club and check them out. They didn't say, "We want you to come to the club and work with us." No, why would they. They had already had their crew, the three of them. I wasn't too hurt because the club that they were working at was a rough area. Grace told me, "Boo, whenever you come, just ask for me, and you don't have to pay anything. You can get in for free. I did what Grace told me to do. When I got to the club, I asked for her, and they told me that it would be ten dollars. I told them again, "Grace is down here working, and she told me to ask for her."

And they still told me, "It will be ten dollars."

I paid the ten dollars to get in and said to myself, "I guess boo ain't had no pull after all!"

When I got inside the club, it was jumping, and I walked to the back to where my girls were cooking. I was already feeling good before I got there. I sat where there were other people ordering their food, and I also put in an order for some chicken and fries. Since my girls were busy cooking, I told them that I was going on the dance floor and I would be right back. About twenty minutes later, I went back and ask them if my food was ready, but they told me that it wasn't, so I talked to them a few more minutes and told them that I would be back, that I was going to get me a drink. I finished my drink and dance on the dance floor. About thirty minutes later, I went back to get my food, but they told me that it still wasn't ready, so I left again to get another drink, hung around on the dance floor, and about thirty minutes later, I was so hungry, I felt like I was going to pass out.

I went behind the counter where my girls were cooking, and I sat in a chair barely able to sit up. I begged and begged my girls for something to eat. Grace sat on my lap, put her arm around me, and told me, "There were other people before you."

I told her, "Now I know damn well there wasn't that many people before me!"

I got so mad that I cursed them all out and left. The next day, the three of them called me up, and Grace said, "What did you say, Tree didn't you say that the money came first."

Tree said, "Yeah!" To hear those words come out of Grace's mouth hurt, but to hear them from Tree hurt me the most saying that the money came first. I told them, "First of all, if I had ten dollars to get into the club, then what makes y'all think I didn't have money to pay for my food? And let me tell y'all another thang if it was me, and I say that y'all are my homegirls, then that's what it is. I wouldn't give a damn about no money because y'all would have come first before any money or people because that's what true friends do!"

And I hung up the phone in their faces and called the Boys to tell them all about it. I found out that the Boys got on them about that bull crap, and I'm glad that they did because they showed me that they weren't the *true* friends like I thought that they were! Like my brother *always* told me, "Shannon, you don't have any friends!"

I really didn't know what road rage was until my son Shaquille and I were a victim of one. One day, while going home, a white man in a truck was driving slow in front of me while talking on his cell phone, and I politely got from behind him got in the other lane, speeded up to jump back into the lane that I was in because I had needed to turn in that lane. The guy got mad and got from behind me, speeded up just to jump back in front of me, just to get stop by the red light. Once he got to the red light, he jumped out of his truck and started walking back to my car, yelling and cursing about what he was going to do to me, but little did he know I was crazy too. Plus I was afraid for my son and my life, so I raised my motor, stuck my head out of the window, and yelled to him, telling him, "Yeah, and if you bring your a—— back here, I promise you, I'm going to run your a—— over!" and I meant just that because I was going to protect my son and myself! I saw him look over to his left, and the next thing you know he was turning around and walking fast back

324

to his car. When I looked to my right to see what he was looking at, another brother, who was sitting at the light and seeing everything, was getting out of his truck with a gun in his hand! I looked over at him with tears in my eyes and thanked him, and he gave me a nod of the head to say you're welcome.

I ended up getting a job at a small post office not too far from the house. It didn't pay much a little over minimum wages, but it helped. As usual, Nuscey and I are back together, and he dropped me off and took the car. I remember one day before I went to work Nuscey, and I had decided to smoke a blunt before I went in, and boy was I high. I was so high that when I got to work, I was so paranoid. I just knew the people there knew that I was high, and it seemed as though everyone there was staring at me because it was a family business, and most of them were church folks. Someone asked me if I was all right because it looked as if I was crying, so I had to put on my best act every and started crying, telling them that I was upset because I found out that my favorite aunt was in a car accident. They said, "Well, she's okay, isn't she?"

I didn't want to say nothing crazy and put bad luck on my aunt, so I said, "Yeah, she's good."

"Well, the way you are acting, you would have thought that she died or something."

I felt bad that I had to lie on my aunt just because I was high, and I told myself that I wasn't going to do that anymore!

I used to have fun with my other coworkers except when the two gay guys came to work. They always seemed to smell like a——— and cologne, like they sprayed themselves with the cologne just to hide the a——— smell, and believe you me, you would know exactly what I'm talking about if you smelled it. One day, while at work, these two older women were talking to each other, and I happened to walk over and butted into their conversation. They asked me, "Do you smoke?" And my dumb self answered, "What, cigarettes?" They looked at me as if they were saying well what else would we be talking about? I sure put my foot in my mouth that time! My front gold tooth fell out again, but I had just decided to just leave it out for good this time. One day, Nuscey and I had got into a fight and when he grabbed me from behind and wrapped his arm around my neck, he started choking me. I bit down into his arm, and he yanked his arm from out of my mouth, and when he did, my real front tooth came out! The same tooth that I had the gold tooth on. I assume the gold tooth had rotten my real tooth. I was so hurt and embarrassed that I told Nuscey, "Now I gotta look like you!" Except he had about two or three teeth missing in the front of his mouth from when he was a teenager. He said that his teeth had gotten knocked out when someone swung a baseball bat and hit him in the mouth by mistake. Now that I had a missing tooth, Shaquille, as a toddler, his front teeth were also missing. Nuscey front teeth were missing, and his daughter JuJu's front teeth were missing. Now Nuscey's family was calling us the snaggletooth family! It was so embarrassing and kinda funny but not that funny.

I hated going to work trying not to smile or talk as much, and the one thing that I love to do if anyone knows me is talk and laugh. I knew that the workers saw it because one of the guy coworkers imitated the way I was trying to hide it with my mouth. It was so embarrassing! Nuscey got a job working down at the fair ground, and I would pick him up late at night. I hated getting out of my bed because the fair closed late every night. One night, I was waiting for Nuscey to call me so that I could go and pick him up, but he didn't call, so I had decided to just go down there because I was sure that once I had gotten down there, he should have been ready. Shaquille and I went down to the fair grounds to pick him up, and he wasn't there. No one was there. I asked around for him, and someone told me that he had went to the hotel with a couple of the workers.

I'm like a detective, and Nuscey always called me Inspector Gadget. He told me that I should have been a detective because I was always figuring things out. I went to the closest hotel around and found Nuscey in the room with some Mexicans. I believe they were getting high. He was mad that I came there looking for him, but like I told him, "What you forgot that I had to pick you up!" He told me, "Yeah, but you should have waited for me to call you!" He was getting high smoking weed, and he was mad that I busted him. Then a couple of days later, Timark and Shaquille asked me if they could go to the fair, but I told them with a loud voice, "No!" They wanted to know why. I said, "Because your dad is working down there putting up the rides, and I don't trust it. Hell, if they let him help put up the rides, then they letting anybody help put up the rides!"

As far as I was concerned, everyone who was working at the fair was getting high!

One day, Nuscey called me. I thought that he was calling me because he was ready to get picked up from work. He was calling me to tell me that the workers at the fair wanted him to travel with them. I told him, "Oh, so now you want to run off with the circus!" He told me that if he did, he would send us the money back home. I told him that I wasn't trusting him sending me no money home and that I would be there in a minute to pick him up, and I hung up the phone! I worked at the post office for about five months because they started laying people off, so back to the streets I went. Nuscey left again, or I put him out. I don't remember. It was just too much to keep up with!

Mary, the hairstylist, called me up to see if I were working anywhere and asked me if I would come and work for her. She said that she was now in another hair salon but still close by my house, and I had agreed. I enjoyed working for Mary and also with most of the female coworkers. I even enjoyed servicing most of the female customers that came there, but some of them could be real b——! I decided to just stay away from those type of females and mind my own business. Each and every day I made sure that I brought my sword (Bible) with me. Even if I forgot it, I would turn around and go back home to get it so when I wasn't busy, I just read my word. In the hair salon, you hear all about the wannabes who got what and who don't have, and if you didn't have it, then you just didn't fit in. I was one of ones who didn't have, and I didn't care if I didn't fit in with anyone. I was fine just the way that I was because most of the women were fake, and I didn't want to be a part of that. Fake like they didn't know anything about food stamps and how to get them. I told one female, "I bet when I go get in line for mine, I'll see most of you in line for yours!" The stories around the shop was whose man they saw doing what with, who, and where. Yeah, but where was your man and who was he with doing what? I wanted to ask them that!

Even though I worked for Mary as her assistant, I also rented a booth for myself. Why not, I was a stylist, and I had my license. If I didn't start, then when. I didn't have many clients, but the few that I did have was difficult to do because I was too busy working for Mary attending to her clients, and it was very unfair that I had to make my people wait until I finish her clients. Mary had me doing everything except styling and cutting her clients' hair. My job was to apply everyone who was getting a chemical relaxer, color, shampoo, and roller set, and I was only getting paid three to four dollars a person. I didn't care at the time because I felt that I was learning from one of the best hairstylists in Columbia! Mary and I was two of a kind. We were both Aquarius, and we both didn't take no s—— from anyone. We spoke our mind, and we used to argue so much in the salon that people thought that we were about to fight until they realized that was just the way Mary and I rolled. Both of us got along, and that we really loved each other at the end of the day.

Mary, one day, told me, "I know you wanna call me a b——, but you better not let me hear it."

I told Mary, "Yeah, you're right. I call you a b—— from the time I walk in this shop until the time I leave, and you're right, you don't hear it!"

Mary looked at me and rolled her eyes with a smirk on her face! The way Mary's system worked is that everyone are walk-ins, and you must sign your name in the book as you walk-in. One morning, while shampooing the client's hair in order and waiting on Mary to get there, there was some commotion going on up front. Some of the females were saying that another female had put down some more female names who wasn't there, so I took their names off the list, and the female started talking s——. And I told her, "To save the drama for your mama!" That female said, "My mama what!" Yeah, I might go for Ms. Billy Bad A——, but that time, I said to myself, "Ooh s——, maybe I went too far this time. But you better fight if you have to!"

So now I have to play the bad a—— role. Hopefully to keep these females off my a——! I said out loud, "You heard me!"

The female didn't say anything else until her sister and cousin got there, and then I found out that they were Mary's cousin. Mary was tripping and laughing talking about she wouldn't have let them jump on me, and I told Mary, "Oh, I wasn't even worried about it!" But I was.

Mary told them, "Y'all better leave that girl alone. She from Hollywood Hills!"

I guess Mary was trying to tell them that since I was from the Hills, I was a fighter.

Even though I liked being a hairstylist working on women's hair, my love was for cutting. I loved cutting hair. Whenever someone brought their son along and wanted their hair cut, Mary would say, "Let Shannon cut their hair. She knows how to cut boys hair." Cutting was my specialty, and I was good at it. One day, while I was getting ready to work on a walk-in female who came in the shop to get her hair done, Mary whispered in the female's ear, "I hope you ain't about to let Shannon do your hair because she is high."

The female looked at me. I was so pissed off. I told Mary, "First of all, I'm high everyday. I come up in here, but you don't know it because I still do my job, so I don't appreciate you telling nobody no s—— like that!"

Mrs. Joyce, one of the older stylists who also was part owner, came up to me one day and said, "Shannon, that's one thang I can say about you. You're always reading your word."

I mainly stayed out of people's faces because I still hadn't got my front tooth fixed from when Nuscey and I had gotten into that fight, and I just wanted someone to say something to me about it. I said to her, "Yes, ma'am, I gotta have my word. Even if I leave it at home, I would turn around to go back and get it because every day before I come into this shop, I give myself two choices. I say, 'Shannon, now you can either read your word or whoop some a——, and because I need my job, I'ma read my word!"

Mrs. Joyce just laughed then said, "Yeah, don't you let these females around here get you locked up!"

I said, "Yes, ma'am. Yeah, you're right, and you too because you can get on my nerves sometimes!"

Mrs. Joyce and I just burst out laughing.

I finally went to the dentist to get my front *tooth* fixed, and he put in a replacement until I got my permanent tooth. He said that it could take weeks. I sure couldn't wait until the permanent tooth came because every now and then, if I talked too hard or too fast, the temp tooth would shoot straight out of my mouth. It was embarrassing!

My house was known to have the parties, and everybody always came. And we always had a good time. We always had the DJ, which was one of the Boys, Toddrick, and we always had my boy Feet on the grill. We had all-you-can-eat-and-drink plus just about everyone who came brought a twelve pack or a case of beer, so we never ran out. This particular party was one of the funniest parties we ever had.

Nuscey and I were together, and we were seeing everybody out. It was late, and the Boys were the last to leave. We stayed in the door until the Boys drove off, and as we were about to close the door, the Boys came back around the corner on two wheels with the police on their tails. They were throwing beer cans out of the window into our yard. They stopped at the Stop sign for the police, and we closed our door. The next morning, I called McGraw to see what had happened, and he said that Apple Seed and Meat was arguing about who was going to drive DJ's car since DJ was too drunk to drive, and Apple Seed jumped in the driver seat talking about, "This me and DJ car." So Meat sat in the front seat on the passenger side while DJ, Feet, McGraw, and Coot sat in the back. McGraw said that when they got around the corner, they saw the police. And instead of Apple Seed making the left, he made the right, and the police came behind him. And at the same time, he was trying to get Meat to trade places with him, throwing his leg over toward Meat talking about, "Come on, Meat. Come on, Meat!"

Meat was pushing Apple Seed's leg off his, talking about, "Oh no, remember this you and DJ's car!"

McGraw said after the police stopped them, he asked Apple Seed to get out of the car, and he asked Apple Seed his name. And he said, "Apple Seed." The police said, "What's your real name?" and he said, "Apple Seed." So the police asked them in the car what was Apple

Seed's real name, and everybody said, "All we know him as is Apple Seed!" So the police asked everybody in the car their names, and they said, "My name Meat," "My name DJ," "My name McGraw," "My name Feet," and "My name Coot." So the police told Apple Seed to get his driver's license and registration. McGraw said that Apple Seed leaned into the window like he was going to the look in the glove department and looked at everybody talking about "See y'all later!" and hauled off and ran from the police!

McGraw said that the police had time to smoke a cigarette and tied his shoe as a joke and humped Apple Seed's little a—— down and brought him back, jacked up from the back of his collar, while Apple Seed was yelling, "See what they doing? Y'all see what they doing!" McGraw said they started yelling in the car, "Rodney King! Rodney King!"

We laughed so hard on the phone! The Boys who are my Boys are so crazy, and I love them all like crazy!

One day, I got a call from the jail house. Nuscey was in the county jail, and he wanted me to come there for his bond hearing so that I could get him out. While I was waiting along with some other people for their loved ones, a lady and I had started a casual conversation. In the conversation, she told me that she knew me.

I said, "You know me? Where do you know me from because I don't know you."

She said, "Well, I know your daddy."

I said, "You know my daddy? Where do you know my daddy from?"

She said, "I'll tell you," but she didn't say anything else after that. and I'm wondering to myself, she says she knows my daddy, where do she know my daddy from. Now I know they said that my daddy was a rolling stone and wherever he laid his hat was his home, but the first thang that came to my mind was, did my dad mess up her car or something. I wanted to know, so I asked her again, "You said you know me and my daddy so where do you know my daddy from?"

She said, "Well, your daddy told me about your incident and you have two brothers Willis and Jacquis, and I'm their mother."

I said, "I have two brothers? No, I have one sister and one brother from my mama, and I don't know nothing about nobody else!"

She said, "Well, you'll find out."

When I got home and told my mom what had happened, she told me, "Yeah, I knew about those boys, but she didn't have no business telling you some mess like that down there at no jail house!"

My mom was furious, and I was shocked to know about my two brothers that I have never known anything about. About three weeks later, I was on my way to my parents' house and driving my mom's Volvo, a car she and my dad gave me. I saw the same lady I saw at the jail house. The same lady who was telling me that I had two other brothers, and you know what, the heifer tried to run me off the road! I don't think that she thought that it was me who was driving my mom's car. I know that she thought that it was my mom because everybody knows my mom and I are twins. When I noticed who was driving the car, I tried my best to catch up with her and beat the brakes off her, but she got away! That lady was running red lights and Stop signs just to get away! It was probably for the best because I knew that she thought it was my mom who was driving her car, and she was trying to hurt my mom, so I was definitely going to hurt her!

During this time, I wasn't working, but I was still doing my thing hustling, and even though I wasn't in my profession as a hair-stylist, I still kept my hair license up by attending a hair class once a year that was required in order to keep your hair license active. I'm glad I did because if you miss over three years without taking a hair class to renew your hair license, they would revoke your license, and you would have had to go back to hair school for those same fifteen hundred hours plus a fee over ten thousand dollars. So who would be crazy enough to not take a class to renew their hair license once a year? You would be surprised. One year, while at my hair class, I sat at a table that had Mrs. Loretta and her hairstylist there. Mrs. Loretta talked to me about me coming back to work for them again, but this time, I wouldn't be her daughter's assistant. I would be Tasha's assistant. I met Tasha while at the hair class, and she seemed kind of cool, so I accepted the offer and went back to work at Mrs. Loretta's Hair Boutique.

I had really enjoyed working there under Tasha, and Mrs. Loretta was very impressed with my technique on how well I applied the client's chemical relaxer. She told me, "For now on, I want you to apply all of my chemical relaxers as well as blow-dry my clients who were getting their hair hot press with a straighten comb." She said that I blew dry her client's hair so well that she didn't have to do much work when pressing it. The only thing I didn't like about working there was when Mrs. Loretta ran out of the hair relaxer that the customers were paying top dollars for. They didn't know the difference because we would have to go to the back to put the relaxers in a bowl. Mrs. Loretta said that it was not professional for customers to see the products that we were putting in their hair, so they just took our word for it. I told Mrs. Loretta that we were out of the relaxer that a customer wanted and that relaxer cost more than the other relaxers, but she just said, "Just put this relaxer in the bowl. They don't know the difference" That relaxer was supposed to be a lesser price, but the customer still got charged for the higher price relaxer. After that, I lost much respect for Mrs. Loretta!

During my lunch breaks since my grandmama (Mama) lived around the corner from the hair salon where I worked. I mostly went there to eat. I would stop at the fish market and pick up Mama and me some good ole hot fresh fried fish. I would go over to Mama's house with that fish and have a good time. I love my grandma so much, and I'm glad that we shared a lot of our time together. She was and will always be my best friend!

While working at the hair salon, I was still hustling on the side, and my people acted as if they couldn't wait until I got off work, so I started bringing the stuff with me and started leaving my door open with the amount that they asked for under the floormat, and they would leave the money. I only did that with customers whom I really trusted. One day, Mrs. Loretta asked me if I could shampoo one of her clients, a good friend of hers for her, an older lady around her age, and Mrs. Loretta told me that this lady knew my dad. While I was shampooing this lady's hair, she kept looking up at me crazy as if

I was going to do something to her. Something just didn't feel right, so I made sure that I got her name. I was telling my mom about the lady that I had to shampoo at the salon, and it just so happened that this lady was someone who my dad was messing with back in the day!

My mom told me that when we were living on Monstella Street, this same lady came to the house looking for her car. And on this particular day, my dad took us my sister, brother, and me to the country in Allendale driving this lady's car. My mom told the lady that she would make sure that she tells my dad that she came by for her car. My mom said about a week or two later, something came up involving this same woman, and she found out where this woman was living. So she went to this lady's house and confronted her about her coming to her house on that day that she was looking for her car. My mom said that she told the lady that she knew that her and my dad was messing around and that if she knew what was good for her, she would leave her husband alone. The woman told my mom who she was and that my daddy had told her that he was leaving my mom, and that they were getting a divorce.

My mom said that she told this woman, "Now let me tell you one damn thang. Bonnie ain't divorcing me. I'm divorcing his a——, and until I do, b——, don't you bring your a—— back to my house again!" My mama said that she went in her purse, and the woman started yelling and screaming, "Oh, don't shoot me! Don't shoot me!" My mama said that she told the woman, "Shut the hell up. Ain't nobody about to shoot you. I'm getting me a cigarette!"

After that story, my mama and I burst out laughing! My mama told me that she told my dad about what had happened to me at the hair salon, me shampooing this lady's hair. I was like "Ooh boy," but my dad never said anything to me about it. I believe that Mrs. Loretta was being messy on that day, and I didn't appreciate it! I told my mama what had happened. The next day, Mrs. Loretta was sitting down in a chair, and she told me to take her shoes off and massage her feet. Why did I tell my mama that? "Who do that woman think you are to her, a slave or something. I ain't never ask you to take off my shoes, and you ain't never massaged my feet, and I bet you did too, didn't you?"

I said, "Yes."

"Well, you the damn fool, and you better not ever do no s——— like that again!"

One day, while I was at work, it was close to me getting off, and the front desk receptionist told me that there were two women up front looking for me. I was like, "Looking for me?" I walked up front, and standing at the front door were two dirty-looking women. I asked them what did they want, and they said, "Noland sent us up here." My heart hit the floor, and at that moment, I was a ventriloquist. I told them without moving my lips, "If y'all don't get the hell out of here!" Then I had to play it off because everybody was looking at us, so I said out loud, "No, I can't do y'all hair today because I'm about to leave. Just come back tomorrow!"

Do you know these crackheads still asked me, "You straight?"

I said without my lips moving again, "If y'all don't get the hell up out of here, I'll kill ya!" They got the hell on! I couldn't believe that Noland sent them crackheads up on my job like that. Boy you wait until I see him!

Mrs. Loretta asked me, "Shannon, what did those women want?"

I said, "Oh, they wanted their hair done."

She said, "Well, Elaine said that Noland sent them up here. Don't you know Noland?"

Elaine was our receptionist, and I found out later that Elaine used to mess with Noland back in the day. Plus Elaine was cousin to my homegirls back in my old neighborhood, the Hills, Sam and Van, so I had already known Elaine. Mrs. Loretta said, "Elaine said that Noland is a drug dealer?"

I told Mrs. Loretta, "I don't know what he is. I just know that he's my youngest son's uncle, and he probably was trying to send me some customers you see how their hair looked!"

Mrs. Loretta asked me, "Well, why didn't you do their hair?"

I said, "Because I was ready to go, and both of their hair would have been time-consuming."

That was a close call, and I sure talked my way out of that one! After work, I went straight around to Noland's house and confronted him about sending those crackheads to my job. Noland insisted that he didn't. He said that he told those two females that he didn't have any dope at the time, but that his niece probably had some, but that I was at work. He said that they asked him where did I work and what time was I getting off. I told him that they came around to my job and all what had happened. At first, he kinda laughed, and then he said with his funny voice, "All right, you wait until I see them b——— again. I'ma curse their a——— out!"

The last day that I decided to work for Mrs. Loretta was around the time my cousin was going to get married. They wanted my son Shaquille to be in the wedding, and I had to take Shaquille the next following week to get him fitted for his tuxedo. Mrs. Loretta's daughter's assistant quit on her, and Mrs. Loretta asked everyone to start helping even if we have to stay over for a little bit to help Charlene out until they found her another assistant. On this particular day, I asked if I could leave work fifteen minutes early because I needed to take my son somewhere. I didn't tell them where. I just said somewhere, and while I was at home on my lunch break, Mrs. Loretta had her assistant to call me to tell me that "Mrs. Loretta said that wherever you have to take your son, it could wait!"

I said, "Excuse me?" I told her, "You can tell Mrs. Loretta that she don't tell me what I can or can't do for my child."

Ten minutes later, Mrs. Loretta called me talking about, "Yes, ma'am, you said that you couldn't work?"

And I said, "No, ma'am, I didn't say that. I said that I needed to get off work fifteen minutes early to take my son somewhere."

She said, "Well, that's like you're saying you can't work."

I said, "Leaving fifteen minutes early really when I'm already staying over just to help your daughter out."

She said, "Well, the choice is yours," and she hung up the phone!

I said to myself, "Yeah, you are right. The choice is mine." Yeah, she crazy as hell. She don't know who she messing with!

When I got back to work and on my way walking toward the door, Mrs. Loretta daughter's Charlene came and met me outside. She said, "Look, Shannon, you are a good stylist. Don't leave!"

I said to myself, "Wow I wonder how she knew that I was leaving?"

I said, "Naw, I'm good!"

I walked inside and started packing up all my s—— and told them to mail me my check! No, ma'am, and no, sir, I don't play when it comes to my boys! I remember a bill collector called and harassed me about a 250-dollar bill that I owed. He was very nasty talking about if I didn't pay my bills, my credit would get bad, and if my credit gets bad, then I couldn't get a job, and if I couldn't get a job, then I wouldn't be able to take care of my kids. He asked me, "Now how are you going to take care of your kids if you don't pay your bills?"

I told him like this, "Do you know how I'm going to take care of my boys?"

He said, "How?"

I said, "With the money I owe y'all" and hung up the phone in his face! I never paid that bill, nor did I ever get a call back!

Another time I got disrespected about my kids over a bill was when I was paying on some furniture at Kimbrells, and I went inside to finish paying them the last $150, and the white chick was talking about "I called you about your bill, and your brother said that you took your kids to the fair!"

I said, "And?"

She said, "And how can you take your kids to the fair but can't pay your bill."

Boy, I started to curse this heifer out, and when I looked over at the other black female sales associate, she gave me the look like, "Are you going to let her talk to you like that?" So what I did was tell the lady, "Oh, I left my money in the car!"

I got back in the car and pulled off and said to myself, "That b—— is crazy talking about how I can take my kids to the fair and can't pay my bills. I'ma take them back to the fair, as a matter of fact, with the money I owe y'all!" I never got a call back from them either! Honey, I'm a child from God. Don't mess with me, nor my boys and when I start realizing that I was a child from God, I used to warn people about messing with me, and that vengeance is His says the Lord!

The weekend was my time to hang out because my mom said that she didn't mind watching my boys. My boys were her boys, and I love her for it! One of the Boys was having a party, and since Nuscey's aunt Bebop had a crush on him, she wanted to go alone with me, so we picked up two of the Boys, and we all rode out to the party. After the party coming home, we were feeling pretty good. I was feeling so good that as I was getting off the interstate exiting off the ramp. I didn't look back to see if there was any coming traffic because I was really out of it, and the next thing I knew—*wham!*—something had hit us on my driver's side, busted out my driver's side window, and broken my rearview mirror, and I almost lost control of my car, which would have sent us driving off a cliff, but I got my composure and got control of the car.

I realized that a van had hit me as I was coming off the ramp. I started to stop, but I remember that I was driving DUI! I saw that the van had stopped, but I kept going. Everyone in the car was okay, but Bebop was panicking. She asked me if I wanted her to drive. Now what makes her think I wanna sit here and switch seats next to the van that I just hit! I told her, "No, I just want you to sit back and ride!"

I got the hell out of there! When I looked back in my rearview mirror, the van was still sitting there, and I prayed that whoever was driving the van was okay, but looking back, my car suffered the most damages. When we got into the Hills to drop the Boys off, I drove down my old street, and just when I was coming up the hill to go down another hill, I saw a police car coming up the hill. I didn't even get to McGraw's house. I stopped on point and back straight into Shorty's house like I lived there two houses up from McGraw.

Four police troopers were cruising up the hill and you talking about someone who's heart dropped and sobered up quick. I just knew right then I was going to jail, but they all looked our way and kept on going until they passed us by. I pulled out, dropped McGraw and Scott off at McGraw's house, and I took the backroads to take Bebop home. I dropped her off, got home, and parked my car in the front of my house, went inside, and passed out. I woke up the next morning, called the police, and told them that somebody done hit my car! They told me to come in and fill out some paperwork. I called my homegirl Tree and was telling her all about it, and she was too happy to volunteer to drive me down to the police station. It made me feel like it was a setup by the police telling me to come in. My homegirl Tree wasn't no better. I told her, "You must want me to get locked up!" Everything went well, I guess, the other driver didn't report the accident. I said to myself God is good. Twice God has saved me from a wreck, and both times the other driver was dirty also! McGraw and Scott both called me and started singing on the phone, and you could hear them hitting on a table singing "Hit and Run" just for fun by the Bar Kays. They both started laughing! I told them that they weren't funny, but they were!

The one thing that I liked about Nuscey was that he was still cool with me hanging out with the Boys or the Boys coming over every now and then to hang out with us to play cards and drink some beer. On this particular day, Nuscey and I went over to one of the Boys' house to play cards and drink some beer plus McGraw and Scott was there. Nuscey got up to use the bathroom, and when he came back to sit down, I noticed Scott was trying to get Nuscey's attention. When I looked up, Scott was trying to tell Nuscey that he had something on his face. When I looked up, Nuscey had cocaine powder on his nose. Scott and McGraw kind of chuckled. That was my first time finding out that Nuscey was snorting powder. I was so embarrassed!

I was doing very well in the hustling business and was making very good money. I started making more money off my cousin and her two girlfriends just by themselves, but what I couldn't understand was that my cousin told me that the only reason she and her girlfriends were buying the crack from me was because they were lacing their joints since the weed that they were buying wasn't that good. But when they started calling me just about every day, I said to myself, "They don't seem like they are just putting it in their weed because they are calling me a little too much and was spending plenty of money!"

The next time I saw my cousin, I told her that I loved her too much for me to keep selling this s—— to her! She told me that she appreciated that, and she didn't call me anymore. Even if she still bought it from someone else, at least it wasn't from me. I was feeling bad enough as it was just selling it because she's one of my favorite cousins more like an aunt, so I really felt bad for selling it to her. One day, while I was sitting in the area where I normally did my hustling, I was sitting in an area where most crackheads hung out, and this female crackhead who was well-known in the neighborhood was just chilling out with me keeping me company. I'll tell you one thang about crackheads, they sure can be funny as hell at times, and this female crackhead was a very fast talker, you could barely keep up with. She was talking a hundred miles a minute. This cab had pulled up, and Al got out of the cab from work, tired and walking slow. Al is Vib's ole man, and Vib and I were always cool even though they both smoked dope. At least Al worked still. It was said that Vib didn't like any females around and especially when Al was around, but I was an exception not because I sold dope. She said because there was just something about me that she liked. So when Al stepped out of the cab, Beb, the female crackhead, had stop talking. I mean she just like froze and waited until Al passed us by, and when he did, Beb looked at Al and shook her head and said, "Boy, I'll tell you that's one ugly motherf—— right there!" To be honest, Al isn't anything to look at, but Vib loves him, and that's all that mattered. I thought that I would die from laughing so hard! You had to be there. It was one of the funniest times I had.

I was told by one of the Boys' niece in my old neighborhood, the Hills, that I needed to watch my back and to get off the streets doing what I was doing because there was a guy who told her that when he catches up with me, he was going to kill me! My mouth dropped! I was like, "Kill me for what?"

She said, "Because he said that he was tired of you selling on his block."

I said, "Well, he don't have a block, and there's enough money out here for everybody!"

This guy didn't know that I knew her, and after Nuke told me this, I knew that she wasn't lying. This guy was someone I knew of, but I also knew that he didn't care about taking someone out, the crackheads said that he was very nasty and disrespectful toward them and that they were going to stop dealing with him because they were tired of how he was treating them and talking to them like they were a piece of s—— and that they weren't about to keep spending their money with someone like that.

They said that they loved the way I treated them, like human beings, plus my dope was better anyway! I told them, "Why should I not treat y'all like somebody because a drug is a drug. It don't matter what kind of drug it is. It could be weed, cocaine, crack, heroin, alcohol. It doesn't matter. A drug is a drug, and I ain't no better than you because my drug is weed!"

It was because of my character and the way that I treated people! Alone with my good dope that no one else had around. I had a particular person where I got it from my cousin on my dad's side, and that was the reason my clientele was off the chain.

I ended up running into E one day, the same guy who said that he was going to kill me, and yes, I confronted him on what was told to me. "E, I heard that you felt that this neighborhood wasn't big enough for the both of us and that you wanted me off your block or else you were planning on taking me out. I feel there's enough money out here for the both of us." E just laughed about it and said, "No, now you know damn well I ain't say no s—— like that, and hell yeah, there's enough money out here for the both of us. If I said anything about you, I said that you were fine as hell!" E and I laughed about it and talked a little bit longer before we parted ways, but something in the back of my mind told me not to trust him at all.

Even though I was still selling, something about me was starting to feel nervous, a little on the scared side. Scared of going to jail, scared of losing my boys, and scared of losing my life! I'll never forget that I was trying to make some ends meet, and my cousin Trapp was doing very well for hisself. He was selling big time weight, and he had his own place with a good friend of his someone whom I loved like a brother. One day, I went to my cousin Trapp, and I was a little short, but I told my cousin that I would be sure to bring him his money back off my first sell. You know what my cousin told me? He couldn't do it. It hurt me to my heart because I helped him when he didn't have a place to stay plus he brought his women up in my house. Not only that, it was my money that got us started in the first place. And now he was too good for me to bring him his money back? Cool! I never went back to him again unless I had all of my money, but since my other cousin Andy had the best around town, I didn't need him anymore.

While I was growing up in the Hills, there were a few of the Boys that I knew liked me, but because they were best friends of Timark's dad Jeff, I couldn't or wouldn't dare date them out of respect for Jeff and myself even though they used to joke around saying, "Oh, Jeff, ain't my homeboy. He's just someone I know," which I knew wasn't true because they have known each other since they were kids. I'm not going to lie. I did find a couple of them attractive, but that's as far as it went because I had the up most respect not only for Jeff but myself. It wasn't like I still had feelings for Jeff or anything. I just wasn't that kind of female. In order for anyone to have respect for you, you have to have the up most respect for yourself.

Strokes was another one of Jeff's homeboys that I knew really liked me, but I told him the same thing: "I could never date you because you and Jeff grew up together, and you both are best friends and even though we're not together, I still couldn't do that out of respect." Even though Strokes was cute, he was just too short. Shorter than me, where we both looked like Betty and Barney on *The Flintstones*. Strokes made it seem as though he and Jeff were only just cool, not best friends, and that's it, but I still didn't budge. Strokes and I got close, the cool kinda close, and I put him on my payroll and had him doing some work for me. Strokes was a loyal worker, and I think he was doing it just to be around me. We would both sometimes go together to different spots to handle our business, and he said that he wanted to come for my protection because he felt I needed it since I didn't own a gun to protect myself.

Most of the time, Strokes and I would just hang out drinking, smoking weed, and playing cards. Strokes and I had started hanging out so much until I really started liking him. Even though he was short, he was still cute and cool, so I said to myself, "Well, since Strokes have been so nice to me, maybe I'll think about giving him a chance?"

A couple of days later, I had to go over to Strokes house to pick up some money that he had for me from his sales. When I walked in the house, I could see that he kinda had a strange look on his face. I was wondering what was wrong. My cousin Squeaky walked out of the bathroom with a towel wrapped around her. I shouted, "Cuz!" and when she saw me, she had a big smile on her face, and she too was like, "Hey, cuz, what's up?"

Strokes was like, "Cuz? Y'all cousins?"

"Yeah, first cousin. You didn't know that?"

"No."

"I don't see why not everybody else knew we were cousins."

After that encounter, I knew for sure that Strokes and I definitely couldn't be anything else but partners in crime!

My girl Grace's house was the ultimate house for the best parties. Not a hood party where everybody and their kids came, no. We had casual parties that only and always the same crew like 90210 crew, just the black verging, and boy did we have fun. I remember at one of Grace's parties, we were all sitting around, talking about doing a couple thing up in the mountains. There were a few couples there who were talking about going. My friends know that I'm the life of the party, and they wanted me to come, but they also knew that I was single, so they were trying to hook me up with this guy name Tanoka. I felt he had a little crush on me, and the crew knew it too, so they were like, "Yeah, Shannon, you and Tanoka should go. It's only $350. Tanoka said that he would pay for everything so all you need is just some spending money."

Tanoka looked at me and said, "Yeah, I'll pay for the room. Just bring yourself!"

We all laughed about it, and I said, "Well, I'll think about it."

Tanoka and I ended up getting each other's number that night and giving each other a call. I found out that he too was a street hustler. No wonder he didn't have a problem paying the bill. I found out what kind of business he was hustling in, and I ended up going over to his house one day to buy some wacky, wacky weed but in a large amount. And before I left, I gave him some sex, got my wacky, wacky weed, and left. Not long after that, Tanoka stopped over to my house, and I gave him some more sex. After we had finished, he went into my bathroom. As I were walking by, he had the door open, and he was standing in the mirror combing his disgusting chest hair with my comb talking about, "Boy, I can't wait to get you to the mountains, so we can have sex all night long! I want to sex you out by the river and in the bathroom and in our room!"

I told him, "First of all, it ain't that kind of party. What is $350, something I could have paid myself if I really wanted to go, so what makes you think you getting ready to be sexing me all over the place like that. I don't think so. As a matter of fact, I ain't even going. Goodbye!"

What really pissed me off was him standing in my bathroom mirror, combing his chest hairs with my comb like he just got finished doing something. Hold up, little minute man!

The crew and Tanoka all went to the mountains. I didn't care but would have liked to have gone but, not under those terms, I wasn't. Tanoka and I remained business associates, and one day, Tanoka gave me a quantity size of the wacky, wacky weed on my face and told me the amount to bring him back. I didn't give him the whole amount that he wanted back at that time. I gave him some of his money back and the rest I told him that I was going to use with the money that I had to make a profit from a seafood party that I was having where you could buy a plate for $10. A plate of crab legs, shrimps, fish, corn on the cob, hush puppies, and a drink. Now that's a seafood plate!

I even rented a portable john for the guest. Things didn't go as planned. Plus it rained. I spoke with Tanoka and told him what I was trying to do to flip my money to make a profit to be able to give him all his money as well as have some left over, so I could get some more weight to flip. I told Tanoka that I would still have his money and not to worry about it. The next day, I got a phone call from Tanoka talking s—— about his money. I didn't know that he called me while he was sitting in my driveway. Now what he did that for! I walked outside and asked him, "What the hell you doing sitting up in my driveway like you live here! You should have called me before you came. I don't appreciate this s——!"

Tanoka said while sitting in his nice truck, like he was Scarface or somebody talking about, "Look, I was trying to help you and your boys out by doing what I did, and you do me this. But that's all right, you can have it. You need it!"

I told him, "First of all, I don't appreciate you pulling up in my yard talking about what you did for me and my boys because my boys don't need nothing from you. I told you that I would give you your money, but since I can have it, thank ya. Now get the hell up out of my yard!" I didn't have any more problems out of him, but he did tell my cousin Piazo what I did to him. Oh, jive sucka!

I'm a hairstylist, but I was getting tired of styling my hair as well as paying to get it done, so I had decided that I would cut it down really short like a boy, but not shaved. Just enough to run my fingers through. I decided that I would put a texturizer in it and let it just look naturally curly, but after putting the texturizer in my hair, my hair looked like what Cedric the Entertainer said about Luther Vandross on one of his stand-ups, "Well, the curl just wouldn't never curl all the way around." No matter how hard I tried, my hair just would not curl for anything. Nuscey didn't like it at all and kept telling me that I looked like a he-she and for me to grow my hair back out, but I thought that I was kinda cute.

My girlfriends Tree, Tonya and, Grace was calling me Florida from off *Good Times*, and every time they saw me, they would all holler, "Damn, damn, damn!" like Florida did on *Good Times* when James died! It was funny, and I laughed, but because everyone was making fun of me, I said that I would just grow it back! Also during that time, when my hair was short, I remember totally losing my car. I had a red Beretta. Shaquille and I was going home at the time, and I think that he was around four or five years old. I knew that he should have been in a car seat, but he wasn't. He was just sitting in the front seat with his seat belt around him. I was driving, and the next thing you know, this SUV was getting over in my lane, but he got over on top of my car on the passenger side, the side that Shaquille was on. This SUV really did a lot of damage to my car where my car was totally wrecked. The man who hit us got out raising hell talking about it was I who hit him even after his wife and the police told him, "No, sir, you hit her." He was disputing the accident so much until the police just told me, "I know he hit you, ma'am. You can go!" What I should have done was call an ambulance and went to the hospital, but we were not hurt, but I did go to a lawyer's office, so that my child and I could get compensated for our pain and suffering!

At this point in my life, I had really gotten tired of selling drugs. I remember just driving one day by myself, and I started talking to the Lord with a heartfelt sincere conversation, and I said, "Lord, if you promise me that you will help me pay my bills, then I will stop selling drugs!"

About a week later, I started telling everyone that I had stopped selling drugs. Nuscey and I had gotten back together. It was in the winter time because we were using the fireplace. I remember Nuscey showing me a way that we could start the wood to burn quicker, without using all the starter wood and paper. Nuscey put some gas into a spray bottle and sprayed the wood with it. He waited for about three minutes before lighting the wood, and when he did, the fire slowly wrapped itself around the wood just as nice because we really used to catch hell, trying to keep that wood lit.

I looked at Nuscey as another MacGyver. He knew all kind of tricks and trades. He said that he was going to show the boys a magic trick by putting rubbing alcohol on his finger. He lit his finger and blew it out before the fire touched his skin. The boys were amazed, and they all laughed, but I told him not to ever teach or show them something like that again, especially with fire! One day, Nuscey and I decided to get romantic by the fireplace. I had on a two-piece lingerie, and Nuscey just had on his boxers. We were going to eat our dinner and drink our wine (liquor) while sitting by the fireplace. I told Nuscey while I get the food and drinks he could get the fire going. I was in the kitchen getting the things to take by the fireplace, and I could see Nuscey getting the fire ready. He grabbed the spray bottle, sprayed the wood like he normally does, and as soon as he sprayed the gas on the wood, it blew up like a fireball and went straight through him.

I stood there with my mouth wide open, praying that he was all right. Nuscey was standing there frozen in shock. The fire had singed the hair over his entire body including his eyebrows. I said to myself, "I'm glad the only thing he had on was a pair of boxers because his clothes could have caught on fire!" It wasn't funny when it happened, but I sure had a good laugh after I knew he was okay.

A couple of days later on this particular day, Timark and I were home, and Shaquille was with Nuscey. I had decided to light the fireplace since our boys loved for us to burn the fireplace so they could roast smores. I sprayed some gas on the wood, not knowing that it was still hot from the night before. It was like speed of lightning. It happened so fast. When I sprayed the gas bottle, it blew up in flames. The flames followed the gas straight back to the bottle. I was so scared that I threw the gas bottle in the fireplace, and the fire blew up even bigger and started burning outside of the fireplace onto the walls.

I just knew that I was about to burn my house down. Timark was panicking, so I ran to get some wet towels, and Timark and I started smothering the fire with the wet towels, and we were able to get the fire under control. I've never been so scared like that in my life. When Nuscey got home, I told him what had happened, but everything was fine by then. Around three o'clock in the morning, our smoke alarm went off! We were shocked that the smoke alarm even went off because that was something we never checked or knew if it needed new batteries because we never changed it since we lived there for six years. We knew without a shadow of a doubt that it was God who woke us up! When we woke up, the whole house was full of smoke, and we all panicked; we couldn't see or breathe. We had to crawl on the floor to see where we were going to get out of the house. Once the four of us got outside, Nuscey ran around the back of the house, and I told Timark and Shaquille not to move while I ran back inside the house to get my purse and car keys, because it was cold outside, and I wanted my boys to be safe and warm in the car.

I ran back into the house, crawling on the floor, and even though it was dangerous, I didn't care. I had to get my purse and keys to put my babies in the car. I got my purse, and when I got back outside coughing, choking, and trying to get my breathe, both of my boys was already in the car looking around for us. I was like, "What the hell, how did y'all get in the car." They said, "The door was already open!" When I turned around, Nuscey was on the top of the roof with the water holes that didn't even reach close to where the fire was at, but he was still trying to put the fire out, poor lil thang, until the firemen came! It wasn't funny, but it was funny in the way the black firemen was looking at Nuscey up and down. Nuscey was wearing his boxers and some cowboy boots. The fireman looked at Nuscey and said, "Now let me tell you something, Mr. Spiderman, don't you take your butt back up on no burning roof again, you hear!" He was saying it in a serious but joking way.

After the firemen put the fire out, we found out that the fire was trapped in between the wall and the fireplace and was burning slowly during the night. I thanked the firemen and started walking toward the house as if we were able to go back inside and get back in the bed. The fireman told us that our home was unlivable, but thank God that only the fireplace and roof above it was the only thing that was damaged, but that still meant that my boys, and I had to move back in with my parents, and Nuscey went back home to his mom. The next day, I called the phone company to set up arrangements to have all my home calls routed to my mom's phone line. After I did it, I panicked! I said to myself, "Oh, Lord, people are going to be calling my mama house looking for drugs!"

My mom wanted to know how much money was I supposed to give her for me staying there, and I was looking at her like, "Nothing, damn. Can my boys and I get ourselves together first." After the insurance adjuster examined the damages of the fire, they gave me a check with both my name and my insurance company's name on. The check for $16,000. My dad was telling me that he wanted to help me get my house back right, and I was saying to myself, "Hell, he ain't never help all this time nor ever stepped foot in my house so why now?" My dad was telling me that I didn't need to give no contractor my check because if I did, then he was going to take the whole check, and I wouldn't get anything out of it. What I should do is subcontract the work out to different people. After that, I would have some money left over to do whatever I needed to do with, but I couldn't cash the check until all the work was completed in the house because my insurance company had to sign the check over to me.

One day, my dad asked to see my check, and since I'm a daddy's girl, I gave him my check without any questions. My boys and I were at my parents' house for about three weeks, and my dad didn't say anything to me about my money or when he was getting someone to start on my house or nothing. So I called my dad up and asked him about my check, and that's when he told me that my check was with a buddy of his that worked at a loan company. I asked my dad, "Why is my check at a loan company?"

He said, "Because, Shannon, you don't have any money of your own to get your house fixed, and I told you that if you give a contractor that check, he's going to take the whole thang!"

I told my dad, "Yeah, but won't the loan company get a percentage of my check?"

He said, "Yeah, a small percentage."

I told my dad, "I don't want no loan company getting no percentage of my money."

As I was talking to my dad on the phone in the house, my mom was sitting outside on the patio listening on the other phone. My dad started getting mad and started talking to me all mean and nasty. I told him that I just wanted my check back, and that I would handle my own business. My dad told me, "Well, since you don't wanna listen to me, then you and your kids can get y'all s—— and get the hell out of my house because I was just trying to help you, but since you are so smart and know-it-all, you can just get your s—— and get the hell out of my house, and I mean it!" My dad has never ever in his life talk to me the way he talked to me all over money and my money at that. After I hung up the phone, I asked my mom if she heard what my dad had said to me. She said, "Yeah, I heard him talking to you like he was on crack or something, a mad man!"

I was so very hurt about what my dad had said to me, but I was more hurt that he was putting my boys and me out, knowing that we didn't have anywhere to go. But see, what my dad didn't know was I did have money in the bank to subcontract all the work out because my son Shaquille and I were in a car accident where another car hit us, and I totally lost my car, and both of us got paid for the accident. I decided that I would just use that money to get my house fixed. God is good, and won't he make a way!

While I was packing up my boys' and our stuff, my mom called my sister to tell her what had happened, and my sister told me that we could come and stay with her and her husband for a little while. I enjoyed being there, but it was a little crowded because my two nieces and nephew were there also. My sister's husband is in the Navy, and we loved each other, but we both bumped heads because he sometimes wants to act more like my dad than my brother-in-law. Plus we are both Aquarius with our birthdays on the same day wow! So while we were there, my sister and her family were going out of town. I was going through a lot, so I asked my brother-in-law if I could have the rest of his Hennessy that was on the bar and that I would replace it. The bottle was about a quart size but only about a pint of liquor was left in the bottle. He said yes, and I drank that bottle like it was the last bottle on the earth.

When I went to the store and saw how much that same quart size bottle cost, I went down to the next size. When my sister and her family got back home, my brother-in-law raised so much hell about the bottle of Hennessy that I brought, which was more than what I drank out of his bottle. My brother-in-law got up in my face and told me, "The next time you tell somebody you was going to do something, you need to do just that. I don't care if you didn't drink the whole bottle, you said that you were going to replace it, and you should have replaced it!"

I told him, "Well, I didn't know that that big bottle was going to cost that much."

He said, "Well, you should have never said that you were going to replace it!"

The next day, my mom called me and told me, "Shannon, you need to just get y'all stuff and come on back here to the house because you are about to make your sister and her husband get a divorce."

I said, "For what? All over a bottle of liquor? If they are going to get a divorce, that's because the n—— been wanted to leave!"

I packed our stuff up again and moved back in with my parents. While we were there, my dad and I didn't say two words to each other. I couldn't believe being a daddy's girl that we weren't speaking because of money. Now I see when they say money is the root of all evil. It's not the money but the person behind it!

I had decided that even though our house wasn't ready to move back in, I still needed to find a job, so I got a job working outbound at a call center where I would be calling customers. I didn't stay there long. For one, the supervisors there had their own clique of people, gay men and women, and if you wasn't down with the clique, because I sure wasn't down with that clique, then you weren't going to be there long. Every day after work, I would go home to check on my house and my dog JB as well as sit on my back porch and smoke me a blunt before I went home to my parents' house. My mom started noticing me coming home late every day, so she asked me, "What do you do when you get off work?"

I told her, "I go to check on my house and my dog."

She said, "And get high!"

I said, "And why do you say that?"

She said, "Girl, I ain't stupid. I know when you are high, so you go home with you friends and get high."

I told her, "No, I go home and get high by myself!"

She said, "By yourself?"

I said, "Yes, ma'am. I don't need no one to get high with!"

My mama just looked at me, shook her head, and walked off.

During this time, I was going over to my house to clean it up and get it in order. Nuscey and I were on our off again relationship, so Strokes came over to lend me a hand. Strokes brought his baby brother Mike with him, which was a mistake because both Mike and I were instantly attracted to each other but without Strokes knowing it. Mike became very helpful. He started coming over by himself helping me with getting things back together in my house until one thing led to another. About a week or two meeting Mike, we were both making love on the sofa. It was nice, and we really enjoyed each other's company. I didn't want Strokes to know that I was messing with his baby brother because I knew that Strokes really cared about me, but I was just a little crazy over Mike. He was cute, sexy, sweet, and helpful. I couldn't stay away; Strokes found out about it anyway, and it broke his heart. Strokes said that he was the one who had introduced us, so he felt betrayed. Strokes was so hurt that he had tears in his eyes, and because I hurt Strokes like that, I called it quits with Mike even though he said that he wasn't having it. We saw each other a few more times after that. Then we eventually ended it, but each time we saw each other, we knew that there was still something special between us!

While working at the call center, I met this guy who worked in front of me in the next stall. A guy who acted like he was so holy than thou and claimed that he always prayed over his food before he ate and that I should do the same thing until I caught him tearing his food up one day without saying a word! I brought it to his attention where he said, "Oh yeah, I forgot!"

All he wanted was to use me, someone, or anyone for a ride home. The job stated that we were not to have any casual conversations on the phone with our customers and because our calls were inbound. We didn't know who the next caller would be until we answered the call. My coworker got a call from someone who lived in a different state, but he found out that it was someone he knew.

He started having a casual conversation with the person on the phone, and the next thang you know, I started smelling something bad. I didn't know where the smell was coming from. I looked around and looked under my desk. This joker had gotten so comfortable on the phone like he was at home that he done took his shoes off, legs crossed, and rubbing his feet together making friction! His feet were stank as hell!

I said, "That's where the smell was coming from, his feet!" I got so mad and said, "Why do you have your feet over here on my side because they stank!"

He said, "My feet ain't stank!"

I said, "Yes, like hell they are. You can't smell them because you're used to the smell!"

It took about six or seven months before the house was finished. Nuscey came back home and got a good friend of their family who was a fireman to replace the fireplace, which was the biggest task of all. This guy tore down our old fireplace and rebuild us another one, better than the one we had. He had extended the bricks farther out because he said that the walls were too close to the fireplace inserter, and that was the reason the walls caught on fire. The only thing that Nuscey and I were upset about was the fireplace inserter. This guy had already inserted the fireplace before we decided if it was what we wanted! This fireplace was much smaller than the old one and a lot cheaper. Our old fireplace was wider and deeper that you could put about six logs in at one time. This fireplace you could only put three. Our old fireplace had a gold frame around it and a glass face, which I loved. This fireplace only had the closing chain that keeps the fire from popping out. We were so mad, but what could we do. He had already framed the bricks around it.

Nuscey and his dad did the dry wall, and I had gotten one of the Boys who was a painter to paint the whole inside of the house. I brought some beautiful carpet and paid good money for it just to have a shade tree carpenter come in to mess it up, but I learned that you get what you pay for! God blessed me to be able to get all the work in the house that I needed done! The insurance adjuster came to view the house, and once they were satisfied, they signed the check over to me. I was able to pay off some bills and get Timark a brand-new bedroom set. I too should have gotten a bedroom set, but instead I fell in love with this old antique-looking bed that the frame by itself was a thousand dollars! My mom thought that I was crazy spending that kind of money just for a bed and not the mattress included, but when other people saw it, they too fell in love with it.

I brought a new refrigerator and stove, a Kenwood surround sound stereo system, and some clothes for my boys and me, and the rest went into the bank. After moving back home, I looked back on how good God was to me. I couldn't believe the whole entire time while I was staying with my parents for those seven months that I didn't get not one phone call from anyone of my many customers wanting drugs! I just knew that it was no one but God who had stopped the calls and answered my prayers when I prayed and asked him to help me. What else could it have been because when have you ever known someone who wanted their drugs care about you telling them you stopped selling drugs, especially since I was selling it to them for so long! When have you ever known a crackhead not calling looking for drugs? When have you ever known a crackhead to believe that you were no longer selling drugs? But I cried out one day, "Lord, if I stop selling drugs, will you please help me to pay my bills!"

I stopped selling drugs, and the Lord heard my cry and helped me pay all my bills.

The Lord kept all those people from calling me. It was amazing I can't explain it! I couldn't explain it then, but I could now! When you pray, ask and believe it may not be on your time, but God is always on time! When you ask the Lord to help you, he will, but you have to love him and trust him to do what you ask, and he will do what you ask. If it is in his will. But don't be greedy thinking you can get everything you want! It is said that you should be careful of what you pray for because you just might get it! Everything we pray for isn't always what God wants for us!

I came home one afternoon from work, and when I walked in the kitchen, something had really hit me. Nuscey had changed the kitchen around, and I was puzzled. I felt as if I've seen this scene before. It felt like déjà vu! I knew that I've seen this scene before, but where? I remember now! I used to dream about this same scene every night for a whole entire year at the age of fourteen, years before I had my boys! The kitchen table, the stove, and the refrigerator was all set up exactly the same way in my dream. It was fifteen years ago since I had the dream, but I remembered it like it was yesterday! I was sitting in the middle of the kitchen table with Timark sitting on my right facing Shaquille who was sitting on my left, with a silhouette of a man's figure standing behind me at the stove as though he was cooking something for us to eat!

Wow! Now ain't that something. I get it now. This house that we are now living in is the same house that I was dreaming about the whole entire time! This white guy, who was sitting in my chair at the barbershop getting his hair cut, told me in my dream what my dream represented. He said, "Remember, you told me you saw you and your boys faces while sitting at the kitchen table while the silhouette of the man at the stove didn't have a face because it was a silhouette. Remember, Jesus didn't have a face, and by him standing at the stove while you and your boys were sitting at the kitchen table waiting to be served is just a way of Jesus telling you that he came to the world to serve, not to be served. So Jesus is letting you know that he's taking care of you and your boys!" Chills ran through my body. Mark 10:45 (NKJV) says. "For even the Son of Man did not come to be served, but to serve, and to give His life a ransom for many."

I broke down in tears! Thank you, Lord!

About the Author

Shannon Hammonds was born in South Carolina. She is a mother, grandmother, comedienne, cosmetologist, barber, truck driver, and now a writer. She considers her faith and family to be most important to her.

She's a very passionate, giving, and people person who meets no strangers. She loves to read and listen to inspirational, motivational, and most importantly, God's Word in her spare time.

She knows that without God in her life, she would have never made it this far.

She thanks God for using her as a vessel in sharing her story in this book and others that's on its way. She gives God all the praises, glory, and honor that he deserves. She will continue to confess one of her favorite quotes: "I can do *all* things through Christ who strengthens me!" (NKJV).

Printed in the USA
CPSIA information can be obtained
at www.ICGtesting.com
LVHW092307050824
787261LV00001B/35

9 781684 981694